What's in the Name?

How the Streets and Villages in Singapore Got Their Names

What's in the Name?

How the Streets and Villages in Singapore Got Their Names

Ng Yew Peng

NEW JERSEY · LONDON · SINGAPORE · BEIJING · SHANGHAI · HONG KONG · TAIPEI · CHENNAI · TOKYO

Published by

World Scientific Publishing Co. Pte. Ltd.
5 Toh Tuck Link, Singapore 596224
USA office: 27 Warren Street, Suite 401-402, Hackensack, NJ 07601
UK office: 57 Shelton Street, Covent Garden, London WC2H 9HE

National Library Board, Singapore Cataloguing in Publication Data
Names: Ng, Yew Peng, 1946–
Title: What's in the name? : how the streets and villages in Singapore got their names / Ng Yew Peng.
Description: Singapore : World Scientific, [2017]
Identifiers: OCN 990571127 | 978-981-32-2139-0 (paperback) | 978-981-32-2135-2 (hardcover)
Subjects: LCSH: Street names--Singapore--History. | Names, Geographical--Singapore--History. | Singapore--Name--History.
Classification: DDC 915.9570014--dc23

British Library Cataloguing-in-Publication Data
A catalogue record for this book is available from the British Library.

Copyright © 2018 by World Scientific Publishing Co. Pte. Ltd.

All rights reserved. This book, or parts thereof, may not be reproduced in any form or by any means, electronic or mechanical, including photocopying, recording or any information storage and retrieval system now known or to be invented, without written permission from the publisher.

For photocopying of material in this volume, please pay a copying fee through the Copyright Clearance Center, Inc., 222 Rosewood Drive, Danvers, MA 01923, USA. In this case permission to photocopy is not required from the publisher.

Desk Editor: Tay Yu Shan

Typeset by Stallion Press
Email: enquiries@stallionpress.com

Printed in Singapore

ABOUT THE AUTHOR

Ng Yew Peng came to Singapore from Nan An County of Fujian Province, China, at the age of 11. He was awarded the Overseas Scholarship under the Colombo Plan and graduated with a Degree in Mechanical Engineering from the University of Canterbury, New Zealand. He returned to Singapore and worked as an engineer in the Civil Service and various commercial organisations. From 1994 to 1998, he was stationed in Shanghai. After his retirement, he pursued further studies in Chinese Language and Literature at Peking University and the University of Nanjing in China. The first part of this book is an adaptation of his graduation thesis for the Master of Arts degree from the University of Nanjing.

The paintings on the front cover and inside the book were works of art by the late Mr. Chua Ek Kay and are now properties of his wife. Reproductions in any form requires written permission from Mrs. Chua Ek Kay (Mdm Yeo Yang Kwee).

This book is supported by

The author is grateful to the National Heritage Board for its financial support towards the printing of this book. However, the views expressed here are solely those of the author in his private capacity and do not in any way represent the views of the National Heritage Board and/or any government agencies.

CONTENTS

About the Author — v

Part I A Study of Singapore Place Names — 1

Section 1 Introduction — 3

Section 2 Nomenclature of Singapore Place Names — 7

    1. Simplex Name — 7
    2. Duplex Name — 7
    3. Complex Name — 7
    4. Generic Elements Used in Singapore Place Names — 8
    5. Irregular Structure — 9
    6. Derivative Place Names — 10
    7. Multi-Language Complex Place Names — 10
    8. Homonyms in Different Languages — 11

Section 3 The Contents of Singapore Place Names — 13

    1. Roads Named after Foreign Places — 13
    2. Anthroponyms — 14
    3. Economic Development and Place Names — 15
    4. War and Place Names — 20
    5. Political System and Place Names — 21
    6. Historical Sites and Place Names — 23
    7. Religion and Place Names — 24
    8. Place Names Linked to Families — 26
    9. Education and Place Names — 28
    10. Places Named after Females — 30
    11. Housing Estates with a Theme — 32

Section 4	Place Names of Chinese Origin	35
	1. Place Names in Mainland China	35
	2. Names of Famous Chinese Poets	35
	3. Names of Local Chinese Business Entities	35
	4. Anthroponyms of Local Chinese Residents	36
	5. Others	38
Section 5	Standardisation of Chinese Place Names	41
Section 6	Evolution of Place Names	45
	1. Changes in Spelling	45
	2. Evolution of Generic Elements	46
	3. Evolution of Specific Elements	47
	4. Change of Place Names	47
	5. Homonyms (Same Place Name Used in More than One Location)	48
	6. Reuse of Place Name	52
	7. Linguistic Refinement of Place Names	54
	8. Omissions and Repetitions in Street Directories	54
Section 7	Conclusion	57
Part II	Singapore Gazetteer Since 1936 and Annotations (Gazetteer of 3,900 place name groups with more than 6,000 place names)	63
Abbreviations and References		445
Acknowledgements		453

PART I

A STUDY OF SINGAPORE PLACE NAMES

SECTION 1

INTRODUCTION

A place name is the specific label of a geographical entity. It may represent the location of the geographical entity, its genre, or its physical or geographical characteristics. From a literary perspective, place names are the products of a society's socio-economic and cultural history and its development; thus, they reflect the particular characteristics of that society at certain moments in time. Because place names are not frequently changed, they can preserve historical and cultural information for long periods of time.

Singapore was originally known as *Temasek/Tumasik* (meaning watertown in Javanese). According to local legend, a Sumatran Prince named Sang Nila Utama was sailing from Riau Island when a strong wind swept his boat to a small island. There, he saw a lion and subsequently named the island *Singapura* — *singa* means lion and *pura* means city. This was the origin of the name "Lion City", as Singapore is otherwise known today.

Singapore has many historical names. On a nautical map drawn by J C Bellin in 1755, it was called *Pulau Panjang* (which means long island in Malay). Early records from 14th century China identified the island using various transcriptions of the Malay names *Temasek* and *Selat*, or the Chinese names "Long Ya Men" or "Ling Ya Men", meaning dragon tooth gate. The dragon tooth was a huge rock in the sea off the beach of Labrador as well as a shipping landmark. It was later called Lot's Wife by the British and was blown up in August 1848. The name of the island was changed to Singapore after Britain took control of the island in 1819.

Development of the island began almost immediately; by 1823, a town plan had been drawn up. Early street names can be seen on a map drawn by G D Coleman, which was based on an actual survey conducted in 1829 and published in 1835. In addition, two lists of Street and Road Names in Singapore were published in *The Straits Times* in 1853.

The first study of Singapore's place names was written by H T Haughton. His list of 73 place names was published in Volume 20 of the *Journal of the*

Straits Branch of the Royal Asiatic Society in 1889. This was followed by a list of 225 colloquial Chinese place names compiled by H W Firmstone in Volume 42 of the same journal in 1905.

The first official publication on Singapore place names was the "Singapore Gazetteer-Index to Roads, 1936". This was an alphabetised table of place names published by the Survey Department of the Straits Settlements. After World War Two ("WW2"), the Survey Department published three editions of its *Road and Street Directory* between 1950 and 1953. The more familiar *Singapore Street Directory* was introduced in 1954. It divided Singapore into 115 small sections and provided a detailed map of street names for each section. All the above publications were only produced in English.

The first book on Singapore's toponyms, *Malayan Street Names*, was produced by Raja Singam. It was published in 1939 and contained notes on nearly 500 place names in Singapore. Unfortunately, a comparison between this book and primary records revealed many discrepancies in the sources of street names.

Next was a Chinese publication *Record of Place and Street Names in South East Asia* by Phua Chay Long, also published in 1939. In a revised edition in 1952, the author listed 1,600 place names in English and Chinese, along with a map of the city.

The first complete Singapore street directory in the Chinese language, titled *Singapore Guide and List of Street Names* was published in 1967. It was compiled by Lee Kian Chye based on the eighth edition of the official *Singapore Street Directory*. It contained street names in both English and Chinese as well as information on places of interest. Most of the Chinese street names listed in this book were the official versions taken from the road signs posted along the streets. However, it quickly became obvious that the Chinese translations of street names lacked uniformity and were sometimes arbitrary. This situation had resulted from the use of Chinese colloquial street names for some streets; in many cases, colonial officials had also made inappropriate selections of Chinese words.

Noting the above problems, a Committee on the Standardisation of Street Names in Chinese ("Committee") was formed on 18 January 1968 under the purview of Singapore's Ministry of Culture. After 14 discussion sessions, the Committee regularised the Chinese names for more than 2,500 streets. The result of this extensive work was the publication of the first bilingual *Singapore Street Directory*, with a comparative index in both English and Chinese, in July 1970. This format of the street directory was retained until the final edition was published in 2007. The publication of the *Singapore Street Directory* was privatised in 2000, when Mighty Minds began publishing the book.

A document titled "Compilation of Singapore Street Names, 1993" by the National Archives of Singapore serves as another record of Singapore place names. It contains details on the historical origins and original meanings of street names. It was written in English and remains unpublished.

More recent publications on Singapore place names can be found in *Street Names of Singapore* by Peter Dunlop and *Toponymics – a Study of Singapore Street Names*; both are without Chinese translations. The latter is the work of V R Savage and Dr. B S A Yeoh, faculty members of the Geography Department at the National University of Singapore. The third edition of this book was published in 2013.

Notably, in recent years, people have become more attentive to the use of the Chinese language for Singapore's place names. A case in point was the negative reaction to the tentative Chinese name for a new Mass Rapid Transit (MRT) station at Bayfront in June 2005. After prolonged discussions among readers of the local Chinese daily, the original transcription of the station name was replaced by a more elegant and meaningful literary translation.

Based on information available in government records, digitised historical newspapers and other reference materials, this book examines the following topics: the formation of place names in Singapore, the basic structure of Singapore's place names, and the unique characteristics of Chinese place names and their standardisation. Through this analysis, it aims to provide readers with a better understanding of Singapore's interesting cultural background and history.

SECTION 2

NOMENCLATURE OF SINGAPORE PLACE NAMES

Place names in Singapore can be divided into the following three categories:
- Simplex name (Single Word)
- Duplex name (Specific Element + Generic Element)
- Complex name (Specific Element + Specific Element + Generic Element)

1. SIMPLEX NAME
Place names in this category are rare, and only five remained in the Street Directory of 2016. They are as follows: Bishopsgate, Bishopswalk, Causeway, Piccadilly and Queensway. Those that have been expunged include: Aldergrove, Chowringhee, Half-Moon and Rimau.

2. DUPLEX NAME
Approximately 56% of current place names in Singapore are duplex names. They can be classified into two categories based on their structure.
- Specific Element followed by Generic Element
  Using Pekin Road as an example, "Pekin" is the Specific Element and "Road" is the Generic Element.
- Generic Element followed by Specific Element
  Using Mount Elizabeth as an example, "Mount" is the Generic Element and "Elizabeth" is the Specific Element.

3. COMPLEX NAME
Approximately 30% of current place names contain three words, approximately 10% contain four words, and less than 4% contain five to six words. Examples are as follows.
- Toa Payoh West
- Tan Boon Chong Avenue
- Choa Chu Kang Avenue 1
- Changi Business Park Avenue 1

- Ang Mo Kio Industrial Park 1
- Sin Ming Industrial Estate Sector A

4. GENERIC ELEMENTS USED IN SINGAPORE PLACE NAMES

There are more than 80 Generic Elements used in place names in Singapore, and they are either in English or in the Malay language.

Among Generic Elements in English, the most common are "Road", "Avenue" and "Street". Other names include "Alley", "Bank", "Circus", "Close", "Court", "Crescent", "Cross", "Drive", "Expressway", "Green", "Grove", "Height", "Highway", "Hill", "Lane", "Park", "Pier", "Place", "Plain", "Quay", "Ridge", "Rise", "Square", "Terrace", "Track", "View", "Walk", "Way" and "Valley".

A few English Generic Elements are used only once.
- "Bow" in Compassvale Bow
- "Concourse" in Tampines Concourse
- "Cross" in Rhu Cross
- "Wood" in Saint Anne's Wood

One interesting point concerns the use of "Mount" and "Hill" in place names. Place names with "Mount" as the Generic Element use the Head-Tail structure, which is consistent with their origin in England; examples are Mount Elizabeth and Mount Sophia. These names can then become double-word Specific Elements, such as Mount Elizabeth Link, Mount Emily Road, Mount Faber Loop, Mount Faber Road, Mount Pleasant Drive, Mount Rosie Road, Mount Sinai Avenue and Mount Vernon Road. On the other hand, place names with "Hill" as the Generic Element use the Tail-Head structure, such as Muswell Hill and Namly Hill. Because Singapore's topography is generally flat, the Generic Elements of "Mount" and "Hill" are usually used for relatively high areas.

Regarding Generic Elements in the Malay language, the most commonly used are "Jalan" (road) and "Lorong" (lane). Other names include "Bukit" (hill), "Kampong" (village), "Ayer" (water), "Padang" (field), "Taman" (garden), "Tanjong" (cape) and "Telok" (bay). One interesting Generic Element used in the past is the word "Pachitan", which is a place name in Indonesia. In line with the grammar of the Malay language, the structure of Malay place names is in reverse order, i.e., Generic Element followed by Specific Element, such as "Jalan Eunos".

From the above, the omission of the Generic Element of "Street" ("Jalanan" or "Lebuh/Leboh") from the Malay names is notable. In contrast, "Leboh" is widely used in Penang, another component of the Straits Settlements. In Penang, the equivalent of Singapore street names such as China Street,

Chulia Street, Farquhar Street and Queen Street are known as Leboh China, Leboh Chulia, Leboh Farquhar and Leboh Queen, respectively.

5. IRREGULAR STRUCTURE

Not all place names in English follow the composite structure of Specific Element + Generic Element or the reverse. There are special cases, as described below.

Place Name Beginning with Definite Article "The" Followed by Specific Element

There are seven such structures, of which four have been expunged ("e").
- The Arcade (e)
- The Cut (e)
- The Duckway (e)
- The Inglewood
- The Knolls
- The Loop (e)
- The Oval

Specific Acronym + Generic Element

Examples of this structure are as follows.
- Anzac Road (e)
  Anzac is the acronym for Australia and New Zealand Army Corps.
- Koyli Road (e)
  Based on a 1910 article in the *Singapore Free Press*, Koyli is the acronym for King's Own Yorkshire Light Infantry.
- Seac Road (e)
  Seac is the acronym for South East Asia Command.
- T1 Arrival Crescent
  T1 is Terminal 1 of Changi Airport.
- ALPS Avenue
  ALPS is the acronym for Airport Logistics Park of Singapore.
- SUT Avenue
  SUT is the acronym for Sembawang Utilities Terminal.

Place Names Without A Generic Element

There are very few place names without a Generic Element. Examples are the following.
- Kallang Tengah
  "Kallang" is a district name and "Tengah" means middle in Malay.

- Kallang Bahru
  "Bahru" means new in Malay.
- Geylang Bahru
  "Geylang" is a district name.

Place Name Without A Specific Element
Lengkok Bahru is a place name with this structure. "Lengkok" is a Generic Element that means bay, and "Bahru" means new in Malay. The word "new" is an adjective.

Place Name With Two Specific Elements
Geylang Serai is an example of this structure. Geylang Serai is a combination of "Geylang" (a district name) and "Serai" (lemongrass in Malay), both are Specific Elements.

6. DERIVATIVE PLACE NAMES
The Derivative Method is now frequently used for large estate developments, such as public housing and industrial estates. This method is used to derive or create a large number of street names by combining a single Specific Element with a series of Generic Elements. An example is the use of "Bishan" as the Specific Element combined with the Generic Elements of "Lane", "Place", "Road" and "Street" to create Bishan Lane, Bishan Place, Bishan Road, Bishan Street, etc.

7. MULTI-LANGUAGE COMPLEX PLACE NAMES
Because there are at least three components in a complex place name, it is possible to use more than two languages in such names. Examples are as follows.
- Bukit Ho Swee Crescent
  "Crescent" is the Generic Element in English, and "Bukit Ho Swee" is the Specific Element. "Bukit Ho Swee" is a combination of "Bukit" (hill in Malay) and "Ho Swee" (name of a Chinese merchant in the Hokkien dialect).
- Jalan Wat Siam
  This is a unique combination, as it uses "Wat", meaning temple in the Thai language; "Siam" is the alternate English name for Thailand; and the Generic Element of "Jalan" is road in Malay. This place name means Siam Temple Road and uses three languages.

8. HOMONYMS IN DIFFERENT LANGUAGES
Due to the use of multiple languages in place names, there are three pairs of street names that look different on the surface but are actually the same name. They are as follows.
- Redhill Road and Jalan Bukit Merah
  The Generic Element of "Road" is equivalent to "Jalan" in Malay. Bukit Merah means red hill in Malay.
- Sea Breeze Road and Jalan Angin Laut
  Angin Laut means sea breeze in Malay.
- Inggu Road and Jalan Inggu
  These two roads are in close proximity.

SECTION 3

THE CONTENTS OF SINGAPORE PLACE NAMES

The speedy development of entrepot trade in Singapore led to an influx of immigrants from surrounding countries, especially China, Indonesia, India and the Middle East. In the early stages of town planning, place names in Singapore were generally functional, such as Market Street, Hospital Road and Commercial Square. In addition, foreign country or district names were used for the purpose of segregating settlers along racial or religious lines, such as Bugis Kampong, Chulia Kampong, Arab Kampong and Chinese Kampong (*kampong* means village in Malay). These were later expanded into Pekin Road, Hokkien Street, Macao Street, Arab Street, etc. Subsequent foreign place names adopted were mainly British in the various fortifications built to defend the island against the Dutch and the pirates initially, and against the Japanese before WW2. Anthroponyms (personal names) were also used extensively in place names. They were mainly names of colonial officials and business leaders who made political or economic contributions to society.

1. ROADS NAMED AFTER FOREIGN PLACES
Britain and the British Empire
A large number of place names in Singapore have their origins in Britain and the British Empire and they are mainly found in the former British military areas. Approximately 40 roads in the former Royal Air Force (RAF) Changi were named after air stations in Britain, more than 100 roads in the former British army barracks were named after towns in Britain and streets in London, and about 40 roads in the former Singapore Naval Base were named after former colonies of the British Empire. British place names are also found in many residential estates such as Serangoon Gardens, the former Grove Estate in Tanjong Katong and Frankel Estate.

Others
Place names originating from the surrounding region are mainly from Malaysia and Indonesia. Malaysian names include Borneo Road, Ipoh Lane, Johore Road, Malacca Street, Penang Road, Perak Road and Bernam Street; Indonesian names include Bali Lane, Bencoolen Street, Deli Street, Java Road and Siak Street.

Indian place names can be found in Anamalai Avenue, Bombay Road, Delhi Road, Ganges Avenue, Kadayanallur Street and Karikal Lane.

Burmese place names, such as "Burmah", "Moulmein" and "Rangoon" are concentrated in the Balestier Road area.

There are about 20 place names from China and they can be found in China Street, Hokien Street, Canton Street, Amoy Street, Shanghai Road, Tew Chew Street, Soochow Road, etc.

2. ANTHROPONYMS

Anthroponyms of Non-Residents
Anthroponyms of non-residents can be grouped as follows.
- Members of the British royal family. This will be discussed in paragraph 8 of this section.
- Governing authority of the Straits Settlements. Initially, Governors/Governor Generals in British India, such as Canning Lane, Ellenborough Street and Minto Road; after the transfer of the Straits Settlements from the East India Company to the Colonial Office in London in 1867 ("Transfer"), Heads of the Colonial Office in London, such as Holland Road.
- British generals who contributed to the colonisation of India and the successful repression of the 1857 Indian Mutiny. Examples are Hastings Road, Havelock Road, Neil Road and Outram Road.
- Generals of the British Royal Navy, mainly found in the former Singapore Naval Base and Harbour area, such as Cochrane Road, Drake Avenue, Exmouth Road, Grenville Road, Hawke Road, Nelson Road and Keppel Road.
- British war heroes in World War One ("WW1"), such as Allenby Road, Beatty Road, Byng Road and Kitchener Road.
- British Generals in WW2, such as Mountbatten Road, Leese Road and Slim Road.
- Non-residents of other nationalities include French generals in WW1, such as Clemenceau Avenue; famous Asian poets and writers such as Iqbal Avenue, Li Po Avenue, Munshi Abdullah Avenue, etc.

Anthroponyms of Residents
Places named after residents formed the largest section of the anthroponyms. There are more than 600 of such names and they are grouped as follows.

Residents of European Origin
Roads named after residents of European origin occupy the largest number of anthroponyms at 46% of the 600 names. These are mainly names of colonial officials, such as Governors, members of the Legislative Council or Municipal Commission, surveyors and engineers. These names will be further discussed under paragraph 5 of this section. Within this group of names, a notable one is J T Thomson, the Chief Surveyor in Singapore from 1841 to 1853. Currently there are 19 roads named after him.

Besides the colonial officials, many European anthroponyms were names of prominent landowners. They include the following list of streets and roads.
- Angus Street (Gilbert Angus of Cluny Hill)
- Cuppage Road (William Cuppage of Emerald Hill Estate)
- D'Almeida Street (Jose d'Almeida of The Everton)
- Napier Road (William Napier of Tang Leng Estate)
- Oxley Rise (Dr. Thomas Oxley of Oxley Estate)
- Palmer Road (John Palmer of Mount Palmer)
- Prinsep Street (C R Prinsep of Prinsep Estate)
- Scotts Road (William Scott of Claymore Estate)

Residents of Chinese Descent
Roads with names of Chinese residents formed 42% of total anthroponyms since the Chinese race formed a large majority of the population in Singapore. This will be further deliberated under Section 4 — Place Names of Chinese Origin.

Others
Out of the remaining 12% of anthroponyms, 9% were Malay names. The rest were names of Indians, Sri Lankans, Arabs, Jews, etc. With regard to the Malay names, the most significant is Mohamad Eunos bin Abdullah, a Malay community leader, who has a group of 24 roads named after him.

3. ECONOMIC DEVELOPMENT AND PLACE NAMES
The main objective in the founding of Singapore was to establish a trading post in this region. Singapore did prosper as an entrepot due to its strategic geographical position as well as the early decision to maintain it as a free port. In the early stage, agriculture was also encouraged for tax revenue.

Entrepot Trade and Place Names
Efficient cargo handling facilities were needed for the development of entrepot trade and many far-sighted merchants built their own quays and piers for efficient transfer of goods to and from the ships. The main ones located around the city area are shown in Table 1.

Table 1   Quays and Piers Located in the City

Name of Quay	Named After
Alkaff Quay	Owned by the Alkaff family.
Boat Quay	This quay was known as Cheang Hong Lim Quay and renamed Boat Quay in 1914.
Clarke Quay	Named after A Clarke, Governor of Singapore.
Collyer Quay	G Collyer, a Colonial Engineer, built this impractical defence structure around 1862.
Earle Quay	T E Earle was Manager of the Straits Steamship Co. Ltd.
Ho Puah Quay	Lim Ho Puah was a shipowner.
Johnston Pier	Built by A L Johnston, one of the earliest European settlers and the owner of the first trading company in 1820. The pier was rebuilt in 1933 and renamed Clifford Pier.
Peng Siang Quay	Lim Peng Siang was the son of Lim Ho Puah.
Raffles Quay	Named after Sir Thomas Stamford Raffles, the founder of Singapore.
Robertson Quay	J H Robertson was a doctor and Municipal Commissioner for many years. The quay was known as Gulam Mydin Quay before 1900.

Larger ships that could not berth at the quayside would anchor at sea with small boats ferrying goods to and fro between the ships and the warehouses along the Singapore River. The river was the economic lifeline of Singapore for many years, especially after the failure of the agriculture economy, which will be discussed later.

With the arrival of steamships and the opening of the Suez Canal in 1869, Tanjong Pagar Dock, and later New Harbour along Telok Blangah Road were built. The harbour was renamed Keppel Harbour in 1900 and the road leading to the harbour was correspondingly changed from New Harbour Road to Keppel Road.

Entrepot trade in early Singapore's economy involved trading in spice, gambier, tin and later on, rubber and petroleum. However, the main source of revenue for the government was the opium trade (opium was only banned in 1943 during the Japanese Occupation). For example, the tax from opium and spirits in 1853 formed about 75% of the revenue collected by the government. Major British trading houses in the Far East including A L Johnston and Jardine Matheson were rich and powerful from opium trade and had their own wharfs in Singapore. The wealth generated from entrepot trade made many local merchants rich and they had the monetary means to make contributions to build public works, hospitals and schools for the common good of the society.

Many European trading houses in sole proprietorship or partnership format were established, mostly as agency houses for companies in Britain and Continental Europe. Numerous roads were named after these merchants since they purchased land for business or residential purposes. The more significant ones are as follows.
- Holt Road (Alfred Holt & Co.)
- Johnston Street (A L Johnston & Co.)
- Guthrie Lane (Guthrie & Co.)
- Henderson Road (Henderson Bros. Rubber Factory)
- Spottiswoode Park (William Spottiswoode)
- Paterson Road (William R Paterson)

Among the above examples, Johnston Street and Guthrie Lane have been expunged. As for the businesses, only Guthrie as a commercial enterprise founded by A Guthrie in 1821 is still in existence in Singapore, albeit with new owners.

Agriculture and Place Names

Besides trading, agriculture formed the other significant sector of the economy in early Singapore. Many kinds of plantations were experimented with including coffee, lemongrass and sugar cane. However, due to the soil condition on the island, the more successful plantations were gambier pepper, nutmeg, coconut, pineapple and rubber. In 1849, gambier and pepper took up most of the agricultural land with nutmeg and coconut in second place.

Gambier and Pepper

Extracts from gambier were the source of leather softening agents before its equivalent synthetic material was developed. When the British took control of Singapore in 1819, Chinese migrants such as Tan Ngun Ha were already growing pepper and gambier on the island. These two produce were complementary in life cycles and were usually planted together. The peak in gambier planting was around 1840, during which there were about 6,000 people working in approximately 600 plantations. Seah Eu Chin (1805–1883) was known as the King of Gambier as he was the largest gambier plantation owner. Gambier plantations rapidly disappeared when synthetic material was found and were gone by 1866 (Makepeace, vol. 2 at 80).

Place names relating to gambier and pepper include Gambier Avenue, Lorong Gambier, Lorong Lada Hitam, Lorong Lada Merah and Lorong Lada Padi in the Sembawang area; and Gambir Walk and Jalan Lada Puteh in the centre part of Singapore.

Nutmeg

Nutmeg and mace were once the prized produce of the Moluccas Islands in Indonesia. In the 1830s, European migrants began planting nutmeg on a large scale in Singapore. Notable ones were Prinsep's Estate, Oxley Estate, Cairn Hill, Sri Menanti Estate and Claymore Estate. These plantations covered an area from what is now Tanglin through Orchard Road to Prinsep Street. Nutmeg cultivation was profitable until the trees were fatally hit by widespread disease in 1855. By 1862 the cultivation of nutmegs had entirely ceased, leaving behind the names of Nutmeg Road and Orchard Road.

Rubber

The next development of agriculture in Singapore was the introduction of rubber trees. Rubber seeds were brought in from South America with the first tree planted in the Singapore Botanic Gardens. The rubber industry began with H N Ridley when he was appointed the Head of the Botanic Gardens in 1888. Ridley devoted his time to the research of rubber tree cultivation and the method of tapping rubber sap without impeding its growth. He made available his findings to local Chinese merchants who were interested in this new venture. Tan Chay Yan (1871-1916) started tapping rubber in 1896 with a rubber plantation in Malacca. He was followed by Lim Boon Keng (1869-1957), Teo Eng Hock (1871-1959), Tan Kah Kee (1874-1961), Lim Nee Soon (1879-1936, nephew of Teo Eng Hock), Tan Chor Nam (1884-1971) and others who established rubber plantations in the rural districts of Singapore. They were joined by major British companies such as the Bukit Sembawang Rubber Company and the Singapore United Rubber Plantation (SURP). These two companies were the largest plantation companies in 1920 and were responsible for about 20,000 acres of land. The cultivation of rubber was most opportune because it was at the same time that the automobile industry in the West started to boom. Rubber was in great demand for the production of car tires; this brought about high prices for the commodity and led to the wealth of the early pioneers of rubber plantations. During this time, old gambier plantations laid in waste were replaced by rubber and pineapple plantations.

Rubber and pineapple plants were complementary in economic cycles and often planted together. Thus, it was only natural that the most wealthy local rubber plantation owner at that time, Lim Nee Soon, was anointed both Rubber King and Pineapple King. After WW2, rubber plantations shared the same fate as gambier plantations upon the introduction of synthetic material. Exacerbated by high land and labour costs, rubber plantations were only seen in Peninsula Malaya and Indonesia by the early 1950s.

In addition to some of the personal names mentioned above, place names connected to the rubber industry are Ridley Park (after H N Ridley) and Lorong Getah (*getah* means rubber in Malay). In respect of pineapples, there are Jalan Darat Nanas (which means pineapple land), Bukit Nanas (which means pineapple hill) and Lorong Ong Lye. "Ong Lye" is also pineapple in the Hokkien dialect. The district name of Buangkok (also the name of a MRT Station) was the Teochew transcription of the Chinese name of SURP, "Wan Guo".

Others
Other place names related to agriculture activities are Balestier Road (sugar cane), Geylang Serai (lemongrass) and Bukit Brown (known as "Coffee Hill" by the locals).

Other Economic Activities

Tin Smelting
There is no historical record of the existence of tin mining in Singapore. However, tin was a major trade item for Singapore as early as the 14th century. This was based on a journal written by Wang Da Yuan (1311-1350), a Chinese merchant and navigator who lived during the Yuan dynasty (1271-1368) in China. When Malaya became the top tin producer in the world during the colonial days, Singapore became the world's largest tin smelting centre. Place names like Adam Drive, Adam Park and Adam Road were named after Frank Adam who was the Managing Director of a major tin smelting company.

Besides tin smelting, a lesser known industry in Singapore was the production of sago from the starch of palm trees for markets in England and India. Sago Lane and Sago Street in the Chinatown area was the centre of sago production.

Other notable place names linked to early economic development are as follows.

Pender Road
This was named after John Denison Pender, President of the Eastern Telegraph Company. The company was responsible for the laying of undersea cables that linked the British Empire from London via Singapore to New Zealand in 1876.

Whampoa Road
This road was named after Mr. Whampoa or Hoo Ah Kay, a wealthy merchant and land owner. Being one of the very few Chinese who could speak English

during his time, he was the first Chinese to be appointed an unofficial member of the Legislative Council in 1867 and was made a Companion of St. Michael and St. George ("C.M.G.") in 1878. His relation to place names will be discussed further in this chapter under "Historical Sites and Place Names".

Kim Seng Road
This road was named after Tan Kim Seng, a prominent Peranakan merchant in the 19th century. He was a Chinese community leader in Singapore and Malacca.

4. WAR AND PLACE NAMES

As mentioned in "Anthroponyms of Non-Residents", many roads in Singapore were named after war heroes in the colonisation of India, repression of the Indian Mutiny and the two world wars. Foreign place names were also used to commemorate famous battle fields during the two world wars and the colonisation of native states in Malaya and Burma. In addition, the following are noteworthy.

Opium Wars and Elgin Bridge

During the two Opium Wars between Britain and China, Singapore served as the transit point between India (the main source of British forces) and China. The Esplanade area, what is now the Padang, was used as the barracks for the army enroute to China.

Yuan Ming Yuan was a summer palace in Beijing. It was built over 150 years during the height of the Ching Dynasty in China and was known as the Versailles of the East. The palace also served as an imperial museum that had a large collection of important books, treasures and cultural artefacts. During the Second Opium War in 1860, James Bruce (who was later created as the Earl of Elgin) led a successful joint military mission of Britain and France to Beijing. At the end of the siege, Yuan Ming Yuan was completely burnt down with all the valuable treasures and artefacts within looted by the attackers. For his efforts in this war, Elgin was appointed Governor-General of India in 1862 and Thomson's Bridge in Singapore was renamed to commemorate him. Unfortunately Elgin died in India in 1863.

WW1 and Sohst Road

This road was named after T H Sohst, a wealthy German aristocrat who settled in Singapore before WW1. It was renamed Mount Rosie Road (after his wife) in 1920 on account of WW1.

WW2 and Percival Road, Fort Canning

In a rather contrasting scenario, Percival Road was named after General Percival who surrendered to the Japanese army during WW2. Due to poor strategy and lack of reinforcements, the British army with about 100,000 personnel was not able to defend the island from the attack of the Imperial Japanese Army of 20,000 personnel. The surrender was described by Sir Winston Churchill as the "worst disaster and largest capitulation in British history". Nevertheless, a road in Fort Canning Hill was named after him after the war.

Post WW2, Japan Street and Grove Road
Japan Street was the first street to be renamed after WW2. It was renamed Boon Tat Street in 1946. Shortly after that, Grove Road was renamed Mountbatten Road to commemorate Lord Mountbatten's victory in the Far East at the end of WW2.

5. POLITICAL SYSTEM AND PLACE NAMES
Rulers of the Original Malay Settlers
Place names related to the political system before British rule were "Sultan" (which means king in Malay) and "Temengong" (equivalent to Interior Minister). Examples are Jalan Sultan, Sultan Gate, Sultan Palace and Temengong Road.

Colonial Governors
From 1819 (when colonial rule began) to 1959 (the beginning of internal self-government), there were altogether 3 Residents and 25 Governors in Singapore. They were Farquhar, Crawfurd (changed to Crawford for road name), Prince (a more senior post of Governor was created during his term), Fullerton, Ibbetson, Murchison, Bonham, Butterworth, Cavenagh, Blundell, Ord, Clarke, Jervois, Robinson, Weld, Smith, Mitchell, Swettenham, Anderson, Young, Guillemard, Clifford, Clementi, Thomas, Gimson, Nicoll, Black and Goode.

With the exception of Ibbetson, Murchison, Blundell, Mitchell, Young, Thomas, Gimson, Black and Goode, all residents and governors have places named after them. In addition, there were 7 places named after Sir Thomas Stamford Raffles ("Raffles").

Members of the Legislative Council
The Governors of the Straits Settlements were supported by an Executive Council and a Legislative Council ("LC"). The Executive Council was made up solely of senior government officers while the LC had some members of the public who were appointed by the Governor. From 1924, the number of LC members was increased to 26 with Governor-appointed members increased from 4 to 13. This political system was maintained until after the end of

WW2. In 1948, partial voting began for 6 members of the LC. Voting was expanded to 25 out of a total of 32 members in 1955. Many place names were named after members of the LC. Examples are as follows.
- Read Crescent (W H M Read, 1867)
- Whampoa Road (Hoo Ah Kay, 1867)
- Liang Seah Street (Seah Liang Seah, son of Seah Eu Chin, 1883–1890)
- Jiak Kim Street (Tan Jiak Kim, grandson of Tan Kim Seng, 1889)
- Boon Keng Road (Lim Boon Keng, 1895–1901)
- Veerasamy Road (N V Veerasamy, 1900)
- Tessensohn Road (E Tessensohn, 1927)

Members of the Municipal Commission

More places were named after members of the Municipal Commission ("MC") compared to the LC; this may be due to the fact that the MC had the authority to approve street names. There are more than 40 names under this category. Examples are as follows.
- Choon Guan Street (Lee Choon Guan)
- Chander Road (A C Chander)
- Dunman Road (Robert Dunman)
- Elias Road (J A Elias)
- Farrer Road (R J Farrer)
- Jalan Eunos (M Eunos bin Abdullah)
- Kheam Hock Road (Tan Kheam Hock)
- Lornie Road (J Lornie)
- Marshall Lane (H T Marshall)
- Sims Avenue (W A Sims)

Others

In addition to the above, roads were named after the following groups of colonial officials.
- Judges and law enforcement officers (Maxwell, Pickering, Goodman)
- Surveyors and engineers of the Municipality (Coleman, Thomson, Newton, Pigott)
- Members of the Rural Board (Nee Soon, Chong Pang, Andrews)

Traces of nepotism can be seen in some of the appointments during the colonial days. Raffles appointed his friend Farquhar as the first Resident of Singapore after signing the key agreements on Singapore. He also appointed his brother-in-law, Captain Flint, as Singapore's first Harbour-Master Attendant and gave a small hill (later known as Wallich Hill) in town to his friend,

N Wallich. Farquhar then appointed his son-in-law, Francis Bernard, as the Police Commissioner. There was a Farquhar street, two Flint Streets and a Bernard Street in the early days. Subsequently, one of the Flint Streets was renamed Prinsep Street and Wallich Hill was flattened for land reclamation leaving Wallich Street on the map today.

Post-independence
Place names related to political figures after Singapore's independence include the following.

Sheares Bridge, Sheares Avenue
Benjamin Henry Sheares was the second President of Singapore.

Jalan Ahmad Ibrahim
Ahmad Ibrahim was the Minister of Labour in 1961.

Hon Sui Sen Drive
Hon Sui Sen was the Finance Minister in the 1970s.

6. HISTORICAL SITES AND PLACE NAMES
Many place names in Singapore have connections with historical sites and personalities. Therefore, embedded in these place names are some interesting facets of the history of multi-racial society in Singapore.

Bras Basah Road
This road was known as *brass bassa* (which means wet rice in Malay). This was a place used by rice merchants to sun wet rice along Sungei Brass Bassa.

Club Street
This street was named after the Chwee Lan Teng Chinese Club, a Hokkien business club, which existed up to 1884. The club had a palatial club house at Gemmill Hill on a land area of five acres. After the dissolution of the club in 1884, the land was divided into building lots and sold. The club house was retained by its subsequent owners and finally became The Weekly Entertainment Kee Lam Club in 1898.

Kreta Ayer Street
This street is located in Singapore's Chinatown. *Kreta* means wheeled vehicle and *ayer* means water in Malay, whereas the Chinese name for Kreta Ayer ("Goo Cia Chwee" in the Hokkien dialect) means bullock, cart and water respectively. Prior to the installation of fresh water pipelines in Singapore, fresh water was supplied to the Chinatown area from Ann Siang Hill and Spring Street using bullock carts as transportation vehicles.

Dhoby Ghaut
Dhoby Ghaut is now the name of a major MRT station. It is a Hindi name that means laundry (*dhoby*) and open space (*ghat*). The original Dhoby Ghaut was at the bank of Sungei Brass Bassa (later renamed Stamford Canal) where Indian laundry workers walked down the open space to do their laundry. The canal has since been filled.

Orchard Road
As mentioned previously, the renowned shopping district along Orchard Road was once lined with many nutmeg plantations. Its Chinese name, 乌节 ("Wu Jie" in pinyin), was derived from a transcription of the English word "Orchard" into the Hokkien dialect.

Toa Payoh
The original name for Toa Payoh was "Toah Pyoh" in the early days. This name is not of Malay origin. In an 1849 press article which provided the interpretation of the name, "Toah" was long or large and "Pyoh" was an irregular path formed by wooden planks thrown into marshy or muddy place by the Chinese. The modern name of Toa Payoh (which means kiln in a big plot of undeveloped land in Mandarin) could come from the brick kilns as well as a huge municipal brickfield in this area around the 1860s.

Whampoa Road and Bendemeer Road
Whampoa Road was named after the hometown of Hoo Ah Kay, a wealthy merchant born in Whampoa, in the province of Guangdong, China. Hoo's fortune began with the supply of foodstuff to the British Navy in Singapore. He became a big land owner and built a large bungalow with a huge Chinese garden known as Whampoa Garden in the Serangoon area. The garden was well known as it was opened to the public during holidays. After Hoo's death, the property was sold to Seah Liang Seah who renamed it Bendemeer Garden. Although the property has been demolished for new developments, the names of "Whampoa" and "Bendemeer" have been retained in roads in this area.

7. RELIGION AND PLACE NAMES

Table 2 shows the spread of religions among the local population based on a population censor in 2000.

Table 2 Spread of Religion among the Population in Singapore in 2000

Religion	Buddhism/Taoism	Christianity	Muslim	Hinduism	Others/No religion
(%)	51	15	15	4	15

Roads Named after Places of Worship

Ama Keng Road
"Ama Keng" is the name of a Taoist temple worshipping the Sea Goddess.

Armenian Street
This street was named after the Armenian Church of St. Gregory The Illuminator, the first church in Singapore.

St. Andrew's Road
This road was named after St. Andrew's Cathedral, the Cathedral church of the Anglican Diocese.

Lutheran Road
This road was named after the Lutheran Church of Our Redeemer.

Bright Hill Crescent/Drive
This is the site of Kong Meng San Phor Kark See, a Buddhist Temple. "Kong Meng San" is the Hokkien transcription of Bright Hill.

Jalan Novena
This was named after the Church of St. Alphonsus (Novena Church), a Catholic Church.

Temple Street/Mosque Street/Synagogue Street
The diversity of religions in Singapore is best seen in a mix of religious buildings in this small area in Chinatown. In 1827, an Indian temple (Sri Mariamam) was built between Pagoda Street and Temple Street. Parallel to Pagoda Street in the north is Mosque Street, which was named after the Masjid Jumae Chulia (built in 1835). Less than a kilometre away from Mosque Street is Synagogue Street, where the Maghain Aboth Synagogue was originally built in 1840.

Roman Catholic Church
Despite the fact that members of the Catholic Church only formed less than 5% of the population, the Catholic Mission in Singapore started as early as 1821. The church made enormous contributions to Singapore in philanthropic activities and education. This can be seen in roads bearing names of saints of the Catholic Church, such as St. Anne's Wood, St. Barnabas Lane, St. Francis Road, St. Helena Road, St. Helier's Avenue, St. Lawrence Road, St. Nicholas View, St. Patrick's Road, St. Wilfred Road and St. Xavier's Lane.

American Missionary
Footprints of American missionary work can be seen in Dickenson Hill (named after J T Dickenson) and Zion Road (Keasberry Mission).

Place Names Which Appear to be Linked to Religion

Beo Crescent in Bukit Ho Swee

The original dwellers of Bukit Ho Swee were mainly from the southern part of Fujian (or Hokkien) Province. "Beo" means temple in Hokkien. The road name was derived from the three temples in this location which were all destroyed in a huge fire in 1960. The fire also destroyed more than 2,200 attap houses on the hill and made 16,000 people homeless. When public housing was subsequently built on the fire site, only the street name of Beo Crescent was retained.

Church Street

This street was named after Thomas Church, the Resident Councillor in Singapore from 1837 to 1856. It is therefore natural that the Chinese name for this street is a phonetic translation.

8. PLACE NAMES LINKED TO FAMILIES

The British Royal Family

Being a former British colony, the most significant group of place names linked to a single family is none other than the British royal family. There are about 50 roads linked to its members. Examples are in Table 3.

Chinese Families

Lim Nee Soon

The most significant group of place names linked to a local family is the family of Lim Nee Soon, with about 18 names. This excludes more than 40 street names in Yishun New Town that were named after him. Lim was known as the Pineapple King and Rubber King during his lifetime. The name Nee Soon (in Teochew dialect) was later refined to become "Yishun", which is the transcription of his name in Mandarin pinyin. He also had other names which were used in road names, including Wei Hua, Kee Hua, Bah Soon Pah (his Peranakan name), Chong How, Chong Sin, Chong Nee and Huang Long. Names related to Lim Nee Soon which have been used in road names include Teo Lee (maternal grandfather), Peng Nguan (grandfather), Eng Hock (maternal uncle), Peck Hay (wife), Chong Kuo (eldest son), Chong Pang (second son), Thong Aik (name of his rubber factory) and Thong Bee (name of his shop).

Cheang Hong Lim

The next longest list of street names related to a Chinese family is that of Cheang Hong Lim. Cheang Hong Lim had five places named after him. In addition, five streets were named after his sons Jim Hean, Jim Chuan and Jim Khean; and four streets were named after his shop, Chop Wan Seng.

Table 3 Places Named After Members of the British Royal Family

Place Name, Date Named	Title of the Royalty and Reign	Relation to Queen Elizabeth II
Queen Street, before 1844	Queen Victoria (1837–1901)	Great great grandmother
Victoria Street, before 1853	Queen Victoria	Great great grandmother
Albert Street, 1858	Prince Albert, consort of Queen Victoria	Great great grandfather
King's Road, 1902	King Edward VII (1901–1910)	Great grandfather
Alexandra Road, 1864	Queen Alexandra, consort of Edward VII	Great grandmother
King George Road, 1926	King George V (1910–1936)	Grandfather
Prince Edward Road, 1923	The heir to George V, became Edward VIII (1936) and abdicated within a year.	Uncle
King's Avenue (Naval Base), 1940	King George VI (1936–1952). The dock at the Base was also named after him.	Father
Queen's Avenue, 1940	Queen Elizabeth, consort of George VI.	Mother
Elizabeth Drive, 1952	Queen Elizabeth II ("QE2") (1952- present)	Self
Prince Philip Avenue, 1952	Prince Philip, the Duke of Edinburg	Consort
Prince Charles Crescent, 1952	Prince Charles	Son
Princess Anne Close, 1952	Princess Anne	Daughter

Other examples are as follows.

- Tan Tock Seng (Tan Tock Seng Link, Jalan Tan Tock Seng)
  Son: Bukit Kim Cheng, Kim Cheng Street, Tan Kim Cheng Road
  Grandson: Teck Guan Street
  Great Grandson: Chay Yan Street

- Tan Kim Seng (Kim Seng Road, Kim Seng Bridge)
  Sons: Beng Swee Place, Beng Gum Road
  Grandsons: Jiak Kim Street, Jiak Chuan Road

- Seah Eu Chin (Eu Chin Street, Seah Street)
  Sons: Liang Seah Street, Peck Seah Street
  Shop: Chin Hin Street

The Contents of Singapore Place Names

- Wee Ah Hood (Ah Hood Road)
  Son: Kim Yam Road
- See Hood Kee (Hood Kee Street)
  Sons: Eng Watt Street, Moh Guan Terrace
  Grandson: Ewe Boon Road
- Cheong Chun Tin (Chun Tin Road)
  Son: Cheong Chin Nam Road, Chin Nam Street
  Daughters-in-law: Yuk Tong Avenue, Tham Soong Avenue

Others
There are few examples of family-linked place names in other races and they are as follows.
- Raffles (seven roads), Mount Sophia (wife) and Flint Street (brother-in-law)
- Farquhar Street, Bernard Street and George Street (sons-in-law)
- De Souza Street, Mount Rosie Road (daughter) and Sohst Road (son-in-law)

9. EDUCATION AND PLACE NAMES

Raffles Institution
Raffles made the significant first step to the development of education in Singapore by allocating 100 acres of land and a personal cash donation of 2,000 Spanish Dollars (currency used at that time) to build the Singapore Institution. The area was later named Institution Hill and remains so today. The school was however only opened in 1834 at the city centre and renamed Raffles Institution after Raffles retired and returned to England. The land at Institution Hill then reverted to the government.

University of Singapore
The University of Singapore started as the Straits Settlements and Federated Malaya States Government Medical School in 1905. It was established upon the petition by Tan Jiak Kim (grandson of Tan Kim Seng) to the colonial government. The initial cost for establishing the school was funded by him and the local non-European community. The medical school subsequently received an endowment from the King Edward VII Memorial Fund and was renamed King Edward VII Medical College in 1921. It became part of the University of Singapore in 1962. A street not too distant from the medical college was named Jiak Kim Street to commemorate Tan Jiak

Kim for his valuable contributions in many ways to the local community. MacAlister Road, at the side of the medical college, was named after Dr. George H K MacAlister, the Principal of the college from 1918 to 1930.

Nanyang University

In early 1953, the Hokkien Association, under the leadership of Tan Lark Sai, initiated the establishment of a Chinese university in Singapore to cater to the need for higher education in the Chinese language. After much lobbying and hard work, he was able to obtain sufficient financial support from the Chinese communities, both in Singapore and other parts of South East Asia. The Nanyang University, the first Chinese university outside greater China, started classes on 15 March 1956. It was built in Jurong on a former rubber plantation land called Yunnan Estate. The university was closed in 1980 and reconstituted as the Nanyang Technological University at the same location. With the exception of two Specific Elements of "Nanyang" (meaning south sea) and "Yunnan", other street names in the original campus were expunged.

School Names

Many schools in Singapore are named after the Specific Element of the road they are located. For example in the Bedok area, there are Bedok North Secondary School, Bedok South Secondary School, Bedok Town Secondary School, and Bedok View Secondary School. The Chinese names for these schools may have no relation to the place names at all. The problem with naming the school based on its location arises when the school is relocated to another part of the island and its name becomes a misfit in its new environment. Examples are as follows.

River Valley High School
Originally located in Jalan Kuala, off River Valley Road, this school was moved to various locations a few times and is currently at Boon Lay Avenue. Boon Lay Secondary School, originally at Jalan Boon Lay, is now located in Jurong West.

Changkat Primary School
Originally located in Changkat Changi, the school was relocated to the Simei area.

Anderson Secondary School
Originally located at Anderson Road, this school is now in Ang Mo Kio.

Scholars and Educators
The following roads are named after scholars and educators.

Boon Keng Road
The name of Lim Boon Keng was already mentioned under "Political System and Place Names" as a member of the Legislative Council. He was also noted as the first local Chinese to receive the Queen's Scholarship to study Medicine at Edinburgh University. He taught at the medical college after graduation. In 1899 he co-founded the Singapore Chinese Girls' School with Song Ong Siang, with major initial funding from Khoo Siok Wan (see below). He served (without salary) as the Chancellor of Amoy (now Xiamen) University in Fujian, China between 1921 and 1937. Amoy University was founded by Tan Kah Kee.

Siok Wan Close
Khoo Siok Wan was a scholar and famous poet from a wealthy traditional Chinese family who passed the pre-qualification exams to participate in the Imperial examination in Beijing, China. It was reported that he inherited 500,000 dollars from his father and spent it within 5 years, mostly due to his generosity to others. For example, he donated more than 50% of the initial fund raised to set up the Singapore Chinese Girls' School. The Chinese synonym for Singapore — "Xing Zhou", or "Sin Chew" (星洲) was adopted from his poem about Singapore in 1896.

Blackmore Drive
This road was named after Sophia Blackmore, a missionary from Australia. During her stay in Singapore from 1887 to 1927, she founded two Methodist girls' schools. The first was originally named Tamil Girls' School and later renamed Methodist Girls' School. The second, Anglo-Chinese Girls' School was established in 1888 and later renamed Fairfield Methodist Girls' School.

St. Andrew's Schools
Three roads in the campus of St. Andrew's schools were named after their founder and former principals. These include Graham White Drive, Francis Thomas Drive and Sorby Adams Drive.

10. PLACES NAMED AFTER FEMALES
Relatively few places in Singapore are named after women, probably due to their lack of social and economic status in the past. Apart from names of the British royal family previously mentioned, Table 4 is a list of places named after women in Singapore.

Table 4 Places Named After Females

Place Name	Woman Named After
Blackmore Drive	S Blackmore, missionary from Australia.
Bukit Teresa Road	Named after Saint Teresa from France.
Da Silva Avenue	Bertha Da Silva, wife of a rich merchant.
Eng Neo Avenue	Tan Eng Neo, wife of Gaw Boon Chan, a landowner.
Florence Road	Florence Yeo, wife of Lim Ah Pin.
Iduna Road	Iduna, a goddess in Norse mythology, is the keeper of the Apples of Immortality.
Jalan Mariam Lengkok Mariam Mariam Close	Mariam is the Malay equivalent of Mary. There is no information on the source of this name.
Joan Road	Joan could be the daughter of the Colonial Secretary, Andrew Caldecott.
Lorong Fatimah	Fatimah was a Malay lady who developed this area.
Maria Avenue	Maria is the Italian equivalent of Mary. There is no information on the source of this name.
Marlene Avenue	There is no information on the source of this name.
Mount Elizabeth Road	T Hewetson was an early dweller on this hill. There is no information on the source of this name.
Mount Emily Road	Emily Prinsep, related to C R Prinsep.
Mount Rosie Road	Rosie was the wife of T H Sohst, a German resident.
Mount Sophia	Sophia Hull, the wife of Sir Stamford Raffles; or Sophia Cooke, of Chinese Girls' School (now St. Margaret's School).
Peck Hay Road	Wee Peck Hay was the wife of Lim Nee Soon.
Queen Astrid Park	Astrid was Queen of Belgium.
Rebecca Road	There is no information on the source of this name.
St. Anne's Wood	Saint Anne was the mother of Virgin Mary.
St. Helena Road	Saint Helena was the mother of Constantine I of the Roman Empire.
St. Margaret's Road	Saint Margaret's Road originated from a place name in Kent, England. The name Margaret refers to Margaret of Antioch or Margaret, Queen of Scots. Both are saints venerated by the Anglican Church.
Tham Soong Avenue	Tham Soong, wife of Cheong Chin Heng or daughter-in-law of Cheong Chun Tin.
Yuk Tong Avenue	Yuk Tong, wife of Cheong Chin Nam.

11. HOUSING ESTATES WITH A THEME

Prior to the use of derivative place names, many housing estates in Singapore use street names around a particular theme, such as trees, flowers, writers, nuts, etc. Examples are as follows.

Trees
Sennett Estate was built on the original site of Alkaff Garden. Roads in part of the estate are named after tropical trees such as Angsana, Belimbing, Camphor, Cedar, Chempaka, Kenanga, Lichi, Mulberry and Willow. Among these roads named after trees is a Butterfly Avenue. On the other hand, tree names from the temperate zone, such as Cherry, Cypress, Fir, Maple, Oak and Redwood are found in an estate in the Bukit Timah area.

Flowers
Names of flowers are used for an estate in the Upper Thomson area; they include Carnation, Daffodil, Gladiola, Jasmine and Marigold.

Limes
Names of different species of lime in the Malay language (*limau* means lime in Malay) are found in the Bedok/Changi area. The types of lime include *limau bali*, *limau kasturi*, *limau manis*, *limau nipis* and *limau purut*. Together with Limau Garden, Limau Grove, Limau Rise, Limau Terrace and Limau Walk, there are 10 roads in this area with the lime theme.

Operas
As the name suggests, roads in Opera Estate were named after operas and stage productions. The names of operas include *Aida*, *Carmen*, *Dafne*, *Ernani*, *Figaro*, *Fidelio*, *Lakme*, *Norma*, *Rienzi* and *Tosca*.

Literary Masters
Roads in the Teachers' Housing Estate used names of literary masters in Asia as Specific Elements. The names are as follows.
- Iqbal Avenue (Muhammad Iqbal, Pakistani poet, 1877–1938)
- Kalidasa Avenue (Kalidasa, Indian playwright and poet, 5th century)
- Li Po Avenue (Li Bai, Chinese poet, 701–762)
- Munshi Abdullah Avenue (Munshi Abdullah, Malay writer, 1796–1854)
- Omar Khayyam Avenue (Omar Khayyam, Persian mathematician and poet, 1048–c.1131)
- Tagore Avenue (Rabindranath Tagore, Indian writer and painter, 1861–1941, Nobel Prize winner, 1913)
- Tu Fu Avenue (Du Fu, Chinese poet, 712–770)
- Tung Po Avenue (Su Shi, also known as Su Dong Bo, Chinese writer and poet, 1037–1101)

Precious Stones
Four roads in the Serangoon area were named after precious stones. They are Moonstone Lane, Opal Crescent, Ruby Lane and Topaz Road.

Animals and Birds
In a small area between Orchard Road and Grange Road, roads were given names of animals and birds in Malay. These roads are not concentrated in one single estate like the examples above but are quite close to each other. They are Jalan Arnap (rabbit), Jalan Kelawar (bat), Jalan Tupai (squirrel), Lengkok Angsa (goose) and Lengkok Merak (peacock). Similarly in the Jalan Eunos area, there are Jalan Punai (pigeon), Jalan Rimau (tiger) and Jalan Singa (lion). In Little India, there are Buffalo Lane, Buffalo Road, Lembu Road (cow), Kerbau Lane (buffalo) and Kerbau Road. In the vicinity of these roads named after buffalos is the Kandang Kerbau Women's and Children Hospital. *Kandang kerbau* means buffalo shed in Malay. Fortunately, the original hospital was built in 1924 on a bamboo plantation and it became the source of its nicer colloquial name of Tekka Hospital ("Tekka" means end of bamboo plantation in the Hokkien dialect). Finally, in the Shepherd's Hill Estate in Queenstown, there are Shepherds Drive, Angora Close, Barbary Walk and Merino Crescent. Angora, Barbary and Merino are three different species of sheep.

Science Park
Reflecting the nature of this park, buildings in the Science Park are all named after scientists such as Isaac Newton, Thomas Edison, Blaise Pascal, Michael Faraday, etc.

SECTION 4

PLACE NAMES OF CHINESE ORIGIN

Place names of Chinese origin are used only for the Specific Element. There are about 700 of them and can be categorised as follows.
- Place names in mainland China
- Names of famous Chinese poets
- Names of local Chinese business entities
- Anthroponyms of local Chinese
- Others

1. PLACE NAMES IN MAINLAND CHINA
Place names in mainland China that were adopted in street names in Singapore are mostly located in the southern part of China where most Singaporean Chinese originated. Other than major cities such as Beijing and Nanjing, some remote places like Xinjiang and Tibet were once used in the former Nanyang University and have since been expunged. Existing street names with Chinese place names (pinyin name in parentheses) in their Specific Elements include the following: Amoy ("Xiamen") Street, Canton ("Guangdong") Street, Hokien ("Fujian") Street, Hong Kong Street, Nankin ("Nanjing") Street Mall, Pekin ("Beijing") Street, Quemoy ("Jinmen") Road, Shanghai Road, Soochow ("Suzhou") Drive and Tew Chew ("Chaozhou") Street.

2. NAMES OF FAMOUS CHINESE POETS
There are only three such names and they are: Li Po Avenue, Tu Fu Avenue and Tung Po Avenue. These names are all located in the Teachers' Housing Estate mentioned in Section 3.

3. NAMES OF LOCAL CHINESE BUSINESS ENTITIES
There are more than 20 roads with names of local Chinese business entities. Examples are as follows.

Aik Hoe Road
This road was named after the Aik Hoe Rubber Factory owned by Tan Lark Sai.

Ban San Street, Hock Lam Street
The above streets were named after the Chinese medicine shop and remittance house owned by Low Kim Pong.

Chin Hin Street
Chin Hin was the name of a shop owned by Seah Eu Chin.

Hoe Chiang Road
This road was named after Hoe Chiang Company owned by Lim Teck Kim.

Jalan Teck Kee
This road was named after Teck Kee Company owned by Sim Lian Hong.

Thong Aik Road, Thong Bee Road, Thong Soon Avenue
Thong Aik, Thong Bee and Thong Soon were business units of Lim Nee Soon.

Whampoa Road
Whampoa Company was the business entity owned by Hoo Ah Kay.

4. ANTHROPONYMS OF LOCAL CHINESE RESIDENTS

A majority of place names of Chinese origin are personal names. They can be categorised into three groups based on the component(s) of the name used, as follows.
- Only family name used as the Specific Element
- Only last name used as the Specific Element
- Full name used as the Specific Element

Only Family Name Used as the Specific Element (more than 50 of them)

Choa Chu Kang
Choa Hock Yi was the first to develop this area. There are more than 20 roads in Choa Chu Kang New Town using this name as the Specific Element. See Choa Chu Kang in Part II for the meaning of "Chu Kang".

Lim Chu Kang
This area was first developed by a Lim family. Subsequent clearing of the land was completed by Neo Tiew in 1914 for use as coconut plantations. There are about 20 roads in Lim Chu Kang New Town using this name as the Specific Element.

Seah Street
This street was named after the Seah family led by Seah Eu Chin.

Yio Chu Kang
This area was first developed by a Yio family. There are five streets bearing this name in the same vicinity.

Only First Name Used as the Specific Element

This category is the most common among the Chinese anthroponyms. The more familiar names under this category are listed in Table 5 with the full name, birth-death range and dialect group of the person concerned, when available.

In addition to the above, the names of Lim Nee Soon and Tan Soo Bee are used as the common Specific Element for about 50 streets in Yishun New Town and Simei New Town.

Table 5 First Names of Chinese Residents Used as Place Names

Ah Hood Road	Wee Ah Hood (1826–1875), Teochew
Ann Siang Hill	Chia Ann Siang (1832–1892), Hokkien
Boon Keng Road	Lim Boon Keng (1868–1957), Hokkien
Boon Tat Street	Ong Boon Tat (1888–1937), Hokkien
Bo Seng Avenue	Lim Bo Seng (1909–1944), Hokkien
Cheng Cheok Street	Khoo Cheng Cheok, Hokkien
Cheng Tuan Street	Tan Cheng Tuan (1864–1902), Hokkien
Chin Swee Road	Lim Chin Swee, Hokkien
Choon Guan Street	Lee Choon Guan (1864–1924), Hokkien
Keong Saik Road	Tan Keong Saik (1850–1909), Hokkien
Kim Yam Road	Wee Kim Yam (1855–1914), Teochew
Liang Seah Street	Seah Liang Seah (1850–1925), Teochew
Nee Soon Road (Yishun)	Lim Nee Soon (1879–1936), Teochew
Peck Seah Street	Seah Peck Seah (died 1939), Teochew
Peng Nguan Street	Lim Peng Nguan (died 1887), Teochew
Peng Siang Quay	Lim Peng Siang (1872–1944), Hokkien
Seng Poh Road	Tan Seng Poh (1830–1879), Teochew
Seok Wee Road	Kiong Seok Wee (1839–1888), Hokkien
Jalan Soo Bee (Simei)	Tan Soo Bee (1875–1964), Hokkien
Teck Lim Road	Ong Teck Lim (1896–1912), Hokkien
Yan Kit Road	Loke Yan Kit (1849–1931), Cantonese
Wee Nam Road	Lee Wee Nam (1880–1964), Cantonese

Table 6 Full Names of Chinese Residents Used as Place Names

Cheang Hong Lim Street	(1825–1893), Hokkien
Cheang Jim Chuan Lane	(1878–1940), Hokkien
Chia Eng Say Road	(1881–1942)
Choa Lam Street	Hokkien
Ee Teow Ling Road	Pre-WW2, Teochew
Eu Tong Sen Street	(1877–1944), Cantonese
Lim Tua Tow Road	Teochew
Lim Teck Kim Road	(died 1938), Hokkien
Loke Yew Street	(1846–1917), Cantonese
Tan Quee Lan Street	(died 1904), Hainanese
Woo Mon Chew Road	(1887–1958), Cantonese

Full Name Used as the Specific Element

Table 6 lists examples of the roads under this category with the birth-death range and dialect group of the person concerned, when available.

5. OTHERS

There are more than 300 place names of Chinese origin under this category and they are concentrated in the following areas.

- Ang Mo Kio New Town (approximately 40 streets with "Ang Mo Kio" as the Specific Element)
- Bishan New Town (approximately 10 streets with "Bishan" as the Specific Element)
- Hougang New Town (more than 20 streets with "Hougang" as the Specific Element)
- Toa Payoh New Town (more than 20 streets with "Toa Payoh" as the Specific Element)
- Defu Industrial Estate (approximately 20 names with "Defu" as the Specific Element)
- Marsiling Industrial Estate (approximately 20 names with "Marsiling" as the Specific Element)
- Sin Ming Industrial Estate (approximately 10 names with "Sin Ming" as the Specific Element)

Jurong New Town and Industrial Estate

Chinese place names in the Jurong New Town and Industrial Estate require special mention as they were translated into English using romanised

Table 7 Groups of Place Names in Jurong New Town and Industrial Estate

Names with good wishes (in Industrial Estate)	Chia Ping Road ("Jia Pin", good product)
	Chin Bee Road ("Zhen Mei", beautify)
	Fan Yoong Road ("Fan Rong", prosperity)
	Joo Kun Road ("Yu Qun", abundant)
	Joo Yee Road ("Ru Yi", wishful)
	Kian Teck Road ("Jian De", establish morality)
	Kwong Ming Road ("Guang Ming", bright)
	Liu Fang Road ("Liu Fang", passing on good name)
	Soon Lee Road ("Shun Li", smoothly)
	Wan Lee Road ("Wan Li", very profitable)
	Wan Shih Road ("Wan Shi", many generations)
Names containing the word "forever" (in New Town)	Yung An Road ("Yong An", forever safe)
	Yung Ho Road ("Yong He", forever peaceful)
	Yung Kuang Road ("Yong Guang", forever bright)
	Yung Loh Road ("Yong Le", forever happy)
	Yung Ping Road ("Yong Ping", forever smooth)
	Yung Sheng Road ("Yong Sheng", forever rising)
Names containing the word "view" (in New Town)	Ho Ching Road ("He Jing", river view)
	Kang Ching Road ("Gang Jing", hill view)
	Tah Ching Road ("Ta Jing", pagoda view)
	Tao Ching Road ("Dao Jing", island view)
	Yuan Ching Road ("Yuan Jing", garden view)

Chinese. These names (with Mandarin pinyin and English translation in parenthesis) can be classified into three groups as shown in Table 7.

The use of a large number of place names with Chinese origin is due to the fact that ethnic Chinese form the majority of the population in Singapore. Before Mandarin Chinese became the common mother tongue of ethnic Chinese, the main dialects spoken were Hokkien, Teochew and Cantonese; and the composition of these three dialect groups among the Chinese population was 26:13:10. As Teochew was considered a variation of the Hokkien dialect, Hokkien can be considered the most frequently spoken dialect in Singapore. Therefore it is no surprise that most Chinese personal names seen in place names were transcribed from the Hokkien dialect.

After Singapore's independence, translation of Chinese origin place names to English was initially changed from dialect transcription to romanised Chinese as seen above for the Jurong area. This was subsequently changed to Mandarin pinyin, such as "Bishan", "Hougang" and "Defu".

SECTION 5

STANDARDISATION OF CHINESE PLACE NAMES

All place names in Singapore are in English or Malay. However, recognising that the majority of the population is ethnic Chinese, it was necessary to have street names in Mandarin to facilitate communication. The early Chinese street names posted along the road were either colloquial names or phonetic translations. In many cases the Chinese words used were inappropriate and in some instances hilarious. For example, Raffles Place became "Raffles Impolite" in Mandarin; North Boat Quay was translated as "Angry, Kiss, Base" and Frankel Walk was translated as "Jew's Nest". In addition, there was also no standard translation for some of the newer Generic Elements. On 18 January 1968, the Committee on the Standardisation of Street Names in Chinese ("Committee") was officially set up by the Ministry of Culture with Committee members from government ministries, the press and universities. After 14 discussion sessions, a report of the Committee was submitted to the Ministry on 10 February 1970 with two important milestones: the standardisation of Generic Elements (such as "Avenue", "Park" and "Place") and standardisation of Chinese translations for more than 2,500 street names. The Committee continued to exist in different formats under various Ministries until 1 January 2003, when the Street and Building Names Board (SBNB) was formed under the purview of the Ministry of Finance.

Currently, the SBNB is the authority for naming streets and buildings, including new names and change of names. Under the present system, developers or the concerned party would submit a name application for new street or building to the SBNB for approval. The approved English name for the street or building would be given to the Ministry of Information, Communications and the Arts to suggest a Chinese name. The final SBNB-approved names in both English and Chinese are given to the Land Transport Authority, which is the authority for usage and deletion of place names.

It can be seen from the above that great efforts have been made to improve the Chinese place names to make them more presentable, and with a higher standard of Mandarin Chinese. However, due to the deep-rooted use of some names, discrepancies in translation for the same word are at times unavoidable. Therefore the current version of the Chinese place names still have inconsistencies in the following areas.

Translation of the Same English/Malay Word in Two Ways
The same English/Malay word is translated literally in one place and phonetically in another place. An example is the translation of "Queen". It is translated phonetically in Queen Street while Queen Road is translated literally. Similarly, two Chinese translations of the Malay Generic Element of "Lorong" are in use. They are translated as "lane, 巷 ('Xiang' in pinyin)" or transcribed as "罗弄 ('Luo Nong' in pinyin)" in Mandarin. For example, Lorong 5 Bukit Gombak is translated as "武吉甘柏5巷 ('Wu Ji Gan Bo Wu Xiang' in pinyin)", and Lorong Ampas is translated as "罗弄安拔士 ('Luo Nong An Ba Shi' in pinyin)".

Translation of the Same English/Malay Word with Different Chinese Words
The same English/Malay word is translated into different Chinese words, some of them in the same vicinity. An example is the word "Albert" in King Albert Park and Albert Street.

Translation of the Same Chinese Name into Different English Names
This is the case of Koh Sek Lim Road and Xilin Avenue in the Simei area. "Xilin" is the Mandarin pinyin for Sek Lim, in Hokkien. Both roads were named after the same person but the Chinese road name for "Xilin" became west woods and not the name of Koh Sek Lim.

Changes in Method of Translating Chinese Words in English Road Names
Maintaining the different ways of transcribing Chinese names into English road names have led to inconsistencies and confusion. During the colonial days, city names such as Pekin, Nankin and Amoy were generally used outside China. These names have since been officially changed by China into Mandarin pinyin transcriptions of Beijing, Nanjing and Xiamen but road names in Singapore remain unchanged. Among local names, "Nee Soon" (in Teochew dialect) was changed into "Yishun" using pinyin. However, the original Nee Soon Road in the same area was left unaltered. The romanised Chinese names used in the 1970s for roads in the Jurong area have also been left unchanged. For example, Yung Kuang Road would be Yong Guang Road in pinyin and Ho Ching Road would be He Jing Road.

Disappearance of Colloquial Road Names

The standardisation of Chinese place names also led to the disappearance of many interesting old colloquial place names that provided some precious glimpses into the life of our pioneer generation. Names like "Hai Sun Kue" (Upper Cross Street), "Tan Pin Kue" (Upper Pickering Street), "Toa Bey Lor" (South Bridge Road) or "Giao Geng Kao" (China Street) no longer mean anything nowadays. The abovementioned colloquial names are all in the Hokkien dialect, and "Kue" means street and "Lor" means road. Upper Cross Street was the base of the "Hai Sun" secret society. "Tan Pin" means single side; this name was given to Upper Pickering Street because buildings were built only on one side of this street. "Toa Bey Lor" means big road as South Bridge Road was the first major trunk road through the city. "Giao Geng Kao" means the entrance to the gambling dens and the China Street area had many of them.

SECTION 6

EVOLUTION OF PLACE NAMES

1. CHANGES IN SPELLING

Many place names, particularly those in Malay, have had changes in spelling over time. In the case of Chinese place names, the changes were mainly caused by the transition from dialect to romanised Chinese and then to the pinyin transcription as discussed in Section 5. Examples of changes in spelling are as follows in Table 8.

Table 8   Examples of Changes in Spelling of Place Names

Present Spelling	Old Spelling	Source
Xiamen (not used)	Amoy, Amoi	SFP, 1838.2.15:12. See Amoy Street.
Bedok	Bidoh, Bedoh	SFP, 1848.2.3:2; SFP, 1898.7.29:2
Beijing (not used)	Peking, Pekin	See Pekin Road.
Bras Basah	Brass Bassa	SFP, 1838.2.22:14
Changi	Changhi	SFP, 1847.9.2:3
Kampong	Campong	SFP, 1831.1.27:1
Dhobies	Dobies	ST, 1849.12.18:6
Gul	Gull, Gool	SFP, 1848.10.26:3; ST, 1904.5.31:5
Geylang	Gaylang	SFP, 1848.11.30:2
Kranji	Kranjee	SFP, 1848.5.18:3
Nanjing (not used)	Nanking, Nankin	See Nankin Street.
Pasir Panjang	Passir Panjang	SFP, 1836.5.28:3
Paya Lebar	Pyah Lebar	SFP, 1849.4.12:2
Ponggol/Punggol	Pongul	SFP, 1848.5.18:3
Pulau	Pulo	SFP, 1831.11.24:2
Serangoon	Sirangoon	SFP, 1845.1.23:2
Silat	Selat	ST, 1856.12.16:5
Tampines	Tampenis	ST, 1856.5.27:6
Telok	Teluk, Tulloh	SFP, 1833.10.31:3; SFP, 1841.11.25:1
Toa Payoh	Toah Pyoh	SFP, 1849.11.2:2

2. EVOLUTION OF GENERIC ELEMENTS

As shown in Table 9, Generic Elements of place names have evolved from a list with "Road" and "Street" forming 65% of place names in 1936 to a more varied format today. "Road" and "Street" as Generic Elements formed only 32% of all place names in 2010. On the whole, the main changes in the distribution of Generic Elements were due to higher usage of "Jalan" in the 1960s and the active use of "Avenue" from the 1970s onwards.

"Road" as a Generic Element is still the most frequently used today but its proportion in the total population of place names was reduced from 48% in 1936 to 23% in 2010, reflecting a more frequent use of other Generic Elements over the years.

The use of "Street" was originally concentrated in the city area. When the city became saturated, development was extended to the suburbs and the proportion of the use of "Street" in the total population of road names was reduced from 17% to a mere 5% by 1970. Its place as the second-most frequently used Generic Element was overtaken by "Jalan" during the 1960s. The use of "Street" as Generic Element was revived following the use of the Derivative Method of naming streets in new towns. The new towns have a

Table 9 Distribution of Generic Elements in Singapore Street Names

Name	1936	1950	1970	1990	2000	2010
Road	47.67%	47.53%	27.43%	26.15%	24.50%	23.40%
Street	17.26%	10.58%	5.36%	7.61%	8.61%	8.98%
Avenue	0.98%	2.92%	5.07%	9.47%	10.29%	10.40%
Jalan	2.50%	5.32%	21.07%	13.75%	11.56%	10.93%
Lorong	9.23%	6.72%	12.70%	7.63%	4.22%	3.64%
Drive	0.54%	1.08%	2.36%	4.08%	5.95%	6.45%
Lane	6.51%	5.07%	3.33%	4.69%	4.07%	4.24%
Track			3.45%	1.26%	0.41%	0.31%
Kampong	3.15%	4.82%	2.80%	0.85%	0.66%	0.12%
Village	1.85%	2.60%	1.65%	0.39%	0.02%	
Close	0.22%	0.38%	1.62%	2.01%	2.19%	2.07%
Terrace	0.87%	1.01%	1.15%	1.99%	2.29%	2.34%
Crescent	0.22%	0.70%	1.15%	2.50%	3.12%	3.30%
Place	1.30%	1.08%	1.12%	1.65%	1.83%	2.29%
Hill	1.52%	1.77%	1.03%	0.83%	0.85%	0.84%
Park	1.19%	1.84%	0.77%	1.44%	1.76%	1.73%
Garden(s)	0.22%	0.32%	0.35%	0.34%	0.41%	0.39%

schematic way of using "Avenue" as the main trunk road and "Street" as branches of the avenue. As a result the use of "Street" in the total population of road names rose moderately to 9% by 2010.

The word "Avenue" is commonly used as Generic Element for place names in France and the United States. In the Singapore Gazetteer Index to Roads 1936 ("1936 Gazetteer"), there was only one avenue, Alkaff Avenue. The use of "Avenue" rapidly increased in recent years due to the scheme of streetnaming in new towns mentioned above. In 1990 the use of "Avenue" as a Generic Element in road names was higher than "Street"; by 2010 the use of "Avenue" almost caught up with "Jalan" as the second most frequently used Generic Name.

The significant increase in the use of "Jalan" and "Lorong" as Generic Elements in road names took place in the 1960s when Singapore was part of Malaysia. In fact, by 1970, the proportion of road names with "Jalan" and "Lorong" exceeded "Road" and "Street" (34% vs. 33%). However, the use of "Jalan" and "Lorong" gradually fell after the 1970s due to the extensive use of "Avenue". In 2010 the proportion of "Jalan" and "Lorong" in the total population of street names had dropped to 15%.

Kampong means village in Malay. The Street Directory of 1972 listed 148 kampongs and villages. These kampongs and villages have disappeared due to urbanisation and almost all Singaporeans have become city dwellers. "Tracks" are small roads found within the kampong and they follow the same fate of the kampong they belonged to. Only a few kampongs and tracks remain as place names today.

3. EVOLUTION OF SPECIFIC ELEMENTS

The language source of Specific Elements can be categorised into English, Chinese, Malay, Indian and Others, in line with the racial composition of the country. The *Road and Street Directory* published in 1936 and 1950 showed that more than half of the Specific Elements in place names used English as the source language. The use of Malay as the source language for Specific Elements increase significantly when Singapore was part of Malaysia. This was shown in the Street Directory of 1970, which showed that Specific Elements in Malay exceeded Specific Elements in English by 9%. This changed again after Singapore's independence and English regained its ground as the main language source for Specific Elements, as shown in Table 10.

4. CHANGE OF PLACE NAMES

Singapore has a relatively short history and stable political system with no event to call for massive changes in place names. The only major change made was to standardise the translation of place names into the Chinese

Table 10 Distribution of Languages Used for Specific Elements of Place Names

Language of Specific Elements	1936	1950	1970	1990	2000	2010
English	50.92%	50.19%	36.42%	40.93%	42.86%	43.99%
Malay	27.36%	27.69%	45.61%	36.96%	36.67%	36.05%
Chinese	15.42%	14.64%	13.67%	18.16%	16.63%	16.30%
Indian	2.82%	2.85%	1.94%	1.68%	1.46%	1.35%
Others@	3.48%	4.63%	2.35%	2.27%	2.39%	2.31%

@ Includes special names with unknown origins and from Burmese, Middle Eastern and British Commonwealth countries.

language as discussed in Section 5. Most of the actual changes in place names were made to reduce homonyms or to avoid confusion caused by similar names. Nevertheless, the following events are noted.

- Renaming of 12 streets in town in 1858. Three of the new names were in honour of Generals who participated in the repression of the 1857 Indian Mutiny.
- Renaming of 9 streets in 1914, out of which 7 names belonged to the family of Cheang Hong Lim. New names given were varied, including Bombay, Calcutta and Hare.
- Renaming of 12 streets in the West Hill area around 1960. Almost all new names belonged to the family of Lim Nee Soon.
- Renaming of 12 streets in Taman Jurong in 1971. New names were of Chinese origin and were transcribed in romanised Chinese.
- Renaming of 15 streets in the former Nanyang University in 1971. New names were given the Specific Element of "Faculty" or "Nanyang".

Examples of changes in names are shown in Table 11.

5. HOMONYMS (SAME PLACE NAME USED IN MORE THAN ONE LOCATION)

Homonyms appear to be quite common in England. This can be seen from the maps of London and England. Many place names are used for multiple locations. A similar scenario was seen in Singapore during the colonial days with homonyms usually occurring in the British military areas. Examples as seen in the street directories are shown in Table 12.

It should be noted that homonyms in the military areas marked (#) were subsequently renamed by adding the word "Old" in front of the name to avoid confusion. However, almost all of these roads are no longer in existence and the only exception is the Old Bird Cage Walk in Seletar.

Table 11 Changes in Place Names

New Place Name	Year Changed	Old Place Name
Baghdad Street	1909	Little Cross Street
Balam Road	~1970	Jalan Balam
Beng Hoon Road	1898	Upper Chan Wan Seng Road
Beng Hoon Road	1924	Taipeng Road
Berwick Drive	~1955	Stirling Drive
Bombay Street	1914	Cheang Jim Khean Street
Boon Lay Road	1949	Chin Teck Road
Boon Lay Road	1949	Hock Seng Road
Boon Tat Street	1946	Japan Street
Bras Basah Road	<1881	Church Street (part)#
Bussorah Street	1909	Sultan Road
Calcutta Road	1914	Cheang Jim Hean Street
Canning Lane	1954	Chong Long Road
Chatsworth Park	1931	Davie Road
Chiku Road	1934	Lorong 207
Chin Swee Road	<1898	Upper Chan Wan Seng Lane
Chin Swee Road	1924	Beng Hoon Road (old road)
Chong How Road	~1962	West Hill Avenue 8
Chong Nee Road	~1962	West Hill Avenue 9
Chong Pang Road	1957	West Hill Avenue
Chong Pang Road	1957	West Hill Road
Chong Pang Village	1957	West Hill Village
Chong Sin Road	~1962	West Hill Avenue 6
Clementi Road	1947	Reformatory Road
Coronation Road West	1949	Coronation Road (part)
Corporation Drive	~1971	Taman Jurong
Crane Road	1934	Lorong A, Siglap
Crawford Street	1858	Market Street#
Elliot Road	1939	Kee Sun Avenue (part)
Eng Hock Road	~1962	West Hill Avenue 4
Eu Tong Sen Street	1920	Wayang Street (part)
Faculty Road	~1971	Muisian Lane
Faculty Road	~1971	Taipu Lane
Faculty Road	~1971	Fuchow Lane

(*Continued*)

Table 11 (*Continued*)

New Place Name	Year Changed	Old Place Name
Faculty Road	~1971	Tibet Road
Faculty Walk	~1971	Amoy Lane
Fowlie Road	1934	Lorong C, Siglap
Greenfield Drive	~1955	Padang Terbakar
Hare Street	1914	Cheang Hong Lim Lane
Ho Ching Road	~1971	Taman Jurong 8
Hock Chwee Road	~1962	West Hill Avenue 1
Hu Ching Road	~1971	Taman Jurong 4
Huang Long Road	~1962	West Hill Avenue 5
International Road	~1968	Jalan Utasan+Jalan Bekalan
Jalan Peng Kang	1971	Corporation Road
Jurong Port Road	1971	Jalan Gudang
Kee Hua Road	~1962	West Hill Avenue 3
Kee Sun Avenue	1956	Tay Lian Teck Avenue
Keppel Road	1900	New Harbour Road
Koon Seng Road	1934	Lorong E, East Coast Road
Lorong Tai Seng	1940	Lorong Serai
Lower Delta Road	~1970	Gagak Selari Selatan
Lower Delta Road	~1970	Gagak Selari Utara
MacRitchie Circus	~1970	Bulatan MacRitchie
Mangis Road	1934	Lorong 205
Marshall Road	1934	Lorong 201
Merpati Road	~1970	Jalan Merpati
Mountbatten Road	1946	Grove Road
Neil Road	1858	Silat (Salat) Road (part)
Newton Road	1915	Syed Ali (Allie) Road
Old Anson Road	~1977	Anson Road#
Old Balmoral Road	~1977	Balmoral Road#
Old Birdcage Walk	~1977	Birdcage Walk#
Old Canberra Road	~1977	Canberra Road#
Old Choa Chu Kang Rd	~2002	Choa Chu Kang Rd (part)
Old Clementi Road	~1968	Clementi Road (part)
Old Halifax Road	~1977	Halifax Road#
Old Holland Road	~1980	Holland Road (part)

(*Continued*)

Table 11 (*Continued*)

New Place Name	Year Changed	Old Place Name
(Old) Jurong Road	~1978	Jurong Road (part)
Old Keppel Road	<1950	Keppel Road (part)
Old Lim Chu Kang Road	~1987	Lim Chu Kang Road (part)
Old Middle Road	~1977	Middle Road#
Old Nelson Road	~1977	Nelson Road#
Old Pier Road	~1977	Pier Road#
Old Stirling Road	~1977	Stirling Road#
Old Tampines Road	~1997	Tampines Road (part)
Old Toh Tuck Road	~1984	Toh Tuck Road (part)
Old Upper Jurong Road	~1987	Upper Jurong Road (part)
Old Upper Thomson Rd	~1968	Old Thomson Road
Old Valley Road	~1977	Valley Road#
Old Yio Chu Kang Road	Not 91	Yio Chu Kang Road (part)
Outram Road	1858	Cantonment Road (part)
Penhas Road	1929	French Road
Pennefather Road	1934	Lorong B, Siglap
Pickering Street	1925	Macao Street
Pipit Road	~1970	Jalan Pipit
Plantation Avenue	1951	Jalan Phua Pak Tiong
Prinsep Street	1858	Flint Street
Pukat Road	1930	Braddell Road
Pulasan Road	1934	Lorong 209
Rambai Road	1934	Lorong 208
Rambutan Road	1934	Lorong 206
Saint Patrick's Road	~1935	Lorong P Telok Kurau
Sembawang Road	1939	Seletar Road (part)
Serangoon Garden Way	1953	Jalan Chye Lye
Shan Ching Road	~1971	Taman Jurong 10
Still Road South	1978	Karikal Lane
Stirling Road	1956	Soo Bin Road
Tah Ching Road	~1971	Taman Jurong 12
Tao Ching Road	~1971	Taman Jurong 6
Tay Lian Teck Avenue	1947	Kee Sun Avenue
Tay Lian Teck Drive	1947	Kee Sun Drive

(*Continued*)

Table 11 (*Continued*)

New Place Name	Year Changed	Old Place Name
Tay Lian Teck Road	1947	Kee Sun Road
Transit Road	1964	Loop Road
Tyrwhitt Road	1932	Fisher Road
Upper Dickson Road	1930	Dunman Street
Upper Pickering Street	1925	Upper Macao Street
Upper Thomson Road	1939	Seletar Road (part)
Veerasamy Road	1927	Jalan Tambah
Verapillay Road	~1962	West Hill Avenue 7
Victoria Street	<1841	Marbro Street
Waterloo Street	<1858	Church Street#
Watten Park	1926	Watten Estate
Wei Hua Road	~1962	West Hill Avenue 2
Yuan Ching Road	~1971	Taman Jurong 2
Yung An Road	~1971	Taman Jurong 9
Yung Kuang Road	~1971	Taman Jurong 5
Yung Loh Road	~1971	Taman Jurong 1
Yung Ping Road	~1971	Taman Jurong 3
Yung Sheng Road	~1971	Taman Jurong 7

Homonyms.
New place names listed above may appear earlier in the newspaper.
Note: circa (~); before (<).

6. REUSE OF PLACE NAME

Some place names that have disappeared from the map are seen to reappear later either in the same location or at a different place. Examples are as follows.

Abbotsingh Road
The road was located in the former RAF Changi, as showed in the Gazetteer and Street Directory since 1950. It was expunged in the year 2000 but reappeared at the same location in the 2015 Street Directory.

International Road
The road was originally located in the former Alexandra Barracks, as recorded in the Street Directory of 1950 and 1953. It was expunged in 1954.

Table 12   List of Homonyms

Place Name	Locations		Year
Akyab Road	Balestier	RAF Changi (e)	1950
Anson Road	City	RAF Tengah (e)#	1975
Balmoral Road	Stevens Rd	Nee Soon Cantonment (e)#	1975
Bird Cage Walk	B Mati Artillery Barracks(e)	RAF Seletar (e)#	1975
Canberra Road	Singapore Naval Base	RAF Tengah (e)#	1975
Falkland Road	Singapore Naval Base	Kallang (e)	1950
Hillside Drive	Upper Serangoon	RAF Changi (e)	1954
London Road	Pasir Panjang Barracks(e)	Nee Soon Cantonment (e)	1953
Middle Road	City	Singapore Naval Base (e)#	1975
Pier Road	Pulau Brani(e)	RAF Changi (e)	1970
Rangoon Road	Serangoon	RAF Changi (e)	1950
Stirling Road	Queenstown	RAF Tengah (e)#	1975
Valley Road	Upper Serangoon	Nee Soon Cantonment (e)	1954
		RAF Changi (e)#	
York Road	Alexandra	RAF Tengah (e)	1975

The place name was reused for the joined roads of Jalan Utasan and Jalan Bekalan in Jurong.

Stirling Road
This road only appeared in the Street Directory in 1953 as located in the former Nee Soon Cantonment. In 1958, Stirling Road reappeared in the Alexandra area and again in 1961, in the former RAF Tengah. The latter was renamed Old Stirling Road around the 1980s. Old Stirling Road has since been expunged.

Tasmania Road
This road was originally located in the former Singapore Naval Base in Sembawang, as shown in the Street Directory in 1961. It was expunged in 1995 but reappeared at the same location in 2015.

Tembusu Road
This road was originally located in the Upper Thomson area as recorded in the 1958 Street Directory. It was expunged in 1966 but reused in 2007 for a road in the Jurong area.

Braemar Drive
This road was originally located in the former RAF Changi as recorded in the Street Directory of 1950. It was expunged in 1953 but later reused in Serangoon Gardens Estate in 1955.

7. LINGUISTIC REFINEMENT OF PLACE NAMES

Linguistic refinement played an important role in the formulation of place names in Singapore, especially in the Chinese version of place names. The publication of various books in the early days eradicated many unsuitable translations during the colonial days when place names were mainly translated phonetically with no regard to the meaning of the words used.

In more recent times, linguistic refinement is also seen in the change of name of Pulau Blakang Mati to Sentosa in 1972. The Malay name for this island meant death upon entering the island. *Sentosa* means peace and comfort in Malay, which is a suitable name for a resort island.

Linguistic refinement also played a role in the present Chinese name for Ang Mo Kio. The original Chinese name means red hair (man)'s bridge ("Ang Mo", i.e. red hair, means white man or Caucasian in the Hokkien dialect). The bridge was built by J T Thompson, the so-called "Ang Mo". Thompson was the Chief Surveyor in Singapore from 1841 to 1853. During colonial days, Ang Mo Kio was already a district name as evident in early maps after the 1870s. However, the name of Ang Mo Kio was not used for street names until after 1970 when a new town was built in the area, with 40 streets using "Ang Mo Kio" as Specific Element. The Chinese name for "Ang Mo Kio" was changed to mean a spacious and abundant bridge with almost the same pronunciation.

8. OMISSIONS AND REPETITIONS IN STREET DIRECTORIES

Omissions in Singapore Street Directories
Place names are permanent features that would not disappear unless the names have been changed or the place or roads have been demolished for new development. Table 13 shows a list of place names omitted in Street Directories.

Repetition in Naming and Adoption
Some roads are officially named or adopted more than once. Table 14 shows examples of such instances.

Table 13 Omission of Place Names in Street Directories

Edition	Place Names Omitted
1981	Kampong Eunos, Java Road, Jalan Durian (Ubin), Alkaff Avenue (Moved), Padang Jeringau
1991	Java Road, Jalan Durian (Ubin), Alkaff Avenue (Moved), Jalan Hwi Yoh
2000	Fort Canning Link, Loyang Terrace, Moh Guan Terrace, Nanyang Crescent, Paya Lebar Close, Punggol Way, Sunrise Walk
2007	Holland Plain, Hon Sui Sen Drive, Jalan Hwi Yoh, Jalan Kemaman, Jalan Murai, Jalan Novena Selatan, Jalan Novena Utara, Jalan Sikudangan, Jalan Sotong, Jalan Telawi, Jervois Hill, Keng Kiat Street, Khiang Guan Avenue, Klang Lane, Klang Road, Lorong Payah, Loyang Terrace, MacPherson Lane, Maritime Square, Middlesex Road, Moh Guan Terrace, Mohamed Ali Lane, Mowbray Road, Orchard Spring Lane, Padang Jeringau, Prince Edward Link, Siloso Beach Walk, Simei Road, Springwood Height, Springwood Terrace, Springwood Walk, St. Barnabas Lane, Sunrise Walk, T2 VIP Drive, Tai Gin Road, Tai Keng Lane, Tanah Merah Kechil Ridge, Teck Lim Road, Telegraph Street, Trevose Place, Waringin Park, Worcester Road

Table 14 Repetitions in Naming Streets in Official Records

	Date of Naming or Adoption	Date of Repetition
Boundary Road	1929 (adoption)	1957
Buckley Road	1919 (named)	1922
Gentle Road	1919 (named)	1922
Nathan Road	1910 (named)	1912
Sturdee Road	1928 (named)	1930
Yow Ngan Pan Street	1910 (named)	1919

Evolution of Place Names   55

SECTION 7

CONCLUSION

A review of the 6,200 place names that have been used in Singapore since 1936 shows the following developments, as presented in Table 15.

Increase in Number of Place Names
On the whole, the total number of place names in Singapore increased from about 920 in 1936 to 4,440 in 2015, a net increase of 3,520 names. Significantly, during the years of rapid economic development from the 1950s to the 1980s, the number of place names more than doubled from 1,580 to 3,490 in 1981. This represents an increase of 1,910 names in a short span of 30 years. The pace of development slowed down after the Asian Financial Crisis in 1979. Between 1981 and 2015, place names increased by only 950. Comparing the total of 6,200 names used over time and what was left in 2015, there was a net loss of 1,760 names to history and together with them, many stories behind the names.

Increase in Number of Generic Elements
The increase in number of Generic Elements was gradual and this has made the road names in Singapore more interesting, as shown in Table 16. In 1950 there was a total of 73 Generic Elements (including Simplex names) as compared to 99 in 2000.

Table 15 Total Number of Singapore Roads According to Street Directory

Year	1936	1950	1970	1990	2000	2010	2015
No. of Streets	920	1,580	3,400	3,880	4,110	4,160	4,440

Table 16 Increase in Number of Generic Elements Over the Years

Street Directory	1950	1970	1981	2000	2010
Total no. of Generic Elements and Simplex names	73	81	95	99	99

Creation of New Words for Specific Elements
Together with the increase in number of Generic Elements, the number of Specific Elements also increased significantly in number and in genre. In contrast with the old practice of using personal names and place names in foreign countries, newer place names contained many new English words not found in the *Oxford Dictionary* (1979 paperback edition) such as Amberwood, Anchorvale, Bayshore, Bayfront, Eastwood, Greenleaf, Greenwood, etc. These naming styles may have their origin in North America.

The steep increase in land price and increasing scarcity of usable land in Singapore have made it more difficult for a single person to purchase a large piece of land and name the roads with personal names. In addition, any new place names or change of place name would require the approval of the SBNB. Therefore, it is logical to conclude that new anthroponyms will be few and will probably be reserved for dignitaries or very distinguished persons.

Evolution of Colloquial Place Names
As part of the consequence of standardising Chinese place names, together with decades of compulsory education in English and the use of Mandarin as the common language for ethnic Chinese, almost all colloquial place names have passed on to history. Only a few of these colloquial names are left today, such as "Ang Mo Kio", "Toa Payoh" and "Niu Che Shui" (Kreta Ayer in Mandarin).

While the old colloquial names in dialect might have been forgotten, new colloquial names have appeared in other forms. Starting with Little India, where immigrants from India would reside during the colonial days, there are now Little Thailand (at Beach Road), Little Vietnam (at Joo Chiat Road) and Little Philippines (in the Lucky Plaza area). While Little India is a commercial centre for Indian businesses, all these places now cater to the migrant workers from India, Thailand, Vietnam and Philippines, where they congregate during their weekend rest days. There is also a Little Guilin in Bukit Gombak, although the name was given due to its similarity to the scenery in Guilin, China.

Place Names Losing Its Connection with History
Following the massive developments that have taken place during the last few decades, many old roads have been demolished and mostly replaced with new names. Some of the popular new place names such as "Plaza", "Square" and "Garden" are far from the reality of their environment. For example, not many trees are found in Eastwood, and Seabreeze Road is not close to the sea. Xilin Road is in the east but has a Chinese name that means

west woods. In the course of these developments, the history connected with the old roads would soon be forgotten.

Increase in Derivative Place Names

Derivative place names as explained in Section 2 is a method of street naming that originated from England and was used sparingly during the colonial days. It is now used extensively in Singapore starting with Toa Payoh New Town in 1966. Using "Toa Payoh" as the Specific Element with "Lorong + number" or "Lorong + direction" as Generic Elements, 17 place names were created for the new town, such as Toa Payoh Lorong (1-8), Toa Payoh Central, Toa Payoh East and Jalan Toa Payoh.

Since then derivative place names have been adopted for all other new towns such as Bedok, Ang Mo Kio, Whampoa, Woodlands, Jurong and Tampines. The only change made in other new towns was the use of Generic Elements in English rather than the Malay Generic Elements of "Jalan" and "Lorong" used in Toa Payoh.

This method of road naming was also adopted in the Changi area. "Changi" is the name of a tropical tree which is now thought to be extinct. Places named after "Changi" include Changi Business Park Avenue, Changi Business Park Crescent, Changi Business Park Vista, Changi Coast Road, Changi Coast Walk, Changi East Drive, Changi East Way and Changi Ferry Road, etc. The name was also adopted for the civilian airport in this area.

The first break from such monotony was seen in the street naming of Seng Kang New Town. The town was built in the late 1990s on a site that was close to a former pier; and in line with this background, three new words ("Anchorvale", "Compassvale" and "Rivervale") were created as Specific Elements. Together with "Seng Kang" there are four Specific Elements used for this new town. Whether or not more creativity will be seen in place names for future new towns, it appears that derivative place names are here to stay.

Increase in the Use of Alphanumeric Characters as Specific Element

Before the development of Toa Payoh New Town in 1966, the use of numeric or alphanumeric characters as Specific Elements in road names were only seen in the Geylang area, and they were named before WW2. With the use of the derivative road naming system in new towns, the use of numeric or alphanumeric characters in road names increased by leaps and bounds. By 2005, this kind of road names formed about 14% of roads in Singapore.

Few place names use only alphabets as Specific Elements and are only found in the Telok Kurau area. More recently, alphabets in place names have been used in the streets in port areas.

Lack of Cultural Contents in New Place Names
As noted above, most new place names came from the development of new towns and the Derivative Method has been used for naming the streets in these new towns. While the methodology may be neat and efficient for the planners, it is nevertheless monotonous and not easily differentiated on the map. Such place names may also overlook the important cultural or historical significance connected to the location.

Generic Elements Created with Modernisation
The rapid development of science and technology has resulted in a more closely connected world with quick exchange of information. As a result, many Generic Elements that are commonly used in other parts of the world have found their way into Singapore place names. Such new names include "Plaza", "Mall", "Field", "Interchange", Gateway", "Grande" and "Promenade". Interestingly "Square", "Plaza" and "Mall" have been translated into the same Chinese words although "Square" has been in existence for a long time while "Plaza" was seen in the 1980s and "Mall" in the 1990s.

Modernisation also entailed the enhancement of the country's infrastructure, one of which was the construction of a network of expressways connecting the whole island. In this connection, new Generic Elements such as "Parkway", "Expressway", "Viaduct" and "Flyover" were introduced.

Missing Historical Anthroponyms
Reviewing the list of anthroponyms shows that some pioneer personalities are missing in our place names and may be worth recording.
- Tan Ngun Ha
  Tan was one of the pioneers who planted gambier and pepper in Singapore before 1819.
- Chow Ah Chay
  Chow was the leader of a reconnaissance party who landed in Singapore before Raffles' arrival on 29 January 1819. He was rewarded with a piece of land in the Rochor area.
- Dr. W Montgomerie
  Dr. Montgomerie was the medical doctor who came with Raffles in 1819. He became the first Assistant Surgeon and one of the first Magistrates appointed by Raffles in the Settlement. Montgomerie was also credited for bringing the properties of Gutta Percha to the attention of the West. The product was later used as the protective material for undersea cables until newer technology replaced it. Nevertheless the Montgomerie Bridge in Whampoa area may be named after him.

- Major James Low
  Major Low was the Superintendent of Police who kept a detailed journal on life in Singapore between 1840 and 1841. He was a writer on early agriculture, geology and history of the Straits and Malay Peninsula.
- Lieutenant P Jackson
  Lieutenant Jackson was the first appointed Executive Engineer and Surveyor in Singapore in 1824. The early maps of Singapore and land surveys were some of his work.
- Thomas Dunman
  All places named to honour Thomas Dunman, the first Police Commissioner of Singapore, have either been expunged or renamed. According to Municipal records, the present Dunman Road in Tanjong Katong was named by the Municipality after his son, William Dunman.
- Maria Dyer
  Maria Dyer was the founder of the first girls' school in Singapore. The Chinese Girls' School, subsequently renamed St. Margaret's School, was founded in 1842 by Maria Dyer. She was a missionary of the London Missionary Society.
- Tan Lark Sai
  Tan made a huge contribution to education in this region and led the initiative in the founding of Nanyang University.
- Tan Kah Kee
  Tan Kah Kee was noted for his contribution to education in South East Asia and the establishment of Amoy (now Xiamen) University in China. Similar to Lim Nee Soon, he was highly honoured in China. The Chinese erected a monument for him in the compound of Huang Di Lin, a temple worshipping the Great Ancestor of the Chinese race, in the ancient capital city of Xian. In 2009, a new MRT Station was named after him in Singapore.
- Lee Kong Chian
  Lee was a prominent businessman and the Founder of the Lee Foundation.
  In addition to the case of Thomas Dunman mentioned above, the following place names connected to prominent pioneers in Singapore have been expunged.
- Farquhar Street (W Farquhar, the first Colonial Resident Officer)
- Bernard Street (Francis Bernard, the first Chief of Police Department)
- Johnston Street (A L Johnston, a Magistrate who established the first commercial company)

PART II

SINGAPORE GAZETTEER SINCE 1936 AND ANNOTATIONS

(Gazetteer of 3,900 place name groups with more than 6,000 place names)
(Translations of Malay place names were based on the dictionaries of Sir R J Wilkinson)

Abbotsingh Road (former RAF Changi)
This road was located in the domain of the former Royal Air Force (RAF) Changi. RAF Changi was first completed as a British artillery base in 1941. The change to an airbase was initiated by the Imperial Japanese Army between 1943 and 1944 using the British and Australian Prisoners of War ("POWs") as labourers. After WW2, the Japanese POWs in turn were used as labourers to further improve the airfield. The airfield facility became a RAF station in 1946 with most of the roads renamed after well known RAF stations in Britain. As it was originally an artillery base, there are a few roads named after British places (nomenclature of roads in army barracks) and military commanders. The air station names include: Abbotsingh, Aberdeen, Aldergrove, Beverley, Biggin Hill, Calshot, Cosford, Debden, etc.

Abbotsingh may have been derived from Abbotsinch Air Station in Glasgow.

Source: *Probert: 23, 53, 55*

Aberdeen Road (e) (former RAF Changi)
This road was named after RAF Aberdeen, Scotland. Aberdeen is a seaport and the third largest city of Scotland. *See Abbotsingh Road.*

Abingdon Road (former RAF Changi)
This road was named after RAF Abingdon (now Dalton Barracks) in Oxfordshire, South East England. *See Abbotsingh Road.*

Access Road (e) (former Singapore Naval Base)

Adam Drive/Park/Place (e)/Road
Adam Road was named after Frank Adam (1856–1925). He was the General Manager of Straits Trading Company and the Managing Director of Pulau Brani Tin Smelting Works. He returned home to Scotland after his retirement in 1923.

Adam Road was known earlier as Adam's Road or Adams Road. It was taken over by the Municipality in 1890 and recognised as "Adam Road" in 1922.

Adam Park was officially named in 1928.

Source: *MC, 1890.5.14; MC1, 1922.2.3; SFP, 1925.2.12:7; MC1, 1928.5.1; MP, vol.2:226; Singam*

Adis Road
This road was named after Nissim N Adis (1857–1927, Jewish) in 1905. Adis was the owner of the Grand Hotel de l'Europe at the present site of the National Gallery. The hotel was affected by the World Economic Depression of the 1930s and closed in 1932 with the land sold to the government. It was reported in the news in 1928 that he passed away in India.

Source: *SFP, 1905.12.2:5; ST, 1928.1.24:3*

Admiralty Drive/Lane/Link/Street
Admiralty Road/Admiralty Road East/West
Some of these roads were the main roads surrounding the former His Majesty's Naval Base, Singapore or Singapore Naval Base located in Sembawang. Within the compound is the Admiralty House, the residence of the Flag Officer.

The Naval Base was built before WW2. It was part of the British government's strategy to deter the increasingly ambitious Japanese Empire in the Far East. The military fortifications in Sembawang included the Naval Base, RAF Sembawang and HMS Simbang (a Royal Naval Air Station). All three installations were completed in 1939/1940 at a staggering cost of 60 million pounds.

The Naval Base itself covered 21 square miles and had the largest dry dock in the world at the time of completion. Road names in the Naval Base were mainly divided into three groups: the first group relates to facilities within the Naval Base, such as Armament Office, *Kedai* (shop in Malay), Dock, etc. The second group of roads in the dock area was mostly named after navy commanders or naval ships such as Cochrane and Exmouth. The third group of roads in the wharf area was named after British Overseas Territories or colonies before WW2.

Source: *NLB-Sembawang Naval Base*

Adur Road (e) (former Pulau Brani military area)
This road was located in Pulau Brani, the site of the navy and military fort of the British Army in 1889, housing the Commissariat and the Ordnance Department. Two other road names on this island begin with letter A: Alde Road and Arun Road. All three roads were named after rivers that flow through the county of Sussex, south of England. This could be due to the fact that the Royal Sussex Regiment was stationed here around the 1920s.

Ah Hood Road
This road, located off Balestier Road, was named after Wee Ah Hood (1826–1875, Teochew), a pepper and gambier plantation owner. It became a public street in 1957. Wee owned one of the four classic Chinese mansions built by Teochew tycoons in the late 19th century. The house of Wee Ah Hood was located at Hill Street, the present site of the Singapore Chinese Chamber of Commerce and Industry (SCCCI). The SCCCI purchased the mansion in 1912 and demolished it in 1961 to make way for the current building.

Source: *ST, 1875.3.13:4; CCAR, 1957:5; Kua: 172; Singam*

Ah Soo Garden/Ah Soo Walk
See Lorong Ah Soo.

Ahmadiyya Cemetery Path 1
Ahmadiyya is the name of a Muslim sect which originated from the borders between Punjab in India and Pakistan.

Aida Street (Opera Estate)
This is one of the streets in Opera Estate which were all named after operas or other stage productions such as *Aida, Carmen, Dafne, Dido, Fidelio, Figaro, Tosca,* etc. *Aida* is an opera by Giuseppe Verdi. Aida Street was named in 1953.

Source: *RBAR, 1953:7*

Aik Hoe Road (e)
This road appeared after WW2, around 1950. Aik Hoe was the name of a rubber factory along this road owned by Tan Lark Sye (1897-1972, Hokkien). Tan was a one of the leading businessmen of his time. He led in the establishment of the former Nanyang University, the only Chinese university outside Greater China.

One other account mentioned that this road was named after Chop Aik Hoe, a ship chandler firm owned by Kiong Seok Wee (1838-1888). This is unlikely as Chop Aik Hoe was destroyed by fire with no insurance cover and Kiong's other businesses failed by 1869. *See Seok Wee Road.*

Source: *Dunlop; Phua, 1952:2; Song: 39*

Airline Road/Airport Boulevard/Airport Cargo Road
These roads are located in the Singapore Changi Airport.

Airport Road/Link (e)/Service Road (e)
These roads were located in the former Paya Lebar Airport. Paya Lebar Airport was completed in 1955 and officially named the following year. Upon commencement of civil aviation services in Changi Airport, Paya Lebar Airport was converted into a military airbase in 1981. Airport Road now leads to the Paya Lebar Air Base.

Source: *RBAR, 1956:9*

Akyab Road
Akyab Road (e) (former RAF Changi)
Akyab is an area along the west coast of Myanmar.

Akyab Road is one of the Burmese roads in the Balestier area. *See Burmah Road.*

Albert Street

This street was named after Prince Albert (1819-1861), the Consort of Queen Victoria of United Kingdom (UK). One account mentioned that it was to commemorate the visit of Prince Albert Victor (Grandson of Queen Victoria) in 1892; this was unlikely as the street was named in 1858.

Source: *SFP 1858.4.1:6; Singam*

Albert Winsemius Lane

This lane was named in 2009 after Albert Winsemius (1910-1996), a Dutch economist and former economic advisor to the Singapore government from 1961 to 1984.

Source: *ST, 2009.10.23:8*

Alde Road (e) (former Pulau Brani military area)

Alde is one of the three rivers that run through the county of Sussex. See *Adur Road*.

Aldergrove (e) (former RAF Changi)

This road was named after RAF Aldergrove (1918-2009) in Belfast, Northern Ireland. The road name was changed from Alder Grove to a single word in 1961. See *Abbotsingh Road*.

Alexandra Avenue (e)/Circus (e)/Close (e)/Lane/Road/Terrace/View

Alexandra Road was completed in 1864 and named after Queen Alexandra, consort of King Edward VII and grandmother of Queen Elizabeth II ("QE2").

Source: *ST, 1864.11.19:4; Singam*

Aliwal Street (Kampong Glam)

Aliwal is a village in the State of Punjab in India. This street name is the only Indian place name in Kampong Glam. The victory of the East India Company in the Battle of Aliwal in 1846 greatly enhanced the position of the British in India. This street was named in 1909. See *Arab Street*.

Source: *MC, 1909.10.1; Dunlop*

Aljunied Avenue 1 to 5
Aljunied Crescent/Aljunied Road/Aljunied Way (e)

Aljunied Road was named in 1926 after the family of Syed Sharif Omar bin Ali Al Junied, a wealthy Arab merchant from Palembang, Indonesia. The family originated from Yemen and was well respected as they were considered descendants of the Islamic prophet Muhammad. Syed Omar was a philanthropist who contributed towards construction of mosques and schools for the Muslims.

Source: *MC, 1926.5.28; Singam*

Alkaff Avenue (e)/Gardens (e)/Quay (e)

The name Alkaff came from the Alkaff family, a wealthy Arab family with ancestry in Yemen, Arabian Peninsula. The Alkaffs arrived in Singapore in 1852 and were great traders in local produce and later in properties. As one of the major property owners in Singapore, the Alkaffs built The Arcade at Raffles Place in 1909. It was Singapore's first indoor shopping centre. The property was sold in 1962 and rebuilt by new owners with no change in name.

Alkaff Avenue was named in 1929.

Alkaff Gardens was named in 1926. It was demolished around the 1950s and redeveloped into Sennett Estate. *See Angsana Avenue.*

Alkaff Quay was officially named in 1907.

Source: *MC, 1907.12.13; MC, 1926.7.1; MC, 1929.2.27; Millet: 112; Singam*

Allamanda Grove

Allamanda is a flowering plant with the common name of golden trumpet.

Allanbrooke Road/East (former Blakang Mati Artillery Barracks)

These two roads were named after Field Marshal Alan Francis Brooke (1883-1963), who was the chairman of the Chiefs of Staff Committee, the foremost military advisor to Winston Churchill during WW2. After the war, Brooke was honoured by the British Crown and given the title of Viscount Allanbrooke in 1946. *See Artillery Avenue.*

Allenby Road (WW1 roads)

In 1926, the Municipal Commission decided to name the streets off Lavender Street to honour Great War (WW1, 1914-1918) leaders. This decision was extended to battlefields and altogether more than 20 roads were named.

Allenby Road was named after Sir Edmund H H Allenby (1861-1936). He was the Commander of the British Army in the Middle East who defeated the Turks in Palestine during WW1.

Source: *MC, 1926.8.27; Singam*

Almeida Road (e)/Almeida Street (e)

Almeida Road was renamed Balmoral Road in 1908.

Almeida Street was named after Joaquin d'Almeida. It was renamed Temple Street in 1908.

The above changes were made to avoid confusion caused by similar road names that were located far apart from each other. *See D'Almeida Street.*

Source: *MC, 1908.2.28*

Almond Avenue/Crescent/Street
Almond Hill (e) (former Pulau Brani military area)
Almond Avenue/Crescent/Street are located in the Upper Bukit Timah area together with a group of roads that were named after nuts. Other roads in this group include Cashew Crescent, Chestnut Avenue and Hazel Park Terrace.

Alnwick Road (Serangoon Gardens)
Serangoon Gardens Estate is a private housing estate built in the 1950s with all roads (about 45) named after heritage towns and villages in Britain. Many of these towns and villages are the locations of famous castles, old buildings or seaside resorts. In addition to Alnwick, there are Brighton, Chartwell, Chepstow, Conway, Kensington Park, Raglan, Stokesay, etc. The roads in this estate were all named between 1953 and 1955.

Alnwick Road was named in 1953 after the town of Alnwick in Northumberland County, North East England, where Alnwick Castle is located.

Source: *RBAR, 1953:8*

ALPS Avenue
ALPS is the acronym for Airport Logistics Park of Singapore, part of Changi Airport.

Alsagoff Estate (e)
The estate was named after Syed Abdul-rahman Alsagoff, founder of an Arab merchant family in Singapore. He came with his son, Syed Ahmed, from Arabia to Malacca and then Singapore in 1824. Ahmed married the daughter of Princess Hadjee Fatima (*see Lorong Fatima*), a Bugis royalty in Malacca who maintained a trading post in Singapore. Syed Ahmed became a successful businessman and acquired a large plot of land in what was later known as Geylang Serai (the site of Alsagoff Estate). He served as a Municipal Commissioner and established an Arabic school. Some prominent descendants of Syed Abdul-rahman who were leaders of the Arabian community in Singapore include: grandson Syed Mohamed bin Ahmed Alsagoff (died 1906); great grandsons, Syed Omar Alsagoff (1849-1927) and Abdul Kadir Alsagoff (1862-1907, he was assassinated). *See Geylang Serai Village.*

Source: *SFP, 1908.9.30:5; Buckley: 564*

Ama Keng Road/Ama Keng Village
Ama Keng Village, as mentioned in a news article in 1947, was named after the Ama Temple in the village. Ama is the Sea Goddess, Mazu, worshipped by sailors from Fujian (or Hokkien) Province. Ama Keng Road was named in 1954.

Source: *ST 1947.11.6:1; RBAR, 1954:8*

Amber Close (e)/Gardens/Road

Amber Road was named in 1921 after prominent Jewish businessman Joseph Aaron Elias (1881–1949) using his telegraphic code and the name of his horse. *See Elias Road.*

One other account states that this road was named after his mother, Amber Serena Balzar Elias.

Source: *MC, 1921.1.28; ST, 1949.7.17:1; Savage & Yeoh, 2004*

(Amberwood Close 1/2/3/4/5) (e)

Amoy Lane (e)/Street

Amoy (also spelt Amoi), now known as Xiamen, is a sub-provincial city in Fujian Province, China.

Amoy Street is one of the old streets in the city and was shown as Amoi Street in G D Coleman's Map of Singapore based on an actual survey in 1829.

Amoy Lane, in the former Nanyang University, was renamed Faculty Road in 1971. *See Faculty Avenue and Nanyang Avenue.*

Source: *NAS, SP002997*

Ampang Walk

Ampang means easy, light in Malay. Ampang is also a district in Kuala Lumpur, Malaysia.

Anamalai Avenue

This road was named in 1955 after A Annamalai (1839–1920), a surveyor and landowner. He was the community leader of Ceylonese (now Sri Lanka) in Singapore. *See Namly Avenue and King's Road.*

Source: *ST, 1920.7.22:6; RBAR, 1955:9*

Anchorvale Close (e)/Crescent/Drive/Lane/Link/Road/Street/Walk (Seng Kang New Town)

Anderson Road

In May 1901 the Municipal Commission approved the cutting of a new road through Ardmore property joining Orange Grove Road to Balmoral Road with the agreement of Messrs. Thomas Scott and John Anderson; both were directors of Guthrie & Co. which owned the land. This was followed by an invitation to tender for the supply of laterite for Anderson Road in January 1902. It appears that the road was named in 1902 after John Anderson (1852–1924), the Chairman of Guthrie & Co. Ltd from 1903 to 1924. He was a member of the Legislative Council (1886–1888 and 1905–1909) and Chairman of the Singapore Chamber of Commerce. He was conferred a knighthood when he returned to England in 1912. The name of Anderson Road was officially approved by the Municipal Commission on 22 April 1904.

Coincidentally one other Sir John Anderson, the Governor of Straits Settlements from 1904 to 1911, arrived in April 1904. Governor Anderson was subsequently commemorated by a new bridge over the Singapore River in 1909 when the Municipal Commission accepted his proposal to name the bridge after him.

Source: *ST, 1901.5.9:3; ST, 1902.1.29:2; ST, 1903.3.31:5; MC, 1904.4.22; MC, 1909.9.16; SFP, 1924.12.20:9; SFP, 1924.12.22:8*

Andover Road (former RAF Changi)
This road was named after RAF Andover in Hampshire, England. The Andover Station was built by German prisoners of war in 1917. *See Abbotsingh Road.*

Andrew Road/Terrace (e)
Based on a report in 1939, this road was named after Andrew Caldecott. *See Caldecott Close.*

Source: *ST, 1939.5.1:10*

Andrews Avenue/Road (e)/Terrace
Andrews Road was named in 1953 after Thomas Edward Andrews (1897–1949), the General Manager of Bukit Sembawang Rubber Estate. He was a member of the Singapore Rural Board from 1940 to 1949.

Source: *ST, 1949.6.16:7; RBAR, 1953:8; Lim HS: 245*

Ang Chuan Lam Park (e)
This road was seen in newspaper articles between 1957 and 1961 but it was not listed in the Street Directory of those years.

Chop Ang Chuan Lam was a business enterprise owned by Hong Ze Shi (in pinyin). *See Jalan Lam Huat.* The road was subsequently renamed Windsor Park Road around 1961.

Source: *ST, 1961.1.3:11; ZB Special Supplement, 2014.11.20:19*

Ang Mo Kio Avenue 1 to 6, 8 to 10, 12
Ang Mo Kio Central 1 to 3
Ang Mo Kio Drive
Ang Mo Kio Electronics Park Road
Ang Mo Kio Industrial Park 1, 2, 2A, 3
Ang Mo Kio Street 11 to 13, 21 to 24, 31, 32, 41 to 44, 51 to 54, 61 to 66
Ang Mo Kio Village (e)
Ang Mo Kio is a transcription of the Hokkien name for this area. "Ang Mo" means red hair literally and was the colloquial name for a Caucasian or

white man. "Kio" is a bridge in Hokkien. The white man's bridge was the bridge built by J T Thomson (Chief Surveyor, Singapore, 1841–1853) located at the junction of Upper Thomson Road and Ang Mo Kio Avenue 1. Besides Ang Mo Kio village (named in 1938), Ang Mo Kio as a district existed in official maps as "Amokiah" and "Ang Mo Kio" in 1873 and 1885 respectively. "Ang Mo Kio area" appeared in press reports as early as 1855.

Ang Mo Kio as a road name was only used after 1970 with the development of the new town. As it was a colloquial name in Hokkien, the Chinese name was refined with a new name meaning spacious and abundant bridge with almost the same pronunciation in Mandarin.

Ang Mo Kio Avenue 1 was opened in 1977.

Source: *ST, 1855.1.2:5; SFP, 1938.8.12:3; ST, 1977.3.25:17; NAS, TM000003; NAS, SP006819*

Angklong Lane
Angklong is a music instrument from Indonesia made of bamboo. *See Jalan Angklong.*

Angora Close
Angora is a breed of domestic goat that is named after Ankara, Turkey. It produces lustrous fibre known as mohair.

Angora Close became a public street in 1957. *See Shepherds Drive.*

Source: *CCAR, 1957:5*

Angsana Avenue (Sennett Estate)
Angsana is *Pterocarpus indicus*, a common wayside tree in Singapore.

Angsana Avenue was built during the second phase of the Sennett Estate development on the site of the old Alkaff Garden. The roads in this phase were named in 1951 with names of trees such as Angsana Avenue, Belimbing Avenue, Camphor Avenue and Willow Avenue.

Source: *CC, 1951.9.28; Boo: 690*

Angsana Drive/Road (e)
Angsana Drive is located on Jurong Island, among a group of roads with tree names.

Angullia Park/Road (e)
Angullia Park was named after the Angullia family. The family's first generation immigrant was E M S Angullia, an Indian trader from Surat, Gujarat, who came to Singapore via Sumatra in 1838. He started his import/export business by opening a shop at Kling Street (now Chulia Street). By the third generation, the family was wealthy enough to acquire land to build a mosque (Angullia Mosque in Serangoon Road) in 1890. The land in the Orchard Road

area was acquired by Ahmed Mohamad Salleh Angullia, E M S Angullia's great grandson.

Angullia Park was renamed Simons Road in 1919 and reinstated in 1920.

Angullia Road, near Queen Street, was made a public street in 1909.

Source: *MC, 1909.6.25; MC, 1919.12.31; MC, 1920.11.26; Singam*

Angus Street (Kampong Malacca)

Streets in Kampong Malacca South were named in 1882. Angus Street was named after Gilbert Angus (1815-1887), a member of the Municipal Commission, an auctioneer and at one time, partner of Hoo Ah Kay in Whampoa & Co. (see *Whampoa Road*). He had nutmeg plantations and owned a number of hills around Tanglin at different times as well as lands in other parts of the island. Interestingly, Angus Street is situated together with three other streets which were named after British merchants of the same era: Fisher, Cumming and Kerr. Angus, Cumming and Kerr were appointed members of the Grand Jury from 1856 to 1857.

Source: *MC, 1882.4.19; Buckley: 658; Singam*
Colloquial Name: Teo Chew Warehouse Lane (*Phua, 1952:149*).

Ann Siang Hill/Road

These roads were named after Chia Ann Siang (1832-1892, Hokkien) from Malacca. Chia joined Boustead & Co. in 1848 and worked for 42 years, first as a clerk and then the chief produce storekeeper. In 1863, he started a warehousing and agency business with two other partners and later expanded into the timber business. He was a shareholder of the Tanjong Pagar Dock Company in 1883. He retired in 1890.

Ann Siang Hill was previously known as Gemmill Hill. The name change took place around 1893.

Ann Siang Road became a public street in 1928.

Source: *ST, 1892.10.5:5; ST, 1928.12.21:11; Kua: 194; Song104*
Colloquial Name: "Chwee Lan Teng" (*Phua, 1952:149*). See Club Street.

Annamalai Chetty Lane (e)

Annamalai Chetty is one of the common names of a Chettiar. Chettiars are a sub-group of the Tamils originating from Chettinad, Tamil Nadu, India. The term *Chettiar* is a caste label; they were traditionally merchants and traders in precious stones but later became involved in money lending. The first wave of Chettiar immigrants arrived in Singapore around the 1820s, following British expansion into this region. They established their businesses in the Singapore River area which was close to the trading houses and banks. Since the Chettiars had long-standing commercial ties with the British in

India, they were able to obtain credit from the banks at favourable rates and give out small loans (without collateral) at good margins. The Chettiars were important players in the banking and finance sectors in early Singapore as there were more money lending firms than banks at that time.

This lane was probably named after either A R Annamalai Chettiar, who set up the Natukottai Chettiar's Trade Association in Tank Road in 1931, or Rajah Sir S R M Annamalai Chettiar. Sir Annamalai (1881-1948) was an Indian banker, educationist and philanthropist. He had extensive businesses in India and South East Asia. He was the founder of Annamalai University in Chidambaram, India.

Source: *MSP, 1931.5.23:32; SFP, 1948.6.17:8; Evers*

Anson Circus (e)/Road
Anson Road (e) (former RAF Tengah)
Based on a report in 1935, Anson Road in the city was named after Major-General Sir Archibald E H Anson (1826-1925), the Lieutenant Governor of Penang from 1867 to 1882 and Acting Governor of the Straits Settlements for short periods between 1878 and 1880.

Anson Road in RAF Tengah was named after the Avro Anson, a multi-role aircraft that served with the RAF during WW2. *See Hornet Road.* The road was renamed Old Anson Road in the 1970s.

Source: *ST, 1925.2.27:9; SFP, 1935.9.19:3; Makepeace, vol.1:25*

Anthony Road
This road was named in 1928 after P A Anthony who was the General Manager of the Malayan Railway from 1910-1924.

Source: *SFP, 1924.8.15:4; MC, 1928.12.28; ST, 1928.12.29:12*

Anzac Road (e) (former Gillman Barracks)
Anzac is the acronym for Australian and New Zealand Army Corps. *See Gillman Close.*

Approach Road (e) (former Singapore Harbour Board)

Arab Street (Kampong Glam)
Arab Street was the main thoroughfare in the Muslim Quarter or Kampong Glam. In addition to land set aside for Sultan Hussein Mohamed Shah, Kampong Glam was allocated to the Malay, Bugis, Javanese and Arab immigrants. Therefore, roads in this area are mostly named after places in the Middle East, Malaya and Indonesia. The Kampong Glam area (bounded by Jalan Sultan, Beach Road, Victoria Street and Ophir Road) was gazetted a conservation area in 1989.

Source: *NLB-Arab Street*

Arang Drive (e)
Arang means charcoal and *kayu arang* is the Ebony tree, *Maba buxifolia* in Malay.
Source: *SFP, 1893.4.3:2*

Arcade (e)
The Arcade was Singapore's first indoor shopping centre built by the Alkaff Family in 1909. *See Alkaff Avenue.*
Source: *Millet: 112*

Arcadia Road
This road was named after a residential development The Arcadia.

Architecture Drive (NUS)

Ardmore Park
Ardmore was the name of the mansion owned by lawyer J G Davidson (1838-1891). He was one of the founders of Rodyk and Davidson. *See Davidson Road.*
Source: *Singam*

Ark Lane (e) (Off Rochor Road)

Armament Office Road (e) (former Singapore Naval Base)

Armenian Lane (e)/Street
These streets were named after the Armenian Church of St. Gregory The Illuminator. The church was completed in 1835 and was the first church in Singapore.

Armenian Street was known as "Seng Poh Au" (meaning behind Seng Poh's residence in Hokkien) by the Chinese in early days. In 1930, there was a suggestion to rename Armenian Street in memory of Tan Seng Poh. The Commissioner decided to leave his name on hold for naming streets in the Tiong Bahru district. *See Seng Poh Road.*

Armenian Lane was on the south side of Armenian Street and was named in 1930.
Source: *MC1, 1930.7.2; MC, 1930.10.31*

Arnasalam Chetty Road
See Annamalai Chetty Avenue.

Aroozoo Avenue/Lane
Aroozoo Avenue was named after Simon Joaquim Aroozoo (1849-1931). He was an employee of Guthrie & Co. from age 16 and retired after 57 years of service. Aroozoo Avenue became a public street in 1956.
Source: *SFP, 1931.5.26:10; RBAR, 1956:9; Braga: 94*

Arrival Crescent (e)
The above was renamed T1 Arrival Crescent.

Arthur Road/Terrace (e)
Arthur Road was named in 1921 after Arthur Henderson Young (1854-1938), Governor of Singapore between 1911 and 1919.

Source: *MC, 1921.2.25; SFP, 1938.10.31:2; Singam*

Artillery Avenue/Close (e)/Link (e) (former Blakang Mati Artillery Barracks) Artillery Avenue was named after the Artillery Barracks on Pulau Blakang Mati (now Sentosa Island).

Blakang Mati Artillery Barracks was built around 1904 to secure the Keppel Harbour and coastal defence as well as to provide soldiers to man the guns at the four forts on the island. Between 1934 and 1937, heavy artillery and several artillery regiments arrived in Changi and Blakang Mati Barracks such that at the time of the outbreak of WW2 in the Pacific (December 1941), Singapore was touted as the most fortified secure British possession in the East. However, this was not to be the case and the British surrendered on 15 February 1942 to the Imperial Japanese Army. The gun batteries were deliberately destroyed before the surrender to prevent them from falling into Japanese hands. They were repaired or salvaged after the war by the Royal Artillery for reuse during the Malayan Emergency (1948-1960). The island was redeveloped into a resort island in the 1970s after withdrawal of the British Army. Prior to the 1970s, roads on the island were all named after artillery installations or leading artillery commanders such as Siloso, Imbiah, Allanbrooke, Carlton, Carrhill, Ironside, Larkhill and Woolwich.

Source: *SFP, 1934.3.23:6; DM, 1937:26-27*

Artisans Road (e) (former Singapore Harbour Board)

Arts Link (NUS)

Arumugam Road
Arumugam is an Indian personal name.

Arun Road (e) (former Pulau Brani Military area)
Arun is one of the three rivers that flow through the county of Sussex, England. *See Adur Road.*

Arundel Road (e) (former Clementi Barracks)
This road was located in Sussex Estate in the Clementi area. The estate was developed in the 1950s to house British senior non-commissioned officers of the army. Roads in the area were all named after places in Sussex County in South East England. Arundel is a market town in West Sussex.

Sussex Estate was demolished in 1997 to make way for a new housing estate along Clementi Avenue 1.

Ascot Rise
This road was named in 1953 after the Ascot Racecourse, a prestigious horse racing venue in Berkshire, England. It is located near the former race course at Dunearn Road.

Source: *RBAR, 1953:7*

Ash Grove
This road was named in 1954. Ash is the name of a tree native to Europe.

Source: *RBAR, 1954:9*

Ashwood Grove
This road is located in Woodlands in an area with roads named after different species of wood. Besides Ashwood Grove, there are Beechwood Grove, Cedarwood Grove, Oakwood Grove, Pinewood Grove and Rosewood Avenue.

Asia Gardens (e) (off Everton Rd)

Asimont Lane
This road was named after W F C Asimont, a surveyor during the 20th century. In 1903, the Municipal Commission accepted his suggestion to name two new roads as Asimont Lane and Barker Road.

Source: *ST, 1903.12.5:5; Singam*

Astrid Hill
See Queen Astrid Park.

Attap Road (e)
Attap Valley Lane/Road (former Singapore Naval Base)
Attap means roof in Malay. The material used for this kind of roof is made from palm fronds. *See Admiralty Road.*

Auckland Road East/West (former Singapore Naval Base)
These roads were named after Auckland, the largest city in New Zealand. *See Admiralty Road.*

Ava Road
Ava (now Inwa or Innwa), located in upper Mandalay, is an ancient imperial capital of successive Burmese kingdoms between 1364 and 1841. This capital city was abandoned after it was destroyed by an earthquake in 1839. *See Burmah Road.*

Avenue A Sakra
See Sakra Avenue.

Aviation Drive
This road is located in Singapore Changi Airport, leading to the Singapore Aviation Academy.

Aviation Park Road

This road is located near Singapore Changi Airport, leading to the Changi Exhibition Centre.

Avon Road (former Grove Estate)

Avon Road was named in 1939 together with three other roads in the Tanjong Katong area, all after English towns in Hampshire and Dorset (Lyndhurst, Cranborne and Wimborne). River Avon is in Hampshire, South East England. See Grove Road.

Source: *SFP, 1939.7.1:2*

Ayer Chawan Place (e)

Ayer chawan is a tea cup in Malay. Ayer Chawan Place was located in former Pulau Ayer Chawan, one of the seven main offshore islands that were amalgamated to form Jurong Island through land reclamation. The other islands were Pulau Ayer Merbau, Pulau Merlimau, Pulau Pesek, Terumbu Pesek, Pulau Sakra, Pulau Seraya and some other small islands. Jurong Island is now the largest outlying island in Singapore.

Source: *Haughton: 78*

Ayer Merbau Road

Merbau is a tree with the scientific name of *Intsia palembanica*; its timber is very durable and termite resistant. This road is located on Jurong Island. It was named after the former Pulau Ayer Merbau. See Ayer Chawan Place.

Source: *Haughton: 78*

Ayer Rajah Avenue/Crescent/Expressway/Industrial Estate (e)/Road (e)

Ayer rajah means amulet water in Malay. The above roads were named after Sungei Ayer Rajah, shown in a 1873 Map of Singapore by J McNair. Ayer Rajah Road was mentioned as a road to be repaired in Municipal records of 1883.

Source: *ST, 1883.4.16:5; NAS, SP006819*

Ayer Samak (e)/Ayer Samak Darat (Pulau Tekong)

Samak is tannin, a chemical used to treat skins and hides of animals to produce leather. *Ayer samak* is tanning liquid in Malay. *Darat* means land in Malay.

In 1905, a Chinese man named Lee Chan planted gambier in this area for the production of tannin.

Source: *ST, 1905.1.13:5*

Baboo Lane (Kampong Kapor)

This lane is in Little India. *Baboo* or *Babu* is a Hindi courtesy title for a man or a Hindu who is literate in English. For example Hoo Ah Kay was addressed as Babu Whampoa (*see Whampoa Road*) by the Hindus. This road was named in 1906.

Source: *MC, 1906.11.30; Makepeace, vol.2:83*

Baghdad Street (Kampong Glam)
This street was a rename of Little Cross Street in 1909. Baghdad is the capital of the Republic of Iraq. *See Arab Street.*
Source: *MC, 1909.10.1*

Bah Soon Pah Road
"Bah" is the short name for Baba. It is a courteous form of address for a Peranakan man. "Soon" refers to Lim Nee Soon. "Pah" is a rural plantation in Hokkien. "Bah Soon Pah" is a transcription from Hokkien that means the (pineapple) plantation of Baba Soon. This road was named in 1950. *See Nee Soon Road.*
Source: *RBAR, 1950:9; Lim HS: 118*

Bah Tan Road (e)
This road in Chong Pang Village was named after Teo Bah Tan, uncle of Lim Nee Soon. *See Nee Soon Road.*
Source: *Lim HS: 118; Song: 34*

Bahtera Track
Bahtera is a stately ship in Malay. This track is off Lim Chu Kang and leads to the historical site of Sarimbun Beach Landing by the Imperial Japanese Army during WW2.

Bain Court (e)/Street
Bain Street was the site of the property once owned by Maclaine Fraser & Co. Gilbert Angus Bain (1809–1886) and Robert Bain (they were brothers) were partners of the firm.
  Bain Court was renamed Colombo Court in 1914.
Source: *ST, 1886.4.29:1; MC, 1914.7.31; Singam*

Bajerai Lane (e)
This road was spelt Badjerai when it was named in 1906. Bajerai was named after Shaik Abdullah Bajerai or his son, who were cattle traders.
Source: *MC, 1906.11.30; Singam*

Bakau Lane (e)
Bakau is the Malay name of a mangrove tree. It was used for making the foundation of buildings.

Baker Street (former RAF Seletar)
This road was located in RAF Seletar (now Seletar Airport). It is noted that roads in this air station were all named after roads and district names in London, such as Battersea, Bayswater, Brompton, Edgeware, Hyde Park, Oxford, Park Lane, Piccadilly, Regent Street, etc. Baker Street is a street in Marylebone district in London.

Balam Road
This road was previously known as Jalan Balam until 1970. *Balam* is a kind of turtle-dove in Malay.

Balestier Road
This road was named after Joseph Balestier (1788-1858), the first United States of America (USA) consul in Singapore. It was listed as a country road in 1853.

Based on a report in 1899, Balestier was in Singapore between 1837 and 1852. His estate in Balestier Plain was a 1,000 acre sugar cane plantation together with processing facilities for sugar and rum. However, the venture was not profitable and was closed.

Source: *SFP, 1853.7.8:4; SFP, 1899.9.20:3*
Colloquial Name: "Oh Kio", Black Bridge (*Phua, 1952:151*).

Bali Lane (Kampong Glam)
This lane is located within the Kampong Glam conservation area. Bali (also known as Bally in the past) is a resort island in Indonesia. *See Arab Street.*

Source: *SFP, 1852.1.23:1*

Ballater Close (e)
Ballater Close was named in 1956 after Ballater, a town in Aberdeenshire, Scotland.

Source: *RBAR, 1956:9*

Balmeg Hill
Balmeg Hill was named after Villa Balmeg which was completed around 1902.

Source: *SFP, 1902.3.14:4*

Balmoral Crescent/Park/Road
Balmoral Road was known as Almeida Road before 1908.

Balmoral Crescent was named in 1928.

Balmoral Park appeared in the Street Directory in 1954.

One other Balmoral Road located in the former Nee Soon Cantonment was expunged.

Source: *MC, 1908.2.28; MC, 1928.11.30*

Ban San Street
"Ban San" ("Chop Ban San") was the name of the Chinese Medicine shop owned by Low Kim Pong. Ban San was also the name of his son. Ban San Street became a public street in 1909. *See Kim Pong Road.*

Source: *MC, 1909.6.25; SFP, 1911.12.9:6; Kua: 24; Singam*

Banda Street
Banda Street first appeared in the news in 1883. It was probably named after Banda Islands, a group of islands in the Banda Sea, in the province of Maluku, Indonesia. Until the mid-19th century the Banda Islands were the world's only source of nutmeg and mace spices, produced from the nutmeg tree. This resulted in frequent wars between the British and Dutch forces in that area in the early 19th century. Hostilities ended with the Anglo-Dutch Treaty in 1824. Up to around 1920, the price of mace in Banda was the reference price quoted in Singapore. Banda Street became a public street in 1901.
Source: MC, 1901.12.18

Bangkit Road
Bangkit means to rise in Malay.

Banyan Avenue/Drive/Place/Road/View
These roads are in Jurong Island next to the Banyan Basin where tree names are used to name the roads: Banyan, Meranti and Tembusu. Banyan tree is a kind of fig tree.

Barbary Walk
Barbary sheep is a species of caprid native to the mountains of North Africa. This road became a public street in 1957. *See Shepherds Drive.*
Source: CCAR, 1957:5

Barganny Lane (Love Lane) (e)
See Oxley Rise.

Barker Road
This road was named after Arthur Barker (1857-1937). Barker came to Singapore in 1889 and started working for Guthrie & Co. for a few years before setting up his own trading company. He was active in church work and was a member of the first executive committee of the YMCA. He served as a member of the Municipal Commission from 1900 to 1905. This road name was proposed by W F C Asimont together with Asimont Lane and approved by the Municipal Commission in 1903.
Source: ST, 1903.12.5:5; ST, 1937.1.31:9; Singam

Barrack Road (e) (former Tanglin Barracks)
This road was located in the former Tanglin Barracks (now Tanglin Village). Tanglin Barracks was built by Colonel G C Collyer on Mount Harriet, a nutmeg plantation owned by Colonial Treasurer William Wilans, and land owned by Hoo Ah Kay. It was completed in 1861 and served the British garrison infantry battalion until the fall of Singapore in 1942. Its first occupiers were members of the 67th Regiment relocated from China in 1862. Tanglin

Barracks was the headquarters of the Far East British Force and most of the roads have names related to regiments in the UK or characteristics of an army camp.

Source: *ST, 1861.6.1:2; ST, 1862.3.15:2; Dhoraisingam: 254*

Bartley Road/Bartley Road East
These roads were named after William Bartley (1885–1961) who was the District Officer, Commissioner of Lands and Under Secretary in Singapore. He was the President of the Municipal Commission from 1931 to 1939 and in 1945 after WW2. This road was named in 1940.

Source: *SFP, 1940.7.27:7; ST, 1961.4.1:10*

Basement Drive (e)
This road was renamed T1 Basement Drive, in Changi Airport.

Bassein Road
Bassein (now Pathein) is a port city about 200 kilometres west of Yangon. It lies on the Pathein River which is a western branch of the Irrawaddy River. This road became a public street in 1960. *See Burmah Road.*

Source: *CCAR, 1960:7*

Bath Road (former Nee Soon Cantonment)
This road might be named after Bath city in Somerset, England. It was listed as Barth Road in the 1950 Street Directory.

Battersea Road (former RAF Seletar)
This road was named after Battersea, a residential district in London. *See Baker Street.*

Battery Road
This was the location of the battery at Fort Fullerton which was built in 1830. The name of Battery Road for its extension to Raffles Square (Place) was approved in 1913.

Source: *ST, 1913.8.30:9; ST, 1950.10.28:6*

Battle Road (e) (former RAF Tengah)
This road was named after Fairey Battle, a single engine light bomber built by the Fairey Aviation Company in the 1930s for the RAF. *See Hornet Road.*

Bay East Drive (Marina East)

Bayfront Avenue/Lane 1, 2/Link (Marina Bay)

Bayshore Road (Upper East Coast Road)

Bayswater Road (e) (former RAF Seletar)

This road was named after Bayswater Road, a main road running along the northern edge of Hyde Park in central London. *See Baker Street.*

Beach Lane (e)/Road/Street (e)/View
Beach Road was at the sea shore in G D Coleman's map of Singapore printed in 1836. It was the seafront residential area of the Europeans in the early days.

The road became an inland road after land reclamation in 1843.

Beach View is on Sentosa Island.

Source: *NAS, SP002997*
Colloquial Name for Beach Lane: "Mee Sua Hang", Noodle Lane (*Phua, 1952:151*).

Beatty Lane/Road (WW1 roads)
These roads were named after Admiral D E Beatty (1871–1936), who was the commanding officer of the battle of Jutland against the German Navy.

Beatty Road was named in 1928. *See Allenby Road.*

Source: *MC1, 1928.10.2*

Beaulieu Road/East (e)/West (e) (former Singapore Naval Base)
These roads were named after the Beaulieu House, a bungalow at the end of the road. *Beaulieu* is a French word for beautiful place. Beaulieu Estate (the possible source of this road name), in Hampshire, England, was once a major naval shipyard which constructed many British Naval vessels, including many of Admiral Nelson's fleet.

The property was originally a holiday bungalow owned by J B David, a prominent Jewish businessman in the early 1900s. It was acquired by the colonial government in the early 1930s to build the Naval Base, which was when the house was named. Beaulieu House was used as the residence of senior officers of the Royal Navy. *See Admiralty Road.*

Source: *NLB-Beaulieu House*

Bedford Road (former Alexandra Barracks)
Bedford is a county town of Bedfordshire, East of England. *See Berkshire Road.*

Bedok Avenue/Central/Close/Garden
Bedok Industrial Park C/E
Bedok Junction/Bedok Lane
Bedok North Avenue 1/2/3/4
Bedok North Drive/Interchange/Road
Bedok North Street 1/2/3/4/5
Bedok Place
Bedok Reservoir Crescent/Road/View

Bedok Ria Crescent/Drive/Place/Terrace/Walk
Bedok Rise/Bedok Road
Bedok South Avenue 1/2/3
Bedok South Road/Bedok Terrace/Bedok Village (e)/Bedok Walk
The Malay word *bedok* has been written in many ways including *bedoh*, *bidoh*, *booloh* and *buddoh*. *Bedok* or *beduk* is a kind of large drum used in the mosque.

Bedok (Buddoh) Road and Bedok Village were shown in a survey map of Tanah Merah Kechil district by J T Thomson in 1844. The village was located at the former seashore near the mouth of Sungei Bedok.

Bedok Avenue was named in 1955.

Bedok New Town was developed in 1973.

Source: *RBAR, 1955:9; NAS, SP000137; Haughton: 76*

Bee San Avenue

Beechwood Grove
See Ashwood Grove.

Belgravia Drive (e)

Begonia Crescent/Drive/Lane/Road/Terrace/Walk
Begonia is a flowering plant in the family of *Begoniaceae*.

Belilios Lane/Road
Belilios Road was named after Isaac Raphael Belilios (died 1910, Jewish) a wealthy cattle trader. He once owned a large parcel of land in the Serangoon area before leaving for Calcutta in 1898. There was a Municipal decision in 1896 for frontagers of Belilios Road to repair the road at their own expense before it could be declared a public street.

Belilios Lane was part of Klang Road before 1923.

Source: *ST, 1896.8.15:3; ST, 1910.10.18:11; MC, 1923.3.29*

Belimbing Avenue (Sennett Estate)
Belimbing is star fruit in Malay. This road was named in 1951. *See Angsana Avenue.*

Source: *CC, 1951.9.28*

Belmont Road
Belmont means beautiful mountain. This road became a public street in 1952. Belmont is a multiple place name in England.

Source: *RBAR, 1952:8; Watts*

Belvedere Close
The word "Belvedere" is derived from two Italian words, *bel* means beautiful and *vedere* means view. Belvedere is a multiple place name in England.

Bencoolen Lane/Link/Street

Bencoolen was a British possession in Sumatra based in the area of what is now Bengkulu City. In 1817, Stamford Raffles was appointed Governor-General of Bencoolen. During his tenure he founded Singapore in 1819 as a new trading port in the region. He encouraged Bencoolen merchants to migrate to Singapore.

Bencoolen Street existed in 1829 as seen in G D Coleman's map printed in 1836.

Source: *NAS, SP002997*
Colloquial Name for Bencoolen Street: "Go Beh Lor", 5th Road (*Phua, 1952:152*).

Bendemeer Road

This was the location of Hoo Ah Kay's mansion, Nam Sang Garden, which was sold to Seah Liang Seah in 1895 after Hoo's death (*see Whampoa Road*). It was said that Seah adopted the suggestion of W E Maxwell, Acting Governor (1893–1895) and changed the name of the mansion to Bendemeer House. The name Bendemeer might have come from a line in an 1817 poem by Thomas Moore: "There's a bower of roses by Bendemeer's stream," which became a song. Coincidentally, Mr. Kua, the author of *A General History of Chinese in Singapore*, also thinks that Bendemeer was the name of a song since Seah was a music lover. The estate was acquired by the government in 1964 for the Kallang Basin housing and industrial project.

Bendemeer Road was named after the property in 1929.

Source: *SFP, 1895.3.29:2; MC, 1929.3.27; Kua: 105; Conversation between the writer and Mr. Kua on 7 April 2012*

Beng Gum Road (e)

This road was named after Tan Beng Gum (1832–1893, Hokkien), the second son of Tan Kim Seng and younger brother of Tan Beng Swee. He took over the management of Kim Seng & Company and the leadership of the Chinese community after the death of his father and brother.

Source: *ST, 1893.9.19:5; Kua: 82; Singam*

Beng Hoon Road (e)

This road name was changed twice: it was first changed from Upper Chan (Cheang) Wan Seng Road to Beng Hoon Road in 1898. In 1924 it became part of Chin Swee Road.

As a side note, the name of Beng Hoon was used to rename Taipeng Road in 1924 but it was eventually expunged.

Source: *SFP, 1898.7.7:3; MC, 1924.10.31*

Beng Huat Road (e)

Beng Swee Place (e)
This was Kim Seng Place before its name was changed to Beng Swee Place in 1928. Tan Beng Swee (1828–1884, Hokkien), was the son of Tan Kim Seng. He inherited his father's business and position in the Chinese community as the President of the Chinese Temple in Malacca (Qing Yun Ting) for 17 years. He was on the list of Grand Jurors in 1864 and appointed Justice of the Peace in 1879. He was noted for donating three hospital wards in Tan Tock Seng Hospital.

Source: *ST, 1884.11.8:90; MC1, 1928.5.1; Kua: 80; Singam*

Beng Wan Road
This road was named after Tan Beng Wan (1851–1891), Director of an insurance company and son of Tan Kim Tian. He inherited his father's shipping business and was a member of the Municipal Commission for two terms. This road became a public street in 1957.

Source: *ST, 1891.12.30:7; CCAR, 1957:5; Kua: 81*

Benoi Crescent/Lane/Place/Road/Sector
Sungei Benui was listed as one of the creeks and rivers in the west side of Singapore in a Government Surveyor's report in 1848. Benoi was probably derived from Benui.

Source: *SFP, 1848.10.26:3*

Beo Crescent/Lane (e)
"Beo" is a transcription of temple in Hokkien. Beo Lane was named in 1907 after the three temples in this area. The temples were all destroyed in the Bukit Ho Swee fire in 1961.

Source: *MC, 1907.12.13*

Berkshire Road (former Alexandra Barracks)
Alexandra Barracks was probably named after Princess Alexandra of Denmark, Queen of Edward VII (1901–1910), and the mother of George V. The Barracks existed in the early 1900s as it was the station for the 95th Russell Infantry on duty in Singapore at that time (*see Hyderabad Road*). It was probably used as the barracks for Indian Regiments as it was the starting point of the Indian Mutiny initiated by the Indian 5th Light Regiment in 1915. After the mutiny, the barracks became the main British Army Ordnance Depot. Roads in Alexandra Barracks were mostly named after towns in England, such as Bury, Canterbury, Cornwall, Warwick and Winchester.

This road was named after Berkshire, a county in South East England, with notable landmarks such as Windsor Castle and the Ascot.

Source: *ST, 1915.3.23:7*

Bermuda Road (former Singapore Naval Base)
Bermuda is a British Overseas Territory in the North Atlantic. It was first discovered by Portuguese J Bermudez in 1522 and the island was named after him. *See Admiralty Road.*

Bernam Street (Malayan Streets in Tanjong Pagar)
This street was named based on a Municipal Commissioners' decision on 28 September 1898 "to name some streets (about 13) in Tanjong Pagar, ...they should be given Malay names as they are simpler and can be pronounced by all classes of the community...,they might perhaps pick a few names from the map of the Peninsular, taking for instance the names of some of the rivers and small towns." Other streets named under this directive include Enggor Street, Gopeng Street, Rambau Street, Raub Street and Tras Street.

Bernam is a river (Sungei Bernam) located between the Malaysian states of Perak and Selangor. Bernam Street was named in November 1898.

Source: *ST, 1898.09.29:2; MC, 1898.11.8*

Bernard Street (e)
F J Bernard was the son-in-law of William Farquhar, the first Resident of Singapore. He was appointed the Acting Master Attendant and later Chief of Police Department in Singapore. Bernard Street was declared a public street in 1907. *See Farquhar Street.*

Source: *MC, 1907.4.19*

Berrima Road
The road name Berrima was possibly taken from Berrima, a historic village in the Southern Highlands of New South Wales, Australia. Roads in this location were all named after scenic towns in Australia and Britain.

Berwick Drive (Serangoon Gardens)
This road was initially named Stirling Drive in 1954 and was changed to Berwick Drive the following year. There are two possible sources of the name Berwick. The first is Berwick Village in East Sussex, South East England. The second is Berwick-upon-Tweed in Northumberland, North East England, and the location of the Berwick Castle. *See Alnwick Road.*

Source: *RBAR, 1955:9*

Beting Kusa Road (e)/Village (e)
Beting kusa means danger in shoaling sand in Malay. These places were located at the end of Tanah Merah Coast Road. Beting Kusa was seen in J T Thomson's survey map of Singapore in 1852. Both names disappeared in the 1950s.

Source: *NAS, SP006362; Haughton: 76*

Beverley Drive (e) (former RAF Changi)
This road was named in 1954 after Beverley at East Riding of Yorkshire, where RAF Leconfield was located. *See Abbotsingh Road.*

Source: *RBAR, 1954:9*

Bhamo Road
Bhamo is a city of Kachin State in the northernmost part of Myanmar. *See Burmah Road.*

Bicester Road (e)
The name may be taken from Bicestor, a town in Oxfordshire, England.

Bidadari Park Drive
Bidadari means nymph or fairy in Sanskrit.

Bideford Road
This road was named in 1927 and was possibly named after the town of Bideford in Devon, South West England.

Source: *MC, 1927.10.29*

Biggin Road (e)/Biggin Hill Road (former RAF Changi)
Biggin Road was listed in the 1950 and 1953 Street Directory. The road reappeared as Biggin Hill Road in 1961, located in RAF Changi. It was named after RAF Biggin Hill in Kent, South East England. *See Abbotsingh Road.*

Bilal Lane
See Jalan Bilal.

Bin Tong (Bintong) Park

Binchang Rise/Walk
See Jalan Binchang and Jalan Berjaya.

Binjai Hill/Park/Rise/Walk
These roads are located in Bukit Timah. Binjai, *Mangifera caesia*, is a large tree in the mango family and is native to Singapore.

Biomedical Grove (Part of Biopolis)

Biopolis Drive/Link/Road/Street/Way
Biopolis is an international research and development centre for biomedical science.

Birch Road
This road was named after J W W Birch (1826–1875), Colonial Secretary of the Straits Settlements between 1870 and 1874. Following the signing of the Pangkor Treaty that established Perak as a British protectorate state,

he was appointed the first British Resident in Perak on 4 November 1874. However, he was assassinated by local Malays the following year. In 1896, frontagers along this road were required to repair the road at their own cost before it could be declared a public street.

Source: *ST, 1896.8.15:3; Singam*

Bird Cage Walk (e) (former Blakang Mati Artillery Barracks, former RAF Seletar)
In Blakang Mati, Birdcage was the nickname of the fighter aircraft F4U Corsair with a unique inverted gull wing. The framed birdcage style canopy when the wings are folded gave rise to its nickname. Designed in the USA, it was used actively towards the end of WW2. *See Artillery Avenue.*

Bird Cage Walk in RAF Seletar was named after a road of the same name in the Westminster district of London. It was renamed Old Birdcage Walk around 1977. *See Baker Street.*

Bird Park Circus (e)/Bird Park Drive
Located in Jurong Bird Park, the park covering 0.2 square kilometres was opened on 4 January 1971.

Source: *ST, 1971.1.5:15*

Biru Lane (e)
Biru means blue in Malay.

Bishan Lane/Place/Road
Bishan Street 11 to 15, 21 to 25
"Bishan" is the Mandarin pinyin of "Peck San". The latter is a transcription of turquoise-colour hill from Cantonese. The name Peck San originated from Kwong Wai Siew Peck San Theng, an organisation established in 1870 to manage the huge burial ground that belonged to 16 clan associations. The land was acquired by the government and redeveloped into Bishan New Town in the 1980s. The organisation now operates columbariums and temples at Bishan Lane. The name Peck San was changed to "Bishan" (in pinyin) during the development of the new town. *See Kampong San Teng.*

Source: *ST, 1985.5.28:14*

Bishops Place (Serangoon Gardens)
Bishopsgate (Road)/Bishops walk (e)
Bishops Place was named in 1953. Bishopsgate and Bishopswalk are both in the Tanglin area. Bishopsgate was named in 1927. It was once the residence of the Bishop in Singapore.

Source: *MC, 1927.6.20; RBAR, 1953:8*

Blackmore Drive
This road was named after Sophia Blackmore (1857-1945), an Australian missionary. She was responsible for establishing a few mission schools for girls, including the Methodist Girls' School. This road leads to the campus of Methodist Girls' School which was opened in 1993.

Source: *ST, 1945.12.7:3; ST, 1993.7.17; Millet: 162*

Blair Road
This road was named in 1906 after John Blair (died 1898) who was the General Manager of the Tanjong Pagar Dock Company between 1881 and 1896.

Source: *MC, 1906.4.20; Makepeace, vol.2:17; Singam*

Blanco Court (e)
Blanco means white in Spanish.

Blandford Drive (Serangoon Gardens)
This road was named in 1955. Blandford Forum is a market town in Dorset, South West England. *See Alnwick Road.*

Source: *RBAR, 1955:9*

Bloxhome Drive (Serangoon Gardens)
This road was named in 1955. Bloxhome could be a variant of Bloxham (derived from the home of Blocc's in Old English), a village in Oxfordshire in South East England. *See Alnwick Road.*

Source: *RBAR, 1955:9*

Bo Seng Avenue
This road was named after Lim Bo Seng (1909-1944), a WW2 hero. Lim came from the province of Fujian, China at the age of 17. He inherited his father's business and was successful in the building construction industry. He was the Chairman of the Singapore Building Industry Association and a Board Member of the Singapore Chinese Chamber of Commerce. During WW2, he was arrested for his involvement in anti-Japanese activities and died in prison in Ipoh. Besides commemorating him with the name of this road, there is a Lim Bo Seng Memorial at the Esplanade Park.

Source: *ST, 1945.12.4:3; Kua: 135*

Boat Quay/Boat Quay Lane
Boat Quay was known as Hong Lim Quay until 1914. *See Cheang Hong Lim Street.*

Boat Quay is a historical quay situated at the mouth of the Singapore River. It was the busiest part of the old Port of Singapore. Boat Quay is also the name of the road along the quay, which is now a pedestrian mall. The quay stopped operations on 31 August 1983 and was gazetted a conservation area in 1989. It has since been converted into a tourist and entertainment area.

Source: *MC, 1914.7.31*

Bodmin Drive (Serangoon Gardens)
This road was named in 1955. Bodmin is a major town in Cornwall, South West England. *See Alnwick Road.*

Source: *RBAR, 1955:9*

Boh Sua Tian Road (e)
"Boh Sua Tian" is a transcription of radio in Hokkien. The road was given this name in 1956 as there was a radio station at this location.

Source: *RBAR, 1956:9*

Bolo Street (e)
Bolo is a kind of knife used by the Malays. This street was named in 1907.

Source: *MC, 1907.12.13*

Bombay Road (e) (former Singapore Naval Base)
Bombay Street (e)
Bombay road was named after Bombay (now Mumbai), the most populous city in India. India was under the control of the British since the 18th century. *See Admiralty Road.*

Bombay Street was in the city area. The street was a rename of Cheang Jim Khean Street in 1914. *See Cheang Jim Khean Street.*

Bond Terrace
This road was named after Lieutenant-General Lionel Vivian Bond (1884–1961) who was the GOC Malaya between 1939 and 1941. Roads around Fort Canning were named after Commanders of WW2. Other roads in the vicinity are: Cox Terrace, Dobbie Rise, Lewin Terrace and Percival Road.

Bonded Store Road (e) (former Singapore Harbour Board)
This was where the bonded store was located in the harbour.

Bonham Street
This street was renamed from Tavern Street in 1858 after Samuel George Bonham (1803-1863). He came to Singapore in 1823 as the Assistant Resident and became the Governor of the Straits Settlements from 1836 to 1848. His tenure was the period of the first Opium War and Bonham was responsible for looking after the British army en route Singapore to China. After the Opium War, Hong Kong was ceded to Britain and Bonham became the third Governor of Hong Kong from 1848 to 1854. He was conferred a Baronetcy in 1852.

Source: *SFP 1858.4.1:6; Makepeace vol.1:85; Singam*

Boon Keng Road

This road was named after Dr. Lim Boon Keng (1869-1957, Hokkien), the first Singaporean to receive a Queen's Scholarship and graduate from the medical college of Edinburgh. Lim was both a good medical doctor and a businessman. He served as a member of the Legislative Council for 14 years. He was noted for pushing social reforms such as female education and regulation of opium consumption. He became the President of Xiamen University (with no pay) for 16 years from 1921. During the Japanese Occupation (1942-1945), Lim was pressured to head the Overseas Chinese Association and had to raise 50 million dollars for Japan. This road was named in 1929.

Source: *MC, 1929.3.27; ST, 1957.1.2:1; Kua: 119*

Boon Lay Avenue/Circus (e)/Drive/Place/Road (e)/Way

These roads were named after Chew Boon Lay (1851-1933), Singapore's early pioneer and successful businessman. He owned large tracts of land in Jurong on which he planted pepper and gambier, and later rubber. He was the father of Chew Hock Seng, the owner of Ho Ho Biscuit Factory. In 1949, Boon Lay Road, Hock Seng Road and Chin Teck Road were merged to become Boon Lay Road.

Boon Lay Way was opened in 1980.

Source: *ST, 1933.6.3:10; RBAR, 1949:9; ST, 1980.6.27:11 NAS, 155:10*

Boon Leat Terrace

This road was named after Tan Boon Leat (1878-1940, Hokkien), a gambier and liquor merchant. He was noted for his keen support for education. He established a school for the poor and provided financial support for a night school for female factory workers.

Source: *Kua: 70*

Boon Tat Link/Street

Originally named Japan Street, Boon Tat Street was one of the two streets to be renamed by the Municipal Commissioners in 1946 immediately after the Japanese Occupation. Ong Boon Tat (1888-1941, Hokkien), the son of Ong Sam Leong (*see Sam Leong Road*) was one of the founders of New World Amusement Park at Jalan Besar. He was a Justice of the Peace and a member of the Municipal Commission.

Source: *SFP, 1941.7.9:3; MC, 1946.6.28; Kua: 3*

Boon Teck Road

This road was named in 1901 after Wee Boon Teck (1850-1888), who inherited a large shipping business from his father Wee Bin. Wee was a generous person who supported various charities including Tan Tock Seng Hospital.

Source: *MC, 1901.12.18; Kua: 171; Song: 115*

Boon Tiong Road
This road was named after See Boon Tiong (c.1807–1888, Hokkien), the son of See Hood Kee. Together with his father, he established the Boon Tiong Company, which had a wide business network all over Malaya. In the second half of the 19th century, he partnered with Cheang Hong Lim in the operation of an opium farm in Malacca. He also acted as an agent for tin mining companies. *See Seng Poh Road.*

Source: *Kua: 211*

Borneo Road (e)
Borneo is the largest island in Asia. It is shared by three countries: Malaysia and Brunei in the north and Indonesia in the south.

This road was located in the Kampong Bahru area off Nelson Road, together with several other roads that were named after towns in Sarawak including Borneo Road, Kuching Road, Miri Road and Sibu Road. Borneo Road was named in 1929.

Source: *MC, 1929.6.28*

Borthwick Drive (Serangoon Gardens)
This road was named in 1955. Borthwick is a hamlet in Midlothian, Scotland. To the east of the village is the 15th century Borthwick Castle. *See Alnwick Road.*

Source: *RBAR, 1955:9*

Boscombe Road (former Grove Estate)
This road was named in 1928 after Boscombe, suburb of Bournemouth. *See Grove Road.*

Source: *MC, 1928.9.28*

Boundary Close (e) (former RAF Changi)
Boundary Close (Serangoon Gardens)
Boundary Road
Boundary Close in RAF Changi was expunged and reused in Serangoon Gardens in the 1950s.

Boundary Road was named in 1921.

Source: *MC1, 1921.9.2*

Bournemouth Road (former Grove Estate)
Bournemouth means river mouth. This road was named in 1928 after Bournemouth, a seaside resort town in Dorset on the southern coast of England. It was the retirement town of Thomas Dunman, the first Police Commissioner and the original owner of Grove Estate. *See Grove Road.*

Source: *MC, 1928.9.28; Watts*

Bow Street (e) (former RAF Seletar)
This road was named after Bow Street, a thoroughfare in Covent Garden, Westminster, London. See *Baker Street*.

Bowmont Gardens (Frankel Estate)
Bowmont Forest is at the border between Scotland and England. See *Burnfoot Terrace*.

Braddell Hill/Rise (e)/Road
These roads were named after Thomas Braddell (1823–1891), the first Attorney-General in Singapore from 1867–1882. The law at that time allowed him to practise as a lawyer at the same time. His sons and grandsons were all prominent legal personalities in Singapore. The law firm, Braddell Brothers, was founded by his two sons. The original Braddell Road in the city was renamed Pukat Road in 1930. Braddell Road as we know today was named before 1935.

Source: *MC, 1930.6.27; Makepeace, vol.2:423-431; Singam*

Braemar Drive (Serangoon Gardens)
This road existed in the RAF Changi between 1950 and 1953. The road name reappeared in Serangoon Gardens in 1955. Braemar (the area of upper Marr in Gaelic) is a village in Aberdeenshire, Scotland. The 17th century Braemar Castle is located close to the village. See *Alnwick Road*.

Source: *RBAR, 1955:9*

Bragi Road (e)
Bragi is the god of poetry in Norse mythology. This road was among the few roads in the Alexandra area with names of legendary gods in European mythology, including Iduna, Odin, Thor and Vulcan. All these roads have been expunged.

Brahmaputra Road (e) (Delta Estate)
Brahmaputra River is also called Tsangpo-Brahmaputra. It originates in the Himalayas and flows across Tibet, China (as Tsangpo); Assam Valley, India (as Brahmaputra); and Bangladesh. It merges with Ganges in the Ganges Delta before emptying into the Bay of Bengal. See *Ganges Avenue*.

Brani Avenue (e)/Causeway/Drive 7 to 9
Brani Terminal Avenue
Brani Terminal Street Y/Brani Way
Brani may be derived from *berani*, which means brave in Malay. These roads are all on the island of Pulau Brani known as Pulau Ayer Brani in the early days. The name possibly came from the story that there was a well in the island with water of potent qualities.

Source: *Haughton: 78*

Branksome Road (former Grove Estate)
This road was named in 1928 after Branksome, a suburb of Poole in Dorset, England. *See Grove Road.*

Source: *MC, 1928.9.28*

Bras Basah Road
Based on an article in 1881, this road was named Church Street in 1823, it was changed to *brass bassa* (which means wet rice in Malay) when the area was used for drying wet rice along Sungei Brass Bassa (Stamford Canal). The name change took place before 1836 as the new name was used in G D Coleman's map printed in 1836. In the 1960s, colloquial names for this road were Bride Street and Bookstore Street as there were many bridal shops and book shops along this road.

Source: *SFP, 1838.2.22:14; STOJ, 1881.5.12:2; NAS, SP002997*

Breeze Road (e)
This road was located off Keppel Road and was named after Breeze Plain, the name of the area in 1929.

Source: *MC, 1929.6.28*

Brickland(s) Road
There were several brick kilns along this road and the largest one was Asia Brick Factory owned by Hokkien businessman Huang Zhong Hang (in pinyin) (1909–1980).

Source: *ZB, Special Supplement, 2014.11.20:19*

Bridport Avenue (Serangoon Gardens)
This road was named in 1954 after Bridport, a market town in Dorset County, South West England. *See Alnwick Road.*

Source: *RBAR, 1954:8*

Bright Hill Crescent/Drive/Road
These roads were named after the Kong Meng San Phor Kark See Monastery at Bright Hill Road. The monastery cum temple was established by Venerable Zhuan Dao in 1920. "Kong Meng San" is the dialect transcription of Bright Hill. In fact, Bright Hill was originally called Hainan Hill. It was probably changed after the establishment of the monastery.

Bright Hill Crescent and Bright Hill Drive were named in 1956.

Source: *RBAR, 1956:9*

Brighton Avenue/Crescent (Serangoon Gardens)
Brighton Crescent was named in 1953 after Brighton, a seaside town in the County of East Sussex, South East England. *See Alnwick Road.*

Source: *RBAR, 1953:7*

Bristol Road (Race Course Road area)
This road was named after Bristol, a city, unitary authority area and county in South West England. The road name first appeared in the press in 1922.

Roads in this vicinity, behind Farrer Park, were all named after counties or county cities in England.

Source: *ST, 1922.12.22:10*

Brizay Park
This road was named after E Brizay, a French engineer, who came to Singapore in 1926 and established E Brizay and Company. The St. Teresa's Church was one of his works.

Source: *Dunlop*

Broadfield Road (e)
This road was off Paterson Road. Broadfield was the name of an estate owned by W Paterson. *See Paterson Road.*

Source: *SFP, 1849.12.7; Buckley: 573*

Broadrick Close/Road (Grove Estate)
These roads were named after E G Broadrick, President of the Municipal Commission from 1904–1910. Broadrick Road was named in 1921. *See Grove Road.*

Source: *MC, 1921.2.25; Singam*

Brockhampton Drive (Serangoon Gardens)
This road was named in 1955. Brockhampton is a multiple place name in Britain, one of which is a small village in Gloucestershire, South West England. *See Alnwick Road.*

Source: *RBAR, 1955:9*

Brompton Road (RAF Seletar)
This road was named after Brompton Road, a street in Knightsbridge, London. *See Baker Street.*

Brooke Road
This road was named in 1928 after Dr. Gilbert E Brooke (1873–1936), the authority on Malaria. He was the Chief Health Officer of Singapore for 26 years.

Source: *ST, 1928.3.29:10; SFP, 1936.1.16:10*

Brooksbank Road (e)
Brooksbank Road was named in 1930. It was probably named after F H Brooksbank (died 1914), a famous seafarer. He joined the Tanjong Pagar Dock Company in 1889 and remained there until the company was closed in 1913.

Source: *ST, 1914.12.1:8; MC, 1930.3.28; Singam*

Brookvale Drive/Walk (Clementi)

Buangkok Crescent/Drive/East Drive/Green/Link
Buangkok North Farmway 1 to 4 (e)
Buangkok South Farmway 1 to 5 (e)
Buangkok View
See *Lorong Buang Kok*. Buangkok Drive and Buangkok Green were opened in 1999.

Source: *NP, 1999.12.21:6*

Buckingham Road (e)
This road was named after Buckingham Palace in London.

Buckley Road
C B Buckley (1844–1912) was an unofficial advisor to the Sultan of Johore and a Partner in the law firm of Rodyk and Davidson. He was the author of the book *An Anecdotal History of Singapore (1819–1867)*. This road was named in 1919 and was listed as a new road again in 1922.

Source: *MC, 1919.11.28; ST, 1922.2.23:8; Makepeace, vol.1:137, 200; Singam*

Buffalo Lane (e)/Road
Located in Little India, this was the area for keeping cattle and goats in the early days.

Bugis Street
Bugis, or Buggis, is a group of seafaring people from Sulawesi Province in Indonesia.

Bukit Arang Road
Bukit is a hill and *arang* means charcoal in Malay. According to an article provided by the Forest Department in 1893, *Kayu arang* is the local name for Ebony tree, *Maba buxifolia*. Ebony was planted in Singapore on a trial basis at that time.

Source: *SFP, 1893.4.3:2*

Bukit Ayam Road (e)
Bukit ayam means chicken hill in Malay. This road was named in 1922.

Source: *MC, 1922.9.29*

Bukit Ayer Molek
Ayer molek means pretty water in Malay. This road is near the Murnane Service Reservoir.

Bukit Ban Kee (e)
This hill was an attap settlement near York Hill. The settlement was destroyed by fire in 1963 when 3,000 people were made homeless.

Source: *ST, 1963.3.9:1*

Bukit Batok Avenue 1
Bukit Batok Central/Batok Central Link/Bukit Batok Crescent
Bukit Batok East Avenue 2 to 6
Bukit Batok Industrial Park A
Bukit Batok Road
Bukit Batok Street 11, 21 to 25, 31 to 34, 51, 52
Bukit Batok West Avenue 2 to 9

Batok is the husk and shell of coconut in Malay. Bukit Batok was known as Japanese Monument Hill after WW2. It was the site of two war memorials erected in 1942 in memory of Japanese and Allied soldiers who were killed during the Battle of Singapore. The monuments were removed after the war.

Bukit Batok Road was opened in 1959.

Source: *SFP, 1948.4.21:5; ST, 1959.2.27:9; BT, 1989.4.18:3*

Bukit Berlayer Road (e)/Village (e)

Berlayer means to sail in Malay. Based on a report in 1848, Bukit Berlayer was named after Batu Berlayer, which was a rock located at the tip of the Singapore mainland opposite Pulau Panjang (old name for Sentosa Island). The rock, also known as Lot's Wife, an ancient navigation landmark of Singapore, was blown up in August 1848. *See Labrador Villa Road.*

Bukit Berlayer Road was named in 1922.

Bukit Berlayer Village was located at the junction of Alexandra Road and Pasir Panjang Road, currently the site of PSA Building.

Source: *SFP, 1848.10.26:3; MC, 1922.9.29; SD, 1954:16*

Bukit Brown Road (e)

This road was named after the original owner of the hill, Henry Brown, a shipowner, trader and broker who came to Singapore in 1840. He purchased the hill, named it Mount Pleasant and built his own residence on the hill (Mount Pleasant Road/Drive). The ownership of the hill subsequently changed hands and a large part of the hill was eventually converted into a Municipal cemetery in 1922. Bukit Brown Road was named in 1923. The colloquial name for the hill was Coffee Hill as there was a coffee plantation on the hill.

Source: *ST, 1923.6.6:10*

Bukit Chermin Road

Chermin was probably derived from Cherimim, which was the name of the river in this area mentioned in an 1848 survey report. *Chermin* means mirror, glass or shadow in Malay. This road was named in 1922.

Source: *SFP, 1848.10.26:3; MC, 1922.9.29*

Bukit Drive (Bukit Timah Reserve)

Bukit Gombak Road (e)
Gombak is the Malay term for loose frontal tuft of hair or feathers; forelock of a horse's mane.

Bukit Ho Swee Crescent/Link
Bukit Ho Swee was named after Tay Ho Swee (1824–1903, Hokkien). He was a gambier and pepper plantation owner and an opium trader. Bukit Ho Swee Crescent was named in 1907.
Source: *MC, 1907.12.13; Kua: 214*

Bukit Kang Kah (e)
Located at the end of Upper Serangoon Road, "Kang Kah" is a transcription from Hokkien that means where the pier meets the land.

Bukit Kasita (e)
Kasita or *kasta* means Indian caste in Malay.

Bukit Kim Cheng (e)
This hill was located in the Cantonment Road area. *See Kim Cheng Street.*

Bukit Mandai Village (e)
This village was named after Bukit Mandai in 1953. *See Mandai Road.*
Source: *RBAR, 1953:7*

Bukit Manis Road (former Blakang Mati Artillery Barracks)
This road was constructed after WW2. *Manis* means light (colour) or sweet in Malay.

Bukit Merah Central
Bukit Merah Lane 1 to 3
Bukit Merah View
Bukit merah means red hill in Malay. This name was probably derived from the Red Hill at this location shown in J T Thomson's survey map of Singapore in 1852. There were several red-brick factories in this area during the 1930s.
Source: *NAS, SP006362; Lee LT: 13*

Bukit Mugliston
This hill was named in 1953 after Gerald R K Mugliston, former Chairman of the Bukit Sembawang Rubber Company Ltd. The company was the owner of this hill. Another road in the vicinity, Gerald Crescent, was named after him in the same year.
Source: *RBAR, 1953:7; NAS, 799:3, 5*

Bukit Nanas (e) (former Singapore Naval Base)
This road was in the depot area of the former Singapore Naval Base. *Bukit nanas* means pineapple hill in Malay. See *Admiralty Road*.

Bukit Panjang Circus (e)/Link/Loop/Ring Road/Road/Village (e)
Bukit panjang means long hill in Malay. Bukit Panjang Village was located close to the junction of Upper Bukit Timah and Choa Chu Kang Road.

Bukit Pasoh Road
Pasoh is derived from *passoo*, which means jar in Malay. Based on a report in 1881, the name came from a ceramic factory on this hill.

Bukit Pasoh (the hill) changed name twice. It was originally called Ryan Hill, and then Dickenson Hill. Reverend J T Dickenson was an American missionary and the Assistant Master of Raffles Institution. He set up a mission school on this hill in the 1850s. Bukit Pasoh as a place name was seen in the press in 1875.

Bukit Pasoh Road was named in 1920. In 1931, the Municipal Commission decided to name another new road in the same area Dickenson Hill Road.

Source: *ST, 1875.12.10:18; STOJ, 1881.5.12:2; MC, 1920.3.26; ST, 1931.3.10:14; Buckley: 346*

Bukit Purmei
Bukit Permai Avenue/Road
Purmei or *permai* means pretty or lovely in Malay.

Bukit Sedap Road
Sedap means delicious or pleasant in Malay. Sedap is also name of a plant, *Pollanthes tuberose*.

Source: *Boo: 373*

Bukit Teresa Close/Road
These roads were named after the Church of St. Teresa in the vicinity. The church building was completed in 1929. St. Teresa of the Child Jesus (1873-1897) was from France.

Bukit Timah Avenue/Circus (e)/Expressway/Lane (e)/Link
Bukit Timah Road/Village (e)
Bukit timah means tin hill in Malay. Unfortunately, there is no record of tin production in this area.

Construction of Bukit Timah Road began in 1827. By 1845, the road reached the Johore Straits at Kranji. In 1929, Bukit Timah Road was divided into Bukit Timah Road (town to Bukit Panjang) and Woodlands Road (Bukit Panjang to Causeway).

Source: *SFP, 1929.12.12:20; SD, 1954:3; Buckley: 198*

Bukit Tinggi Road
Bukit tinggi means lofty hill in Malay.

Bukit Tunggal Road
Located off Chancery Lane, this road was named in 1931. *Tunggal* means unique or lonely in Malay.

Source: *MC, 1931.7.31*

Bukit Way (Bukit Timah Reserve)

Bulatan Gudang (e)
Bulatan is a traffic roundabout or a traffic circus and *gudang* is godown in Malay. The circus was located at a godown area.

Bulatan MacRitchie (e)
James MacRitchie (1848–1895) was the Municipal Chief Engineer in the late 1800s. During his tenure, he was in charge of building bridges, the water supply system and drainage system in Singapore, including the reservoir at Thomson Road. The reservoir was named after him in 1922 to commemorate his contributions to Singapore.

This traffic circus was outside the reservoir; it was renamed MacRitchie Circus in 1970.

Source: *ST, 1895.4.27:3*

Bulatan Pabrik (e)
Pabrik means factory in Malay.

Bulatan Utasan (e)
Utasan means skilled craftsman in Malay.

Bulim Avenue/Drive/Street
Bulim Village (e)
"Bulim" (武林) is the transcription of world of martial arts in Hokkien. Bulim village was located at 13.5 milestone ("ms") Choa Chu Kang Road.

Bulford Road (e) (former Pasir Panjang Barracks)
This road was probably named after Bulford Camp in Wiltshire as the Wiltshire Artillery was stationed in Singapore in 1950. *See Island View Road.*

Source: *ST, 1950.7.7:1*

Buller Terrace (e)
This road was named after the Buller Camp of the British Army when the Singapore Improvement Trust used the site of the camp to build 222 residential units in 1952. It became a public street in 1957.

Source: *ST, 1952.6.16:7; CCAR, 1957:5*

Bunga Rampai Place

Bunga rampai means flower petals mixed with scented leaves in Malay.

Buona Vista Road (e)/Village (e)

Buona Vista Road was divided into north and south roads in 1949. *See North Buona Vista Road.*

Source: *RBAR, 1949:9*

Burgess Road (e) (former Pulau Brani military area)

This road was made in 1954. Burgess Hill is a town in West Sussex, England. *See Adur Road.*

Burghley Drive (Serangoon Gardens)

This road was named in 1955. It was probably named after Burghley House, a grand 16th century house near to Stamford, Lincolnshire. The house was built for Sir William Cecil (1520-1598), who was Lord High Treasurer to Queen Elizabeth I. *See Alnwick Road.*

Source: *RBAR, 1955:9*

Burgundy Crescent/Drive/Rise

Burgundy is a wine production district in France.

Burmah Road

Burmah was the name for Burma when it was colonised by Britain in 1886. This road is off Serangoon Road, between Little India and the former European area near the Race Course Road. In 1896, frontagers along this road were required to repair this road at their own expense prior to its change to a public street.

There are more than 15 roads with Burmese names in this area. British rule in Burma lasted from 1852 to 1948. The first stage was the creation of Lower Burma as a province of British India in 1862. Upper Burma was annexed in 1885 and Burma became a separate British colony in 1937. It was occupied by the Imperial Japanese Army during WW2 between 1942 and 1945.

An analysis showed that there are two stages of naming the roads. The first group of roads were named before 1936 as they appeared in the 1936 Gazetteer. This was the period when Burma was first colonised and exchanges in trade and government officials were thriving. This group includes:

- Burmah (country name), named before 1896;
- Rangoon (capital), named before 1886;
- Mandalay (the last Royal Capital);
- Ava (the old imperial capital);
- Martaban (terminal of railroad from Yangon in the south), named in 1929;
- Mergui (extreme south with pearl and tin production), named in 1922;

- Moulmein (capital of Mon, port for crude oil), named in 1900; and
- Pegu (capital of Bago, source of timber), named in 1931.

The second group of Burmese names were adopted after WW2 as these names appeared in the Street Directories of 1950 and 1953. The names include Irrawaddy, Akyab, Ramree, Bassein, Shan, Bhamo and Prome. These were some of the strategic battle locations in the Allied Forces' Burma Campaign against the Imperial Japanese Army in Burma.

Source: ST, 1896.8.15:3

Burn Road (MacPherson private roads)
Burn is a Scottish colloquial word for small stream. This road was named after Reverend Robert Burn (died 1833) who was the first Resident Chaplain of the Anglican Diocese in Singapore. It was listed in the 1936 Gazetteer and became a public street in 1960. *See Davidson Road.*

Source: CCAR, 1960:7; SG-1936; Buckley: 226; Singam

Burnfoot Terrace (Frankel Estate)
Burnfoot means a place at the foot of the burn (small stream). Burnfoot is a hamlet in the Scottish Borders.

In 1954, the developer of Frankel Estate submitted names for new roads in the estate as follows: Burnfoot Terrace, Cheviot Hill, Dryburgh Avenue, Ettrick Terrace, Jedburgh Gardens, Linton Avenue, Lothian Terrace, Lynhurst Gardens, Melrose Gardens and Yarrow Gardens. The City Council was not inclined to use British names and suggested using bird names in Malay instead. The names suggested were Jalan Elang, Jalan Kaka Tua, Jalan Kasawari, Jalan Kelawar, Jalan Layang Layang, Jalan Merak, Jalan Merbok, Jalan Merpati, Jalan Punggok and Jalan Tiong. After discussions, the developer was allowed to use the above Scottish place names with the exception of Linton, Lynhurst and Melrose. They were replaced by Coldstream, Dunbar and Roseburn. The Malay names, with the exception of Elang, Kawasari and Punggok, were later adopted elsewhere, mainly in Jurong Kechil. *See Jalan Layang Layang.*

Source: ST, 1954.6.15:5; Mills

Buroh Crescent/Drive/Lane/Street
Buroh or *buruh* means labourer in Malay.

Bury Road (former Alexandra Barracks)
This road was named after Bury, a town in Greater Manchester, England. Its notable landmark is the Bury Castle. *See Berkshire Road.*

Bushey Park (e)
The name was taken from Bushey, a town in Hertfordshire, East of England.

Business Link (NUS)/**Park Drive** (International Business Park)

Singapore Gazetteer Since 1936 and Annotations   103

Bussorah Street (Kampong Glam)

This street was a rename of Sultan Road in 1909. Bussorah, also known as Basra or Basrah, is a main port in Iraq. *See Arab Street.*

Source: *MC, 1909.10.1*

Butterfly Avenue (Sennett Estate)

This road was named in 1951. *See Angsana Avenue.*

Source: *CC, 1951.9.28*

Butterworth Lane (Thiam Siew Village, Tanjong Katong)

Butterworth is a town in Penang which was named after Colonel William John Butterworth (1801-1856), Governor of Straits Settlements from 1843 to 1855. He was responsible for the removal of tax for gambier, construction of bridges, harbours, hospitals and offshore lighthouses in the colonies. *See Thiam Siew Avenue.*

Source: *Singam*

Buyong Lane (e)/Road

Buyong means youth or round bottom earthenware with a narrow neck in Malay. Buyong Road was named in 1931.

Source: *MC, 1931.7.31*

Byng Road (e) (WW1 roads)

This road was named after Field Marshal Julian H G Byng (1862-1935), one of the leading commanders in WW1. *See Allenby Road.*

Source: *Singam*

Cable Car Road (e)

This road was located in Sentosa Island, near the Cable Car Station. The cable car system that connects Sentosa Island and Mount Faber has been in operation since 1974.

Cable Road

This road is located between Nathan Road and Jervois Road. It was the property of Eastern Extension Telegraph Co. and was named in 1921 after SS *Cable*, the cable ship of the said company that laid submarine cable.
See Pender Road.

Source: *MC, 1921.2.25; SFP, 1935.10.31:10; Singam*

Cactus Crescent/Drive/Road

Cairnhill Circle/Rise/Road

These roads were named after Charles Carnie (died 1901), from Scotland. Around 1848, Carnie planted 4,370 nutmeg plants in his Cairnie Hill Estate. Cairnie Hill was later shortened to Cairnhill.

Cairnhill Road was approved for construction in 1901.

Cairnhill Circle was named in 1937.

Source: *MC, 1901.4.11; SFP, 1901.5.6:3; ST, 1937.12.10:18; Buckley: 406; Siddique: 9*

Calcutta Hill Estate (e)/Calcutta Road (e)

Calcutta (now Kolkata) is the capital of India's West Bengal state.

Calcutta Hill Estate was located in the Thomson Road area.

Calcutta Road was in the Havelock Road area, it was known as Cheang Jim Hean Street before 1914.

Source: *MC, 1914.7.31*

Caldecott Close

Based on a report in 1939, Caldecott Hill (construction began in 1936) was named after Sir Andrew Caldecott (1884-1951). He was the Colonial Secretary of the Straits Settlements from 1933 to 1935, Governor of Hong Kong for a short time and the second last Governor of Ceylon.

Roads in the vicinity of Caldecott Hill were named after Sir Andrew Caldecott and members of his family, including Caldecott Close, Andrew Road, Olive Road (named after his first wife), Joan Road (named after his daughter) and possibly, John Road (named after his son).

Source: *ST, 1939.5.1:10*

Calshot Road (former RAF Changi)

This road was named after RAF Calshot (1913-1961) in Hampshire, south of England. *See Abbotsingh Road.*

Camborne Road

This road was probably named after Camborne, a town in west Cornwall, England. *See Berrima Road.*

Cambridge Road (Race Course Road area)

This road was named in 1930 after Cambridge, the university town and the county town of Cambridgeshire, England. The University of Cambridge was founded in 1209. *See Bristol Road.*

Source: *SFP, 1930.6.14:12*

Camden Park

This road was named in 1949 after Camden, a town in South East England.

Source: *MC, 1949.5.27*

Cameron Court (e)

Cameron Court was named after John Cameron (1835-1881). In 1861, Cameron partnered with a friend and bought over *The Straits Times* and became its Chief Editor. Under his charge, the newspaper expanded from a weekly newspaper to become a daily press.

Source: STOJ, 1881.12.31:2; Buckley: 715

Camp Road (former Tanglin Barracks)

Campbell Lane (Kampong Kapor)
Construction of roads in Kampong Kapor was planned in 1883, with the appearance of street names in the press beginning in 1886. Most of the streets, including Campbell Lane, appeared in a survey map of Singapore in 1893.

The source of this road name is said to be Robert Campbell, a Partner at Martin Dyce & Co. in the 1870s and a member of the Legislative Council for about two years from 1878 to 1880. He passed away in England shortly after leaving Singapore in 1881. Martin Dyce & Co. ceased operations in 1885.

However, Campbell Lane is one of the four parallel roads in Kampong Kapor with the other three roads named after senior colonial officials involved with the annexation of the Native States in Malaya. The other three roads are: Dunlop Street, Weld Road and Dickson Road. Therefore, Campbell Lane may be named after George W Robert Campbell, the Acting Lieutenant Governor of Penang from 1872 to 1873. He was a key person in the settlement of the Larut War in Perak and was made a C.M.G. in 1887 for his services during this period.

Source: ST, 1878.12.21:4; ST, 1881.6.2:1; ST, 1883.5.23:9; ST, 1887.8.3:2; NAS, SP002987; Makepeace, vol.2:205; Singam

Camphor Avenue (Sennett Estate)
Camphor is found in the wood of *Camphor laurel*. This road was named in 1951. *See Angsana Avenue.*

Source: CC, 1951.9.28

Canada Road (former Singapore Naval Base)
Canada (which means small cluster of houses in Red Indian language) became a British colony in 1867. *See Admiralty Road.*

Source: Wagner: 45

Canal Road (e)
This road was located between New Bridge Road and Magazine Road. It was listed as a street in town in 1853.

Source: SFP, 1853.7.8:4

Canberra Drive/Lane/Link/Road/Square (e)/Street/View/Walk/Way
Canberra Road was located in the former Singapore Naval Base. It was named after HMAS *Canberra*, the flagship of the Royal Australian Navy

in commemoration of the visit of the Royal Australian Navy to Singapore in 1937.
Source: ST, 1937.9.2:12

Canberra Road (e) (former RAF Tengah)
The road was named after English Electric Canberra, a British first-generation bomber manufactured in large numbers through the 1950s. See *Hornet Road*.

Canning Lane/Rise/Walk
These roads were named after Fort Canning as they are in the vicinity of the fort. See *Fort Canning Link*.

Canning Lane was the rename of Chong Long Road in 1954.

Canning Rise was named in 1915 and declared a public street at the same time.
Source: MC, 1915.5.28; ST, 1954.6.12:12

Canterbury Road (former Alexandra Barracks)
This road was named after Canterbury, a historic English cathedral city in Kent, South East England. Canterbury Cathedral is the cathedral of the Archbishop of Canterbury, leader of the Church of England. See *Berkshire Road*.

Canton Lane (e)/Street
Canton (now Guangdong) is a province in South China.

Canton Lane was located in the former Nanyang University.

Canton Street is in Boat Quay. It was listed as a street in town in 1853.
Source: SFP, 1853.7.8:4

Cantonment Close/Link/Road
Cantonment is a military garrison or camp. This cantonment refers to the barracks of East India Company's Sepoy (see *Sepoy Avenue*) troops stationed in this area between 1824 and 1858.

Cantonment Road was listed as a country road in 1853. In 1858, part of this road became Outram Road.
Source: SFP, 1853.7.8:4; SFP, 1858.4.1:6

Capetown Crescent (e) (former Singapore Naval Base)
This road was named after Cape Town, the legislative capital of South Africa. See *Admiralty Road*.

Capricorn Drive
This road is located in the Upper Thomson area among a group of roads named after planet and zodiac signs. In addition to Capricorn, there are Jupiter Road, Leo Drive, Libra Drive, Venus Drive and Venus Road. This road was named in 1961.
Source: SFP, 1961.1.6:6

Cardiff Grove (Serangoon Gardens)
There are more than ten road names starting with the alphabet C in Serangoon Gardens. In addition to Cardiff Grove, there are Chepstow Close, Chartwell Drive, Chiselhurst Grove, Coniston Grove, Conway Circle, etc.

This road was named in 1955 after the city of Cardiff, the capital and largest city in Wales. The Cardiff Castle, a medieval castle built in the 11th century, is located within the city. *See Alnwick Road.*

Source: *RBAR, 1955:9*

Carey Road (e)
This road was named in 1907 after E V Carey (died 1914) who cultivated rubber in Malaya.

Source: *MC, 1907.12.13; ST, 1914.4.27:9; Singam*

Carisbrooke Grove (Serangoon Gardens)
This road was named in 1955 after Carisbrooke, a village near Newport, Isle of Wight and is best known as the site of Carisbrooke Castle. *See Alnwick Road.*

Source: *RBAR, 1955:9*

Carlisle Road (Race Course Road area)
This road became a public street in 1930. Carlisle is a town in Cumbria, north of England. *See Bristol Road.*

Source: *SFP, 1931.8.17:12*

Carlton Avenue (Siglap)

Carlton Hill (e)/Hill Road (e)/Walk (e) (former Blakang Mati Artillery Barracks)
Carlton Avenue is in the Siglap area. Carlton is a multiple county name in England.

The roads in Blakang Mati were likely named after Carlton Barracks in Leeds in West Yorkshire, England. The Yorkshire (West Riding) Artillery was a volunteer unit of the British Army. Its 122nd Field Regiment was sent to the Far East in the beginning of the Pacific War in 1941 and more than 200 members of the regiment died in Singapore, mainly as POWs. *See Artillery Avenue.*

Carmen Street/Terrace (Opera Estate)
Carmen is an opera by French composer Georges Bizet. *See Aida Street.* Carmen Street was named in 1953.

Source: *RBAR, 1953:7*

Carmichael Road

This road was named after A T Carmichael, Manager of Chartered Bank. He served as a Municipal Commissioner from 1869 to 1872. He, with Gilfillan of Borneo Company, was responsible for introducing half-day work on Saturdays in 1862.

Source: *STOJ, 1869.4.13:8; Buckley: 691*

Carnation Drive

This road was named in 1954. It is part of a group of roads named after flowers in the Upper Thomson area. Besides Carnation Drive, there are Daffodil Drive, Gardenia Road, Gladiola Drive, Jasmine Road, Marigold Drive and Orchid Drive.

Source: *RBAR, 1954:8*

Carnie Street (e)

This road was located between Rochor Road and Farquhar Street. It was the city residence of Charles Carnie. It became a public street in 1907. See *Cairnhill Circle*.

Source: *MC, 1907.4.19; Buckley: 377*

Carpenter Street

Carpenter Street was listed as a street in town in 1853. There were many carpenter and furniture shops along this street in the early days.

Source: *SFP, 1853.7.8:4*
Colloquial Name: "Hee Guan Kwe", Opera House Street (*Phua, 1952:158*).

Carpmael Road

This road was named after Harold Carpmael (1871-1927), a surveyor in government service. The road name was changed from Lorong 202 in 1934.

Source: *SFP, 1934.1.11:8*

Carrhill Road (e) (former Blakang Mati Artillery Barracks)

Carrhill is a village in Durham, North East England. In 1940, the 125 (Northumbrian) Field Regiment re-roled as the 125 Anti-Tank Regiment was deployed to the Far East. They were captured and many of them ended up as POWs. As the regiment had most likely camped on Blakang Mati, it may be the reason for the road to be named after the village in Durham. See *Artillery Avenue*.

Source: *(http://en.wikipedia.org/wiki/205_(3rd_Durham_Volunteer_Artillery)_Battery_Royal_Artillery_(Volunteers), 19 Jan 2012)*

Carver Street

This street was named after C I Carver or his nephew G S Carver. They were both partners at Donaldson and Burkinshaw and members of the Legislative

Council. Both returned to England after retirement, the former in 1918 and the latter in 1928.

Source: *SFP, 1928.3.8:9; Singam*

Caseen Street

This street was named in 1898. Caseen was spelt Casseen and Kasseen.

Source: *NLB-Caseen Street*

Cashew Crescent/Link/Road/Terrace

See Almond Avenue.

Cashin Street

This road was named after Joseph William Cashin (1844–1907), a lawyer's clerk with the firm of J P Joaquim. He made his fortune in opium farming and real estate and was the first Eurasian millionaire.

Source: *ST, 1907.8.7:7; ST, 1947.10.7:7; Singam*

Cassia Crescent/Drive/Lane (e)/Link/Square (e)

Cassia is the scientific name for Cinnamon.

Cassia Drive, off Linden Drive, was named in 1954.

Cassia Crescent/Link are located between Guillemard Road and Old Airport Road. In 1956, a new road in Sembawang Estate was named Cassia Crescent but was soon changed to Seraya Crescent in the same year.

Source: *RBAR, 1954:9; RBAR, 1956:9*

Casuarina Road/Walk

Casuarina is a tree known as *rhu* in Malay. Casuarina Road was named in 1956.

Source: *RBAR, 1956:9*

Catterick Circle (e)/Road (former RAF Changi)

The above roads were named after RAF Catterick in Yorkshire, England. *See Abbotsingh Road.*

Causeway (to Johor Bahru)

Causeway (to Pulau Damar Laut, Jurong)

The Causeway leading to Johor Bahru was completed in 1923. It was partially destroyed (about 20 meters) on 27 January 1942 to obstruct the invasion of the Imperial Japanese Army. The repair of the bridge took one year.

Cavan Road (WW1 roads)

This road was named after the tenth Earl of Cavan (Field Marshal F R Lambart, 1865–1946), one of the leading commanders in WW1. Cavan was the Commander-in-Chief ("C-in-C") of British Forces on the Italian Front in

1918 when he dealt a decisive victory against the Austro-Hungarian Army. *See Allenby Road.*

Cavenagh Road
This road was named after Sir William Orfeur Cavenagh (1821–1891), the last India-appointed Governor of the Straits Settlements. He was badly injured in the Battle of Maharajpore and his leg was severed just above the ankle. Nevertheless he continued his work with the East India Company in India. He governed the Straits Settlements from 1859 to 1867. This road was built in 1865.
Source: *ST, 1865.12.2:2*

Cecil Street
This street was named by the Municipal Commission in 1881 after Sir Cecil Clementi Smith (1840–1916), when he was the Colonial Secretary in Singapore. He was appointed Governor of the Straits Settlements from 1887 to 1893.

He was known for quelling Chinese secret societies in the Straits Settlements and was the Governor who established the Queen's Scholarships for Singaporeans in 1889.

It was reported in 1935 that Cecil Street was named after Robert Cecil, the Queen's Council appointed by the Tanjong Pagar Dock Company. This is unlikely as Robert Cecil arrived in Singapore in 1905, after this street was named.
Source: *STOJ, 1881.4.18:2; ED, 1905.10.13:3; ST, 1935.9.19:13*

Cedar Avenue (Sennett Estate)
Cedar is the common name for cedarwood. This road was named in 1951. *See Angsana Avenue.*
Source: *CC, 1951.9.28*

Cedarwood Grove
See Ashwood Grove.

Cemetery Central Street/North Street/South Street (Lim Chu Kang)

Central Boulevard (Marina South)

Central Circus (General Hospital)

Central Exchange Green (Fusionpolis)

Central Expressway

Central Lane 1 (Marina South)

Ceylon Lane/Road
Ceylon is now known as Sri Lanka. *Ceylon* is the Sanskrit word for Lion Island.
Source: *Wagner: 53*

Chai Chee Avenue/Drive/Lane/Road/Street

"Chai Chee" is a transcription of vegetable market in Hokkien. These roads were named after Kampong Chai Chee which had a vegetable and farm market.

Chai Chee Drive was a rename of a stretch of Upper Changi Road in 1987.

Source: *ST, 1987.10.30:23*

Chain Lane (e)

This lane was named in 1953 and only appeared once in the 1953 Street Directory. It was marked as a military area off Yio Chu Kang Road.

Source: *RBAR, 1953:7*

Champions Way (Singapore Sports School in Woodlands)

Chancellor Road (e)

This road was named in 1928 after A R Chancellor, who was the Inspector-General of Police from 1914 to 1923.

Source: *MC, 1928.9.28; Singam*

Chancery Hill Road/Walk/Chancery Lane

The name probably had an English source such as: (1) Chancery Lane, name derived from the Court of Chancery, an equity court, in London. (2) Chancery village in Ceredigion, Wales.

Chancery Lane appeared in Municipal records in 1861.

Chancery Hill Road was named in 1928.

Source: *ST, 1861.12.14:1; MC, 1928.2.24*

Chander Road

Situated in Little India, this road was named after Anukul Chander Chander (died 1936), the President of the Indian Association from 1924 to 1926. He was the representative of the Hindu Advisory Board in the Municipal Commission from 1922 to 1934.

Source: *SFP, 1936.8.28:9; Singam*

Chang Charn Road

This road first appeared in the 1958 Street Directory. The name "Chang Charn" is a transcription of increase production in Cantonese, a suitable name for the factory area here. *See Hoy Fatt Road.*

Change Alley (e)

Two names were proposed for this lane: Change Lane and Change Alley. The Municipal Commission decided on the latter on 11 November 1890. The name was probably taken from Change Alley (or Exchange Alley) in London.

Change Alley became a place where locals conducted barter trade with regional sea merchants and Europeans.
Source: *ST, 1890.11.12:9; DA, 1890.11.12:3*
Colloquial Name: "Tor Kor Hang", Agency Houses Lane (*Phua, 1952:159*).

Changi Business Park Avenue 1, 3
Changi Business Park Central 1, 2
Changi Business Park Crescent/Vista
Changi Coast Road/Walk
Changi East Close Road/Drive/Way
Changi Ferry Road/Changi Hill (e)
Changi North Crescent/Rise
Changi North Street 1, 2/Changi North Way/Changi Road
Changi South Avenue 1 to 4/Changi South Lane
Changi South Street 1 to 3
Changi Village (e)/Changi Village Road

Changi was spelt Changhi or Changei in early days. Based on a survey report in 1848, Changei was the name of a river. According to the National Parks Board, Changi, *Sindora wallichii,* is a large tropical tree which belongs to the bean family. In other literature, species like *Balano corpas* (Makepeace, vol.2:64), *Sepetir daun tebal* and *Neobalanocarpus helmii* (Chengai) are also said to be Changi.

The British government started building fortifications in the Changi area in 1927, originally to protect the Singapore Naval Base in Sembawang. The conversion into an air base during WW2 has been discussed under Abbotsingh Road. The air base became an RAF headquarters for the Far East after WW2. It was transferred to the Singapore government on 5 December 1971 when Britain decided to withdraw its military presence from Singapore.

Changi (Changie) Road was listed as a country road in 1853.

Changi Village Road was a rename of a stretch of Upper Changi Road in 1987.

Source: *SFP, 1848.5.18:3; SFP, 1853.7.8:4; ST, 1987.10.30:23; Probert: 45*

Chapel Close/Road
There was a chapel (Church of the Holy Family) at this location.

Charlton Lane/Road
Charlton and Carlton are the same in Old English. Just like Carlton, Charlton is a multiple place name in England. Charlton Road was made a public street in 1956.

Source: *RBAR, 1956:9*

Chartwell Drive (Serangoon Gardens)
This road was named in 1953. Chartwell is an estate in the county of Kent, South East England. It was the principal adult home of Sir Winston Churchill from 1922 to 1965, when he passed away. See *Alnwick Road.*

Source: *RBAR, 1953:8*

Chatham Court (e)
Chatham Road (e) (former Pasir Panjang Barracks)
Chatham Court was located off St. Thomas Walk.

Chatham Road was a former British Army residential area. Chatham is a multiple place name in England. See *Island View Road.*

Chatsworth Avenue/Park/Road (former Sri Menanti Estate)
Chatsworth Avenue/Road were named in 1909 after Chatsworth Mansion, which was a property owned by G G Nicoll (1814-1897). Nicoll was the owner of the largest nutmeg plantation in Singapore. See *Sri Menanti Estate.*

Chatsworth Park was known as Davie Road before 1931. See *Davie Road.*

Source: *MC, 1909.12.29; MC, 1931.2.27; Buckley: 406*

Chay Yan Street
This road in Tiong Bahru district was named after Tan Chay Yan (1870-1916, Teochew), son of Tan Teck Guan and grandson of Tan Tock Seng. Tan Chay Yan was the first pioneer of the rubber industry in Singapore and Malaya. See *Seng Poh Road.* Chay Yan Street was listed in the 1936 Gazetteer and was officially named in 1941.

Source: *MC 1941.4.25; Kua: 75*

Cheang Cheoh Street (e)
See *Cheng Cheok Street.*

Cheang Hong Lim Lane (e)/Market (e)/Place/Street (e)
Cheang Hong Lim ("CHL") (1825-1893, Hokkien) was the son of Chang Sam Teoh. Both were operators of opium and liquor farms (see *Cheng Teo Place*). Cheang was a philanthropist and leader of the Chinese community. His community contributions included the building of Hong Lim Park, schools, convents and temples. He even owned a private fire brigade. His family name in English was Chiang before 1892. From 1892 onwards, both Chiang and Cheang were used concurrently and finally only Cheang was used. Some Street Directories (1950, 1954, 1961 and 2007) erroneously used "Cheong" as his family name.

At one stage, many streets were named after the Cheang family, including his sons (Jim Hean, Jim Chuan and Jim Khean), and his business names (Wan Seng). However, the change began in July 1914 when seven of the streets were renamed. CHL Lane was split into two parts and renamed Hare Street and Covent Row. CHL Market was changed to Covent Garden.

Source: ST, 1861.5.25:3; ST, 1893.2.11:2; MC, 1914.7.31; Song: 168

Cheang Jim Chuan Lane (e)/Place (e)/Street (e)

Cheang Jim Chuan (c.1878-1940) was the third son of CHL and the main Administrator of CHL's Estate. Cheang Jim Chuan Lane was located between Havelock Road and Chin Swee Road. Cheang Jim Chuan Place was located between 22 and 24 Prinsep Street.

Cheang Jim Chuan Street was renamed Covent Street in 1914.

Source: MC, 1914.7.31; ST, 1940.5.23:2; Kua: 166

Cheang Jim Hean Street (e)

Cheang Jim Hean (died 1901) was the eldest son of CHL. He established the Cheang Jim Hean Free School for the poor after his father passed away. However, the school did not last too long as Cheang Jim Hean died at a young age of 29 and the school was closed soon after. His only son died of a sudden illness at the age of 12 in the midst of a law suit over his inheritance initiated by his stepmother. This road was renamed Calcutta Road in 1914.

Source: ST, 1901.5.13:2; MC, 1914.7.31

Cheang Jim Khean Street (e)

This street was named after the fourth son of CHL. In the Municipal Commissioner's minutes of 31 July 1914, it was to be renamed Covent Alley. However, it was actually renamed Bombay Street.

Source: MC, 1914.7.31

Cheang Wan Seng Lane (e)/Place/Road (e)

These streets were named after the Chop Wan Seng owned by CHL. Cheang Wan Seng Place became a public street in 1901. Cheang Wan Seng Road was renamed Taipeng Road in 1914. *See Cheang Hong Lim Street.*

Source: MC, 1901.12.18; MC, 1914.7.31; Singam; Kua: 166

Chee Hoon Avenue

This road was named in 1951. "Chee Hoon" is the transcription of purple cloud in Hokkien. It is the name of a main branch of the Huang family which originated in central China. This is confirmed in the minutes of the Public Works Committee (PWC) which mentioned that the owners of this road belonged to the surname Oei. "Oei" is the Indonesian version of the surname "Huang" in Hokkien.

Source: MC, 1951.5.31; PWC, 1951.5.4

Chelsea Road (e) (former Pasir Panjang Barracks)
Chelsea is a multiple place name in England. *See Island View Road.*

Chempaka Avenue (Sennett Estate)
Chempaka Avenue was named in 1951. *See Angsana Avenue.*

In 1956, a new road in Sembawang area was named Chempaka Avenue (originally Chempaka Road). It was renamed Nemesu Avenue in the same year.

Source: *CC, 1951.9.28; RBAR, 1956:9*

Chempaka Kuning Link
See Jalan Chempaka Kuning.

Chencharu Lane/Link
Chencharu is horse mackerel in Malay.

Cheng Cheok Street (e)
Khoo Cheng Cheok (1820–1896) was the brother of rice merchant Khoo Cheng Tiong. In 1896, frontagers were required to repair this street before it could become a public street. This street was originally known as Cheang Cheoh Street.

Source: *ST, 1896.8.15:3; T Pagar: 133; Song: 101*

Cheng Lim Farmway (e)/Cheng Lim Farmway 1 to 6 (e)
These farmways existed around 1983 to 2006 before they gave way to housing estates in Punggol and Seng Kang. Based on a tape recording material in the National Archives of Singapore, these farmways were named after Tan Cheng Lim who worked in Asia Insurance Company.

Source: *NAS, 172:4*

Cheng San Road (e)
This road was located near Serangoon Gardens Way; it was named after Kampong Cheng San in this vicinity.

Source: *RBAR, 1957:8*

Cheng Siong Avenue (e)
This road was named after Tan Cheng Siong (1874–1922, Hokkien), a banker. He was the father of Tan Chin Tuan, former Chairman of OCBC Bank.

Source: *Kua: 90*

Cheng Soon Crescent/Garden/Lane
These roads were named after Wee Cheng Soon, a prominent building contractor before WW2. Construction of Cheng Soon Garden began in 1975.

Source: *ST, 1911.9.18:6; ST, 1975.1.11:14*

Cheng Teo Place (e)
Cheng Teo Place was built by Chang Sam Teoh in 1859 and it was to be named using his first and last name. However, his name was given as Chang Say Teok to the Municipal Commission. Therefore the road was originally named Chang Teok Place and subsequently changed to Cheng Teo Place.

Chang Sam Teoh, of Hokkien ancestry, was the founder of Teong Tai Association. He became wealthy operating an opium and liquor farm with Tay Ho Swee. He was the father of CHL.

Source: *ST, 1859.10.8:3*

Cheng Tuan Street (e)
This street was named in 1898 after Tan Cheng Tuan (1864–1902) who was in the ship chandler business. He served as a central district member of the Municipal Commission.

Source: *MC, 1898.11.8; Kua: 73*

Cheng Yan Place
The road was named after Lee Cheng Yan (1841–1911, Hokkien), with businesses in trading, finance and property investments. He was a member of the Chinese Advisory Board. This road was named in 1906 when Lee built ten houses along this private road and requested for the road to be named after him. It was approved by the Municipal Commission.

Source: *MC, 1906.1.12; Kua: 50*

Cheong Chin Nam Road
Cheong Chin Nam (died 1924, Cantonese) was the son of Cheong Chun Tin. Chin Nam Street was also named after him. *See Chun Tin Road.*

Source: *ST, 1924.6.20:8; Kua: 112*

Cheong Hong Lim Street (e)
See Cheang Hong Lim Street.

Cheow Keng Road
This road was named in 1931 after Wee Cheow Keng (1860–1939, Hainanese). He owned rubber plantations, land and was a banker.

Source: *MC, 1931.9.25; Kua: 5*

Chepstow Close (Serangoon Gardens)
This road was named in 1953. Chepstow is a town on the River Wye in Monmouthshire, Wales. Chepstow castle is situated on a cliff top above the Wye and is often cited as the oldest surviving stone castle in Britain. *See Alnwick Road.*

Source: *RBAR, 1953:8*

Cherry Avenue
This is one of the roads named after trees off Bukit Timah Road. The trees are Cherry, Cypress, Elm, Fir, Maple, Redwood and Oak.

Chertwell Drive (e)
This was a misprint of Chartwell Drive in the Street Directory of 1954.

Cheshire Road (e)
Cheshire means Roman army camp. Cheshire County is in North West England.

Source: *Wagner: 133*

Chestnut Avenue/Close/Crescent/Drive/Gardens/Lane/Terrace
See Almond Avenue.

Cheviot Hill (Frankel Estate)
This road was named in 1954. Cheviot Hill is at the border between England and Scotland. *See Burnfoot Terrace.*

Source: *ST, 1954.6.15:5*

Chia Eng Say Road (e)
Chia Eng Say (1881–1942) was one of the founders of Chung Cheng High School. He died during WW2 in the hands of the Imperial Japanese Army.

Source: *Kua: 195*

Chia Keng Village (e)
This village, named in 1938, was located at 6 ms Yio Chu Kang Road. "Chia Keng" is a transcription of car repair shop in Hokkien. There were apparently many car repair shops in this village.

Source: *SFP, 1938.8.12:3*

Chia Ping Road
This road was first seen in the 1969 Street Directory. During the late 1960s and 1970s road names of Chinese origin began to use romanised Mandarin Chinese particularly in the Jurong area. The names (all good wishes) in the industrial area were as follows.

- "Chia Ping": good product
- "Fan Yoong": prosperity
- "Joo Yee": wishes fulfilled
- "Kwong Min": bright
- "Soon Lee": smooth
- "Wan Lee": plentiful returns

Chiap Guan Avenue
This road was first seen in the 1958 Street Directory.

Chiku Road
Chiku is the Malay name for Sapodilla, *Achras sapota*. This road was known as Lorong 207, Siglap Road before 1934. *See Tembeling Road.*
Source: *ST, 1934.3.8:19*

Chiltern Drive (Braddell Heights Estate)
Chiltern is a place name in England, it means higher (hill). This street was named in 1950.
Source: *ST, 1950.8.26:7*

Chin Bee Avenue/Crescent/Drive/Road
The above were named after Chin Bee Village in this location.
Source: *NAS, 165:10*

Chin Cheng Avenue
This road was first seen in the 1953 Street Directory.

Chin Chew Street
"Chin Chew" is a transcription of pearl in Hokkien. The name was given as it was located near the foot of Pearl's Hill. Chin Chew Street existed in 1829 as seen in G D Coleman's map of Singapore printed in 1835.
Source: *NAS, SP002997*

Chin Chong Road (e)
This road was located in Jurong. It was probably named after Khoo Chin Chong, an assistant of Lim Nee Soon. He derived his wealth from building houses in the Nee Soon area (now known as Yishun).
Source: *NAS, 606:2*

Chin Hin Street (e)
This street in the Merchant Road area was owned by Seah Eu Chin. His request to name Chin Hin Street was approved by the Municipal Commission on 22 November 1870. Chin Hin was the name of a shop owned by Seah.

The suggestion that this road was named after Lim Chin Hin, a merchant and award-winning sharp shooter, is doubtful.
Source: *ST, 1870.12.17:1; Singam*

Chin Hong Road (e)
This road was only seen in the 1950 Street Directory. It was probably named after Chew Chin Hong, grandson of Chew Boon Lay. The road was described in the directory as "off Boon Lay Road".

Chin Lye Street (e)
This street was named in 1898 together with Tian Lye Street at the same location. It is possible that Chin Lye is related to Lee Tian Lye. See *Tian Lye Street*.

Source: *MC, 1898.11.8*

Chin Nam Street (e)
This street was named in 1905 at the request of Cheong Chin Nam. See *Chun Tin Road*.

Source: *MC, 1905.1.27*

Chin Swee Road
This road was named after Lim Chin Swee (died 1905), owner of Chop E. Thye. He is the son of Lim Eng Keng (see *Eng Keng Street*). Both father and son were well known merchants at the end of the 19th century. This road was originally known as Upper Chan Wan Seng Lane. The change in name was confirmed by the Municipal Commission in 1898. In 1924, the road was lengthened further by merging with Beng Hoon Road.

Source: *MC, 1898.6.8; MC, 1924.10.31; Song: 188*

Chin Teck Road (e)
This road was renamed Boon Lay Road in 1949.

Source: *RBAR, 1949:9*

Chin Terrace
This street was named after Toh Chin Joo, a Hokkien businessman. See *Toh Avenue*.

Source: *ZB-Special Supplement, 2014.11.20:19*

China Street
China Street existed in 1829 as seen in G D Coleman's map of Singapore printed in 1835. The colloquial name for this street in Hokkien was "Giao Geng Kao", meaning the entrance to the gambling dens. There were many gambling dens in this part of Chinatown in early Singapore.

Source: *NAS, SP002997*

Chinese Cemetery Path 1 to 22, 26, 28, 30, 32, 34, 36, 38 (Choa Chu Kang)

Chinese Garden Road
The Chinese styled garden in Jurong was opened in 1975.

Chiselhurst Grove (Serangoon Gardens)
The name of this road was proposed as Chislehurst in 1955. However, Chiselhurst was the name adopted. Chislehurst was a village in Kent until

1934 and is now an affluent suburban district in southeast London. *See Alnwick Road.*

Source: *RBAR, 1955:9*

Chitty Lane (e)/Road (Kampong Kapok)
Chitty means businessman in Tamil, or a Hindu descendent of a Hindu Indian who married a local Malay woman. These two roads became public streets in 1914.

Source: *MC, 1914.11.27; Dhoraisingam: xi*

Choa Chu Kang (CCK) Avenue 1 to 7
CCK Central/Crescent/Drive/Grove/Link/Loop
CCK North 5 to 7
CCK Road
CCK Street 51 to 54, 62, 64
CCK Terrace
CCK Track (2, 2A, 2B, 4 to 12) e, 14, 33
CCK Village (e)/Walk/Way

"Kang" is transcription of pier in Hokkien. "Kang Chu" is the owner of the pier who is entitled to cultivate the land on both sides of the river. Choa is a family name. Choa Chu Kang implies that the port was once owned by a Choa family. According to a book by Lim Soon Hock, Choa Hock Yi was the first person who cultivated land in this area. The original Choa Chu Kang Road had been renamed Old Choa Chu Kang Road.

Source: *Lim SH: 11*

Choa Lam (Lan) Street (e)
Choa Lam, a Hokkien shipowner, was a prominent businessman at the end of the 19th century. He owned a large estate in the King's Road area around 1905 (*see King's Road, Empress Road and Coronation Road*). Choa Lam Street, located near Chin Swee Road, was named in 1901.

Source: *MC, 1901.12.18; Kua: 208*
Colloquial Name: "Jiu Long Lye", inside the brewery. (*Phua, 1952:160*)

Chong How Road (e)
Chong How was one of the many names of Lim Nee Soon. Based on a news article in 1985, the road name was changed from West Hill Avenue 8 around 1962. *See Nee Soon Road and West Hill Avenue.*

Source: *ST, 1985.2.1:21*

Chong Kuo Road
This road was named in 1955 after Lim Chong Kuo (1902-1938), the eldest son of Lim Nee Soon. He married Tan Lay Ho, the second daughter of Tan Kah Kee. Lim Chong Kuo fell ill shortly after arranging his father's funeral in Shanghai in 1936 and passed away two years later. *See Nee Soon Road.*

Source: *RBAR, 1955:9; Kua: 128*

Chong Long Road (e)
Choa Chong Long (c. 1788-1838, Hokkien) was from a wealthy family in Malacca. He was the son of Kapitan China Choa Su Cheong of Malacca when it was under the Dutch. It was reported that Raffles stayed in one of Choa's mansions when he made a visit to Malacca in 1810. Choa became a big landowner and a Chinese community leader in Singapore. He was murdered in Macao in 1838. Chong Long Road was renamed Canning Lane in 1954.

Source: *ST, 1954.6.12:12; Kua: 206*

Chong Nee Road (e)
Chong Nee was one of the many names of Lim Nee Soon. Based on a news article in 1985, the road name was changed from West Hill Avenue 9 around 1962. *See Nee Soon Road and West Hill Avenue.*

Source: *ST, 1985.2.1:21*

Chong Pang Road (e)/Village (e)
Lim Chong Pang (1904-1956) was the second son of Lim Nee Soon. He married Lee Poh Neo, the youngest daughter of Lee Choon Guan. He ventured into the cinema business in 1927 and was active in community work. He served as a member of the Rural Board from 1929 to 1938. Chong Pang Road and Chong Pang Village were originally named West Hill Avenue and West Hill Village. They were renamed by the Rural Board in 1957. *See Nee Soon Road and West Hill Avenue.*

Source: *ST, 1956.7.22:11; ST, 1957.7.18:5; RBAR, 1957:8; Kua: 125*

Chong Sin Road (e)
Chong Sin was one of the many names of Lim Nee Soon. Based on a news article in 1985, the road name was changed from West Hill Avenue 6 around 1962. *See Nee Soon Road and West Hill Avenue.*

Source: *ST, 1985.2.1:21*

Choon Guan Street
Lee Choon Guan (1868-1924, Hokkien) was a banker. He was the son of Chinese community leader Lee Cheng Yan. He served in the Municipal Commission from 1900-1905 and was a member of the Legislative Council in 1919 and 1923-1924. During WW1, he and Lim Peng Siang made a joint

donation of an aeroplane to the British government. *See Cheng Yan Place and Pang Seng Road.*

Source: *SFP, 1924.9.16:12; Kua: 50*

Chowringhee (e)
This place was named after Chowringhee, a commercial and business district in Calcutta (now Kolkata).

Christian Cemetery Path 1 to 9, 11, 13, 15

Chu Lin Road/Chu Yen Street
The above roads first appeared in the Street Directory of 1969. "Chu Lin" is the transcription of bamboo forest in Mandarin. Similarly, "Chu Yen" is bamboo garden.

Chua Keh Hai Road (e)
This road was named in 1948 after Chua Keh Hai (1891-1939, Hokkien), a banker. He served in the Municipal Commission from 1935 to 1939.

Source: *ST, 1939.1.30:12; RBAR, 1948:7; Song: 538; Kua: 205*

Chuan Close/Drive/Garden/Chuan Lane/Link/Place/Terrace/View/Walk
Chuan Garden was previously Taman Serangoon. *See Lorong Chuan.*

Chuan Hoe Avenue
Lim Chuan Hoe (1904-1968, Hokkien) was a lawyer. He represented the Chinese Chamber of Commerce in testifying the atrocities of the Imperial Japanese Army at the War Commission after WW2. This road was named in 1948 and was subsequently extended by merging with the Japanese Cemetery Road in 1957.

Source: *RBAR, 1948:7; RBAR, 1957:8; Kua: 131*

Chulia Street
The name Chulia refers to the old Chola kingdom of Tamil Nadu in India.

This street was known as Kling Street before 1 January 1922. Kling was the short name given by the Malays and Javanese to the Kalinga, people of the Telinga nation of Southern India. It was later used by the British and Dutch for Indians in general, including the coolies and the soldiers. There were some other explanations for the word "kling", one of them was the "kling" noise made by metal harness on the convict labourers from India. In 1862, there was a decision to change the name of this street to Canning Street. However, the decision was not implemented. The change to Chulia Street was made in 1921 based on a request by the Indian community, who felt that the term was derogatory.

Source: *ST, 1862.8.23:1; MC, 1921.6.24; Buckley: 73; Makepeace, vol.1:344*

Chun Tin Road/Terrace
Cheong Chun Tin (died 1898, Cantonese) was the first qualified Chinese dentist in Singapore. He had two sons who were also dentists.

Other roads named after his family members are: Cheong Chin Nam Road, Chin Nam Street, Yuk Tong Avenue and Tham Soong Avenue.

Source: *Kua: 111*

Chungking Road (e)
Chungking (or Chongqing) is a municipality in Southwest China in Sichuan Province. Chungking Road was renamed Nanyang Valley in 1971. *See Faculty Avenue and Nanyang Avenue.*

Church Lane (e)
The above was named after the Bethesda church in the vicinity.

Source: *Savage & Yeoh, 2004*

Church Street
This street was named after Thomas Church (1798-1860) who was a Resident Councillor in Singapore. He was appointed Acting Governor of the Straits Settlements from April to October 1834 and became the Resident Councillor of Singapore from 1837 to 1856.

Church Street was shown in G D Coleman's map of Singapore in 1836.

One other Church Street (named after a Catholic Church) in the past was renamed Waterloo Street in 1858.

Source: *ST, 1856.9.30:4; SFP, 1858.4.1:6; NAS, SP002997; Buckley: 637; Corfield J, Historical Dictionary of Singapore: 62*

Chwee Chian Road/View
Lim Chwee Chian (1868-1923, Hokkien), was a banker and Chinese community leader. He founded the Ee Hoe Hean Club and was appointed a Justice of the Peace in 1918. He was nicknamed the Wolfram King of Malaya.

Source: *ST, 1923.2.13:8*

Chye Kay Road (e)/Village (e)
Chye Kay Village was named in 1954 after Tan Chye Kay (Teochew). Tan was a rubber plantation owner who died before WW2. His son, Tan Bok Hee, was the Chairman of the Sembawang Rural District Committee.

Source: *RBAR, 1954:9; NAS, 606:2*

Circuit Link/Road
Circuit Road was previously known as Pesiaran Keliling.

Circular Road
The road was probably named based on the shape of the road. This was one of the early roads built before 1830. In that year, a major fire disaster started from a shop in Circular Road and spread to Philip and Market Street. That fire was the subject of the poem "Singapore Terbakar" by Moonshi Abdulah. *Terbakar* means fire disaster in Malay.

Source: *Buckley: 209; Song: 28*

Clacton Road (former Grove Estate)
Under the heading of "Seaside Echoes in Suburban Nomenclature" in the news report, roads south of Grove Road (now Mountbatten Road) were named by the Municipal Commission in 1928 after seaside towns in England. They were Clacton, Margate, Ramsgate and Walton. Clacton-on-Sea is a seaside resort in Essex, England. *See Grove Road.*

Source: *MC, 1928.9.28; ST, 1928.9.8:12*

Clarence Lane
Clarence Walk (e) (Princess Elizabeth Estate)
Clarence Lane is located in the Alexandra Road area.

Clarence Walk was named in 1952. It was part of the Princess Elizabeth Estate which was built to commemorate the wedding of Princess Elizabeth (later QE2) to Prince Phillip in 1947. At the time of completion of the estate, the royal couple had two children, Prince Charles and Princess Anne. Therefore, besides Clarence Walk, road names in this estate included Elizabeth Drive, Philip Walk, Prince Charles Rise and Princess Anne Hill. Clarence Walk was named after Clarence House, a royal residence in London's City of Westminster. It was the residence of the royal couple until Princess Elizabeth's ascension to the throne. This estate was demolished around 2000.

Source: *RBAR, 1952:8*

Clarke Quay/Road (e)/Street
Clarke Quay and Clarke Street were named after Sir Andrew Clarke (1824–1902). He was the Governor of the Straits Settlements from 1873 to 1875. Clarke Street was named in 1896.

Clarke Road was known as Swiss Club Road before 1938. It was renamed Clarke Road after J A Clarke, director of a rubber firm who owned the land through which the road was made. However, the old name of Swiss Club Road was reinstated in 1947 due to confusion with Clarke Street.

Source: *ST, 1896.8.3:3; SFP, 1947.6.20; SFP, 1947.10.17:5; Singam*

Claymore Drive/Hill/Road

These roads were named after Claymore Estate, owned by Captain William R Scott (1786-1861). Captain Scott was the Harbour and Post Master from 1836 to 1847. It was reported in 1851 that a tiger foot print was discovered in the woods of this area. *See Scotts Road.*

Claymore Drive and Claymore Road were named in 1926.

Claymore Hill was named in 1920.

Source: *ST, 1851.10.28:4; SFP, 1861, 12.21:1; ST, 1919.3.8:9; MC, 1920.6.25; MC, 1926.8.27; Singam*

Clemenceau Avenue/Clemenceau Avenue North

G Clemenceau (1844-1929) was the Prime Minister of France. He led the nation during WW1 by persuading the Allies to agree to a unified military command and eventually achieved victory over Germany. Clemenceau visited Singapore in 1920 when Clemenceau Avenue began construction.

Source: *SFP, 1920.10.23:14*

Clementi Avenue 1 to 6
Clementi Close/Crescent/Loop/Road/Service Road
Clementi Street 11 to 14
Clementi West Street 1, 2
Clementi Woods Drive

Clementi Road was named in 1947 after Sir Cecil Clementi (1875-1947), the Governor of the Straits Settlements from 1930 to 1934, soon after the death of the Governor in Britain. The road was originally known as Reformatory Road, which was named after the Reformatory Centre.

In most accounts, this road was believed to be named after Cecil Clementi Smith, uncle of the abovementioned Cecil Clementi, Governor of the Straits Settlements from 1887 to 1893 (*see Cecil Street*). This author would like to think otherwise as the road name was changed a few months after the passing of Cecil Clementi. In addition, road names are usually given using the first or the last name of the persons concerned, as seen in Cecil Street.

Source: *SFP, 1947.10.17:5*

Cliff Road (e) (former Nee Soon Cantonment)

Many roads in the Nee Soon Cantonment were named after geographical features such as The Crest, The Cut, Edgeway Lane, Loop Road, Lower Road, Mount Road and Valley Road.

Clifford Pier (e)

Sir Hugh C Clifford (1866-1941) was the Governor of the Straits Settlements from 1927 to 1930.

The pier was built in 1853 and originally named after its owner, A L Johnston, as Johnston Pier. It was rebuilt in 1932 and renamed Clifford Pier. The colloquial name for this pier was red light pier or "Ang Tang Beh Tao" in Hokkien as red navigation lights were turned on at night.
Source: ST, 1853.10.25:5; SFP, 1932.6.11:8

Clifton Vale (Braddell Heights Estate)
Clifton means a dwelling place on a slope or riverside. Clifton is a common place name in England. Clifton Vale was named in 1951.
Source: CC, 1951.11.28

Clive Street (Kampong Kapor)
This street is located in Kampong Kapor (now Little India) with a group of roads named after colonial masters and war heroes in the colonisation of India. Parallel to Clive Street is Madras Street; Madras was a Presidency in British India. Clive Street was named after Major-General Robert Clive (1725-1774), First Baron Clive, C-in-C of British India. Clive was one of the most controversial figures in British military history. He helped achieve control over much of India and laid the foundation of the British Raj. Other names in this vicinity include Hastings, Dalhousie and Mayo.
Source: *Singam*

Clover Avenue/Close/Crescent/Rise/Way (Bishan)
Clover Hill (e) (former Pulau Brani military area)

Club Street
Based on Municipal minutes, Club Street existed before 1883 and was the heart of the Chinese business quarter. It was most likely named after the Chwee Lan Teng Chinese Club, a private Hokkien club that was sited at Gemmill's Hill (also known as Lessuden Hill), at the end of China Street. Lessuden Hill was listed in a survey map by J T Thomson in 1852 and was identified by C B Buckley as the location of the Chinese Club. It is not known when the club was formed but it was in the news in 1884 when the club was dissolved by the Court due to disagreement between its members. According to press reports in 1884, the club property at Gemmill Hill had a land area of five acres and was sold by the Court for 50,000 dollars. The land was subsequently cut up into building lots after the sale.

Tan Quee Lan was the subsequent owner of the club building as his address in 1889 was Gemmill Hill (see *Tan Quee Lan Street*). In 1898, the building at Gemmill Hill became the new club house of the Weekly Entertainment Kee Lam Club. Other clubs like Ee Hoe Hean followed in establishing their club premises at Club Street subsequently. Club Street became a public street in 1900.

Gemmill Hill was renamed Ann Siang Hill between 1893 and 1901.

The account that Club Street was named after the Weekly Entertainment Club which was formed in 1891 does not fit in with the history of the street.

Source: *ST, 1883.11.24:11; ST, 1884.3.22:2; ST, 1893.11.21:5; ST, 1898.5.7:2; MC, 1900.7.12; Buckley: 573*

Colloquial Name: "Chui-lan Teng" (*Firmstone, 1905:80*); "Toa Meng Lau", building with big door (*Phua, 1952:161*).

Cluny Hill/Park/Park Road/Park Way/Road

The name Cluny could have originated from the parish of Cluny, in Aberdeenshire, northeast Scotland, where the Cluny Castle is located; or a small settlement in the Fife County of Scotland. According to some accounts, Cluny might be derived from Jacob Clunis, the P&O pilot, who arrived in Singapore as a blacksmith and shipwright in 1845. He died suddenly in 1866. He once owned part of Pulau Brani in an attempt to build a dry dock.

Cluny Hill (the estate) was first seen in the press in 1852. It was the property of G Angus as reflected in Municipal records. The hill was marked in a survey map c.1850s as located near Dalvey/Bukit Timah Road.

Cluny Road was initially called Cross Road when it was first constructed in 1856 to connect Napier Road to Bukit Timah Road. The name of Cluny Road was first seen in the press in 1864 and shown in a survey map c.1860–1870.

Cluny Hill (the road) and Cluny Park were named in 1925.

Cluny Park Way is in the Singapore Botanic Gardens.

Source: *ST, 1852.8.3:3; SFP, 1856.10.2; SFP, 1864.11.17; MC, 1925.8.26; NAS, SP000041; NAS, SP006818; Buckley:732; Singam*

Clyde Street (e)/Terrace (e)

These roads were located off Beach Road. The name Clyde probably came from First Baron Clyde, Field Marshall Colin Campbell (1792–1863). He was the C-in-C in India during the Indian Mutiny of 1857. For this he was raised to the peerage as Baron Clyde in 1858. He was also involved in the two Opium Wars with China: as the Commander of the 98th Regiment of Foot during the First Opium War and by helping to organise the army sent East in the Second Opium War.

Clyde Terrace was named after Clyde Terrace Market. The market existed in the 1860s and was rebuilt on reclaimed land in 1872.

Source: *ED, 1906.4.24:3*

Cochrane Crescent (e)/Road (e) (former Singapore Naval Base)
These two roads were probably named after Admiral Thomas Cochrane (1775-1860), Tenth Earl of Dundonald, a daring and successful captain of the Napoleonic Wars. Two ships in the British Navy were named after the Admiral: HMS *Cochrane* (1950) and HMS *Cochrane* (1938). *See Admiralty Road.*
Source: *Buckley: 196; Dunlop*

Cockburn Drive (e)
This road led to St. Andrew's School and was probably named after John R Cockburn. He retired in June 1933 after teaching in the school for 34 years.
Source: *ST, 1933.12.4:12*

Coconut Road (e)
This road was renamed MacPherson Road around 1892.
Source: *ST, 1893.2.15:2*

Colchester Grove (Serangoon Gardens)
This road was named in 1955 after Colchester, a historic town in Essex, East of England. Colchester (meaning Roman Town along Colne River) is the oldest town in Britain and was for a time the capital of Roman Britain. It is home to the Colchester Castle. *See Alnwick Road.*
Source: *RBAR, 1955:9; Watts*

Coldstream Avenue (Frankel Estate)
This road was named after Coldstream, a town in the Scottish Borders. *See Burnfoot Terrace.*

Coleman Lane/Street
Based on an article in 1906, G D Coleman (1795-1844) was the first Government Superintendent of Public Works. He was Singapore's pioneer architect who planned, surveyed and built much of government offices, commercial buildings and churches using convict labourers from India. Coleman Street was listed as a street in town in 1853.
Source: *SFP, 1853.7.8:4; ED, 1906.4.24:3*
Colloquial Name for Coleman Street: "Jiu Diam Kue", Hotel Street (*Phua, 1952:162*).

College Avenue East/West/Link (NUS)
College Green (former University of Singapore)
College Road
This was named after King Edward VII Medical College, now College of Medicine in the General Hospital area.

Collyer Quay
The quay was named after George Chancellor Collyer (1814–1897). An army engineer from the Madras Engineers who was appointed Chief Engineer in Singapore in 1862 for the fortification of the colony. He built Collyer Quay which was actually used for commercial purposes after its completion.
Source: *ED, 1906.4.24:3*

Colombo Court (e)
Colombo Road (e) (former Singapore Naval Base)
  Colombo Court was known as Bain Court until 1914.
  Colombo Road was named after Colombo, the capital of Sri Lanka (previously Ceylon). *See Admiralty Road.*
Source: *MC, 1914.7.31*

Commerce Street (Marina South)

Commercial Square (e)
The Square was renamed Raffles Place in 1858.
Source: *SFP 1858.4.1:6*

Commonwealth Avenue/Avenue West/Close/Crescent/Drive/Lane/Link
Commonwealth, or British Commonwealth, is an organisation of member states that were territories of the former British Empire. It was formally constituted by the London Declaration in 1949.
  Commonwealth Avenue was named in 1956.
  Commonwealth Avenue West was opened in 1980.
Source: *RBAR, 1956:9; ST, 1980.6.27*

Compassvale Bow/Crescent/Drive/Lane/Link/Road/Street/Walk
(Sengkang New Town)

Computing Drive (NUS)

Coniston Grove (Serangoon Gardens)
This road was named in 1955. Coniston is a multiple place name in England. Coniston Village in Cumbria, North West England, is at the south of the Lake District National Park. *See Alnwick Road.*
Source: *RBAR, 1955:9*

Connaught Drive
This road was named in 1907 after Prince Arthur, Duke of Connaught and Strathean (1850–1942), to commemorate his visit to Singapore on 2 March 1906.
Source: *MC, 1907.3.1; Singam*

Conway Circle/Drive (e)/Grove (Serangoon Gardens)
These roads were named in 1955 after Conwy (formerly known in English as Conway), a walled market town on the north coast of Wales. Notable structures in this town are the Conwy Castle and the town walls. *See Alnwick Road.*

Source: *RBAR, 1955:9*

Cook Street
This street was named in 1925 after W W Cook, the General Manager of Straits Trading Company from 1910 to 1918. He was a member of the Legislative Council from 1911 to 1918.

Source: *MC, 1925.6.26; ST, 1918.5.28:7; Makepeace, vol.1:155, vol.2:223; Singam*

Cooling Close (Serangoon Gardens)
This road was named in 1955 after Cooling, a village in Kent, South East England. A notable building in the village is the Cooling Castle. *See Alnwick Road.*

Source: *RBAR, 1955:9*

Copeland Avenue (Jurong Island)

Coral Island (Sentosa Island)

Corfe Place (Serangoon Gardens)
This road was named in 1955. Corfe is derived from the Saxon word for gap or pass. The road could be named after the village of Corfe in Somerset county or the Corfe Castle, a village in Dorset county. Both are in South West England. The Corfe Castle dates back to the 10th century. *See Alnwick Road.*

Source: *RBAR, 1955:9; Mills*

Cornish Lane (e) (East Coast Road)

Cornwall Gardens
Cornwall Road (former Alexandra Barracks)
Cornwall Street (e)
Cornwall Road was located in the former Alexandra Barracks. It was named after Cornwall, a county in South West England, or possibly King Edward VII or King George V, who were both Duke of Cornwall at the relevant time. *See Berkshire Road.*

Cornwall Street (e) in the Chin Swee Road area was named in 1901 to commemorate the visit of the Duke of Cornwall and York in that year. The Duke ascended the throne as King George V in 1910.

Source: *MC, 1901.12.18*

Coronation Drive/Road/Road West/Walk
Coronation Road was a private road and was officially named in 1905 together with Empress Road and King's Road. The three roads were earlier named in 1902 to commemorate the coronation of King Edward VII (1841-1910). *See King's Road.*

Surrounding Coronation Road is a series of road names with titles of the royal family. In addition to Empress and King mentioned above, there are Duke's Road, Duchess Avenue, Prince Road, Princess of Wales Road, etc. Part of Coronation Road was renamed Coronation Road West in 1949.

Source: *MC, 1905.7.14; RBAR, 1949:9*

Corporation Drive/Rise/Road/Walk
Corporation Drive was Taman Jurong and Corporation Road was Jalan Peng Kang. Both names were changed in 1971.

Cosford Road (former RAF Changi)
This road was named after Cosford airbase in Warwickshire, West Midlands, England. *See Abbotsingh Road.*

Cotswold Close (Braddell Heights Estate)
Cotswold is a place name in England. This street was named in 1950.

Source: *ST, 1950.8.26:7*

Cottesmore Road (former RAF Changi)
This road was named after RAF Cottesmore (1938-2012) in Rutland, England. *See Abbotsingh Road.*

Countryside Grove/Link/Place/Road/View/Walk

Court Road (Serangoon Gardens)
This road was named in 1953.

Source: *RBAR, 1953:8*

Cove Avenue/Drive/Grove/Way (Sentosa Island)

Covent Garden (e)/Row (e)/Street (e)
The above places were known as CHL Market, CHL Lane and Cheang Jim Chuan Street respectively before 1914.

Covent Garden is the name of a famous farm market in London.

Source: *MC, 1914.7.31*

Cowdray Avenue (Serangoon Gardens)
This road was named in 1953. It was probably named after the 16th century Cowdray Castle in Midhurst, West Sussex County, South East England. *See Alnwick Road.*

Source: *RBAR, 1953:8*

Cox Terrace
This road is located in Fort Canning. There are two possible sources of this road name. The first is Group Captain C R Cox of the RAF. He was the Officer Commanding of RAF Seletar in 1936. During the Japanese air raid of Singapore in December 1941, he was the HQ Army Co-operation Command. The second source of road name is Major General L H Cox (1893-1949) who was the General Officer Commanding ("GOC"), Singapore District from 1944 to 1948.

There is an account that this road was named after Sir William Henry Lionel Cox (1844-1921). William Cox was the Chief Justice of the Straits Settlements from 1893 to 1906. This is unlikely as Cox Terrace was not listed in the 1936 Gazetteer. Additionally, roads in the Fort Canning area were named after senior officers of WW2. See *Bond Terrace*.

Source: *Savage & Yeoh, 2004*

Craig Road
The word "Craig" is derived from Scottish Gaelic meaning rock. Based on auctioneer's advertisements in 1856, both Craig Hill and Duxton Hill belonged to the Estate of the late Dr. Montgomerie. The auction advertisements indicated that each hill had about 900 nutmeg trees with a dwelling house. Therefore Craig Road was only built after the land was subdivided, sold and developed, and was named after the hill.

Dr. William Montgomerie, who came to Singapore as the first surgeon shortly after Raffles founded the island, was also a horticulture enthusiast. He was the person who introduced the use of Gutta Percha to the Western world. In addition to the nutmeg plantation above, he had a large sugar plantation in the Serangoon area which was later purchased by R C Woods (*see Woodsville Circus*). He died in India in April 1856.

The account that this road was named after Captain J Craig of the Merchant Service Guild in 1819 and succeeded Farquhar as the Resident of Singapore from 1823 to 1826 is doubtful. J Craig was the President of the Masters and Mates Association only in 1889, and later a member of the Merchant Service Guild. The second Resident of Singapore was John Crawford (*see Crawford Lane*).

Source: *ST, 1856.9.9:4; Makepeace, vol.2:316; Mills; Singam; T Pagar: 134*

Cranborne Road (former Grove Estate)
This road was named in 1939 after Cranborne, a village in Dorset, England. See *Grove Road*.

Source: *SFP, 1939.7.1:2*

Crane Road
T O Crane, an auctioneer, arrived in Singapore around 1824. He married the daughter of Jose d'Almeida (see *D'Almeida Street*). They had 14 children. This road was known as Lorong A before it was renamed in 1934.

Source: *ST, 1934.3.8:19; Lee KL: 16; Singam*

Cranwell Road (former RAF Changi)
This road was named after RAF Cranwell, in Lincolnshire, England. It was a rename of part of the Quarry Road when the area was converted to an air station. *See Abbotsingh Road.*

Source: *Probert: 11*

Crawford Lane/Street
John Crawford (1783-1868) was the second British Resident in Singapore, holding office from 1823 to 1826. His original family name was Crawfurd. Crawford was a qualified doctor with keen interest in languages.

Crawford Street was the rename of Market Street in 1858.

Based on a 1988 news article, Crawford Lane was known as Sumbawa Road. The change took place around 1981.

Source: *SFP 1858.4.1:6; ST, 1988.1.26:4*

Create Way (NUS)

Crescent Lane

Crescent Road (former Grove Estate)
Crescent Road was named in 1921; its name probably came from the curving shape of this road.

Source: *MC, 1921.2.25*

Crest Road (e) (former Nee Soon Cantonment).

See Cliff Road.

Crichton Close (Serangoon Gardens)
This road was named in 1955 after Crichton, a small village in Midlothian, Scotland. The 14th century Crichton Castle is situated close to the village. *See Alnwick Road.*

Source: *RBAR, 1955:9*

Cross Street
At the time of construction, this street connected two parallel roads of Telok Ayer Street and South Bridge Road, which gave it its name.

Cross Street was shown in G D Coleman's survey map of Singapore printed in 1836. Its extension to Robinson Road was officially named and declared a public street in 1895.

Source: *MC, 1895.2.27; NAS, SP002997*
Colloquial Name: "Kek Leng Kwe", Indian Street (*Phua, 1952:163*).

Croucher Road

This road was named after Dr. F B Croucher (born 1866), Chief Medical Officer and Principal Chief Medical Officer in charge of the General Hospital between 1914 and 1920. He served as Municipal Commissioner and was a member of the Legislative Assembly.

Source: *ST, 1920.4.10:8; Makepeace, vol.1:519; Singam*

Crowhurst Drive (Serangoon Gardens)

This road was named in 1953. Crowhurst is a multiple place name in England. Among them are two villages in South East England: one in East Sussex and another in Surrey. A few historic buildings and castles are close to Crowhurst in Surrey. *See Alnwick Road.*

Source: *RBAR, 1953:8*

Crown Lane (e)

This road appeared only once in the 1950 Street Directory. It was indicated as "off Upper Serangoon Road".

Cuff Road (Kampong Kapor)

This road was named in 1906 after J C Cuff, a highly skilled electrician with the Eastern Extension Telegraph Co. at the end of the 19th century.

Source: *MC, 1906.11.30; Singam*

Cumberland Lane (e) (Race Course Road area)

Cumberland is a historic county of North West England. It is now part of Cumbria. Cumberland Lane was named in 1941. *See Bristol Road.*

Source: *MC, 1941.9.26*

Cumming Street

Streets in Kampong Malacca South were named in 1882 and Cumming Street started to appear in the press in 1884. It was likely to be named after J Bannerman Cumming, who started in Singapore as a clerk in the firm of Maclaine Fraser & Co. in 1833 and became a Partner in 1855. He left the firm in 1861 to set up Cumming Beaver & Co., an insurance agent. Cumming was the Secretary and Treasurer of the Zetland Lodge (Free Masons) in 1845. He was active in commercial and political activities in the Settlements. *See Angus Street.*

One other J B Cumming (1858-1899) came to Singapore in 1891 after Cumming Street was named. He was the Manager, and later Partner, of

Fraser & Co.'s brickworks. He died while swimming at his residence in Beting Kusa, Changi in 1899.

The account that this street was named after J Purss Cumming is doubtful because the senior Cumming was only in Singapore from 1843 and he passed away in 1859.

Source: *ST, 1859.7.2:2; SFP, 1863.9.17:3; MC, 1882.4.19; ST, 1884.3.8:2; SFP, 1899.12.30:10; Buckley: 66, 383, 696; Makepeace, vol.2:195; Singam*

Cuppage Road

This road was officially named and declared a public street in April 1914. It was named after William Cuppage (1807-1872), who was an officer in the Post Office. He was appointed the Post Master in 1856 after 26 years of employment. When the Post Office was separated from the Harbour Board in 1869, he became the Acting Post Master General and retired in 1871. He owned a large nutmeg plantation on Emerald Hill and his residence on the hill was named Fern Cottage. Cuppage Road appeared in Municipal minutes in 1891 before Emerald Hill Estate was put up for sale in 1900. *See Koek Road.*

Source: *STOJ, 1871.4.26:6; STOJ, 1872.3.28:1; ST, 1891.12.2:5; SFP, 1900.11.13:4; MC, 1914.4.24*

Cuscaden Road/Walk

W A Cuscaden (1853-1936) was the Inspector-General of Police, Straits Settlements, from 1906 to 1913. He served as a Municipal Commissioner in 1901-1902. Cuscaden Road was named in 1921.

Source: *MC1, 1921.6.7; SFP, 1936.8.7:6; Singam*

Cypress Avenue

See Cherry Avenue.

Cyprus Road (former Singapore Naval Base)

Cyprus is an island country in the Eastern Mediterranean Sea. It was under British administration before WW2. *See Admiralty Road.*

D'Almeida Street

Named after Joze (or Jose) d'Almeida (1784-1850), a naval surgeon who was one of the earliest European settlers. d'Almeida came from Macau in 1825. He initially set up a dispensary in Commercial Square (renamed Raffles Place) and later established a trading firm, which became one of the largest and most respected firms in Singapore.

Source: *ST, 1850.10.22:4; Singam*

Da Silva Avenue (e)/Lane

The above were named after Bertha Da Silva (died 1949).

Source: *Braga: 94*

Daffodil Drive
This road was named in 1954. *See Carnation Drive.*
Source: *RBAR, 1954:8*

Dafne Street (Opera Estate)
Dafne is the earliest known musical work that could be considered an opera. *See Aida Street.* Dafne Street was named in 1953.
Source: *RBAR, 1953:7*

Dahan Road (former Singapore Naval Base)
Dahan means branch of a tree in Malay. *See Admiralty Road.*

Dairy Farm Crescent/Heights/Road
Dairy Farm Road was named in 1954 after the Singapore Dairy Farm, a dairy producer.
Source: *RBAR, 1954:8*

Daisy Avenue/Road

Dakota Close/Crescent
Dakota means friend in West Indian language. The road was probably named after the Dakota DC-3, a RAF aircraft that crashed in a thunderstorm at Kallang Airport on 29 June 1946, killing all 20 military personnel on board.

Dalhousie Lane (Kampong Kapor)
This lane was named after James Andrew Broun-Ramsay (1812–1860), First Marques of Dalhousie, a Scottish statesman and the Governor-General of India from 1848–1856. There is also a Dalhousie Obelisk (now located at Empress Place) which was built to commemorate his visit to Singapore in February 1850. *See Clive Street.*
Source: *Singam*

Dalkeith Road
Dalkeith means meadow beside the woods. This road was probably named after Dalkeith, a town in Midlothian, Scotland. *See Berrima Road.*
Source: *Mills*

Dalvey Estate/Dalvey Gate Road (e)/Dalvey Road
Dalvey Estate was named in 1923.
    Dalvey Gate Road is in the Singapore Botanic Gardens.
    Dalvey Road was a public street before 1861.
Source: *ST, 1861.10.12:21; MC, 1923.1.26*

Damai Crescent
This road is located on the island of Pulau Damar Laut. *Damai* means bringing about a good understanding in Malay.

Damar Road (e)

Damar is resin or gum exuded by certain trees in Malay.

Davidson Road (MacPherson private roads)

This road was named after James Guthrie Davidson (1837/1838-1891). In 1861, Davidson partnered with Robert Carr Woods to set up Woods & Davidson, the first legal practice in Singapore. Woods passed away in 1875 and Bernard Rodyk was taken as the new Partner two years later. The firm of Rodyk and Davidson has remained as one of the leading law firms in Singapore today. Besides legal practice, Davidson was the first British Resident of Selangor in 1875 and the third British Resident of Perak from 1876 to 1877.

Davidson Road is located in an industrial area off MacPherson Road together with ten other roads of similar nomenclature. They were all named after influential European personalities in the 19th century including British Residents in Malaya, members of the Legislative Council or Municipal Commission, and an Anglican Chaplain. These roads were listed in the 1936 Gazetteer and mostly remained as private roads until 1960.

Source: *ST, 1891.2.11:8; RBAR, 1960:7; SG-1936; Buckley: 731*

Davie Road (e)

This road was named in 1929 after Charles James Ferguson-Davie (1872-1963), who was the Bishop of the Anglican Church in Singapore from 1909 to 1927. The road was renamed Chatsworth Park in 1931 due to confusion with Dalvey Road.

Source: *SFP, 1927.7.13:10; MC, 1929.5.11; MC, 1931.2.27*

Dawnville Road (e) (off Clementi Road)

Dawson Road

This road was first seen in the 1953 Street Directory. Part of it was declared a public street in 1957.

Source: *CCAR, 1957:5*

Day Road (e)

This road was probably named after E V G Day. He worked in Malaya for 30 years, first as a British Resident in Malacca and later as British Advisor to the State of Kedah. After his retirement in 1951, he became Chairman of the Rural Board in Singapore from 1952 to 1954. This road was named in 1954.

Source: *ST, 1952.12.19:9; RBAR, 1954:9*

De Souza Avenue/Street (e)

Based on a news article in 1933, De Souza Street was named after Manuel Francisco De Souza (1816-1891, Eurasian). He specialised in trading with Indochina and became a big landowner. Mount Rosie was named after his daughter.

Source: *ST, 1891.2.18:11; ST, 1933.7.2:9; Makepeace, vol.1:367*

Deal Road (former Pasir Panjang Barracks)
This road was named after Deal, a town in Kent, England. *See Dover Road.*

Debden Road (e) (former RAF Changi)
This road was named after Debden Air Base (1937–1975) in Essex, East of England. *See Abbotsingh Road.*

Dedap Link/Place/Road
Dedap is a coral tree, *Erythrina variegate* in Malay.

Source: *Boo: 583*

Defu Avenue 1, 2
Defu Lane 1 to 12
"Defu" is the pinyin version of "Teck Hock" in Hokkien. It means good morals. The name was taken from Teck Hock village which was located at 8 ms Tampines Road.

Source: *NAS, 1275:9*

Delhi Road (former Singapore Naval Base)
Delhi is the capital of India, which was under British control before WW2. *See Admiralty Road.*

Deli Street (e)
Deli was a Sultanate in Sumatra with Medan as its capital. It was annexed by the Netherlands in 1854. This area was rich in agriculture produce such as tobacco leaves, coconut and spices, with tobacco as its main export. This street was located just outside the former Tanjong Pagar Dock area. The other street in this area named after a Sumatra Sultanate was Siak Street. Deli Street was named in 1898.

Source: *MC, 1898.11.8*

Dell Lane (Singapore Botanic Gardens)

Delta Avenue/Circus (e)/Road
Delta refers to the delta of the Singapore River.

Dempsey Road (former Tanglin Barracks)
This road was named after General Sir Miles Christopher Dempsey (1896–1969) who fought in both world wars. In 1944, he commanded the British Second Army during the Battle of Normandy and was the first British Army commander to cross the Rhine. After the war he was appointed C-in-C of the Allied Land Force South East Asia between November 1945 and July 1946. *See Barrack Road.*

Source: *ST, 1946.12.28:2*

Denham Close/Road
Denham Close is located off Upper Bukit Timah Road. It was part of the Kilburn Estate built by George Wimpey, a British company. The company was the first residential property developer in Singapore after WW2. Denham Close was named after Denham, the town near Uxbridge, England where the company had its headquarters.

Denham Road is the road outside the Old Police Academy at Thomson Road. It was named in 1929 after Godfrey Charles Denham, Police Commissioner from 1923 to 1925.

Source: *MC, 1929.7.26; ST, 1940.5.5:8; ST, 1947.11.30:7; Singam*

Departure Crescent (e)
This road was renamed T1 Departure Crescent.

Depot Close/Lane/Road/Walk
Depot Road was the location of the depot of the colonial government Central Supply Office. Before this area became part of the Gillman Barracks, it might have been the area of Coolie Line as it had the colloquial name of Labourers' Quarters together with nearby Dog Hill and Friendly Hill Road.

Source: *Edwards: 331*
Colloquial Name: "Gang Lang Xia", Laborers' Quarters. (*Phua, 1952:164*)

Deptford Road (former Singapore Naval Base)
This road was probably named after the Deptford Royal Navy Dockyard, in South East London. *See Admiralty Road.*

Derbyshire Road (Race Course Road area)
This road was named in 1922 together with several other roads in the same area. Derby is a term used for horseracing. Derbyshire is a county in the East Midlands, England. *See Bristol Road.*

Source: *ST, 1922.2.23:8*

Desker Lane (e)/Road (Kampong Kapor)
This road was named after Henry Fillipe Desker (1826–1898), owner of the largest abattoir and butchery in early Singapore. These two roads were approved as public streets in 1914.

Source: *ST, 1898.3.9:2; MC, 1914.11.27; Singam*

Devonshire Road
This road was named after Devonshire, a county in South West England. In 1874, a proposal to take over this road as a public street was under consideration by the Municipal Commission.

Source: *ST, 1874.5.23:2*

Dhoby Ghaut (e)
Dhoby Ghaut was also known as *Dhobi Ghat*, a Hindu term. *Dhoby* means laundry and *ghaut* means open space. It was where the Indians washed their clothes at the side of the Stamford Canal in the early days. Dhoby Ghaut is now the name of a MRT station.

Dickenson Hill Road
This road was named in 1931 after Reverend J T Dickenson, an American missionary. See *Bukit Pasoh Road*.

Source: *MC, 1931.3.27; Singam*

Dickson Lane (e)/Road (Kampong Kapor)
This road was named after J F Dickson, the Colonial Secretary from 1885 to 1892, who worked for Governors Frederick Weld and Cecil Smith. Dickson Lane was made a public street in 1914.

Source: *MC, 1914.11.27; Singam*

Dido Street (Opera Estate)
Dido and Aeneas is an opera written by Henry Purcell (see *Aida Street*). Dido Street was named in 1953.

Source: *RBAR, 1953:7*

Digby Road (former RAF Changi)
This road was named after RAF Digby in Lincolnshire, East of England. See *Abbotsingh Road*.

Din Pang Avenue
This road first appeared in the Street Directory of 1963.

Dinding Place
Dinding is the inner wall or partition in Malay. See *Jalan Bumbong*.

Dix Road
This road was probably named after R A Dix (died 1942), Manager of Singapore United Rubber Plantations Limited. He was a member of the Rural Board from 1928 to 1935. Road names in this area are mostly Scottish place names or names of senior staff of the above plantation company. They include: Glasgow Road, Hillside Drive, Highland Close, Leith Park, Parry Avenue, Rosyth Avenue, etc.

One other account mentioned that the source of this name was C C Dix, Master Attendant of the Straits Settlements in 1931. This is unlikely because the road was located inside the plantation owned by the above company and it remained a private road until 1953, when the Rural Board decided to convert it to a public street.

Source: *ST, 1953.5.29:4; ST, 1946.7.12:6-"Regarding Death and Will"; Dunlop; Lim HS: 245*

Dobbie Rise (Fort Canning Road)
Dobbie Rise was named after Lieutenant General William G S Dobbie (1879–1964). He was the GOC Malaya between 1935 and 1939. General Percival was his Chief Staff Officer during the WW2. *See Bond Terrace.*

Dock Road East/North/South/West (former Singapore Naval Base)
These roads surround the King George VI Dock in the Base.

Dog Hill (e) (Gillman Barracks)
See Depot Road.

Dohan Road (e)
This road was only listed in the 1950 Street Directory as located in the Naval Base. It was probably a misprint of Dahan Road.

Dorset Road (Race Course Road area)
Dorset is a county in South West England on the English Channel Coast. This road was named in 1922. *See Bristol Road and Derbyshire Road.*
Source: *ST, 1922.2.23:8*

Dover Avenue/Dover Close East
Dover Crescent/Drive/Rise/Road (former Pasir Panjang Barracks)
Dover means water in Latin. Dover Road was one of the British Army residential areas in Pasir Panjang. It was named after Dover, a town and major ferry port in Kent, South East England. Other roads in the vicinity such as Deal Road, Folkestone Road, Maidstone Road, Sandwich Road and St. Margaret's Road were all named after places in Kent.
Source: *Watts*

Drake Avenue/Lane (former Singapore Naval Base)
This road was probably named after Vice Admiral Sir Francis Drake (1540–1596). Drake was the key figure in gaining much of England's riches and naval successes. He contributed to the colonisation of the New World. About 20 ships of the Royal Navy were named after Drake. *See Admiralty Road.*

Draycott Drive/Park
Draycott Drive was named in 1940 after Draycot (spelt with only one t), a 19th century bungalow that was the residence of James Robertson, General Manager and Director of Guthrie & Co. The building was given conservation status by the Urban Redevelopment Authority in 2003.
Source: *URA-Draycott*

Dryburgh Avenue (Frankel Estate)
This road was named in 1954. Dryburgh is a village in the Scottish Borders. *See Burnfoot Terrace.*
Source: *ST, 1954.6.15:5*

Dublin Road
Located off Killiney Road, Dublin is the capital of Ireland, UK.
Dublin Road became a public street in 1900.
Source: *MC, 1900.7.12*

Duchess Avenue/Place/Road/Walk (e)
Duchess Road was named in 1949. *See Coronation Road.*
Source: *MC, 1949.5.27*

Duke Street (e) (former RAF Seletar)
Duke's Road
Duke's Road is one of the roads named after the royal family in Bukit Timah. Although it was named in 1928, it remained a private road and undeveloped until the completion of the Lutheran Church at this location in March 1960. *See Coronation Drive.*
Source: *MC, 1928.3.30*

Duku Lane/Place/Road
Duku, *Lansium domesticum*, is the name of a local fruit similar in shape to a longan. Based on a news article in 1935, Duku Road was a rename of Lorong D in 1934. *See Tembeling Road.*
Source: *ST, 1935.12.21:10*

Dunbar Walk (Frankel Estate)
Dunbar is a town in East Lothian on the southeast coast of Scotland. *See Burnfoot Terrace.*

Dundee Road
Located off Alexandra Road, this road was named in 1956. Dundee is a city in the northeast of Edinburgh.
Source: *RBAR, 1956:9*

Dunearn Close/Road
Dunearn Road was named in 1928 after Dunearn, the name of a mansion in Dunearn Estate. Based on a news article in 1939, Dunearn became the Oldham Boarding School. Dunearn is an area in Fife County, Scotland.
Source: *MC, 1928.10.26; ST, 1939.5.1:10*

Dunkirk Avenue
Dunkirk is a multiple place name in Britain. However, the most reputable town of Dunkirk is in France, close to the Belgian border. During WW2, Britain managed to evacuate more than 300,000 soldiers isolated in Dunkirk by the advancing German Army.

Dunlop Lane (e)/Street (Kampong Kapor)
Colonel Samuel Dunlop (1838-1917), C.M.G., was the Police Commissioner from 1872 to 1890. During this period, he helped quell the disturbances in Perak and was appointed the Acting Resident Councillor of Penang in 1885. He was President of the Municipal Commission in 1889. *See Campbell Street.*

Dunlop Lane was approved as a public street in 1914.

Dunlop Street appeared in Municipal minutes in 1887.

Source: *ST, 1887.5.18:8; MC, 1914.11.27; SFP, 1917.8.16:102; Makepeace, vol.1:249; Singam*

Dunman Lane (e)/Street (e) (Kampong Kapor)
Thomas Dunman (1814-1887) was the first Police Commissioner in Singapore (1856-1871) and a Municipal Commissioner. He owned several plantations in Singapore including a large coconut plantation called Grove Estate in Tanjong Katong. He returned to England after his retirement. Grove Estate was later developed into a residential estate by his son, William Dunman. *See Grove Road.*

Dunman Street began construction in 1886. It was named after Thomas Dunman.

However, the street name was changed to Upper Dickson Road in 1930 when the name Dunman was used for a new road in Tanjong Katong. *See Dunman Lane (Tanjong Katong).* The decision to change was not unanimous and was carried through after voting.

Dunman Lane was made a public street in 1914.

Source: *STOJ, 1871.8.26:1; ST, 1886.2.6:7; MC, 1914.11.27; MC, 1930.6.27; MC, 1930.10.31; Buckley: 397*

Dunman Lane/Road/Terrace (e) (Tanjong Katong)
Dunman Road in Tanjong Katong was named in 1930 after William Dunman, son of Thomas Dunman, who was a Municipal Commissioner between 1923 and 1926. In 1930, the President (R J Farrer) of the Commission proposed that the road, which was close to Grove Estate, be named after him for his considerable service to the town.

Dunman Terrace appeared in the Street Directory of 1991. The street was later renamed Dunman Road in 1993.

Source: *MC, 1930.6.27*

Dunsfold Drive (Braddell Heights Estate)
Dunsfold is a place name in England and it means Dunt's sheepfold. This street was named in 1950.

Source: *ST, 1950.8.26:7; Mills*

Durban Road (former Singapore Naval Base)
Durban is the busiest port in South Africa. *See Admiralty Road.*

Durham Road (Race Course Road area)
Durham is a county in North East England. *See Bristol Road.*

Duxford Road (e) (former RAF Changi)
This road was named after RAF Duxford in Duxford, Cambridgeshire. *See Abbotsingh Road.*

Duxton Hill/Duxton Hill Road (e)/Duxton Road
Duxton House on Duxton Hill was the residence of Hugh Syme who established Syme & Co. in 1823 in Singapore. Syme died in 1830 on his way back to Europe and the property was sold by Syme & Co. in 1836. This property together with Craig Hill were listed as properties belonging to the Estate of Dr. Montgomerie in 1856 when the doctor passed away (*see Craig Road*). Duxton Hill Road was declared a public street in 1907. Based on reports in the newspaper, Duxton Road should be named around 1892.
Source: *ST, 1823.5.8:10; SCCR, 1836.4.16:1; MC, 1907.4.19; Makepeace, vol.2:229*

Dyson Road
This road was named after Cecil Venn Dyson, Acting District Judge, who died in the Indian Mutiny of 1915 in Singapore.
Source: *SFP, 1915.5.13:3; Makepeace, vol.1:410; Savage & Yeoh, 2004*

Eagle Avenue (e) (former Pulau Brani military area)

Ean Kiam Place
Tan Ean Kiam (1881–1943, Hokkien) was a rubber merchant and a banker. He was Managing Director of a bank for about 30 years.
Source: *Kua: 79*

Earle Quay (e)
The quay was named in 1907 after T E Earle, the General Manager and Director of Straits Steamship Co. Ltd. He was a member of the Legislative Council in 1900.
Source: *MC, 1907.12.13; Singam*

East Church Road (former RAF Changi)
This road was named after RAF Eastchurch in Kent, south of England. *See Abbotsingh Road.*

East Coast Avenue/Drive
East Coast Park Service Road/East Coast Parkway
East Coast Road/East Coast Terrace

East Gate Road (e) (former Nee Soon Cantonment)
This road was probably renamed Balmoral Road in 1953/1954.

Singapore Gazetteer Since 1936 and Annotations

East Lagoon Link (e) (East Coast Park)

East Perimeter Road (Singapore Changi Airport)

East Reclamation Road (e) (former Singapore Harbour Board)
This road was situated beyond the original shore line.

East Sussex Lane
East Sussex is a county in the south of England. *See Sussex Garden.*

East Wharf Road (e) (former Singapore Harbour Board)

Eastern Link (e)

Eastwood Drive/Green/Place/Road/Terrace/Walk/Way

Eaton Place/Walk
Eaton is an English name, the most reputable being Eaton College in Berkshire, England.

Eber Road
This road was the property of Aberto Eber who worked in J Almeida & Co. in 1850. It became a public street in 1930.
Source: *SFP, 1931.8.17:12; Makepeace, vol.1:373*

Eco Garden Way (Singapore Botanic Gardens)

Eden Grove
This road was named in 1956.
Source: *ST, 1956.2.1:8*

Edgedale Plains/Edgefield Plains/Walk (Punggol New Town)

Edgeway Lane (e) (former Nee Soon Cantonment)
See Cliff Road.

Edgeware Road (former RAF Seletar)
This road was probably named after Edgeware Road, a major road through northwest London. *See Baker Street.*

Edinburgh Road
This road runs from Orchard Road to The Istana. It was named to commemorate the 1869 visit of the Duke of Edinburgh (1844–1900), grand uncle of QE2, to Singapore. In 1870, a request by the Colonial Secretary to convert this road to a public street was turned down by the Municipal Commission as the road was solely for the use of the Colonial Governor.
Source: *ST, 1870.3.26:2; Singam*

Ee Teow Leng Road
This road was named in 1952 after Ee Teow Leng, a Teochew merchant.
Source: *RBAR, 1952:8*

Elias Green/Road/Terrace
Joseph Aaron Elias (1881-1949), E A Elias (1884-1943) and two other brothers were very successful Jewish merchants. They owned trading firms, properties, newspapers, mineral water bottler and ice factories. All were unmarried. J A Elias served as a Municipal Commissioner from 1916 to 1949.
Source: *ST, 1949.7.17:1; Bieder: 56*

Elite Park Avenue/Elite Terrace

Elizabeth Drive (Princess Elizabeth Estate)
This road was named in 1952. *See Clarence Walk.*
Source: *ST, 1952.5.16:9*

Ellenborough Street (e)
Based on a report in 1906, this road was named after the Earl of Ellenborough Edward Law (1790-1871), Governor-General of India from 1841-1844. During his tenor in 1843, he appointed William George Butterworth (1801-1856) as Governor of the Straits Settlements in Singapore. The new market built along this road, completed in 1845, was also named after him. Ellenborough Market was a famous landmark until it was demolished for new developments in early 2000.
Source: *ED, 1906.4.24:3; Buckley: 430*

Ellington Square
Ellington is a multiple place name in England.

Elliot Road/Walk
These roads lead to the St. Andrew's Orthopaedic Hospital for Children. They were named after Dr. Patricia Ruth Elliot (died 1950) by the Rural Board upon completion of the hospital in 1939. Dr. Elliot was the Medical Officer-in-charge of St. Andrew's Mission Hospital and St. Andrew's Orthopaedic Hospital from 1927 to 1950.

The suggestion that the roads were named after F M Elliot, a lawyer and member of the Legislative Council in 1914 is doubtful.
Source: *ST, 1950.9.22:6; NAS, 184:19; Dunlop*

Ellis Road
Sir Evelyn Campbell Ellis (1865-1920) was a Partner at Drew and Napier. A member of the Legislative Council from 1908 to 1916, he was appointed Acting Attorney-General for a short period in 1913. Ellis Road was named in 1922.
Source: *SFP, 1920.9.9:169; MC, 1922.4.27; Makepeace, vol.1: 235; Singam*

Elm Avenue
See Cherry Avenue.

Emerald Hill Road/Emerald Link
Emerald Hill Road was named after the Emerald Hill Estate owned by William Cuppage (see *Cuppage Road*). It was declared a public street in 1913.

Source: *SFP, 1913.2.1:7*

Empress Place/Road
Empress Place was originally proposed to be named King's Place on 1 March 1907. However the name was changed to Empress Place at the same Municipal meeting. In addition, the empress behind this road name was not Queen Alexandra, the Queen in reign in 1907, but Queen Victoria who passed away in 1901. The Victoria Theatre, also named after her, is at the same location.

Empress Road was originally named Queen Alexandra Road in 1902 when King's Road was first named (see *King's Road*). It was changed to Empress Road in 1905 upon an application by Choa Lam, the new owner of the land.

Source: *MC, 1905.7.14; MC, 1907.3.1; Singam*

Eng Hock Road (e)
Teo Eng Hock (1871–1959, Teochew) was the maternal uncle of Lim Nee Soon. He derived his wealth from rubber plantations and mass manufacturing of rubber shoes. With his wealth, he was one of the founders of Dr. Sun Yat-Sen's Tong Meng Hui in Singapore. However, he later joined Wang Jing Wei, another member of Tong Meng Hui in China, who later collaborated with the Japanese during WW2. Wang was appointed head of state in China by the Japanese government and Teo was a member of the Central Supervisory Committee under his leadership. For this he was jailed after WW2.

Based on a news article in 1985, the road name was changed from West Hill Avenue 4 around 1962.

Source: *ST, 1985.2.1:21; Kua: 109; Lim HS: 118*

Eng Hoe Road (e)
This road was named in 1951. It was located at the junction of Holland Road and Buona Vista Road.

Source: *RBAR, 1951:8*

Eng Hoon Street
This street was named after Koh Eng Hoon (1823–1880, Hokkien). He was a wholesaler and commission agent. Eng Hoon Street is located in the (pre-war) Tiong Bahru housing estate and was listed in the 1936 Gazetteer. See *Seng Poh Road*.

Source: *SG-1936; Kua: 31*

Eng Keam Place (e)
This road was listed in the 1936 Gazetteer as east of Parkstone Road.

Eng Keng Street (e)
Lim Eng Keng (1837–1892) was the owner of Lim Lan & Co. (Chop Swee Tye), a wholesaler. He was a Director at the Singapore Insurance Company and Singapore Land Company. Lim served as a member of the Municipal Commission from 1888 to 1892.

Source: *SFP, 1892.2.1:3; Song: 188; Kua: 121*

Eng Kong Crescent/Drive/Garden/Lane/Place/Road/Terrace
These roads serve the residential area which was developed around 1971.

Eng Neo Avenue
This road was named in 1950 after Tan Eng Neo (died 1941). She was the wife of Gaw Boon Chan, a successful businessman from Semarang, Indonesia. Gaw was murdered in 1911 and Tan Eng Neo inherited all his properties including the large piece of land in the Eng Neo Avenue area. After the death of Tan, the land was auctioned off in smaller lots in 1950.

Prior to ownership by the Gaw family, this piece of land was owned by a Goh family and this gave rise to an account that this road was named after Goh Eng Neo, coincidentally a similar name. However, Goh Eng Neo was declared a bankrupt in 1885.

Source: *ST, 1912.5.24:12; ST, 1950.5.27:2; RBAR, 1950:9; Dunlop; Kua: 59, 52*

Eng Watt Street
This street is located in the (pre-war) Tiong Bahru housing estate and was listed in the 1936 Gazetteer. Koh Eng Watt, a Hokkien, was the brother of Koh Eng Hoon. *See Eng Hoon Street and Seng Poh Road.*

Source: *Kua: 31*

Enggor Street (Malayan Streets in Tanjong Pagar)
This road was named in 1899 after Enggor, a town in Kuala Kangsar district of Perak. This area was known for tin and coal production. *See Bernam Street.*

Source: *MC, 1899.12.20*

Engineering Drive 1 to 4 (NUS)

Engku Aman Road
Engku is a Malay title of high rank, meaning prince. Based on a news article in 1994, this road was probably named after Abdulrahman bin Taha Alsagoff (1880–1955, Arabian). He was the nephew and son-in-law of Syed Mohamed Ahmed Alsagoff and the son of Hajjah Fatimah, a member of the Bugis royal family, which explained his title as Engku. Aman is the short name for Abdulrahman or Rahman.

Source: *ST, 1994.8.16:27; ST, 1994.8.20:29; Koh: 30*

Enterprise Road (Jurong Industrial area)

Equestrian Walk (Singapore Turf Club, Woodlands)

Ernani Street (Opera Estate)
Ernani is an operatic drama by Giuseppe Verdi. *See Aida Street.*

Erskine Road
This road was named in 1907 after Samuel Erskine (1839-1917), who was a Partner of a construction company in 1882.
Source: *MC, 1907.7.5; Singam*

Esplanade (e)/Esplanade Drive
The original Esplanade was located at the present Padang area in front of the City Hall. When land reclamation took place after WW2, the Esplanade was moved to the Queen Elizabeth Walk area. Esplanade (the road which had been expunged) was named in 1907.
Source: *ST, 1907.5.13:7*

Essex Road (Race Course Road area)
Essex is a county in South East England. *See Bristol Road.*

Estate Office Drive (NUS)

Ettrick Terrace (Frankel Estate)
This road was named in 1954. Ettrick is a small village at the Scottish Borders. *See Burnfoot Terrace.*
Source: *ST, 1954.6.15:5*

Eu Chin Street
Seah Eu Chin (1805-1883, Teochew) came to Singapore at the age of 18 (in 1823). He was one of the rare educated immigrants from China at that time. He first worked as a clerk, established his own gambier and pepper plantation and married the daughter of Tan Ah Hun, Kapitan China of Perak. He became a successful plantation owner and was known as the King of Gambier. In later years he started trading under Eu Chin Co., with his sons and brother-in-law, Tan Seng Poh, helping with the management of the business. With his wealth, he spearheaded the formation of Ngee Ann Kongsi in 1845 and helped set up Tan Tock Seng Hospital. As a Chinese community leader, he acted as the go-between for the colonial government and the Teochew community and was an early member of the Chamber of Commerce. His public appointments included an unofficial member of the Legislative Council, Justice of the Peace, and member of the Grand Jury. These appointments resulted in another title for him as Emperor Seah.

Eu Chin Street was named before 1936 together with Seng Poh Road and about ten roads in the (pre-war) Tiong Bahru housing estate. *See Seng Poh Road.*
Source: *ST, 1883.12.8:5; Kua: 104*

Eu Tong Sen Street
Eu Tong Sen (1877-1944, Cantonese) was the King of Tin. His assets included tin mines, rubber plantations, banks and medical shops in Singapore, Malaya and Hong Kong. In Singapore, his assets included properties along Eu Tong Sen Road, ownership of Lee Wah Bank and Eu Yan Sang (now listed on the Stock Exchange) and a mansion in Mount Sophia (since redeveloped). In 1919, Eu Tong Sen Street was extended by merging with Wayang Street. It was done at the request of Eu, on the basis that he had bought nearly all the houses along that street.
Source: *MC, 1919.8.1; SFP, 1919.12.13:5; Kua:105*

Eunos Avenue (1, 2) (e), 3 to 8, 5A, 5B, 7A, 8A
Eunos Crescent/Link
Eunos Road 1 to 8
Eunos Terrace
See Jalan Eunos.

Evans Road
This road was named after William Evans (1860-1936) who was the Protector of Chinese in the Straits Settlements, Resident of Malacca and Penang. He retired in 1913. This road was named in 1941.
Source: *SFP, 1936.6.6:8; MC, 1941.4.25; Makepeace, vol.1:140; Dunlop*

Evelyn Road
This road was named in 1919 after Evelyn Anne Kennedy, wife of Arthur Young (1854-1938), Governor of the Straits Settlements from 1911 to 1920.
Source: *MC, 1919.11.28; Singam*

Evergreen Avenue/Evergreen Gardens

Everitt Road/Everitt Road North
These roads were named after Sir Clement Everitt (1874-1934) who became a Partner at the legal firm of Sisson and Delay in 1909. He was a member of the Legislative Council and Executive Council of the Colony. He retired in 1927 and received a knighthood in 1928. Everitt Road was a rename of Lorong 3 Changi in 1931.
Source: *MC, 1931.4.29; SFP, 1934.2.12:3; Singam*

Everton Park/Road
These two roads were named after the Everton, the residence of Jose d'Almeida. *See D' Almeida Street.*

Everton Road was constructed off Neil Road and part of it became a public street in 1901.

Everton Park was named in 1922.

Source: *MC, 1901.12.18; MC, 1922.9.29; SFP, 1904.4.8:4; T Pagar: 135*

Evolution Garden Walk

Ewart Circus (e)/Park

Ewart is a town in Northumberland, England.

Ewart Park became a public street in 1951.

Source: *RBAR, 1951:8*

Ewe Boon Road

See Ewe Boon (1859–1909, Hokkien) was the grandson of See Hood Kee (*see Hood Kee Street*), and the second son of See Eng Watt. He was Comprador of the Hongkong & Shanghai Bank from 1890–1909. This road was named in 1928.

Source: *MC, 1928.3.30; ST, 1909.6.18:6; Kua: 212; Singam*

Exeter Road

This road is connected to Devonshire Road in the Orchard area. It was originally named Paya Lane in 1922 and renamed Exeter Road in 1928. Exeter is a city in Devonshire in South West England.

Source: *MC, 1922.2.24; MC1, 1928.5.1*

Exmouth Road (e) (former Singapore Naval Base)

This road was probably named after Admiral Edward Pellew (1757–1833), First Viscount of Exmouth. Viscount Exmouth was appointed the Commander of the East Indies Station in Penang between 1804 and 1809. A number of ships of the Royal Navy were named after Edward Pellew. *See Admiralty Road.*

Expo Drive/Link (Singapore Expo in Changi)

Faber Avenue/Crescent/Drive/Green/Grove/Heights/Park/Terrace/Walk

These streets were named after Faber Union Ltd, the developer of Faber Hills.

Faculty Avenue/Road (e)/Walk (e)

These are roads in the Nanyang Technological University (NTU). Road names were changed when it took over the campus of the former Nanyang University. Faculty Avenue was the merger of Swatow Lane and Upper Tientsin Road.

Faculty Road was the merger of Fuchow Lane, Muisian Lane, Taipu Lane and Tibet Road.

Faculty Walk was Amoy Lane. *See Nanyang Avenue.*

Fair Drive (e) (Haig Road)

Fairways Drive (former Turf Club in Bukit Timah)

Fairy Point Hill (former RAF Changi)

Fajar Road
Fajar means daybreak in Malay.

Falkland Road (Kallang) (e) (WW1 roads)
This road was named in 1928 after Falkland Islands in the South Atlantic, one of the famous battlefields during WW1. *See Allenby Road and Sturdee Road.*
Source: *MC1, 1928.10.2*

Falkland Road (former Singapore Naval Base)
Falkland is a British Overseas Territory. *See Admiralty Road.*

Fan Yoong Road
This road was first seen in the 1969 Street Directory. *See Chia Ping Road.*

Farey Park (e) (former RAF Changi)
Farey may be derived from Fairey Aviation Company, noted for the design of a number of important military aircrafts, including bombers for the RAF. Due to frequent accidents, the planes were subsequently transferred to British colonies for training purposes.

Farleigh Avenue (Serangoon Gardens)
This road was named in 1953. Farleigh is a multiple place name in England. Farleigh village in Surrey, South East England has several heritage sites including the home of Charles Darwin. *See Alnwick Road.*
Source: *RBAR, 1953:8*

Farnborough Road (former RAF Changi)
This road was named after Farnborough Airfield, in northeast Hampshire, England. This town is also known for its association with aviation, such as the famous Farnborough Airshow. *See Abbotsingh Road.*

Farquhar Street (e)
Major-General William Farquhar (1774–1869) was the first British Resident and Commandant of Singapore from 1819 to 1823. He was part of the negotiating team for the Singapore Treaty and made many positive and practical contributions for the initial development of Singapore. This road was made a public street in 1907.
Source: *MC, 1907.4.19*

Farrer Court (e)/Drive/Farrer Road
Farrer Park Road/Station Road
Farrer Park (or Farrer's Park) was named in 1929 after R J Farrer (1882–1956), President of the Municipal Commission from 1927–1931 and President of the Singapore Improvement Trust.

The park existed long before its official name. It was used as a turf club since 1843. It was also the landing strip for the first aircraft that landed in Singapore in 1919. Farrer Park was officially named in 1929 after a major redevelopment.

Farrer Road, between Holland Road and Bukit Timah Road, was named in 1931.

Source: *SFP, 1929.6.29:20; SFP, 1931.2.28:12; MC, 1931.7.31; ST, 1956.7.26:1*

Felixstowe Road (e) (former RAF Changi)
This road was named after RAF Felixstowe in Suffolk, South East England. *See Abbotsingh Road.*

Fernhill Close/Crescent/Road
Fernhill Road was named in 1922 after the Fernhill Estate off Orange Grove Road.

Source: *ST, 1903.12.31:1; MC, 1922.7.28*

Fernvale Close/Crescent/Lane/Link/Road/Street (Sengkang New Town)

Fernwood Terrace
The above was named after Fernwood Towers in Marine Parade.

Fidelio Circus/Street (Opera Estate)
Fidelio is a German opera by Ludwig van Beethoven. *See Aida Street.* Fidelio Street was named in 1953.

Source: *RBAR, 1953:7*

Fifth Avenue
This is one of the series of six roads in the Bukit Timah area that were named in New York fashion. First, Second and Third Avenue existed before November 1935.

Fifth Avenue was upgraded in 1949 at the expense of frontagers before it was declared a public street.

Source: *ST, 1935.11.3:2; RBAR, 1949:8*

Fifth Lok Yang Road
See Lok Yang Road.

Figaro Gardens/Street (Opera Estate)
The Marriage of Figaro is an opera composed by Wolfgang Amadeus Mozart. *See Aida Street.* Figaro Street was named in 1953.

Source: *RBAR, 1953:7*

Fiji Road (former Singapore Naval Base)
Fiji is an island country in the South Pacific. *See Admiralty Road.*

Finlayson Green
John Finlayson, Manager of Boustead & Co., was Chairman of the Tanjong Pagar Dock Company between 1883 and 1895. He was a member of the Legislative Council in 1887. This road was named in 1895.
Source: *MC, 1895.2.27; Singam*

Fir Avenue/Fir Tree Hill (e)
See Cherry Avenue.

Firestone Park (e)
Firestone Tire and Rubber Company is an American tire company which owned the property at this location. The company is now a part of Bridgestone of Japan. This road was named in 1928.
Source: *MC, 1928.11.30*

First Avenue
See Fifth Avenue.

First Hospital Avenue (General Hospital)

First Lok Yang Road
See Lok Yang Road.

First Street, Siglap
This street was a rename of Siglap, 1st Street.

Fish Court (e)
This street was renamed Swatow Street in 1928.
Source: *MC1, 1928.5.1*

Fish Farm Road 1 to 3 (e)

Fish Street (e) (off Ellenborough Street)

Fisher Road (e) (WW1 roads)
This road was named after Admiral John Arbuthnot Fisher (1841–1920), one of the leading commanders in WW1. *See Allenby Road.* The road was completed around 1929 and renamed Tyrwhitt Road in 1932.
Source: *ST, 1932.8.15:16*

Fisher Street (Kampong Malacca)
Streets in Kampong Malacca South were named in 1882. Fisher Street first appeared in press reports in 1883.

John Fisher (1820–1904) was an engineer by profession. He came to Singapore in 1858 and probably started working as a Manager in Alsagoff's Serai plantation in Perseverance Estate. In 1863 he set up a local telegraph line as a Partner of Fisher and Riley, before the arrival of the Eastern Telegraph Company. However, the telegraph line was destroyed in a thunderstorm after ten years. Before he retired from Singapore in 1880, he was the Manager of Borneo Company's saw mills at Keppel Harbour. *See Angus Street.*

Source: *MC, 1882.4.19; ST, 1883.1.15:6; SFP, 1904.7.18:5; Makepeace, vol.2:84*

Fishery Port Road (Jurong)

Flag Road (e)
This road was located near the Union Jack Club off North Bridge Road. The Union Jack is the national flag of the UK.

Flanders Square (WW1 roads)
This road was named in 1928 after Flanders Fields, one of the famous battlefields during WW1. *See Allenby Road.*

Flanders Field is in an area straddling Belgium and Northern France where fierce fighting between the Allied Forces and Germany took place with heavy casualties totalling more than 200,000. The battles lasted from October 1914 until the end of the war in November 1918.

Source: *MC1, 1928.10.2*

Flint Street
This street was named after Captain William L Flint (1781–1828), the brother-in-law of Raffles. Based on a report in 1935, the properties in this area were owned by Raffles, and were inherited by Flint after Raffles' death. Flint was appointed by Raffles as the first Harbour-Master attendant, a lucrative position during those days. Two Flint Streets were listed as streets in town in 1853, and one of them was renamed Prinsep Street in 1858.

Source: *SFP, 1853.7.8:4; ST, 1858.7.10:2; SFP, 1935.9.19:3*

Flora Drive/Road

Florence Close/Road
These roads were named after Florence Yeo, wife of Lim Ah Pin (*see Lim Ah Pin Road*). Construction of Florence Road was approved by the Rural Board in 1952 and it became a public street in 1955. Florence Close was named in 1953.

Source: *ST, 1952.12.19:4; RBAR, 1953:7; RBAR, 1955:9; NAS, 1935:1*

Florida Road
Florida is a state in the southeast of the USA. This road was named in 1956 together with Toronto Road and Ontario Avenue in the same vicinity.

Source: *RBAR, 1956:9*

Florissa Park
Florissa came from the word "flora".

Flower Road
In 1950, the road was repaired at the expense of frontagers before it became a public street in the following year.
Source: *RBAR, 1950:8; RBAR, 1951:8*

Foch Road (WW1 roads)
This road was named around 1929 after French Marshal Ferdinand Jean Marie Foch (1851–1929). He was the C-in-C of the Allied Forces in 1918 (WW1) who played a decisive role in winning the war. *See Allenby Road.*
Source: *ST, 1926.8.10:10; Singam*

Folkestone Road (former Pasir Panjang Barracks)
This road was named after Folkestone town in Kent, England. *See Dover Road.*

Foo Kim Lin Road
Foo Kim Lin is a Chinese personal name.

Ford Avenue/Street (e)
The property at Ford Avenue (off Holland Road) once belonged to Ford Motors, the American automobile company. In 1926, the company established its first car assembly plant in South East Asia at Anson Road. The factory was later relocated to Upper Bukit Timah Road in 1941. It became a historic site as it was the place where the British Army formalised its surrender to the Imperial Japanese Army in Singapore in 1942.

Ford Street was located in the city. It was named after T Ford, the first Chief Justice of the Straits Settlements from 1886 to 1889.
Source: *ST, 1953.6.16:10; Dhoraisingam: 285; Dunlop; Singam*

Forfar Square (e)
This road was named in 1956. Forfar is the county town of Angus County, North East England. *See Strathmore Road.*
Source: *RBAR, 1956:9*

Fort Canning Link/Road
Based on a report in 1935, Fort Canning, one of the early forts in Singapore, was named after Earl Canning (1812–1862) or C J Canning. He was the Governor-General of India from 1856 to 1858 and Governor-General and Viceroy of India from 1858 to 1862. Fort Canning was installed in 1859.

When Raffles first landed in Singapore, the hill on which the fort was installed was called Forbidden Hill by the locals. It was changed to Government Hill when Raffles built his residence on the hill. It finally became Fort Canning Hill when the fort was installed.

Fort Canning Road was previously named Back Road, as it was at the back of Tank Road. The name was changed in 1901 at the recommendation of W A Cuscaden, a Municipal Commissioner.

Source: *SFP, 1901.7.4:3; ST, 1935.9.19:13*

Fort Road
This road was named in 1921 after Fort Tanjong Katong (1878-1910).

Source: *MC, 1921.2.25*

Fourth Avenue
See Fifth Avenue.

Fourth Chin Bee Road
See Chin Bee Road.

Fourth Lok Yang Road
See Lok Yang Road.

Fourth Street, Siglap
This street was a rename of Siglap, 4th Street.

Fourth Street Sakra
See Sakra Avenue.

Fowlie Road
Dr. P Fowlie was a medical practitioner and a good golfer; he was a member of the Municipal Commission from 1899 to 1917. He retired in 1918 and returned to England. This road was known as Lorong C before the name was changed to Fowlie Road in 1934.

Source: *SFP, 1918.1.22:4; ST, 1934.3.8:19; Singam*

Francis Thomas Drive
This road, leading to St. Andrew's Secondary School, was named after Francis Thomas (1912-1977). He was the Minister for Works and Communication between 1956 and 1959. After leaving politics, he resumed his teaching career at St. Andrew's School and became its Principal from 1963 to 1974.

Source: *ST, 1977.10.15:11*

Frankel Avenue/Close/Drive/Lane (e)/Place/Street/Terrace/Walk
These roads were named after the family of Abraham Frankel (1854-1928), a Jewish family from the Soviet Union. They started with the textile business and extended into furniture and properties.

Source: *ST, 1928.5.28:7; Bieder: 80*
Colloquial Name for Frankel Drive: "Yu Tai Lor", Jew's Road. (*Phua, 1952:169*)

Fraser Road (e) (former Singapore Naval Base)
This road was probably named after Admiral Sir Bruce Austin Fraser (1888-1981), Commander of the British Pacific Fleet in 1944. He was the British signatory to the Japanese Instrument of Surrender at Tokyo Bay on 2 September 1945. See *Admiralty Road*.
Source: *ST, 1945.12.16:1*

Fraser Street
This road was named after John Fraser (1842-1907). He was the co-founder of Fraser and Neave (a company still in operation) with D C Neave in 1898. He also had a joint venture with J B Cumming in a brick factory in the Balestier area.
Source: *SFP, 1907.3.22:5; Makepeace, vol.2:194-195*

Fraser's Place (e)
This lane was located at Hill Street.
Source: *STOJ, 1871.9.23:7*

Frater Road (e)
This was a misprint of Fraser Road in the Street Directory of 1950.

French Road (WW1 roads)
This road was named around 1929 after John Denton Pinkstone French (1852-1925), one of the leading commanders in WW1. See *Allenby Road*.
Source: *ST, 1926.8.10:10; Singam*

Friendly Hill (e)/Friendly Hill Road (e) (Gillman Barracks)
See *Depot Road*.

Fuchow Lane (e)
Fuchow or Fuzhou is the capital of Fujian Province, China. This lane was renamed Faculty Road in 1971. See *Faculty Avenue and Nanyang Avenue*.

Fudu Park/Walk
"Fudu" appears to be a Chinese name meaning wealthy city.

Fullerton Parade (e)/Road/Square
Based on a news article in 1906, Fullerton Road (leading to Fort Fullerton) was named after Robert Fullerton (1773-1831), Governor of the Straits Settlements from 1826 to 1827. The landmark on this road was the Fullerton Building, which was completed in 1928 and mainly housed the General Post Office up to the 1990s.

Fullerton Parade was located between Anderson Bridge and Johnston's Pier (now Clifford Pier), it was named in 1910.

Fullerton Square was named in 1928.
Source: *MC1, 1910.4.8; MC, 1928.7.27; ED, 1906.4.24:3*

Fulton Avenue/Road
These roads were probably named after Fulton, a district in Dumfries and Galloway County, south of Scotland.

Fusion Place (e)

Fusionopolis Link/Place/View/Walk /Way
Fusionopolis is a combination of fusion and metropolis, a new word.

Gagak Selari Barat (e)/Selatan (e)/Timor (e)/Utara (e)
Translations of Malay words are as follows: *Gagak* (crow), *selari* (parallel), *barat* (west), *selatan* (south), *timor* (east), *utara* (north).

Gagak Selari Selatan and Gagak Selari Utara were both renamed to Lower Delta Road in 1970.

Gale Avenue (e) (former Pulau Brani military area)

Galistan Avenue
This road was named in 1953 after Emile Galistan. Based on a news article in 1939, Galistan had worked in the Municipality for 36 years and retired in 1938. After WW2, he returned to serve as a member of the Rural Board from 1946 to 1951. He spent his pastime cultivating orchids and named a specie with his own name.

Source: *ST, 1939.6.9:13; RBAR, 1953:8; Braga: 94*

Gallop Circus/Hill (e)/Park/Park Road/Road/Walk
Gallop Road could be the place where galloping horses were allowed in the past. It was named in 1925.

Gallop Hill was renamed Woollerton Park in 1949.

Source: *MC, 1925.9.25; MC, 1949.5.27; Singam; Wise: 147*

Gambas Avenue
Gambas is pumpkin in Malay.

Gambir Walk
Gambir is gambier in Malay. Gambier is a kind of climbing plant which is the source of tannin, a chemical agent for processing leather. It was one of the main agriculture products in early Singapore.

Gambir Walk was opened in 1986.

Source: *BT, 1986.7.17:3*

Ganges Avenue/Crescent (Delta Estate)
Ganges River is a trans-boundary river which flows through India and Bangladesh. It is about 2,500 km in length. Roads in this area are all named after famous rivers such as Indus, Nile, Tigris, Brahmaputra and Mekong. Except for Indus Road and Ganges Road, all other roads in this group have been expunged.

Gangsa Road
Gangsa is bronze or goose in Malay.

Garage Road (e) (former Singapore Naval Base)

Garden Avenue (e)/Road (e)/Street (e)
Garden Avenue was located on Sentosa Island.

Garden Road was located in the Singapore Botanic Gardens. It was renamed Tyersall Avenue in 1924.

Garden Street was in the Beach Road area.

Gardenia Road
This road was named in 1954. *See Carnation Drive.*

Source: *RBAR, 1954:8*

Garfu Road (e) (former Singapore Naval Base)
Garfu is table fork in Malay. *See Admiralty Road.*

Garlick Avenue
Based on a news article in 1958, Dr. George Herbert Garlick (1886–1958) was the Chief Medical Officer in Johor in 1917 and was appointed the Principal Chief Medical Officer from 1934 to 1942. After WW2, he was responsible for the implementation of X-ray facilities and the establishment of the Singapore Anti-tuberculosis Association (SATA).

Source: *ST, 1958.6.8:1; Dunlop*

Gateway Avenue/Drive/Link
Gateway Avenue links Sentosa Island to Keppel Road.

Gateway Drive/Link are off Jurong Gateway Road.

Gek Poh Road (e)
Lee Gek Poh (1886–1958, Teochew) owned the first Chinese winemaker in Hare Street.

Source: *Kua: 42*

Gemmill Lane
Based on a report in 1850, this road was named after John Gemmill, an English businessman who came to Singapore around 1830. John Gemmill was the first auctioneer and banker in Singapore. In fact, Ann Siang Hill used to be known as Gemmill's Hill as his house stood on the top of the hill.

Source: *ST, 1850.6.8:12; Buckley: 316; Singam*

Genista Lane (e)
Genista is an almost leafless Eurasian shrub of the pea family, which bears a profusion of yellow flowers.

Genting Lane/Link/Road

Genting means a pass between hills in Malay. Genting Lane was named in 1921.

Source: *MC, 1921.12.20*

Gentle Drive/Road

Based on a report in 1924, Alexander Gentle (1839-1923) was a broker and an accountant. He served as President of the Municipal Commission from 1890 to 1900. After which he was a coroner for many years. Gentle Road was first named in 1919, and was again confirmed as a new road in 1922.

Source: *MC, 1919.11.28; ST, 1922.2.23:8; SFP, 1924.1.21:6*

Geok Teat Street (e)

Tay Geok Teat (1832-1893, Hokkien) was elected to replace Lim Eng Keng (*see Eng Keng Street*) as a member of the Municipal Commission in 1892 when the latter passed away.

Source: *SFP, 1893.4.21:2; Kua: 115; Song: 122*

George Street

William Renshaw George (1797-1873) arrived in Singapore in 1823 as a merchant. He was the son-in-law of William Farquhar, the first Resident of Singapore. George Street was listed as a street in town in 1853.

Source: *SFP, 1853.7.8:4; STOJ, 1873.4.24:1; Singam*

Gerald Crescent/Drive/Park/Terrace

Gerald Crescent was named in 1953 after Gerald R K Mugliston, the Chairman of Singapore United Rubber Plantations Limited and Bukit Sembawang Rubber Company Ltd. *See Bukit Mugliston.*

Gerald Drive was a rename of Jalan Woodbridge by the Land Transport Authority in 1998 following the relocation of the Woodbridge Hospital. Since this road is connected to Gerald Crescent, it is logical to assume that the road was also named after G R K Mugliston.

One account mentioned that Gerald Drive was named after Gerald Hawkins (1893-1973), a civil servant with the City Council and a Secretary of Defence after WW2.

Source: *SFP, 1948.7.22:1; RBAR, 1953:7; BT, 1998.6.30:32; ZB, 2006.12.17; NAS, 799:5; Savage & Yeoh, 2004*

Geylang Bahru/Geylang Bahru Lane/Terrace
Geylang Drive (e)
Geylang East Avenue 1 to 3

Geylang East Central/Geylang Road
Geylang Serai/Village (e)
Geylang Square/Geylang Tengah (e)
Gelang was written as Gilang (as in Sungei Gilang) in a survey map c. 1830. It was also spelt Gelang or Gaylang up to the early 1900s.

Gilang means glittering in Malay. Gelang could be from *gelang pasir*, a type of purselane (*Portulaca oleracea*) or *gelang laut*, a creeping plant (*Sesuvium portulacastrum*). Subsequently, Geylang was said to be derived from *kilang*, a machine that crushes coconut husks. Other translations of Malay words are as follows: *bahru* (new), *serai* (lemongrass), *tengah* (middle).

The Geylang Serai Village area is believed to be the early settlement for *orang laut* who originally lived around the mouth of the Singapore River. The name Serai came from the *serai* plantation (cultivated between 1850 and 1890) in the Perseverance Estate owned by the Alsagoffs. The village was demolished in 1965 for new public housing.

Geylang Road was officially named in 1912.

Geylang Serai as an area was named in 1930.

Source: *MC, 1912.12.27; MC, 1930.6.27; ZB Supplement, 2012.09.09:10; NAS, SP006747; Haughton: 77; Makepeace, vol.2:84; Sophia: 377 map*

Ghim Moh Link/Road
Ghim Moh Road was named after Ghim Moh Village at the same location. The village was occupied by a Chua clan from the Anxi County in the province of Hokkien, China. The village was named in 1965.

Source: *NAS, 828:1; NAS, 980:1*

Gibraltar Crescent/Road (former Singapore Naval Base)
Gibraltar is a British Overseas Territory on the south coast of Spain. See *Admiralty Road*.

Gifford Road (e) (former RAF Changi)
This road only appeared once in the 1950 Street Directory.

Gillman Circus (e)/Close (e)/Heights (e)
Gillman Close was named in 1953. However, Gillman Barracks was built before WW2 and named after Lieutenant General Webb Gillman (1870–1933). Gillman came to Singapore for three months from April 1927 to prepare a report on the defence needed to protect the new Naval Base in Sembawang. One of his proposals was to build an artillery base in the Changi area.

Gillman Barracks was completed in 1935 to accommodate the First Battalion, the Middlesex Regiment, in order to double the infantry strength in Singapore.

Source: *SFP, 1927.7.12:9; ST, 1935.6.3:7; RBAR, 1953:7; Probert: 3*

Gilstead Road

This road was named in 1899 after Gilstead, a mansion in the Newton Road area.

Source: *SFP, 1899.7.6:3*

Gladiola Drive

This road was named in 1954. *See Carnation Drive.*

Source: *RBAR, 1954:8*

Glasgow Road

Glasgow is the largest city of Scotland and a major shipbuilding centre in the world. This road was repaired by the Rural Board in 1953. *See Dix Road.*

Source: *ST, 1953.5.29:4*

Gloster Road (e) (former Tanglin Barracks)

Gloster is the short name of Gloucester, England. The Gloucestershire Regiment was stationed at Tanglin Barracks in the 1870s.

Gloucester Road (Race Course Road area)

Gloucester is the county town of Gloucestershire, South West England. *See Bristol Road.*

Godown Road (e) (former Singapore Harbour Board)

Golden Drive/Rise/Walk

Goldhill Avenue/Drive/Place/Plaza/Rise/View

Golf Club Road (e)

This road was named in 1922 after Keppel Club, the first golf club in Singapore.

Source: *MC, 1922.9.29*

Gombak Drive/Rise

See Bukit Gombak Road.

Goodlink Park

Goodman Road (former Grove Estate)

This road was named in 1921 after Sir G A Goodman (1862-1921), one month after he passed away. Goodman was the Chief Justice of the Straits Settlements at the time of his death. *See Grove Road.*

Source: *SFP, 1921.1.27:6; MC, 1921.2.25; Singam*

Goodwood Hill/Road (e)
These roads were named after Goodwood Park, the Sussex estate of the Duke of Richmond and Gordon.

As for its landmark, the Goodwood Park Hotel, a news article in 1935 said that it was built in 1899 for the Tutonia Club, a German Club established in 1855. The premises were confiscated by the colonial government during WW1. It was renamed Goodwood Hall after WW1 and converted into a hotel in 1929.

Source: *ST, 1935.11.10:2; NLB-Goodwood Park*

Gopeng Street (Malayan Streets in Tanjong Pagar)
This street was named in 1899 after the town of Gopeng, district of Kampar, in Perak. Gopeng was once a bustling tin mining town. *See Bernam Street.*

Source: *ST, 1898.09.29:2; MC, 1899.12.20*

Gordon Road (former RAF Changi)
This road was probably named after the Gordon Barracks in Aberdeen. The Second Battalion of the Gordon Highlanders was stationed in Singapore from 1937 to 1941, when Changi was a Royal Artillery Base.

Source: *SFP, 1937.2.20:3*

Gosport Road (former RAF Changi)
This road was named after RAF Gosport in Hampshire, England. *See Abbotsingh Road.*

Grace Park/Walk

Graham White Drive
Based on a news article in 1961, Graham White was the Archdeacon of the Anglican Church (1931–1942) who helped establish the St. Andrew's School. He was sent to Thailand during the Japanese Occupation and passed away in 1945.

Source: *SFP, 1961.8.8:7*

Grandstand Drive (Singapore Turf Club, Woodlands)

Grange Circus (e)/Garden/Road
These roads were named after Grange House, one of the bungalows built by Dr. Thomas Oxley in his estate. Grange Road was extended and declared a public street by the Municipality in 1863. *See Oxley Road.*

Source: *ST, 1863.4.25:1; Singam*

Gray Lane
This road was said to be named after Gray, a Partner of Hamilton Gray. However, a news article in 1922 showed that Gray Lane was one of the winning

entries in a road-naming competition. Four road names were selected at the end of the competition: Green Lane, Rose Lane, Sandy Lane and Gray Lane. Gray Lane was named in 1922.

Source: *MC1, 1922.2.3; SFP, 1922.2.27:6; Singam*

Green Lane

Green Lane was named in 1922. *See Gray Lane.*

Source: *MC1, 1922.2.3*

Greenbank Park (off Jalan Kampong Chantek)

Greendale Avenue/Rise/Greenmead Avenue/Greenpark Avenue/Greenview Crescent

Greenwood Avenue/Crescent/Grove/Lane/Link (e)/Place/Terrace (e)/View (e)/Walk (off Hillcrest Road)

Greenfield Drive (Frankel Estate)

This road surrounds a narrow field; it was previously named Padang Terbakar.

Greenleaf Avenue/Drive/Grove/Lane/Place/Rise/Road/View/Walk (Residential area, off Holland Road)

Greenridge Crescent (off Toh Tuck Road)

Greenville Avenue (e)/Road (e)

Greenville Road was a rename of Grenville Road in the 1980s. *See Grenville Road.*

Greenwich Drive (Tampines LogisPark)

Grenville Road (e) (former Singapore Naval Base)

This road was probably named after Sir Richard Grenville (1542–1591). He died as the captain of the HMS *Revenge* that fought heroically against 53 Spanish warships near Flores in the Azores in 1591. Several Royal Navy ships were named after him. *See Admiralty Road.*

Grove Avenue/Crescent/Drive/Lane/Road (e) (Ghim Moh)

Grove Road (e)

Grove Road was named in 1907 after Grove Estate (named in 1901) and was immediately taken over by the Municipality as a public street. Grove Estate was a 400 acres coconut plantation in Tanjong Katong owned by Thomas Dunman, the first Police Commissioner in Singapore. He retired and returned to England in 1875, and passed away in 1887 in Bournemouth, England. The huge residential development of Grove Estate was the work of his son, William Dunman, who managed and developed the estate between 1900 and 1930. W Dunman (1856-1933) was a businessman and a Municipal Commissioner from 1923-1926. He contributed his expertise in the building of roads and bridges in Singapore.

As for the road names in Grove Estate, a number of roads were named after colonial officials in the early 1900s, such as Broadrick, Goodman and Wilkinson. It is noted that a majority of the roads were named in 1928 after Bournemouth and towns around Bournemouth, at the request of W Dunman. They include: Boscombe, Poole, Parkstone, Wareham, Ringwood and Branksome.

Grove Road was renamed Mountbatten Road in 1946 immediately after WW2. The rename was agreed to by Lord Mountbatten.

Source: SFP, 1901.7.8:3; MC, 1907.7.5; ST, 1923.7.14:8; MC, 1946.6.28

Guan Chuan Street
Soh Guan Chuan (born 1808, Hokkien) was one of the first board members of the Singapore Chamber of Commerce when it was established in 1837. This road was listed in the 1936 Gazetteer and was officially named in 1948. *See Seng Poh Road.*

Source: RBAR, 1948:7; Kua: 53

Guan Soon Avenue
The owner of this road made an application in 1952 to name the road after himself. It was initially rejected on the ground that he had made no contribution to society. Nevertheless, the name was approved in 1954.

Source: ST, 1952.12.19:5; RBAR, 1954:8

Guards Avenue (Bedok Camp)

Guildford Road (e)
This road was named in 1954 after Guildford town in Surrey, England.

Source: RBAR, 1954:9

Guillemard Camp Road (e)/Circus (e)/Crescent/Lane/Road
These roads were named after Laurence N Guillemard (1862-1951), Governor of the Straits Settlements and British High Commissioner in Malaya from 1920-1927. He revised the composition of the Legislative Council by adding representatives from major ethnic groups. Guillemard Road was named in 1931.

Source: MC, 1931.2.27

Gul Avenue/Circle/Crescent/Drive/Lane/Link/Road
Gul Street 1 to 5
Gul Way
The name Tanjong Gool appeared in a survey map c.1830. In a 1848 Survey Report, Sungei Gool was listed as a creek in the present Jurong area. The

present name of Gul for both landmarks was used in J T Thomson's survey map of 1852. *Gul* means rose in Malay.

Source: *SFP, 1848.10.26:3; NAS, SP006362; NAS, SP006747; Sophia: 377 map*

Gulega Road (e)/Village (e)

Gulega means talismanic or curative bezoar in Malay. Gulega Road was named in 1952.

Source: *RBAR, 1952:8*

Gunner Lane (e) (former Blakang Mati Artillery Barracks)

See *Artillery Avenue.*

Gunnesbury Lane (e) (former Nee Soon Cantonment)

Gunnersbury means manor house of a lady called Gunnhildr. It is a place in the London Borough of Hounslow. This road was only listed in the 1950 and 1953 Street Directory.

Source: *Mills*

Guok Avenue

This road was named in 1956.

Source: *RBAR, 1956:9*

Guthrie Lane (e)

This lane, located between Cecil Street and Telok Ayer Street, was named after Guthrie & Co. in 1897. Guthrie was one of the leading agency houses in Singapore during the 19th and 20th centuries. It was established by A Guthrie (1796–1865) and his nephew J Guthrie in 1821. While ownership has changed hands, Guthrie as a company in Singapore is now known as Guthrie GTS.

Source: *SFP, 1897.8.13:2*

Gymkhana Avenue

This road is located in the Mount Pleasant area near the Singapore Polo Club. *Gymkhana* is an Indian term which refers to a place of assembly. In English speaking countries, gymkhana is a multi-game equestrian event.

Hacienda Grove

Hacienda is a manor in Spanish.

Hai Sing Crescent/Road

These roads were probably named after Hai Sing Girls' High School (now Hai Sing Catholic School).

Hai Sing Girls' High School was founded in 1959 by the Franciscan Missionaries of Mary sisters. In 1990 the school became a co-educational institution when it moved to its new premises in Pasir Ris. It was first renamed Hai Sing High School and changed again in 1999 to its present name to emphasise its Catholic status.

Haig Avenue/Lane/Road
Douglas Haig (1861-1928) was the Commander of the British Army and the Allied Forces during WW1. Although he achieved the ultimate victory and ended the war, the casualties from this war numbered more than two million. As such, his achievements were much debated after his death.

Haig Road was named in 1920 after WW1.

Source: *MC, 1920.3.26*

Haigsville Drive
See Haig Road.

Haji Lane (Kampong Glam)
Haji, Hajji or *Hajee* is an honorific title given to a Muslim who has successfully completed the Hajj to Mecca. A lady with the same status is *Hajah* or *Hajjah*. The road name originated from the fact that there were many agencies along this road that helped organise trips to Mecca. *See Arab Street.*

Source: *NAS, 1255:3*

Half-Moon (Road) (e) (former RAF Seletar)
Half-Moon Road was originally listed as Half-Moon in the Street Directories. Half-Moon is a multiple street name in London, one of them is Half Moon Street in Mayfair, London. *See Baker Street.*

Halifax Road
Halifax Road (e) (former RAF Tengah)
Halifax Road was named in 1924 after F J Halifax (1873-1933), who was President of the Municipal Commission from 1911 to 1918.

Halifax Road in RAF Tengah was named after Halifax, a heavy bomber manufactured by Handley Page which was operated by the British RAF during WW2. *See Hornet Road.*

Source: *ST, 1933.2.27:10; MC, 1924.11.28*

Hallpike Street (e)
Based on a report in 1933, this street was named after Stephen Hallpike (died 1844), a blacksmith, who established the first private lodging house in 1831. He also owned a boatyard along Boat Quay.

Source: *SFP, 1844.6.27:1; ST, 1933.8.6:8*

Halton Road (former RAF Changi)
This road was named after RAF Halton in Buckinghamshire, a county in South East England. *See Abbotsingh Road.*

Hamid Lane (e)
Hamid is a Malay proper name.

Hamilton Place (e) (former RAF Seletar)
Hamilton Road (WW1 roads)
Hamilton Place was named after a side street of Piccadilly, close to Hyde Park Corner, in London. *See Baker Street.*

Hamilton Road, in the Jalan Besar area, was named around 1930 after General Sir Ian Standish Monteith Hamilton (1853–1947), one of the leading commanders in WW1. *See Allenby Road.*

One account mentioned that this road was named after William Hamilton, a Partner at Hamilton, Gray & Co. (1832). However, the trading firm was closed in 1886, long before the appearance of this road.
Source: *ST, 1926.8.10:10; Singam*

Hampden Road (e) (former RAF Tengah)
This road was named after Handley Page Hampden, a medium Bomber of the RAF serving in WW2. *See Hornet Road.*

Hampshire Estate (e) (former Ayer Rajah Barracks)
See Nepal Park.

Hampshire Road (Race Course Road area)
Hampshire is the name of a county in the south of England. *See Bristol Road.*

Hampstead Gardens (former RAF Seletar)
This road was named after Hampstead Gardens, a suburb in northwest London. *See Baker Street.*

Handy Road
This road was named after J M Handy (1869–1920, Ceylonese), a medical doctor.
Source: *SFP, 1920.11.9:6; Singam*

Hangchow Road (e)
Hangchow or Hangzhou is the capital of Zhejiang Province in China. Hangchow Road was renamed Nanyang Green in 1971. *See Faculty Avenue and Nanyang Avenue.*

Happy Avenue Central/East/North/West
These places are in the MacPherson area.

Harbour Drive (Pasir Panjang Terminal.)

Harbour Front Avenue/Place/Walk (Keppel Road)

Harding Road (former Tanglin Barracks)
The road was probably named after Field Marshal Allan F J Harding (1896–1989). He was the GOC, Far East Land Forces (FARELF) between 1948 and 1951.
Source: *Dunlop*

Hare Street (e)
This road was part of a street known as Cheang Hong Lim Lane before 1914. It was renamed for George Thompson Hare (1863-1906) who was the Secretary of the Chinese Advisory Board from 1897 to 1906.
Source: *ST, 1906.2.26:5; MC, 1914.7.31; Makepeace, vol.1:133; Singam*

Harlyn Road
This road was probably named after Harlyn Village in the north coast of Cornwall, England, very close to St. Merryn. See *Berrima Road*.

Harper Road (MacPherson private roads)
This road was probably named after R I Harper, who was the Manager of the Chartered Bank in 1870 as well as a broker and a member of the Singapore Exchange in 1887. He was a member of the Grand Jury and Municipal Commission. This road was listed in the 1936 Gazetteer. It was declared a public street by the City Council in 1960. *See Davidson Road.*

One account mentioned that this road was named after Lance Corporal J. Harper who died in the Indian Mutiny in 1915. This is doubtful as none of his superiors, R N Gerrard, Captain Horace Cullimore and Second Lieutenant J Love Montgomerie received such honour.
Source: *CCAR, 1960:8; SG-1936; Makepeace, vol.1:410, vol.2:176, 349; Savage & Yeoh, 2004*

Harrison Road (MacPherson private roads)
This road was named after C H Harrison, who was a Partner at Middleton, Brundell in 1850 (changed to Middleton, Harrison in 1860) and a shareholder of the Tanjong Pagar Dock Company. He was a member of the Municipal Commission from 1861 to 1862. See *Davidson Road*.
Source: *ST, 1862.10.4:1; Buckley: 401*

Hartley Grove (Frankel Estate)
The developer of Frankel Estate, Seacon Ltd, suggested naming this road in honour of Geoffrey Oliver Hartley (1916-1951), who died during the Malayan emergencies. Hartley was a courageous officer who overcame a number of ambush attacks before his death. The last one occurred in July 1951, when his convoy of two vehicles were attacked by about 30 bandits in Kuantan. The Municipal Commission approved the name in August 1951.

The account that this road was named after F W Hartley, Principal of Victoria School in 1897 is doubtful.
Source: *MC, 1951.8.31; Dunlop*

Harvey Avenue/Close/Crescent
Harvey Avenue was named in 1953 after J A Harvey (born 1900). He was the Commissioner of Lands (1949-1953) as well as Chairman of the Singapore

Rural Board, after which he became the British Advisor in the state of Pahang for more than a year before retirement. He returned in 1957 as the Comptroller of the Royal Household of the Sultan of Malaya.

Source: *RBAR, 1953:7*

Harvey Road (MacPherson private roads)
This road was named after John Harvey who was the Managing Director of Borneo Company in 1857. His public appointments included membership in the Legislative Council and Municipal Commission.

This road was listed in the 1936 Gazetteer and became a public street in 1960. See *Davidson Road*.

Source: *ST, 1857.8.23:1; CCAR, 1960:8; SG-1936; Buckley: 381; Singam*

Hasting Road (e) (former RAF Tengah)
This road was named after Handley Page Hastings, a troop carrier and freight transport aircraft designed for the RAF with its first flight in 1946. It was the RAF's standard long-range transport in the 1950s. See *Hornet Road*.

Source: *Probert: 86*

Hastings Road (Kampong Kapor)
This road was named in 1914 after Warren Hastings (1732–1818), the first Governor-General of India from 1773 to 1786. Hastings served as a volunteer in Robert Clive's regiment in the retaking of Calcutta in 1757. He was initially made a British Resident in Bengali in 1758. Upon his return to England in 1787, he was impeached in the House of Commons for crimes during his times in India, only to be acquitted of all charges in 1795. See *Clive Street*.

Another person named Hastings in the history of Singapore was The Marquees of Hastings, Francis Rawdon (1754–1826), who was the Governor-General of India from 1813 to 1823. It was with his agreement that Raffles purchased the island of Singapore.

Source: *MC, 1914.1.30; Singam*

Havelock Link/Road/Square
Havelock Road was named in 1858. Based on a news article in 1906, it was named after Major General Henry Havelock (1795–1857) who died from dysentery after the capture of Lucknow during the Indian Mutiny of 1857.

Source: *SFP, 1858.4.1:6; ED, 1906.4.24:3*

Hawke Road (e) (former Singapore Naval Base)
This road was probably named after Admiral of the Fleet Edward Hawke (1705–1781). He achieved many victories in wars against the French navy

between 1747 and 1759. Several places in the British Commonwealth and navy ships were named after him. See *Admiralty Road*.

Hawkinge Road (former RAF Changi)
This road was named after RAF Hawkinge in Kent, South East England. See *Abbotsingh Road*.

Hawkins Road (e) (former Singapore Naval Base)
This road was probably named after Admiral John Hawkins (1532–1595). Several Naval ships have been named after Hawkins. See *Admiralty Road*.

Hay Market (e) (former RAF Seletar)
This road was named after Haymarket, a street in the St. James area in London. See *Baker Street*.

Hazel Park Terrace
See *Almond Avenue*.

Heap Guan Village (e)
The above was named after Kampong Heap Guan San at the same location in Telok Blangah. The land was originally owned by Chop Kong Cheang, Hood Ing Company formed by Yeo Hood Ing and Yeo Chi Guan. They named it Hood Ing Estate. In 1899, the land was donated to the Hokkien Yeo Clan Association for use as a communal burial ground, which was renamed Heap Guan San ("San" means hill in Hokkien). Following this the village in that location was called Kampong Heap Guan San.

Source: *Savage & Yeoh, 2004; Song: 95*

Hemmant Road (e)
This road was named in 1931 after George Hemmant (born 1880), Under Secretary of the Colonial Office in Singapore.

Source: *MC, 1931.2.27; Singam*

Hemsley Avenue (Serangoon Gardens)
This road was named in 1953. It was initially named Helmsley and changed to Hemsley in 1957. Helmsley is a market town in North Yorkshire, England and is the location of the 900-year-old Helmsley Castle. See *Alnwick Road*.

Source: *RBAR, 1953:8*

Henderson Avenue (e)/Crescent/Drive (e)/Road/Square (e)/Walk (e)
Henderson Road was probably named around 1921 after Henderson Bros. Rubber Factory. Henderson Bros. Ltd was a big operator in the rubber and shipping agency business until 1926, when it went into voluntary liquidation. In an advertisement by Henderson Bros. Ltd in 1920, the factory location

was stated as "Tiong Bahru, near Alexandra Road". When a fire occurred at the back of the factory in 1921, the location of the fire was described in the press as "near Henderson Bros. factory at Henderson Road".

One other account said that it was named after George Henderson who worked in Hamilton, Gray & Co. around 1850. This is doubtful as Hamilton, Gray & Co. closed its operations in Singapore in 1886, long before the road was named.

Source: *ST, 1920.7.9:10; SFP, 1921.7.27:1; Makepeace:200; Singam*

Hendon Road (former RAF Changi)
This road was named after RAF Hendon in Middlesex County, in South East England. *See Abbotsingh Road.*

Hendry Close
This road was probably named after P H Hendry (1887–1961, Sinhalese) who was a Jeweller. A Sinhalese Cricket competition cup was named after him. This road was named in 1953.

Source: *ST, 1961.9.2:8; RBAR, 1953:7*

Heng Mui Keng Terrace

Hertford Road (Race Course Road area)
Hertford is the county town of Hertfordshire, England. This road was named in 1922. *See Bristol Road and Derbyshire Road.*

Source: *ST, 1922.2.23:8*

High Street
This was the main shopping street in town in the early days. It was listed as a street in town in 1853.

Source: *SFP, 1853.7.8:4*

Highgate Crescent/Walk
Highgate is a multiple place name in England.

Highland Close/Road/Terrace/Walk
Highland refers to the highlands of Scotland. *See Dix Road.*

Highland Road became a public street in 1951.

Highland Close was named in 1956.

Source: *RBAR, 1951:8; RBAR, 1956:9*

Hill Street
Hill Street was named after the nearby Government Hill (renamed Fort Canning Hill in 1859). The street was present in G D Coleman's map of Singapore printed in 1836.

Source: *NAS, SP002997*

Hillcrest Road

Hillside Drive/Terrace
Hillside Drive was named by a resident in 1927, most likely after a village in Angus, Scotland.

Hillside Terrace, a branch of Hillside Drive, was named in 1953.

There was one other Hillside Drive within the domain of RAF Changi which had been expunged.

Source: *SFP, 1927.10.12:11; RBAR, 1953:7*

Hillview Avenue/Crescent/Drive/Link/Park (e)/Rise/Road/Terrace/Way
Hillview Avenue and Hillview Road were declared public streets in 1955.

Source: *RBAR, 1955:9*

Hindhede Drive/Lane (e)/Place/Road/Walk
Based on a report in 1936, Hindhede Road was named after J Hindhede, who owned the Hindhede quarry at this location.

Source: *ST, 1936.11.1:28*

Hindoo Road (Kampong Kapor)
This road was originally known as Hindu Lane. Hinduism is the religion for a majority of Indians. *See Hindu Lane.* The road was declared a public street in 1914.

Source: *MC, 1914.11.27*

Hindu Cemetery Path 1/2

Hindu Lane (e)
Hindu Lane was named in 1906 and renamed Hindoo Road before 1914.

Source: *MC, 1906.11.30*

Ho Ching Road
During the late 1960s and 1970s many road names of Chinese origin were translated into English using romanised Chinese. Most of them are found in the Jurong area. Ho Ching Road was among a group of numerical road names in the Jurong residential area that were renamed into romanised Chinese names as follows.

- "Ho Ching", which means river view, was Taman Jurong 8
- "Hu Ching", which means lake view, was Taman Jurong 4
- "Shan Ching", which means mountain view, was Taman Jurong 10
- "Tah Ching", which means pagoda view, was Taman Jurong 12
- "Tao Ching", which means island view, was Taman Jurong 6
- "Yuan Ching", which means garden view, was Taman Jurong 2

- "Yung An", which means forever peace, was Taman Jurong 9
- "Yung Kuang", which means forever bright, was Taman Jurong 5
- "Yung Loh", which means forever happy, was Taman Jurong 1
- "Yung Ping", which means forever smooth, was Taman Jurong 3
- "Yung Sheng", which means forever rising, was Taman Jurong 7

There are two other new roads in this area:
- "Kang Ching", which means hill view
- "Yung Ho", which means forever harmony

The river view of Ho Ching Road refers to Sungei Jurong.

Ho Puah Quay (e)
The above was named after Lim Ho Puah (1840-1914, Hokkien), a ship-owner. He was a member of the Chinese Advisory Board and a Justice of the Peace. He petitioned for removal of the requirement for Chinese women immigrants to be examined naked upon disembarkation in Singapore, which was accepted by the colonial government. The quay was named in 1907.
Source: *MC, 1907.12.13; SFP, 1914.4.1:3; Kua: 128*

Hobart Road (former Singapore Naval Base)
Hobart is the capital of Tasmania, Australia. *See Admiralty Road.*

Hock Choon Road (e)
This road was named in 1955 after Hock Choon Village at the same location.
Source: *RBAR, 1955:9; NAS: 1997019831*

Hock Chwee Road (e)
Based on a news article in 1985, Wi Hock Chwee was the father-in-law of Lim Nee Soon and the road name was changed from West Hill Avenue 1 around 1962.
Source: *ST, 1985.2.1:21*

Hock Lam Street (e)
This street was named after Hock Lam Remittance Co., which was one of the business units of Low Kim Pong (1838-1909). Hock Lam Building still exists today. In 1896, frontagers paid for the repair to this road before the Municipality would declare it as a public street. *See Kim Pong Road.*
Source: *ST, 1896.8.15:3; Kua: 24*

Hock Seng Road (e)
This road was probably named after Chew Hock Seng, the eldest son of Chew Boon Lay. It was renamed Boon Lay Road in 1949.
Source: *RBAR, 1949:9*

Hoe Chiang Road
This road was named in 1929 after Hoe Chiang Company which was owned by Lim Teck Kim. *See Lim Teck Kim Road.*
Source: *MC, 1929.2.27; Kua: 137; Singam*

Hog's Back (or Hogsback) (e) (former Ayer Rajah Barracks)
Hog's Back is part of the North Downs in Surrey, England. *See Nepal Park.*

Hoi How Lane (e)/Road (e)
Hoi How or Haikou is the capital of Hainan Province in China.

Hoi How Lane was renamed Nanyang Hill in 1971. *See Faculty Avenue and Nanyang Avenue.*

Hoi How Road was the road running from Beach Road to the landing steps at the beach front and was known as Hai Lam Kongsi Road. It was renamed Hoi How when the road was declared public.

Hokien Street
This was the area for the Hokkiens in Chinatown during early colonial days. Hokien Street was shown in G D Coleman's survey map of Singapore printed in 1836.
Source: *NAS, SP002997*

Holland Avenue/Close/Drive/Green
Holland Grove Avenue/Drive/Lane/Road/Terrace/View/Walk
Holland Heights/Hill/Lane (e)/Link/Park/Plain/Rise/Road Holland Road North/South/West
Holland Village (e)/Walk
The current etymology for Holland Road is: "Named after Hugh Holland, an early architect and amateur actor". This seems to have been derived from two sources.

Firstly, from Singam: "Holland Road: — (Napier Road to Municipal Boundary) Named after Mr. Hugh Holland R.A., an early resident".

Secondly, from Makepeace, vol.2:400: "In July 1907, a party of amateurs produced a musical....... Mr. A S Bailey... and Mr. Hugh Holland, R.A., also made their debut, and scored successes."

It should be noted that R.A. is the title of an officer in the Royal Artillery. The post-nominals of a British architect would be "RIBA" (Royal Institute of British Architect). From press reports, Hugh Holland appears to be an officer with the rank of Lieutenant from the Royal Artillery that was stationed in Singapore between 1907 and 1908. He married in Brompton, England in 1911. Holland Road started to appear in the press in 1891 and was included as a major road in a Singapore survey map of 1892, before Hugh Holland's arrival in Singapore.

Holland Road was initially built as an extension from Napier Road to Bukit Timah Road by the government. It was handed over to the Municipality in 1887 and named around 1891. Its importance is shown in the fact that progress in the further extensions of this road was mentioned in the Governor's annual address in 1899.

From the above findings, it is more likely that Holland Road was named after Sir Henry Holland, the Secretary of State for the Colonies (Cabinet Minister with the power to name Governors for colonies) in London from January 1887 to 1892, around the time of appearance of Holland Road. Sir Holland was elevated to Viscount Knutsford in 1895.

Holland Grove Avenue/Drive/Lane/Road/Terrace/Walk were named in 1956.

Holland Hill was named in 1929.

Holland Park was named in 1920.

Holland Village was named in 1929.

Source: *ST, 1887.1.31:3; ST, 1887.8.31:6; ST, 1891.10.13:6; ST, 1899.10.3:3; ED, 1907.5.13:6; ST, 1908.3.30:7; ST, 1908.11.10:8; SFP, 1911.12.11:7; MC, 1920.8.27; MC, 1929.10.25; ST, 1929.7.31:12; RBAR, 1956:9; NAS, SP000006*

Holloway Lane (e)

Holloway Lane appeared in the news as early as 1857. The lane runs parallel to Middle Road, Bain Street and Cashin Street. It was probably named after C P Holloway, Director, Registrar of Imports and Exports around the 1840s. Holloway Lane was likely to be the place of his residence. An advertisement by the Chinese Girls' School (now St. Margaret's School) in 1851 mentioned that the school's residence was at 227 North Bridge Road, adjacent to the house of C P Holloway.

Source: *SFP, 1846.3.12:2; ST, 1851.10.7:4*

Holt Road

This road was said to be named after Private A J G Holt, who died in the 1915 Indian Mutiny in Singapore. This is doubtful. *See Harper Road.*

Holt Road was named in 1918 in an application by Swan & Maclaren, Architect/Surveyor of the building project along the new road. The name was approved by the Municipal Commission together with Cable Road in 1921. From correspondence between the owners and Municipal Commissioners in 1925, it is clear that the owners of Holt Road and Cable Road were Mansfield & Co. Ltd and Eastern Extension Telegraph Co. respectively.

In view of the above, Holt Road was likely named after Alfred Holt, the founder of Blue Funnel Line and the Ocean Steamship Company. The company established its main base in Singapore with Mansfield & Co. Ltd as its agent around 1880. Managers of both companies were known to have their residences at Holt Road between 1921 and 1933.

Source: *MC, 1921.2.25; ST, 1921.9.28:8; ST, 1933.9.20:11; NAS, 101-1/1918; Singam*

Holy Innocents Lane (e)
This road was named in 1948; it was located next to the Holy Innocents' School and Church at Upper Serangoon Road.

Source: *RBAR, 1948:7*

Hon Sui Sen Drive
This road was named after Hon Sui Sen (1916-1983), Singapore's Finance Minister from 1970 to 1983.

Hong Hin Court (e)
This road was named in 1908 after Hong Hin Company, one of Tan Kim Seng's business units. *See Kim Seng Road.*

Source: *MC, 1908.1.17; Singam*

Hong Kah Circle (e)/Drive (e)/Lane (e)/Road (e)/Village (e)
Hong Kah Village was situated at 12 ms Jurong Road. "Hong Kah" is the transcription of Christianity in Hokkien. It was named as the majority of the residents in this village were Christians. However, the name of the village was translated into Hong Kah Village in English and then back to Chinese which now means abundant and good.

Source: *NAS, 165:10*

Hong Kong Road (e) (former Singapore Naval Base)

Hong Kong Street
Hong Kong became a British colony after the First Opium War (1839-1842). Its sovereignty was transferred back to China on 1 July 1997. *See Admiralty Road.*

Hong Kong Street was listed as a street in town in 1853.

Source: *SFP, 1853.7.8:4*

Hong Lee Place

Hong Lim Quay (e)/Hong Lim Road (e)
Hong Lim Quay was renamed Boat Quay in 1914. *See Boat Quay and Cheang Hong Lim Street.*

Source: *MC, 1914.7.31*

Hong San Terrace/Walk

Hong San Village was Ang Oon Hui's ancestor home in Nan An County in the province of Hokkien, China. The village name was used for the roads in Comfort Garden, a housing estate which Ang built in Choa Chu Kang. *See Tong Lee Road.*

Source: *ZB Special Supplement, 2014.11.20:19*

Hood Kee Street (e)

This street was named after See Hood Kee (1793-1847, Hokkien). He was the founder of the Hokkien clan in the early days. Other roads named after his family members are: Boon Tiong Road, Ewe Boon Road and Moh Guan Terrace.

Source: *Kua: 213*

Honington Road (e) (former RAF Changi)

This road was named after the Honington airbase in Suffolk, East of England. *See Abbotsingh Road.*

Hooper Road

This road was named in 1924 after William Edward Hooper (died 1939) who arrived in Singapore in 1881. He became the Registrar of Vehicles in 1892 and remained in that post till 1923. The first autocar registered in Singapore was a Benz in 1896; it was the property of C B Buckley (*see Buckley Road*).

Source: *MC, 1924.11.28; ST, 1939.3.26:9; Makepeace, vol.2:362; Singam*

Hoot Kiam Road

Song Hoot Kiam (1830-1900, Hokkien) was fluent in English. He was the father of Song Ong Siang, the author of *One Hundred Years' History of the Chinese in Singapore*. This road was named in 1930.

Source: *MC, 1930.10.31; Kua: 37*

Hornchurch Road (former RAF Changi)

This road was named after RAF Hornchurch in Essex County, East of England. *See Abbotsingh Road.*

Horne Road (WW1 roads)

One account said that this road was named after a Judge named Horne. However, as roads in the vicinity were all named after leading Commanders in WW1, it is more likely that the road was named after General Henry Sinclair Horne (1861-1929). *See Allenby Road.*

During WW1, Horne was the only British artillery officer to command an army in the war. After the war he was raised to the peerage as Baron Horne of Stirkoke in the county of Caithness. In 1929, the Municipal Council decided to construct this road.

Source: *SFP, 1929.8.22:9; Singam*

Hornet Road (e) (former RAF Tengah)
This road was located in RAF Tengah (now Tengah Air Base of the Republic of Singapore Air Force). RAF Tengah was commissioned in 1939 with most roads within its compound named after names of military aircraft. Hornet was a land and naval base fighter aircraft manufactured by de Havilland in 1946. Other names of military aircrafts in this airbase include: Anson, Battle, Canberra, Halifax, Hampden, Hasting, Hurricane, Lancaster, Meteor, Manchester, Oxford, Mosquito, Spitfire, Stirling, Sunderland, Vampire, Warwick and York.

Horsham Road (e) (former Clementi Barracks)
This road was in the Sussex Estate. Horsham is a market town on the upper reaches of River Arun in Sussex, England. *See Arundel Road.*

Hospital Avenue (e)/Hospital Drive/Hospital Road (e) (General Hospital)

Hougang Avenue 1 to 10
Hougang Central
Hougang Street 11, 21, 22, 31, 32, 51, 52, 61, 91 to 93
Hougang Town Centre Road (e)
"Hougang" is the pinyin of the colloquial name "Au Gang", a Hokkien term that means behind the pier. The pier in question was the pier at the mouth of the Serangoon River. *See Upper Serangoon Road.*

Hougang Town Centre Road was renamed Hougang Street 21.

How Sun Avenue/Close/Drive/Road/Walk
The land in this area belonged to Tan Kim Tong, a Hokkien whose ancestor home was in Heshan (meaning grain hill), in the centre of Xiamen city. "How Sun" is the transcription of Heshan in Hokkien.

Source: *NAS, 168:3*

Howard Road (MacPherson private roads)
William Howard was a Municipal Commissioner in 1859. This road was listed in the 1936 Gazetteer and became a public street in 1960. *See Davidson Road.*

Source: *ST, 1859.9.3:3; CCAR, 1960:8; Singam*

Hoy Fatt Road
This road first appeared in the Street Directory of 1958, it was among the first batch of road names in the development of Redhill Industrial Estate. The name "Hoy Fatt" is a transcription of development in Cantonese. The other two Cantonese names in this location are: "Chang Charn" (increase production) and "Kung Chong" (factory).

Hu Ching Road
The lake view in Hu Ching Road refers to Jurong Lake. *See Ho Ching Road.*

Hua Guan Avenue/Crescent

Huang Long Road (e)
Huang Long was the pen name of Lim Chong Pang. Based on a news article in 1985, the road name was changed from West Hill Avenue 5 around 1962. *See Nee Soon Road* and *West Hill Avenue.*

Huat Choe Village (e)
This village was located at 14.5 ms Jurong Road, close to the entrance of the former Nanyang University.

Huddington Avenue (Serangoon Gardens)
This road was named in 1953. Huddington is a village in Worcestershire, West Midlands, England. A famous landmark in this village is the Huddington Court, a 15th century manor house. *See Alnwick Road.*

Source: *RBAR, 1953:8*

Hullet Road
This road was named in 1914 after R W Hullet, the Principal of Raffles College from 1871 to 1906. The naming of this road was proposed by his student Lim Boon Keng.

Source: *MC, 1914.9.25; ST, 1927.2.24:8; Lee KL: 20; Singam*

Hume Avenue/Heights (e)
Hume Avenue was named after the factory of Hume Industries located along this road. Hume Industries in Singapore was the branch of an Australian company owned by W R Hume. The factory was established in 1922 to produce steel pipes. The road was made a public street in 1954.

Source: *RBAR, 1954:8*

Hun Yeang Road/Village (e)
The above road was named in 1941 after Khoo Hun Yeang, a wealthy businessman from Penang who was the Managing Director of a Singapore opium and spirit farm. He died in an accident in Medan, Indonesia in 1917. In 1904, Khoo donated a sum of 3,000 dollars to the Medical College.

Source: *SFP, 1917.7.4:10; ST, 1941.5.16: 12; Kua: 101*

Huntley Close (e) (former RAF Changi)
Huntley is a multiple place name in England. *See Abbotsingh Road.*

Hurricane Road (e) (former RAF Tengah)
This road was named after Hawker Hurricane, a British single seat fighter aircraft built by Hawker Aircraft Ltd for the RAF. *See Hornet Road.*

Hwa San Road (e)
This road was located at 8.5 ms of Upper East Coast Road. It was named in 1954. This road was the route to a Chinese cemetery.

Source: *RBAR, 1954:9*

Hyde Park Gate (former RAF Seletar)
This road was probably named after Hyde Park Gate, a street in Central London on the southern boundary of Kensington Gardens. *See Baker Street.*

Hyderabad Road (former Alexandra Barracks)
This road was named after Hyderabad, India. Hyderabad was historically known as a pearl and diamond trading centre. In 1724 it was declared sovereign under the Nizams of Hyderabad and later became a princely state of the British Raj for 150 years. In 1813, Sir Henry Russell, then British Resident at the court of the Nizam, raised the Russell Brigade with funding provided by the Nizams. The 95th Russell Infantry was stationed at Alexandra Barracks in the early 1900s. Besides Hyderabad Road, there is a Russels Road within the same locality. *See Berkshire Road.*

A newspaper article in 2014 mentioned that Hyderabad Road was given its name because the land was once owned by the Paigah family, linked by matrimony to the Nizams.

Source: *ZB, 2014.9.1 supplement.2; Arnold & Cartwright, 1908:587*

Hylam Street
Hylam is the old name of Hainan, one of the major Chinese dialect groups in Singapore.

Hythe Road (Serangoon Gardens)
This road was named in 1953. Hythe is a small coastal market town on the south coast of Kent, South East England. The town was once defended by two castles, Saltwood and Lympne. *See Alnwick Road.*

Source: *RBAR, 1953:8*

Idris Road (e)
This road was named after Idris Hydraulic Tin Ltd in 1929. *See Kempas Road.*

Source: *MC, 1929.3.27; SIT 1158/28*

Iduna Road (e)
Iduna (or Idun) is the Goddess with apples of youth in Norse mythology. *See Bragi Road.*

Imbiah End (e)/**Hill Road/Road/Walk** (Sentosa Island)
Imbiah End appeared in the Street Directory of 1950 when the island was still an artillery barracks.

Inche Lane (e)
Inche is a courteous address for a man in Malay, equivalent to Mr. in English. There was a Municipal decision to rename Jalan Tambah to Inche Lane in 1906. However, the decision was not implemented. *See Jalan Tambah.*
Source: *MC, 1906.11.30*

Indent Lane (e) (former Pulau Brani military area)
Indent is to make a requisition. *See Adur Road.*

Indus Lane (e)/Road (Delta Estate)
Indus River is a major south-flowing river in South Asia, with a total length of 3,180 km. It flows through Tibet, India and Pakistan. *See Ganges Avenue.*

Inggu Road
Inggu is the oleo-gum-resin of *Ferula spp*, or rue in Malay. *Ikan inggu* is an inedible coral fish, *Holacanthus spp. See Kampong Wak Hassan.*

Inn Lane (e) (Telok Blangah)

Inner Temple (e) (former RAF Seletar)
This road was probably named after Inner Temple, one of the four Inns of Court in London. *See Baker Street.*

Institution Hill
This was supposed to be the site for Singapore Institution, the first school in Singapore that was planned by Raffles. The school was finally built at Stamford Road and renamed Raffles Institution. Institution Hill was sold to A Sykes and M J Martin in 1845. The road and the hill were formally named in 1912.
Source: *MC, 1912.12.27; Buckley: 125*

International Business Park

International Road
International Road was originally connected to Alexandra Road. It was expunged in 1954. The name appeared again around 1968 in Jurong for the newly merged road of Jalan Utasan and Jalan Bekalan.

Inverness Road (e) (former Tanglin Barracks)
Inverness means mouth of the River Ness; it is a city in the Scottish Highlands and is regarded as the capital of the Highlands of Scotland. To the northeast of Inverness is a large 18th century fortress, Fort George, operated by the British Army. In 1877, the 74th Highland Regiment of Foot was stationed in the Tanglin Barracks. This road was renamed Loewen Road in the 1970s. *See Barrack Road.*
Source: *STOJ, 1877.1.25:11; Mills*

Ipoh Lane (Thiam Siew Village, Tanjong Katong)
Ipoh is the former tin mining town in Perak, Malaysia. See *Thiam Siew Avenue*.

Iqbal Avenue (Teachers' Housing Estate)
This road was named after Muhammad Iqbal (1877-1938), a Pakistani poet. It is located in the Teachers' Housing Estate. All roads in this estate were named after literary masters in Asia. Other names include Kalidasa Avenue, Munshi Abdullah Avenue, Omar Khayyam Avenue, Li Po Avenue, Tu Fu Avenue and Tung Po Avenue.

Irau Avenue/Drive
Irau is a variant of *hiru*, which means disturbance in Malay. These two roads were named after the former Kampong Tanjong Irau in this location.

Ironside Link (e)/Road (e) (former Blakang Mati Artillery Barracks)
This road was named after Field Marshal William E Ironside, (1880-1959). He joined the Royal Regiment of Artillery in 1899 and fought in both world wars. Ironside served as the Chief of the Imperial General Staff between 1939 and 1941. See *Artillery Avenue*.

Source: *Dunlop*

Irrawaddy Road
This road was named after the Irrawaddy River, also known as Ayeyarwady River, which flows from north to south through Burma (now Myanmar). It is the largest and most commercially important waterway in the country. See *Burmah Road*.

Irving Place/Road (MacPherson private roads)
Based on a news article in 1936, Charles John Irving (1831-1917) was the Colonial Auditor General to the government of the Straits Settlements in Penang from 1867 to 1879. He became Resident Councillor of Malacca in 1879 and Resident Councillor of Penang from 1885 to 1887. Irving Road was listed in the 1936 Gazetteer. See *Davidson Road*.

Source: *ST, 1936.5.17:10; SG-1936; Singam*

Irwell Bank Road
This road was named in 1859 after the Irwell Estate at the same location.

Source: *ST, 1859.7.2:3*

Island Club Road
This road leads to the Singapore Island Country Club. It was named and declared a public street in 1950.

Source: *ST, 1950.3.17; RBAR, 1950:8*

Island Gardens Walk

Island View Road (e) (former Pasir Panjang Barracks)
Island View Estate was built around 1950 to house the British Army. The estate had three other roads, all named after place names in England: Bulford Road, Chatham Road and Chelsea Road.
Source: *ST, 1951.4.22:3*

Jacaranda Road
Jacaranda, *Jacaranda obtusifolia*, is a flowering tree. This road was named in 1956.
Source: *RBAR, 1956:9; Boo: 626*

Jago Close
This road was named after Frederick E Jago (1861–1924), who became a Partner at Boustead & Co. in 1898 after many years of service. He left the company in 1908 to join Asia Petroleum Company and retired three years later. He served as a member of the Municipal Commission.
Source: *ST, 1924.10.6:8; Ramachandran*

Jalan Abadi (e) (former Jalan Eunos Malay Settlement)
Abadi means eternal in Malay. This road was previously known as Jalan Kaki Bukit. It was renamed in 1961 together with the naming of a group of new roads in the Jalan Eunos Malay Settlement. See *Jalan Panglima*.

The original Malay Settlement in this area was opened in 1935 to resettle Malays residents in the Kallang area to make way for the former Kallang Airport.
Source: *SFP, 1961.6.1:3; Tan: 27*

Jalan Abdul Aziz (e) (former Jalan Eunos Malay Settlement)
Abdul Aziz is a common Malay personal name. Notable persons with this name include Abdul Aziz and Ungku Abdul Aziz. The former was an executive member of the Singapore Malay Union between 1929 and 1930. He was also the Treasurer of the Malay Football Association. Ungku Abdul Aziz was the Acting Mentri Besar of Johore and a member of the Council of Raffles College in 1928. See *Jalan Eunos*.
Source: *SFP, 1928.6.1:8; SFP, 1929.2.1:13; SFP, 1930.4.2:8*

Jalan Abdul Hamid (e) (former Jalan Eunos Malay Settlement)
Abdul Hamid is a common Malay personal name. This road may be named after Abdul Hamid bin Rahmat, who was a member of the Land Board that controlled occupation of land at the Jalan Eunos Malay Settlement in 1936. See *Jalan Eunos*.
Source: *SFP, 1936.9.11:9*

Jalan Abdul Majid (e)
Abdul Majid is a common Malay personal name. Notable persons with this name include Abdul Majid who was the Pilgrim Officer who led a group of Muslims from Singapore and Malaya for pilgrimage to Mecca in 1926 and Abdul Majid bin Mohamed Amin who was a member of the Mohamedan Advisory Board in 1927. He was also one of the founders of the Malay Union.
Source: *SFP, 1926.11.10:2; ST, 1927.5.7:10*

Jalan Abdul Manan (e) (former Jalan Eunos Malay Settlement)
Based on reports between 1926 and 1930, this road may be named after Abdul Manan bin Mohamed Ali who was the honorary auditor of the Malay Union. The Acting Managing Director of *Utusan Malayu* in 1948 was also Abdul Manan. It is not known if they are the same person. *See Jalan Eunos.*
Source: *SFP, 1930.3.21:12; ST, 1948.7.6:8*

Jalan Abdullah (e) (former Jalan Eunos Malay Settlement)
Abdullah is a common Malay personal name. Notable persons with this name are Munshi Abdullah (*see Munshi Abdullah Avenue*) and Dato Abdulah bin Jaffar (1876-1934). Dato Abdullah was the Prime Minister (now Menteri Besar) of Johor from 1923-1928. He resided in Singapore after retirement. Jaffar could be written as Jaafar, Ja'afar or Jafaar. *See Jalan Eunos.*
Source: *SFP, 1934.5.1:2*

Jalan Abdullah Taha (e) (former Jalan Eunos Malay Settlement)
This road was expunged in 1954. *See Jalan Eunos.*

Jalan Adam (e) (former Jalan Eunos Malay Settlement)

Jalan Adat
Adat means custom in Malay.

Jalan Afifi
This road in the Paya Lebar area was named in 1957. It was named after Shaikh Yahya bin Ahmed Afifi (c.1890-1940), an Arab who worked for Alkaff & Co. for more than 30 years and became its General Manager in 1932. He was the President of the Arab Association and Charter member of the Singapore Rotary Club. He served as a Municipal Commissioner in 1932.
Source: *ST, 1932.6.19 19:4; SFP, 1940.7.13:2; RBAR, 1957:8*

Jalan Ahmad Ibrahim
This road was named after Ahmad Ibrahim (1927-1962), former Minister for Health and Minister for Labour of Singapore.

Jalan Aliran (e)
Aliran means current or flow, trend of opinion in Malay.

Jalan Alsagoff (e)
This road in the Geylang Serai area was named in 1952 after the wealthy Alsagoff family, originally from Arabia. *See Alsagoff Estate and Geylang Serai Village.*

Source: *ST, 1952.10.18:4*

Jalan Aman (e)
Aman means peace and safety in Malay; it is also a short name for Abdul-rahman. This road was in the Whampoa area.

Jalan Ambo Sooloh (e) (former Jalan Eunos Malay Settlement)
Based on a report in 1988, Ambo (Ambok) Sooloh bin Haji Omar (1891–1963, Bugis) helped to establish *Utusan Malayu* in 1932. He was also the chairman of the Singapore Malay Union from 1934 to 1939. *See Jalan Eunos.*

Source: *ST, 1988.1.26:4; NAS, 1255:5*

Jalan Ampang
See Ampang Walk.

Jalan Ampas
This road was located off Balestier Road. *Ampas* means refuse (of sugar cane or tapioca) in Malay. This was the location of a large sugar cane plantation together with a processing plant for rum around the 1840s. This road was named in 1901. *See Balestier Road.*

Source: *MC, 1901.12.18; Singam*

Jalan Anak Bukit
Anak means small or young in Malay. *Anak bukit* means small hill. The hill is opposite Bukit Timah, so it is small in comparison.

Jalan Anak Patong
Patong or *patung* means puppet in Malay.

Jalan Ang Sian Kong (e)
"Ang Sian Kong" is a Hokkien name. "Ang Sian" is the name of the deity and "Kong" is a Taoist temple. This road was named in 1957.

Source: *RBAR, 1957:8*

Jalan Ang Teng (e)
"Ang Teng" is a transcription of red light in Hokkien. This road was located near the Paya Lebar Airport; the red light refers to the red navigation light used by the airport.

Source: *NAS, 168:42*

Jalan Anggerek
Anggerik is orchid in Malay. This road is one of roads named after flowers off MacPherson Road which include Jalan Anggerek, Jalan Melati, Jalan Jermin, etc.

However, a news article in 1971 mentioned that Jalan Anggerek was a road with many scrap-iron junkyards and spare-parts workshops.

Source: *ST, 1971.1.27:18*

Jalan Angin Laut
Angin laut means sea breeze in Malay.

Jalan Angklong
Angklong is a music instrument from Indonesia made of bamboo. Roads in this vicinity were named after musical instruments, including *gendang, rebana, seruling* and *tambur*.

Jalan Angkup (e)
Angkup means pincers in Malay.

Jalan Antoi
Antoi, *Cythocalyx sumatranus*, is native to Singapore. It is a large tree in the same family as soursop and custard apple.

Jalan Ara (e)
Ara is a fig tree in Malay. Jalan Ara was opened in 1976.

Source: *ST, 1976.5.15:8*

Jalan Arif
Arif means learned in Malay.

Jalan Arnap
Arnap or aarnab is rabbit in Malay. Several roads in this vicinity were named after birds and animals. They include: Jalan Kelawar (bat), Jalan Tupai (squirrel), Lengkok Angsa (swan), and Lengkok Merak (peacock).

Jalan Aruan
Aruan is mud fish, *Harpodon nehereus* in Malay.

Jalan Asas
This is one of the roads in the Dairy Farm area that have Malay names related to academic studies. *Asas* means foundation in Malay. Other names in this group include: *Uji* (test), *tumpu* (focus), *siap* (prepared) and *tekad* (determination).

Jalan Asuhan
This is one of the four small roads that branched off from University Road with Malay names relating to education. *Asuhan* means bring up (a child) in Malay. The other names are: *Seni* (art), *ilmu* (knowledge) and *bahasa* (language).

Jalan Awan (e)
Awan means clouds in Malay.

Jalan Awang (former Jalan Eunos Malay Settlement)
Awang means young fellow in Malay. See *Jalan Eunos*.

Jalan Ayer
Ayer means water in Malay.

Jalan Ayer Samak (e) (Pulau Tekong)
See *Ayer Samak*.

Jalan Ayu (e)
Ayu means pretty or handsome in Malay.

Jalan Azam
Azam means determination in Malay. *Azam* was the title of a Malay movie. The residential estate in this vicinity was built adjacent to the Cathay-Keris Studios and the roads were named after Malay films produced by the studios. The roads include: Jalan Buloh Perindu (named after *Buloh Perindu*, the Studio's first film in colour), Jalan Azam, Jalan Dondang Sayang, Jalan Puteri Jula Juli, Jalan Saudara Ku and Jalan Selendang Delima.

Jalan Bachang (e) (Kampong Ubi)
Bachang, *Mangifera foetida*, is a large tree native to Singapore. This road was named in 1957.

Source: *RBAR, 1957:9; Boo: 648*

Jalan Bahagia
Bahagia means blissful, lucky or blessed in Malay.

Jalan Bahar
Bahar means great waters in Malay.

Jalan Bahasa
Bahasa means language in Malay. See *Jalan Asuhan*.

Jalan Bahru Selatan (e)/Utara (e)
Special names in Malay are: *Bahru* (new), *selatan* (south) and *utara* (north).

Jalan Bahtera
Bahtera is a stately ship in Malay. This is one of the three roads in Lim Chu Kang with Malay names of boats including Jalan Bahtera, Jalan Kapal and Jalan Perahu.

Jalan Bahulu (e)
Bahulu means egg sponge cakes in Malay.

Jalan Baiduri
Baiduri is opal in Malay.

Jalan Bakar Sampah (e)
This road was located off Chua Chu Kang Road. *Bakar* means being set on fire and *sampah* means rubbish in Malay. *Bakar sampah* means burning rubbish.

Jalan Bakti (e) (former Jalan Eunos Malay Settlement)
Bakti means faithful work in Malay. This road was named in 1961. See *Jalan Panglima*.
Source: *SFP, 1961.6.1:3*

Jalan Balam (e)
This road was renamed Balam Road in 1970. See *Balam Road*.

Jalan Balangkas (e)
This was a printing error of Jalan Belangkas.

Jalan Bangau (Seletar Hills Estate)
Bangau is white egret, *Bubulcus coromandus* in Malay. This road became a public street in 1967.
Source: *ST, 1967.9.16:19*

Jalan Bangket
Bangket is coconut cookies in Malay.

Jalan Bangsawan (Opera Estate)
Bangsa means noble and *wan* is ordinary folks in Malay. *Bangsawan* is a Malay play with dialogues and songs. See *Aida Street*.

Jalan Bangsi (e)
Bangsi is bamboo flute in Malay.

Jalan Basong
Basong is the Malay name for asparagus-like shoots from certain trees such as the perepat. See *Kampong Wak Hassan*.

Jalan Batai
Batai, *Peltophorum pterocarpum*, is the yellow flame tree. This road was named in 1957. See *Jalan Chengam*.
Source: *RBAR, 1957:8; Boo: 671*

Jalan Batalong/East
Batalong means hollow brick in Malay.

Jalan Batu
Batu means stone in Malay.

Jalan Batu Koyok (e) (Pulau Tekong)
"Koyok" is a transcription of medicinal plaster in Hokkien. Batu Koyok is probably gypsum, a material used for making koyok. This road was named after Kampong Batu Koyok in this location.

Source: *Haughton: 76*

Jalan Batu Nilam
Batu nilam is sapphire in Malay. This road branched out from Elizabeth Drive of the former Princess Elizabeth Estate. Besides *batu nilam*, there are *intan* (diamond) and *zamrud* (emerald), all precious stones fitting for the princess.

Jalan Batu Ubin (Pulau Ubin)
Batu ubin is the Malay name for ceramic tiles. This road is near a quarry.

Jalan Bawang (e) (Kampong Ubi)
Bawang is the generic name for onion, leeks, etc. in Malay. This road was named in 1957.

Source: *RBAR, 1957:9*

Jalan Bayam (e) (Kampong Ubi)
Bayam is spinach in Malay. This road was named in 1957.

Source: *RBAR, 1957:9*

Jalan Bedara (e) (Kampong Ubi)
Bedara or *bidara* is red date in Malay. This road was named in 1957.

Source: *RBAR, 1957:9*

Jalan Beka (e)
Beka means discussing in Malay. It is also the name a Malay cake.

Jalan Bekalan (e)
Bekalan means supply in Malay. See *International Road*.

Jalan Belachu (e)
Belachu means unbleached cotton cloth in Malay.

Jalan Belang (e)
Belang means stripes or banded (in colouring), brightly marked in contrasting colours in Malay. It was the honorific name for tiger in the past. This road was named in 1955.

Source: *RBAR, 1955:9; Savage & Yeoh, 2004*

Jalan Belangkas
Belangkas is a female king-crab, *Limulus moluccanus* in Malay. However, since this road is among a group of roads named after flowers, *bunga belangkas* is Chinese rice flower, *Aglaia Adorata*. See *Jalan Anggerek*.

Jalan Belibas
Belibas is the Malay name for a sea fish Black Trevalley, *Teuthis oramin*.

Jalan Belinjau (e)
Belinjau is a small to medium-size tropical tree, *Gnetum gnemon*. The fruit of *belinjau* is widely used in Indonesian cuisine, the most popular of which is the *emping belinjau*, a cracker made from the fruit.

Source: *Boo: 613*

Jalan Bena
This road is located at the side of Changi Prison. *Bena* means caring about in Malay.

Jalan Benaan Kapal
Benaan means structure and *kapal* is a ship in Malay. *Benaan kapal* means shipbuilding. This road runs along the mouth of the Kallang River, a former ship building and repair centre.

Jalan Bendera (e)
Bendera is flag in Malay. This road was named in 1956.

Source: *RBAR, 1956:9*

Jalan Bendi (e) (Kampong Ubi)
Bendi is lady's finger in Malay. This road was named in 1957.

Source: *RBAR, 1957:9*

Jalan Berahi (e)
Berahi means passion in Malay.

Jalan Berangan (e) (Kampong Ubi)
Berangan is chestnut in Malay. This road was named in 1957.

Source: *RBAR, 1957:9*

Jalan Berembang (e)
Berembang is a large and beautiful mangrove apple tree with white flowers, *Sonneratia acida* in Malay. See *Kampong Ubi*.

Jalan Beringin
Beringin is Waringin tree, *Ficus benjamina* in Malay.

Jalan Berjaya
This is one of the four roads in the Bishan area with Malay names, *berjaya* (success), *binchang* (to harp on a subject), *insaf* (fairness) and *peminpin* (leader).

Jalan Bermi (e)
Bermi is the Malay name of a wetland creeping herb, also known as Indian pennywort, *Swintonia spp*. See *Kampong Ubi*.

Jalan Berseh
Berseh or *bersih* means clean in Malay.

Jalan Bersekutu (e)
Bersekutu means partnership in Malay.

Jalan Berseri
Berseri means to brighten up in Malay.

Jalan Besar/Jalan Besar Lane (Kampong Kapor)
Besar means big in Malay. Jalan Besar, which means big road, was the first major road in the Kampong Kapur area and was opened in the early part of 1883. Jalan Besar Lane was declared a public street in 1914.
Source: *ST, 1883.4.5:6; MC, 1914.11.27*

Jalan Besi (e)
Besi means iron in Malay.

Jalan Besi Baja (e)
Besi baja means steel in Malay

Jalan Besut
Besut means refining metal in Malay.

Jalan Betek (e) (Kampong Ubi)
Betek or *betik* means papaya or watermelon in Malay. This road was named in 1957.
Source: *RBAR, 1957:9*

Jalan Bilal
Bilal is the man who summons Muslims to prayer from the minaret of a mosque in Malay. There is a mosque at the end of Jalan Bilal. This road was named in 1956.
Source: *RBAR, 1956:9*

Jalan Binchang
Binchang means to harp on a subject in Malay. See *Jalan Berjaya*.

Jalan Bingka
Bingka is a Malay cake made of rice flour, coconut milk, egg and palm sugar.

Jalan Binjai
See *Binjai Hill*.

Jalan Bintang Tiga (Opera Estate)
Bintang means star and *tiga* means three in Malay. Bintang Tiga was a popular Malay show. See *Aida Street*.

Jalan Biola (e)
Biola is violin in Malay.

Jalan Biru (e)
Biru is blue in Malay.

Jalan Bongkong (e)
Bongkong is a tree, *Artocarpus polyphema* in Malay.

Jalan Boon Lay/Jalan Boon Lay Lama
Lama means old in Malay. *See Boon Lay Avenue.*

Jalan Boyan (e)
This road was located off Syed Alwi Road. Boyan is also known as Bawean, a small island in the Java Sea, 120 km north of Surabaya. *See Kampong Soo Poo.*

Jalan Bruas (e)
Bruas or Beruas, is the ancient name for the State of Perak in Malaysia. It is also the name of a small town in Perak. *See Perak Road.*

Jalan Buang Kok (e)
This road was off 9 ms Punggol Road. *See Buangkok Crescent.*

Jalan Budi (e) (former Jalan Eunos Malay Settlement)
Budi means intelligent, character, or kindness in Malay. This road was named in 1961, *See Jalan Panglima.*
Source: *SFP, 1961.6.1:3*

Jalan Buey (e)
Buey or *bueh* means foam in Malay.

Jalan Bukit Atas (e)
This road was located off 7 ms Yio Chu Kang Road. *Bukit* is hill and *atas* means higher in Malay. This road was named in 1948.
Source: *RBAR, 1948:7*

Jalan Bukit Ho Swee
See Bukit Ho Swee.

Jalan Bukit Merah
See Bukit Merah Central.

Jalan Buloh Perindu
Buloh or *buluh perindu* is a pipe musical instrument made from bamboo. *Buloh Perindu* was the first Malay film in colour. *See Jalan Azam.*

Jalan Bumbong
Bumbong or *bumbung* means roof in Malay. Roads in this area were named after parts of a house, such as *dinding* (inner wall), *gelegar* (beams), *kasau* (rafter), *rasok* (cross beam) and *jendela* (window).

Jalan Bumbun Selatan (e)/Utara (e)
Bumbun is a hunter's small hut for watching wild animals in Malay. *Selatan* is south and *utara* is north in Malay.

Jalan Bunga Mas (e)/Rampai/Raya
Translations for Malay words are as follows: *Bunga* is flower, *mas* is gold and *rampai* is a variety and *raya* is big.

Bunga mas is a flower made from gold foil; it was used as a tribute by vassal states.

Bunga rampai is a bouquet of different types of flowers used as a wedding present.

Bunga raya is Hibiscus, the national flower of Malaysia.

Jalan Bungar (e)
Bungar is the Malay word for first bloom, flower, fruit or egg.

Jalan Buntu (e) (former Jalan Eunos Malay Settlement)
Buntu means blocked (road, door) or clogged in Malay. Jalan Buntu means a dead end road. This road was named in 1957. See *Jalan Eunos*.

Source: *RBAR, 1957:8*

Jalan Buroh
Buroh or *buruh* means labour in Malay.

Jalan Chai Chee (e)
See *Chai Chee Avenue*.

Jalan Chapa (e)
Chapa is the Malay name for a plant, *Blumea balsamifera* or a game suggestive of pitch and toss. Jalan Chapa was opened in 1976.

Source: *ST, 1976.5.15:8*

Jalan Chegar
Chegar means rapids over a pebbly or sandy river bed in Malay.

Jalan Chekor (e) (Kampong Ubi)
Chekor or *chekur* is the Malay name for a creeping weed, *Kaempferia galangal*. This road was named in 1957.

Source: *RBAR, 1957:9*

Jalan Chelagi
Chelagi is tamarind in Malay; it is also known as Asam Chelagi or Asam Java.

Jalan Chempah
Chempah or *chempa* is Chempaka flower or a plant, *Elaeocarpus obtusus* in Malay.

Jalan Chempaka Kuning/Puteh
Chempaka is a large evergreen tree in the *Magnoliaceae* family. *Chempaka kuning* is yellow chempaka and *chempaka puteh* is white chempaka.

Jalan Chempedak
Chempedak, *Artocarpus poly-phema*, is in the same genus as jackfruit, it is native to South East Asia. This road was named in 1957. *See Jalan Chengam.*

Source: *RBAR, 1957:8*

Jalan Chendana (e)
Chendana is sandalwood in Malay.

Jalan Chendawan (e) (Kampong Ubi)
Chendawan is a generic name for poisonous fungi in Malay. This road was named in 1957.

Source: *RBAR, 1957:9*

Jalan Chenderai (e)
Chenderai is a generic name given to several plants, including *C. Argyratus* and *Grewia latifolia*.

Jalan Cheng Hwa (e)
This road was probably named after Cheng Hwa Primary School in this location. The English name of the school had since been converted to pinyin as Zheng Hua Primary School.

Source: *DSM: 395*

Jalan Cheng Kee Siew (e)
This road was only seen in the Street Directory of 1961.

Jalan Cheng Lim (e)
See *Cheng Lim Farmway.*

Jalan Chengam
Chengam is a mangrove shrub, *Scyphiphora hydrophyllacea* in Malay. This road is in the Upper Thomson area in an estate with road names of trees or plants, including Jalan Gelenggang, Jalan Kuras, Jalan Lanjut, Jalan Leban, Jalan Menarong, Jalan Rukam, Jalan Sappan, Jalan Tarum and Jalan Telang.

Jalan Chengam was named in 1957.

Source: *RBAR, 1957:8; Boo: 408*

Jalan Chengkek
Chengkek means thinner at the centre than at the extremities of a post in Malay.

Jalan Cherah (e)
Cherah means clear, unobstructed view in Malay.

Jalan Chermai
Chermai is a tree yielding a small round acid fruit in Malay.

Jalan Chermat
Chermat means neat or well groomed in Malay.

Jalan Cherpen
Cherpen or *cerpen* is short story in Malay. This is one of the four roads with cultural influences in the Sembawang area including Jalan Sajak, Jalan Hikayat, and Jalan Shaer.

Jalan Chichau
Chichau is a bird like a plover in Malay. Jalan Chichau was opened in 1976.

Source: *ST, 1976.5.15:8*

Jalan Chorak
Chorak means scheme of design, motif or scheme of colour in Malay.

Jalan Chuan Seng (e)
This was the location of Chuan Seng Pineapple Factory.

Source: *NAS, 1117:4*

Jalan Chulek
Chulek is a cuckoo bird, *Chalcococyx honorata* in Malay.

Jalan Churam (e)
Churam means falling away steeply in Malay.

Jalan Chwee Khoon (e)

Jalan Chye Lye (e)
This road was named in 1948; its name was changed to Serangoon Garden Way in 1953.

Source: *RBAR, 1948:7; RBAR, 1953:8*

Jalan Daliah
Daliah or Dahlia is a flowering ornamental plant.

Jalan Damai (former Jalan Eunos Malay Settlement)
Damai is peace-making in Malay. This road was named in 1961. See *Jalan Panglima*.

Source: *SFP, 1961.6.1:3*

Jalan Darat Nanas (e)
Darat means land and *nanas* is pineapple in Malay. *Darat nanas* means pineapple plantation. This was also the location of Kampong Darat Nanas.

Source: *DSM: 801*

Jalan Datoh
This road is located off Balestier Road. *Datoh*, also spelt as *Dato'*, *Datok* or *Datuk*, is a title conferred by a ruler in Malaysia. This road was named in 1901 together with Mandarin Road and Tai Gin Road.

Source: *MC, 1901.12.18*

Jalan Datok Burma (e)
This road was located off 8 ms Tampines Road. The Datok in this context is the earth god and Datok Burma is a Burmese earth god. The road was named after the Burmese temple at this location in 1948.

Source: *RBAR, 1948:7; ST, 1951.4.14:6*

Jalan Daud (former Jalan Eunos Malay Settlement)
Daud is equivalent to David in English. A notable person with this name was Daud bin Mohamed Shah, who was the Administrative Officer in various areas in Malaya. After his retirement in 1935, he returned to Singapore and served in the Municipal Commission and Rural Board. He was appointed a Justice of the Peace in 1939. See *Jalan Eunos*.

Source: *ST, 1939.6.9:13; RBAR, 1948:2*

Jalan Dedali (e)
Dedali is a tree, *Strombosia javanica* in Malay.

Jalan Delima (e)
Delima is pomegranate in Malay. See *Kampong Ubi*.

Jalan Demak
The name Demak may refer to the Javanese Muslim Sultanate (1478–1568) in Indonesia. However, it is noted that the road is located in an area where bird names are used. See *Jalan Kuang*.

Jalan Dermawan
Dermawan means charitable, gracious in Malay.

Jalan Derum
Derum is a small tree with attractive white flowers, *Cratoxylon spp.*

Jalan Dinding
Dinding is the inner wall or partition in a house in Malay. See *Jalan Bumbong*.

Jalan Dondang Sayang
"Dondang Sayang" is a kind of Malay folk song. *Dondang Sayang* is the name of a Malay movie. See *Jalan Azam*.

Jalan Dua
This is part of a group of six roads in the Old Airport Road area using numerals in Malay. *Dua* means two in Malay. See *Pachitan Dua*.

Jalan Dulang (e)
Dulang is wooden tray in Malay.

Jalan Durian (Pulau Ubin) (Kampong Ubi)
Jalan Durian in Pulau Ubin was named after Kampong Durian on the Island.

Jalan Durian in Kampong Ubi (e) was named in 1957.

Source: *RBAR, 1957:9*

Jalan Dusun
Dusun is an orchard in Malay.

Jalan Elok
Elok means beauty, charm and loveliness in Malay.

Jalan Emas Urai
Emas urai means gold dust in Malay.

Jalan Empat/Jalan Enam
See *Jalan Dua*.

Jalan Endut Senin (Pulau Ubin)
Endut Senin, a Malay who used to live along the Kallang River, was believed to be the earliest settler in Pulau Ubin.

Source: *ST, 2000.6.19:4*

Jalan Enggang (e)
Enggang is hornbill in Malay.

Jalan Engku Kadir (e) (former Jalan Eunos Malay Settlement)
Engku is a title of high rank or prince in Malay. This road was first named Jalan Tungku Kadir, then changed to Jalan Engku Kadir in 1955. See *Jalan Eunos* and *Jalan Tungku Kadir*.

Jalan Eunos
This road was named after Mohamad Eunos bin Abdullah (or Yunos, 1876-1933, Malay) who founded Malay language newspapers. As a community leader for the Malays, he served as a member of the Legislative Council and the Municipal Commission. In 1927, he petitioned through the Legislative Council to purchase land in the Jalan Eunos area to establish a Malay settlement and succeeded. The settlement was officially opened in 1929. Most roads in the settlement were given Malay names such as Abdul Aziz, Abdul Manan, Abdullah, Adam, Ambo Soloh, Daud, etc. Jalan Eunos was named in 1930.

Source: *MC, 1930.1.28; ST, 1930.4.16:5; Dhoraisingam: 246*

Jalan Fajar (e)
Fajar means dawn in Malay.

Jalan Gagah (e) (former Jalan Eunos Malay Settlement)
Gagah means elephant-like, large or important in Malay. This road was named in 1961, See *Jalan Panglima*.

Source: *SFP, 1961.6.1:3*

Jalan Gaharu
Gaharu is the Malay name for eagle-wood or agila-wood which is very fragrant wood. True agila wood is the diseased core of *Aquilaria malaccensis*.

Jalan Gajar (e)
Gajar means reward in Malay.

Jalan Gajus
Gajus is cashew nut in Malay.

Jalan Gali Batu
Gali means digging or surface mining in Malay. *Gali batu* means stone mining. There was a stone quarry in this location.

Jalan Gapis
Gapis is the Malay name for yellow saraca. See *Kampong Wak Hassan*.

Jalan Gelam
Gelam is a seashore tree, *Melaleuca leuco-dendron*. Its bark is used for caulking boats. It is also called *kayu puteh* and may be the possible source of the name for Kampong Glam. See *Kampong Wak Hassan*.

Jalan Gelatek (e)
Gelatek is a rice-eating finch, *Munia oryzivora* in Malay.

Jalan Gelegar
Gelegar means girder or cross-stick supporting a framework in Malay. See *Jalan Bumbong*.

Jalan Gelenggang
Gelenggang is a herb, *Cassia alata* used as a laxative and remedy for ringworm.

Jalan Gelugur (e)
Gelugur is a large rainforest tree with fruit of fluted appearance. The fruit is bright yellow orange and is a common ingredient in curries. This road was named in 1957.

Source: *RBAR, 1957:9*

Jalan Gemala (e)/Jalan Gemala 2/3
Gemala means luminous bezoar in Malay.

Jalan Gembira
Gembira means passion or excitement in Malay.

Jalan Gendang
Gendang is an Indonesian drum. See *Jalan Angklong*.

Jalan Geneng
Geneng means charming in Malay.

Jalan Geok Siang Nng (e)
"Geok Siang Nng" is a transcription of jade fairy in the Teochew dialect.

Jalan Geylang Serai (e)
See *Geylang Serai Village*.

Jalan Giam (e)
Giam is the Malay name for commercial timber from *Hopea nutans*, a tropical tree.

Source: *Boo: 619*

Jalan Girang
Girang means glad or cheerful in Malay.

Jalan Golok
Golok means machete or sword with a convex cutting edge in Malay.

Jalan Gombak (e)
See *Bukit Gombak*.

Jalan Gotong Royong
Gotong royong means community spirit in Malay.

Jalan Greja
Greja or *gereja* is a church in Malay. This road was named in 1954; it is located next to a Methodist church.

Source: *RBAR, 1954:8*

Jalan Grisek
This road was located in the Kembangan area. *Grisek* or *gresek* means looking for in Malay. See *Jalan Kembangan*.

Jalan Guan Choon (e)
This road was located at 10.5 ms Tampines Road. Guan Choon was the shop name of Teo Kim Eng, a Hokkien businessman. He built a bungalow with a swimming pool in this area which was a popular picnic venue for social groups and students on a rental basis.

Source: *RBAR, 1948:7; Kua: 111*

Jalan Gudang (e)
Gudang is warehouse in Malay. This road was renamed Jurong Port Road in 1971.

Source: *SYrBk, 1971:12*

Jalan Gumilang
Gumilang means dazzling in Malay.

Jalan Gurindam (e)
Gurindam means couplets in Malay.

Jalan Haji (e)
See Haji Lane.

Jalan Haji Alias
Alias is a Malay personal name. This road was named in 1956.
Source: *RBAR, 1956:9*

Jalan Haji Karim (e)
Karim is a Malay personal name. This road was located off 7.5 ms Tampines Road and was named in 1948. *See Kampong Haji Karim.*
Source: *RBAR, 1948:7*

Jalan Haji Salam
Salam means peace, the blessing at the end of a mosque service in Malay. It was reported in 1984 that the family of Fatimah binti Haji Abdul Salam was once the owner of land along this road. Jalan Haji Salam was named in 1950.
Source: *RBAR, 1950:8; ST, 1984.4.26:12*

Jalan Hajijah
This road is located off 7.5 ms East Coast Road. Hajijah or Hajjah is an honorific address for a Muslim lady who had completed her pilgrimage to Mecca. This road was converted to a public street in 1957.
Source: *RBAR, 1957:8*

Jalan Halaman Kedai (e)
Halaman is a courtyard or compound and *kedai* is shop in Malay.

Jalan Halia (e) (Kampong Ubi)
Halia is ginger in Malay. This road was named in 1957.
Source: *RBAR, 1957:9*

Jalan Hang Jebat
Hang is an address for a warrior in Malayan history. Hang Jebat was the closest companion of Hang Tuah (*see Jalan Hang Tuah*). This road was located in the British military area off Portsdown Road.

Jalan Hang Kasturi (e)
Hang Kasturi was one of the five warriors who worked for the Sultan of Malacca in the 15th century. *See Jalan Hang Tuah.*

Jalan Hang Tuah (e)
Hang Tuah was a legendary warrior who lived in Malacca in the 15th century. He is probably the most well known and illustrious warrior figure in Malay history and literature. He and his four close friends Hang Jebat, Hang Kasturi, Hang Lekir and Hang Lekiu were all warriors of the same Sultan.

Jalan Hari Raya
Hari raya means a holiday in Malay. *See Jalan Isnin.*

Jalan Harom Setangkai
Harom or *harum* means perfume and *setangkai* means diffuse in Malay.

Jalan Harum
Harum is perfume in Malay.

Jalan Hassan (e) (Jalan Eunos Malay Settlement)
Hassan is a Malay personal name. *See Jalan Eunos.*

Jalan Hiboran
Hiboran or *hiburan* means entertainment in Malay.

Jalan Hijau (e)
Hijau means green in Malay.

Jalan Hikayat
Hikayat means narrative, story or tale in Malay. *See Jalan Cherpen.*

Jalan Hitam Manis
Hitam means very dark in colour and *manis* means sweet in Malay. *Hitam manis* means dark brown.

Jalan Hock Chye
This road is located off 10.5 ms Tampines Road. It was probably named in 1948 after Cheong Hock Chye (1900-1949), a member of the Rural Board. Cheong founded Cheong Hock Chye & Company, a surveyor and valuer firm in 1940. The firm is now known as Knight Frank Pte Ltd.

Source: *RBAR, 1948:7*

Jalan Hong Keng (e)
This road was located off 8 ms Tampines Road. It was named in 1948.

Source: *RBAR, 1948:7*

Jalan Hormat (former Jalan Eunos Malay Settlement)
Hormat means honour and respect in Malay. This road was named in 1961. *See Jalan Panglima.*

Source: *SFP, 1961.6.1:3*

Jalan Hussein
Hussein is a Malay personal name. *See Jalan Eunos.*

Jalan Hwi Yoh
This road was located off 6.5 ms Yio Chu Kang Road. There were 5 kilns in this location which were specialised in making round ceramic pots with small mouths. This road was named in 1948.

Source: *RBAR, 1948:7; Serangoon: 15*

Jalan Ibadat
Ibadat means God's service in Malay.

Jalan Ikan Merah
Ikan merah is the Malay name for red snapper.

Jalan Ilmu (e)
Ilmu means knowledge in Malay. *See Jalan Asuhan.*

Jalan Inggu
See *Inggu Road* and *Kampong Wak Hassan.*

Jalan Insaf
Insaf means true justice in Malay. *See Jalan Berjaya.*

Jalan Intan
Intan means diamond in Malay. *See Jalan Batu Nilam.*

Jalan Ishak (former Jalan Eunos Malay Settlement)
Encik Ishak bin Ahma was the father of Yusof Ishak (1910–1970), the first President of independent Singapore from 1965 to 1970. Encik Ishak was Acting Director of Fisheries. It is unlikely that the road was named after the President as the road was named before 1950. *See Jalan Eunos.*

Source: *Dunlop; Ramamchandran: 3*

Jalan Ismail (former Jalan Eunos Malay Settlement)
Among the notable persons with this name was M Ismail, who was a member of the Mohamedan Advisory Board in 1927. The road was repaired at frontagers' expense in 1952 with the approval of the Rural Board. It was subsequently made a public street in 1955. *See Jalan Eunos.*

Source: *SFP, 1927.6.18:2; RBAR, 1952:8; RBAR, 1955:9*

Jalan Isnin
Isnin is Monday in Malay. In the same area there are Jalan Rabu (Wednesday), Jalan Khamis (Thursday), Jalan Minggu (week) and Jalan Hari Raya (holiday).

Jalan Istimewa
Istimewa means special case or special rules in Malay.

Jalan Jaffar (e) (former Jalan Eunos Malay Settlement)
Notable persons with this name are brothers Abdullah bin Jaffar and Mustaph bin Jaffar. The former was a Mentri Besar in Johore from 1923–1928.

Younger brother Mustaph took over his position from 1928 to 1931. Jaffar could be spelt Jaafar, Ja'afar or Jafaar. See *Jalan Eunos*.

Jalan Jagong (e)
Jagong is corn in Malay. See *Kampong Ubi*.

Jalan Jamahat (e)
This road was located off East Coast Road. *Jamahat* or *jamadat* means lifeless object in Malay.

Jalan Jamal
Jamal means goodliness in Malay; it is also a masculine personal name.

Jalan Jambatan Lama (e)
Jambatan is bridge and *lama* means old in Malay. There was an old railway bridge in this location.

Source: *NAS, 1117:4*

Jalan Jambu Ayer/Batu/Mawar
Jambu ayer is water apple, *Eugenia aquea* in Malay.

Jambu batu is guava in Malay.

Jambu mawar is rose-apple, *Eugenia jambos* in Malay.

Jalan Janggus
Janggus is cashew nut in Malay. See *Kampong Wak Hassan*.

Jalan Jarak (Seletar Hills Estate)
Jarak is the generic name for the Castor oil plant in Malay. This road was built on the land previously known as 406 Yio Chu Kang Road. It became a public street in 1967.

Source: *ST, 1967.9.16:19; NAS, 799:3; Boo: 388*

Jalan Jasa (e) (former Jalan Eunos Malay Settlement)
Jasa means loyal service in Malay. This road was named in 1961. See *Jalan Panglima*.

Source: *SFP, 1961.6.1:3*

Jalan Jati (e)
Jati is the Malay name for teak wood.

Jalan Jaya (e)
Jaya means triumphant in Malay. This road was named in 1956.

Source: *RBAR, 1956:9*

Jalan Jelawi (e)
Jelawi is the Malay name for a kind of Banyan tree, *Ficus micorcarpa*.

Jalan Jelawi was opened in 1975.

Source: *ST, 1975.10.11:7; Boo: 599*

Jalan Jelita
Jelita means graceful in Malay.

Jalan Jelurai (e)
Jelurai is the Malay shredded wheatmeal bread.

Jalan Jelutong (Pulau Ubin)
This road was named after Sungei Jelutong in Pulau Ubin. Jelutong is the generic name for *Dyera costulata*, a type of hard wood. Its sap was once the main ingredient of chewing gum.

Source: *Boo: 577*

Jalan Jemerlang (e)
Jemerlang, variant of *chemerlang*, means radiant in Malay. *See Kampong Ubi.*

Jalan Jendela
Jendela means window in Malay. *See Jalan Bumbong.*

Jalan Jentera (e)
Jentera is a wheel, especially of the spinning-wheel in Malay. There was a spin mill in this location.

Jalan Jering (e) (Kampong Ubi)
Jering is a medium-size tree with evil smelling pods, *Pithecolobium lobatum*. The seeds are a popular dish in South East Asia. This road was named in 1957.

Source: *RBAR, 1957:9*

Jalan Jermin
Jermin is geranium in Malay. *See Jalan Anggerek.*

Jalan Jeruju
Jeruju is the Malay name of a shrub, *Acanthus ebracteatus*, with white flowers and holly-like leaves.

Jalan Jintan
Jintan is the generic name for spice seeds including caraway, fennel, aniseed and dill in Malay. *See Nutmeg Road.*

Jalan Jitong (Seletar Hills Estate)
Jitong is the rengas tree, well known for its poisonous sap. This road became a public street in 1967.

Source: *ST, 1967.9.16:19*

Jalan Jitu (e) (former Jalan Eunos Malay Settlement)
Jitu means accurate in Malay. This road was named in 1961. *See Jalan Panglima.*

Source: *SFP, 1961.6.1:3*

Jalan Jong (e)
Jong is a sea-going ship in Malay.

Jalan Joran (Seletar Hills Estate)
Joran is a fishing rod in Malay. This road became a public street in 1967.
Source: *ST, 1967.9.16:19*

Jalan Jujor (e) (former Jalan Eunos Malay Settlement)
Jujor or *jujur* means honest or trustworthy in Malay. This road was named in 1961. Jujor was originally approved as Jujur. See *Jalan Panglima*.
Source: *SFP, 1961.6.1:3*

Jalan Jumat (e) (former Jalan Eunos Malay Settlement)
Jumat means Friday in Malay. A notable person with this name is T P Jumat, who worked in the Singapore High Court. He was also the Honorary Secretary of the Singapore Malay Union for several years.
Source: *SFP, 1929.2.1:13*

Jalan Jurong Kechil/Jalan Jurong Kechil Track 1
See *Jurong Road*. *Kechil* means small in Malay.

Jalan Kachang (e)
Kachang means pea or bean in Malay. See *Geylang Serai Village*. This road was opened in 1966.
Source: *ST, 1966.7.30:7*

Jalan Kachip (e)
Kachip is betel-nut scissors in Malay.

Jalan Kakatua
This road was previously spelt Kaka Tua. *Kakatua* is cockatoo in Malay. See *Jalan Layang Layang*.

Jalan Kaki Bukit (e) (former Jalan Eunos Malay Settlement)
Kaki means foot and *bukit* means hill in Malay. This road was named in 1957 and renamed Jalan Abadi in 1961.
Source: *RBAR, 1957:8; SFP, 1961.6.1:3*

Jalan Kamaman (e)
Kamaman means a shed in Malay. This road, located in the Balestier Road area, was named in 1901.
Source: *MC, 1901.12.18*

Jalan Kambing (e)
This road was located off Kim Chuan Road. *Kambing* is goat in Malay.

Jalan Kampong Chantek
This road was named in 1953. *Kampong* is a village and *chantek* means pretty in Malay.

Source: *RBAR, 1953:8*

Jalan Kampong Java Teban (e)
See *Kampong Java Teban*.

Jalan Kampong Paya (e)
Paya means swamp or morass in Malay. This road was opened in 1966.

Source: *ST, 1966.7.30*

Jalan Kampong Sayor (e)
Sayor or *sayur* means green food or edible vegetables in Malay. This road was named after Kampong Sayor (e) in this location.

Jalan Kampong Siglap
This road was named after Kampong Siglap (e) in this location. See *Siglap Road*.

Jalan Kampong Tengah (e)
This road was located off 6.75 ms Punggol Road. *Tengah* means middle in Malay. This road was named in 1948. Kampong Tengah was located quite a distance away from this road, at 8.25 ms.

Source: *RBAR, 1948:7*

Jalan Kandis
Kandis is the Malay name of *Garcina atrolineata*, which is a tree in the same family as the mangosteen. See *Kampong Wak Hassan*.

Jalan Kangkong (e) (Kampong Ubi)
Kangkong is the Malay name for Morning Glory. This road was named in 1957.

Source: *RBAR, 1957:9*

Jalan Kapal
Kapal is a decked ship in Malay. See *Jalan Bahtera*.

Jalan Kasau
Kasau means rafter, part of a beam in Malay. See *Jalan Bumbong*.

Jalan Kasturi (e)
Kasturi is a kind of Malay cake. See *Kampong Ubi*.

Jalan Kathi
Kathi was the Legal Officer in charge of affairs of the Malay community, reporting to the Sultan. This road was named in 1950.

Source: *DSM, 1928:15-A; RBAR, 1950:8*

Jalan Kayu/Jalan Kayu Village (e)

Kayu means wood in Malay. Jalan Kayu was originally named Air Base Road. It was then decided by the British Army to name the access road to RAF Seletar after the Chief Engineer (C E O Wood) who was in charge of the construction of the air station. The name Wood was localised to Kayu.

The name Jalan Kayu was approved by the Rural Board in 1937 and became a public street in 1952.

Jalan Kayu Village was named in 1954.

Source: *ST, 1937.12.10:19; RBAR, 1952:8; RBAR, 1954:8*

Jalan Kayu Manis/Puteh (e)

Kayu manis is the Malay name for cinnamon. See *Nutmeg road*.

Jalan Kayu Puteh is in the Kampong Ubi area. *Kayu puteh* is the Gelam tree. See *Jalan Gelam*.

Jalan Kayu Rural Centre (e)

Jalan Kebaya

Kebaya is the name of a blouse worn by Malay and Peranakan women. The matching long skirt is the *sarong*. An example of the *sarong kebaya* is the uniform worn by stewardesses of Singapore Airlines.

Jalan Kebun Limau

Kebun means garden and *limau* is lemon, lime or orange in Malay.

Jalan Kechil (e)

Kechil means small in Malay.

Jalan Kechot (Jalan Eunos Malay Settlement)

Kechot or *kechoh* means disturbance or noise in Malay.

Jalan Kechubong

Kechubong is the Malay name for *Datura fastuosa*, the Indian Thorn Apple. The plant has smooth, violet or dark purple branches and fragrant flowers. Its seeds are poisonous.

Jalan Kedai (e) (former Singapore Naval Base)

Kedai means shop in Malay. See *Admiralty Road*.

Jalan Kedidi (e)

Kedidi is snippet, sandpiper and small plover in Malay.

Jalan Kekal (e) (former Jalan Eunos Malay Settlement)

Kekal means permanence, enduring or perpetual in Malay. This road was named in 1961. See *Jalan Panglima*.

Source: *SFP, 1961.6.1:3*

Jalan Kekapas (e)
Kekapas is the Malay name for green bulbul, a bird, *Chloropsis spp.* or a silver bream, *Gerres spp.*

Jalan Kelabu Asap
Kelabu means grey and *asap* means smoke in Malay.

Jalan Keladan (e)
Keladan is a large forest tree, *Dryobalanops oblongifolia*, also known as *Kuras*, a close family to the *Kapur* or Camphor tree. Its timber is moderately heavy and can be used for wharf decking, bridges and railway sleepers.

Source: *Boo: 575*

Jalan Keladi (e) (Kampong Ubi)
Keladi means yam in Malay. This road was named in 1957.

Source: *RBAR, 1957:9*

Jalan Kelasi (e)
Kelasi means sailor in Malay.

Jalan Kelawar
Kelawar is the generic name for bats in Malay. See *Jalan Arnap*. This road was named in 1954.

Source: *ST, 1954.6.15:5*

Jalan Keledeh (e)
Based on a news article in 1881, *keledeh* is sweet potato in Malay. The road name was simplified to Jalan Kledek. See *Jalan Kledek*.

Source: *STOJ, 1881.5.12:2*

Jalan Kelempong
Kelempong is a small tree, *Ficus obphyramidata*, also known as Common River Fig.

Jalan Keli
Keli is a catfish in Malay.

Jalan Kelichap
Kelichap is a Malay hummingbird or sun bird.

Jalan Keliling (e)
Keliling means situation around in Malay. This road was named in 1956.

Source: *RBAR, 1956:9*

Jalan Kelulut
See *Kelulut Hill*.

Jalan Kelur (e)
Kelur is a plant, *Moringa pterygosperma* in Malay. This road was named in 1957.

Source: *RBAR, 1957:9*

Jalan Kemajuan
Kemajuan means progress or prosperity in Malay.

Jalan Kemaman
This road is located off Balestier Road. Kemaman is a town in Trengganu, Malaysia, known in the past for its tin mines.

Jalan Kembang Melati
Kembang means blossoming in Malay. *Melati* is Indonesian jasmine.

Jalan Kembangan
Kembangan means expansion in Malay. This was the site of Kampong Kembangan, located next to the former Jalan Eunos Malay Settlement. Several roads in this area use pleasant expressions in Malay, such as Jalan Sayang, Jalan Sentosa, Jalan Selamat, Jalan Senang, etc. See *Jalan Krian*.

Jalan Kemboja
Kemboja is Frangipani in Malay.

Jalan Kemuka (e)
Kemuka means handover in Malay.

Jalan Kemuning
Kemuning is a tree, *Murraya exotica*. This road was named in 1957.

Source: *RBAR, 1957:8*

Jalan Kenarah (Seletar Hills Estate)
Kenarah means trim in Malay. This road became a public street in 1967.

Source: *ST, 1967.9.16:19*

Jalan Kentang (e) (Kampong Ubi)
Kentang means potato in Malay. This road was named in 1957.

Source: *RBAR, 1957:9*

Jalan Kerayong
Petai kerayong is a tree, *Parkia roxburghii* in Malay. See *Kampong Wak Hassan*.

Jalan Keria
Keria in Malay means sweetmeat made of sweet potato or a Sharpe's crane.

Jalan Keris
This road is located in Cathay Garden, the site of the former Cathay-Keris film studio. *Keris* is a Malay short knife. See *Jalan Azam*.

Jalan Kerja (e)
Kerja means work or business in Malay.

Jalan Kerong (e)
Kerong means a smelting-furnace in Malay. *Ikan kerong* is large-scaled Terapon.

Jalan Keruing
Keruing is a tree, *Dipterocarpus baudii*; its resin is used as fire lighter.

Jalan Kesembi (e)
Kesembi or *kesambi* is a tree, *Antidesma ghoesembilla* in Malay.

Jalan Kesoma
Kesoma is a flower, a beautiful woman or youth in Malay.

Jalan Ketapang (e)
Ketapang is the Indian almond tree, *Terminilia catappa* in Malay.

Jalan Ketola (e) (Kampong Ubi)
Ketola is pumpkin in Malay. This road was named in 1957.

Source: *RBAR, 1957:9*

Jalan Ketuka
Ketuka is a small skate in Malay. See *Kampong Wak Hassan*.

Jalan Ketumbit
Ketumbit is a herb used in the treatment of skin diseases, *Leucas zeylanica* in Malay.

Jalan Khairuddin (Opera Estate)
Inche Khairuddin is the pioneer in popularising *Bangsawan*, the Malay operas. See *Aida Street*.

Jalan Khamis
Khamis is Thursday in Malay. See *Jalan Isnin*.

Jalan Khidmat (e) (former Jalan Eunos Malay Settlement)
Khidmat means service or submission in Malay. This road was named in 1961. See *Jalan Panglima*.

Source: *SFP, 1961.6.1:3*

Jalan Kilang/Jalan Kilang Barat/Timor
Kilang is a Malay word for factory or mill. These roads are located in Redhill Industrial Estate. *Barat* and *timor* are west and east in Malay respectively.

Jalan Kimia (e)
Kimia means chemistry in Malay.

Jalan Klapa (Kampong Glam)
This road was named in 1861. It is located within the Muslim Quarter beside Arab Street. *Klapa* or *kelapa* is coconut in Malay. This is one of the series of

streets named after food in the same location which include Jalan Kledek, Jalan Pinang and Jalan Pisang. *See Arab Street.*

Source: *SFP, 1861.1.17:3; STOJ, 1881.5.12:2*

Jalan Kledek (Kampong Glam)

This road was renamed from Jalan Keledeh. *Keledeh* or *kledek* is sweet potato in Malay. *See Jalan Klapa and Arab Street.*

Jalan Klinik

Klinik is the Malay transcription of clinic in English.

Jalan Kluang (e)

Kluang or *keluang* is a fruit bat or flying fox in Malay. There are other streets named after birds in this area such as Jalan Pipit (sparrow) and Jalan Puchong (heron). They were all named in 1956.

Source: *RBAR, 1956:9*

Jalan Kolam Ayer

Kolam is pond or reservoir and *ayer* means water in Malay. *Kolam ayer* was the name given to the impounding reservoirs in the vicinity. The road is now part of the Pan Island Expressway.

Jalan Kong Kuan (e)

This road was at the junction of Bukit Panjang/Upper Bukit Timah/Woodlands Road. There were several clan associations at this location. The premises of clan associations are called "Kong Kuan" in Hokkien, which was the source of the road name.

Jalan Korban (e)

Korban means sacrifice in Malay.

Jalan Korma (e)

Korma is a rich stew of meat in Malay.

Jalan Koswi (e)

Koswi is the name of a Malay cake, *kueh koswi* (now called *ko swee* or *kosui*), which is made from rice and tapioca.

Jalan Koya (e)

Koya means many in Malay.

Jalan Krian

This road is located in the Kembangan area. *Krian* or *kerian* is a district in Perak which was under dispute before the Pangkor treaty (*see Larut Road*). The district was rich with tin mines and rubber, rice and sugar plantations. Jalan Krian is surrounded by Jalan Sayang, Jalan Sentosa, Jalan Selamat and Jalan Senang, perhaps implying that peace and happiness were achieved after the Pangkor treaty. *See Jalan Kembangan.*

Jalan Kuak
Kuak is a night-heron in Malay.

Jalan Kuala
Kuala is the Malay word for river mouth, the point where a tributary falls into the main stream. This is a side road from River Valley Road.

Jalan Kuala Simpang (e)
This road was located off 12.75 ms Sembawang Road. *Kuala* means river mouth and *Simpang* means crossroads in Malay. This road was named in 1948.

Source: *SFP, 1948.7.17:5*

Jalan Kuang
Kuang means pheasant in Malay. This road is located in the Upper Changi area with a few other streets named after birds in the vicinity. There are Jalan Meragi, Jalan Pelatok, Jalan Pergam and Jalan Segam.

Jalan Kuantan (e)
This road was located near Kampong Glam between Victoria Street and North Bridge Road. Kuantan is the state capital of Pahang in Malaysia. Kuantan was printed as Jalan Kwantan in the 1936 Gazetteer. Jalan Kuantan became a public street in 1900.

Source: *MC, 1900.7.12*

Jalan Kubis (e) (Kampong Ubi)
Kubis is cabbage in Malay. This road was named in 1957.

Source: *RBAR, 1957:9*

Jalan Kubor (Kampong Glam)
Located within the Muslim Quarter, *kubor* or *kubur*, is cemetery in Malay. It was probably once a Muslim burial ground. *See Arab Street.*

Jalan Kuchai (e) (Kampong Ubi)
Kuchai is the transcription of chives in Hokkien. This road was named in 1957.

Source: *RBAR, 1957:9*

Jalan Kuda (e)
Kuda means horse in Malay. This name aroused the anger of Malay residents when the road was named in 1958. However, the Rural Board decided that no change would be made as a number of other roads in the vicinity were also named after animals.

Source: *ST, 1958.11.17:4; ST, 1959.3.21:4*

Jalan Kukoh

Kukoh means staunch, of unshaken loyalty in Malay.

Jalan Kundur (e) (Kampong Ubi)

Kundur means wax-gourd in Malay. This road was named in 1957.

Source: *RBAR, 1957:9*

Jalan Kuning

Kuning means yellow in Malay.

Jalan Kunyit (e) (Kampong Ubi)

Kunyit is turmeric in Malay. This road was named in 1957.

Source: *RBAR, 1957:9*

Jalan Kupang

Kupang is a small shell, *Mytilus sp.* in Malay, possibly once used as a currency-token.

Jalan Kuras

Kuras, *Dryobalanops oblongifolia*, is also known as *Keladan*. See *Jalan Chengam* and *Jalan Keladan*.

Source: *Boo: 575*

Jalan Kurnia

Kurnia means bounty or grace from a superior in Malay.

Jalan Kwok Min

This road was probably named after Kwok Min School in this location.

Jalan Labu (e)/Labu Ayer/Labu Manis/Labu Merah

Translation of Malay names are as follows: *Labu* is gourd, *labu ayer* and *labu manis* are pumpkins and *labu merah* is pumpkin or musk melon.

Jalan Labu was named in 1957.

Source: *RBAR, 1957:9*

Jalan Lada (e)/Jalan Lada Puteh

Lada is pepper and *puteh* means white in Malay.

Jalan Lada is in Kampong Ubi. It was named in 1957.

Jalan Lada Puteh is in the Orchard Road area. See *Nutmeg Road*.

Source: *RBAR, 1957:9*

Jalan Ladang (e) (former Jalan Eunos Malay Settlement)

Ladang is the Malay word for unenclosed plantation on dry ground. This road was named in 1949. See *Jalan Eunos*.

Source: *RBAR, 1949:9*

Jalan Lakum
Lakum means wild vine, such as *Vitis diffusa* in Malay.

Jalan Lam Huat
This road was named after the Lam Huat (Hup Kee) Pineapple Factory. The factory was co-founded by Hong Ze Shi (in pinyin) of Hokkien ancestry. Hong (or "Ang" in Hokkien) came to Singapore with his father at the age of four. He first established a provision shop named Chop Ang Chuan Guan and later expanded into the remittance business. "Lam Huat" was sometimes translated as "Nam Wat". Ang was a founder of the Nanyang Ang Clan Association. He passed away in 1969.

Source: *NAS, 1117:4; ZB Special Supplement, 2014.11.20:19*

Jalan Lam Sam
"Lam Sam" is a transcription of south hill in Hokkien. "Lam Sam" was south of Choa Chu Kang Road at 12.5 ms. There was another hill in the north of this road, called North Hill. In 1941, two village schools were merged to become Nam Sam School. Construction of the new school premises was however disrupted by WW2 and only managed to open on 5 February 1946. Nam San Village (or Lam San Village) was officially named in 1948 after the name of the school. Jalan Lam Sam was named after the village. See *Lam San Village*.

In 1990, Nam Sam School was merged again with another primary school and renamed South View Primary School. Following this, the relationship between the school and the road name was terminated.

Source: *ST, 1948.3.19:5; Nam Sam School Souvenir Magazine, 1978:20*

Jalan Lama (e)
Lama means old, a long time in Malay.

Jalan Lana
Lana is the Malay name of a climber, *Ipomoea digitata*.

Jalan Langgar Bedok
Langgar means knocking up against and *bedok* is a big drum used for calling people to the mosque in Malay. *Langgar bedok* means beating the drum in the mosque. See *Bedok Road*.

Jalan Lanjut
Lanjut, *Mangifera lagenifera*, is a source of Machang timber. This road was named in 1957. See *Jalan Chengam*.

Source: *RBAR, 1957:8*

Jalan Lapang
Lapang means spacious in Malay. See *Jalan Kembangan*.

Jalan Lateh
Lateh means practised, trained in Malay.

Jalan Laut (e)
Laut means sea or ocean in Malay. Jalan Laut was a road beside Clyde Terrace Market leading from Beach Road towards the sea. This road was probably used to bring sea produce to the market.

Jalan Layang Layang
Layang layang is a swallow in Malay. This road is one of the streets named after birds located off Jalan Jurong Kechil. There are Jalan Kakatua, Jalan Merbok, Jalan Rajawali, Jalan Selanting and Jalan Tekukor. *See Burnfoot Terrace.*

Jalan Leban
Leban is a tree, *vitex spp.*, in the teak family. *See Jalan Chengam.*

Jalan Lebat Daun (Seletar Hills Estate)
Lebat daun means dense leaves in Malay. This road became a public street in 1967.

Source: *ST, 1967.9.16:19*

Jalan Legundi
Legundi is the Malay name of a large coastal shrub, *Vitex trifolia.*

Jalan Lekar
Lekar is a woven pot stand in Malay.

Jalan Lekub (Seletar Hills Estate)
Lekub is a tree in the mango family. This road became a public street in 1967.

Source: *ST, 1967.9.16:19*

Jalan Lembah Bedok
Lembah means low-lying land in Malay. *See Bedok Road.*

Jalan Lembah Kallang
See Kallang Road.

Jalan Lembah Thomson
See Lembah Bedok and Thomson Road.

Jalan Lembayong (e)
Lembayong is the water-hyacinth, *Eichornea crassipes* in Malay.

Jalan Lempeng
Lempeng means a roll of Indonesian tobacco in Malay.

Jalan Lengkok Sembawang
Lengkok means a bend, curve or twist in Malay, i.e. a curved road in Sembawang. *See Sembawang Road.*

Jalan Lengkuas (e)
Lengkuas is blue ginger, *Alpinia galanga* in Malay.

Jalan Lepas
Lepas means freed or let loose in Malay.

Jalan Lim Sin Tat (e)
This road appeared in the Street Directory of 1961. It was probably named after Paul Lim Sin Tat (1863–1942) who lived in Bukit Panjang Road, a short distance from this road.

Source: *SFP, 1942.1.10:2*

Jalan Lim Tai See
This road was named in 1957 after a deity by the name of Lim Tai See who was worshipped in the Yun Shan Temple nearby. "Tai See" is the title for a senior Taoist disciple. Lim Tai See was born Lin Jie Chun (in pinyin), and was a highly respected person in his prefecture in Fujian Province during the 15th century. He was revered as a deity after his death. "Yun Shan" was his religious name in his old age.

Source: *RBAR, 1957:8; ZB, 2011.4.25:11*

Jalan Lima
See *Jalan Dua*.

Jalan Limau Bali/Kasturi/Manis/Nipis/Purut
Limau is lemon, lime or orange in Malay.

Limau bali is pomelo.

Limau kasturi is calamansi.

Limau manis is orange.

Limau nipis is key lime.

Limau purut is kaffir lime.

Source: *SFP, 1951.10.12:5*

Jalan Limbok
Limbok or *limbuk* is a pigeon in Malay.

Jalan Lobak (e) (Kampong Ubi)
Lobak is Chinese radish in Malay. This road was named in 1957.

Source: *RBAR, 1957:9*

Jalan Lokam
Lokam, variant of *lokan*, is a shell fish, *Cyrena spp.* or a climber, *Trichosanthes nervifolia* in Malay.

Jalan Loyang Besar/Kechil (e)
See *Loyang Avenue*. *Besar* means big and *kechil* means small in Malay.

Jalan Lye Kwee (off 7.25 ms Upper Serangoon Road)
This road was named in 1948 after Goh Lye Kwee. The Rural Board discovered in 1950 that the location of the road sign was switched with Lorong Batawi (reported as Jalan Batawi in the press). However, it was decided that no changes would be made.

Source: *RBAR, 1948:7; ST, 1950.11.17:7; Phua, 1952:179*

Jalan Machang
Machang is horse-mango, *Mangifera foetida*, a tree native to Singapore. See *Kampong Wak Hassan*.

Source: *Boo: 648*

Jalan Madrasah (e) (former Jalan Eunos Malay Settlement)
Madrasah is a Muslim school. This road was named in 1951. See *Jalan Eunos*.

Source: *RBAR, 1951:8*

Jalan Mahasiswa (e)
Mahasiswa means university student in Malay.

Jalan Mahir
Mahir means expert or skilled in Malay.

Jalan Majapahit (e)
This road was named after the Majapahit Empire (1293–1519) based in the island of Java. Singapore was part of the Majapahit Empire around 1365.

Jalan Malu-Malu
Malu-Malu is a sensitive plant, *Mimosa pudica* in Malay. Mimosa is a plant that folds its leaves when touched or exposed to heat.

Jalan Mamam (Pulau Ubin)
Mamam is a climber in Malay. This road was named after Sungei Mamam in Pulau Ubin.

Jalan Ma'mor
Ma'mor or *makmur* means prosperity in Malay.

Jalan Mandar (e)
Mandar is purple teal in Malay. Jalan Mandar was opened in 1976.

Source: *ST, 1976.5.15:8*

Jalan Mandy Kapore (e)
This road only appeared in the 1950 and 1953 Street Directory. It was indicated as located off Changi Road.

Jalan Mangga (e) (Kampong Ubi)
Mangga is mango in Malay. This road was named in 1957.

Source: *RBAR, 1957:9*

Jalan Mangkok
This is a short road off Jalan Piring. *Mangkok* is European cup and *piring* is saucer in Malay.

Jalan Manis
Manis means sweet in Malay.

Jalan Mariam
Mariam is a name in Malay, equivalent to Mary in English.

Jalan Mas Kuning/Mas Puteh
The above Malay names are translated as follows:

Mas means gold, *kuning* means yellow and *puteh* means white.

Mas kuning is yellow gold.

Mas puteh is platinum.

Jalan Mashor
Mashor or *mashhur* means famous in Malay. A famous mosque, Masjid Omar Salmah and MediaCorp are located nearby.

Jalan Masjid
This road is located off Changi Road. *Masjid* is mosque in Malay. This road was named after the Masjid Kassim, which was built by Naina Kassim, an Indian Muslim.

Jalan Mastuli
Mastuli is a kind of heavy and strong silk fabric used for *sarong*.

Jalan Mat Jambol
This road is located off Pasir Panjang Road. It was named after Mat Jambol, a Malay military officer who helped curb the Indian Mutiny of 1915 in Singapore. This road was named by the Rural Board in 1948 for his meritorious service, 33 years after his brave deed.

Source: *RBAR, 1948:7*

Jalan Mata (e)/Mata Ayer
Mata means eye in Malay. *Mata ayer* is spring, source of stream in Malay.

Jalan Mata Ayer in Sembawang leads to the only hot spring in Singapore.

Jalan Mawar
Mawar means rose in Malay. See *Jalan Anggerek*.

Jalan Mayaanam
Mayaanam, also known as *sudalai*, is the funeral rites or cemetery for Southern Indians.

Jalan Mega Mendong (e)
Mega means cloud and *mendong* means overcast in Malay. *Mega mendong* is rain clouds.

Jalan Melati
Melati is a name for jasmine. See *Jalan Anggerek*.

Jalan Melor
Melor or *melur* is the Indian jasmine. See *Jalan Anggerek*.

Jalan Membina
Membina means to build or to construct in Malay.

Jalan Membina Barat (e)
Barat means west in Malay.

Jalan Mempelam (e)
Mempelam means mango in Malay. See *Kampong Ubi*.

Jalan Mempurong
Mempurong is anchovy-herring in Malay. See *Kampong Wak Hassan*.

Jalan Menarong
This road was named in 1957. *Menarong* is a rush used in basket-making. It covers the species *Fimbristylis globulosa* and *Scirpus spp*. See *Jalan Chengam*.

Source: *RBAR, 1957:8*

Jalan Mendaki (e)
Mendaki means to ascend or climb up in Malay.

Jalan Mendong (e)
Mendong means overcast or a tree, *Elaeocarpus parvifolius* in Malay.

Jalan Mengkudu
Mengkudu is a plant of which the root's bark gives a red dye, such as *Morinda citrifolia*. This road was named in 1957. See *Jalan Chengam*.

Source: *RBAR, 1957:8; Boo:659*

Jalan Meragi (e)
Meragi is a bird, *Rostratula capensis*, also known as a painted snipe. See *Jalan Kuang*.

Jalan Merah Saga
Merah means red in Malay. *Saga* is the Malay name for *Adenanthera pavonina*, also known as the coral tree. The seeds of the tree are hard and bright red in colour, often scattered under the tree.

Source: *Boo: 506*

Jalan Merbok
Merbok is the Malay turtle dove, *Turtur tigrinus*. See *Jalan Layang Layang*.

Jalan Merdu
Merdu means tuneful or melodious in Malay.

Jalan Merlimau
See *Merlimau Lane*.

Jalan Merpati (e)
Merpati means dove in Malay. This road was renamed Merpati Road in 1970.

Jalan Mesin
Mesin is the Malay transcription of machine. This road is located in an industrial area.

Jalan Mesra
Mesra means absorption in Malay.

Jalan Minggu
Minggu means week in Malay. See *Jalan Isnin*.

Jalan Minyak
Minyak means oil in Malay. This name may have been derived from the several oil mills and oil warehouses at nearby Havelock Road. There were Bintang Oil Mills, Singapore Oil Mills and the warehouse of Ho Hong Oil Mills, etc. York Hill was once called Ho Hong Hill by the residents around this area. See *Peng Siang Quay*.

Jalan Modin (e)
Modin is the Malay circumciser.

Jalan Molek
Molek means charming or pretty in Malay.

Jalan Muhibbah
Muhibbah or *muhibah* means goodwill in Malay.

Jalan Mulia
Mulia means distinguished or meritorious in Malay.

Jalan Murai
This road was named after Sungei Murai, which was dammed in the early 1980s to create a reservoir. *Murai* is a generic name for many birds, especially for the straits robin, *Copsychus saularis*.

Jalan Murni (e) (former Jalan Eunos Malay Settlement)
Murni means clean, pure or genuine in Malay. This road was named in 1961. See *Jalan Panglima*.

Source: *SFP, 1961.6.1:3*

Jalan Mustika (e) (former Jalan Eunos Malay Settlement)
Mustika is a variant of *mestika*, a talismanic bezoar in Malay. This road was named in 1961. See *Jalan Panglima*.

Source: *SFP, 1961.6.1:3*

Jalan Mutiara
Mutiara means pearl in Malay.

Jalan Naga Sari
Naga sari or *nagasari* is the Malay name for a low thorny shrub, *Acacia farnesiana*, which yields yellow fragrant flowers.

Jalan Nagoh (e)

Jalan Nam Seng (e)

Jalan Nanas (e) (Kampong Ubi)
Nanas means pineapple in Malay. This road was named in 1957.

Source: *RBAR, 1957:9*

Jalan Naung
Naung means shadowing or shelter in Malay.

Jalan Nilai (e)
Nilai means appraising or pricing in Malay.

Jalan Nilayan (e)
Nilayan or *nelayan* is fisherman in Malay.

Jalan Nipah
Nipah is the Malay name for thatch-palm, *Nypa Fruticans*, also known as Attap.

Jalan Nira
Nira is fresh palm sap obtained from the blossom of coconut tree or sugar palm.

Jalan Noordin (Pulau Ubin)
This road was named after the former Kampong Noordin.

Jalan Novena
See *Novena Terrace*.

Jalan Novena Barat/Selatan/Timor/Utara
Barat, *selatan*, *timor* and *utara* are Malay words for west, south, east and north respectively.

Jalan Nuri
Nuri means parrot or lory in Malay.

Jalan Nyiur (e) (Kampong Ubi)
Nyiur is fresh coconut in Malay. This road was named in 1957.

Source: *RBAR, 1957:9*

Jalan Omar Samad (e) (former Jalan Eunos Malay Settlement)

Jalan Pabrik (e)
Pabrik means factory or mill in Malay.

Jalan Pacheli
Pacheli is a brinjal or pineapple condiment in Malay.

Jalan Padang (e) (former Jalan Eunos Malay Settlement)
Padang means treeless plain in Malay. This road was named in 1957. Padang town is in Sumatra, Indonesia.

Source: *RBAR, 1957:8*

Jalan Pagak (e) (former Jalan Eunos Malay Settlement)
This road was probably named after Dr. Abdul Samat bin Haji Pagak (1902–1952), possibly the first Malay medical doctor in Singapore. He was the co-founder of the Malay Institute and a member of the Malay Union in 1929. His father was Haji Pagak bin Daing Armi, also a member of the Malay Union. See *Jalan Eunos*.

Source: *ST, 1937.9.30:10*

Jalan Pakis
Pakis is fern in Malay.

Jalan Pandan
Pandan is the tropical plant in the *Pandanus genus* (with the common name of screwpine) which is widely used for cooking as flavouring.

Jalan Pandu (e)
Pandu means testing, trying or pioneering in Malay.

Jalan Panglima (e) (former Jalan Eunos Malay Settlement)
Panglima means warrior or commander in Malay. This road was named in 1961 together with about 20 other roads in the settlement, all with the same theme. Among the road names are: *Jujor* (honest), *perwira* (hero), *ta'at* (obedient), *damai* (peace-making), *hormat* (respect), *gagah* (important), etc. Incidentally, the mansion of Tan Jiak Kim in River Valley Road area was called Panglima Prang.

Source: *SFP, 1961.6.1:3*

Jalan Pantun (e)
Pantun is the Malay quatrain.

Jalan Papan
Papan means plank, board or flooring in Malay.

Jalan Paras
Paras means good looks, appearance in Malay. *See Jalan Kembangan.*

Jalan Pari Burong/Pari Dedap/Pari Kikis/Pari Unak
Pari is the generic name for stingrays in Malay.

Pari burong is an eagle ray.

Pari dedap is a porcupine ray.

Pari kikis or *Pari kikir* is a rough-skin ray.

Pari unak or *Trygon uarnak* is a sand-loving thorny ray.

Jalan Parit (e)
Parit is drain or moat in Malay.

Jalan Parut (e)
Parut is coconut grater in Malay.

Jalan Pasar Baru (e)
This road was formerly located in Geylang Serai. *Pasar baru* means new market in Malay.

Jalan Pasar Sembawang (e)
Pasar Sembawang is the market in Sembawang. *See Sembawang Road.*

Jalan Pasir (e)/Pasir Merah (e)/Pasir Ria
Pasir means sand or sandy stretch in Malay.

Jalan Pasir was originally located in the Upper East Coast area. It was changed to Sennett Road at the request of residents along the road in 1947. Several years later, Jalan Pasir was used for a road in Geylang Serai. *See Geylang Serai Village.*

Pasir merah means red sand in Malay. It was located on Pulau Tekong.

Pasir ria means delightful sandy stretch in Malay. It is off Pasir Panjang Road.

Source: *ST, 1947.10.17:5*

Jalan Pasiran
Pasiran means sand-like in Malay.

Jalan Paya (e)
Paya means swamp or morass in Malay. Jalan Paya was opened in 1966. *See Geylang Serai Village.*

Source: *ST, 1966.7.30:7*

Jalan Payoh Lai
This road is located off 7 ms Upper Serangoon Road. For "Payoh", see *Toa Payoh Central*. "Lai" means inside in Hokkien.

Jalan Pekan (e)
This road was located between Victoria Street and North Bridge Road, just outside Kampong Glam. *Pekan* means market or trade centre in Malay.

Jalan Pekan Ubin (Pulau Ubin)
Ubin means floor tile in Malay. Pekan Ubin is the market or town in Pulau Ubin.

Jalan Pelajau (Seletar Hills Estate)
Pelajau is the name of the timber from *Pentaspadon motleyi*. This road became a public street in 1967.

Source: *ST, 1967.9.16:19; Boo: 672*

Jalan Pelangi
Pelangi means rainbow in Malay.

Jalan Pelatina
Pelatina means platinum in Malay. This road is surrounded by *taman permata*, which means gem stone garden.

Jalan Pelatok
Pelatok or *pelatuk* is woodpecker in Malay. *See Jalan Kuang*.

Jalan Pelawan (e)
Pelawan is the Malay name for a lofty tree, *Tristania spp*. It yields a durable timber used for building houses. Jalan Pelawan was opened to traffic in 1967.

Source: *ST, 1967.5.16:7; Boo: 743*

Jalan Pelepah
Pelepah is the Malay word for frond or palm-leaf.

Jalan Pelikat
Pelikat or *pelekat* means placard, to caulk a ship or a kind of Indian *sarong* in Malay.

Jalan Pemimpin
Pemimpin means a guide in Malay. *See Jalan Berjaya*.

Jalan Peng Kang (e)
This road was named after the former Peng Kang district shown in J T Thomson's survey map of 1852. It was renamed Corporation Road around 1971.

Source: *NAS, SP006362*

Jalan Penggaga (e)
Penggaga is the Malay name for a creeping plant, Indian Pennywort, *Hydroctoye asiatica*. This road was named in 1957 and was accessible to motor vehicles in 1966.

Source: *RBAR, 1957:9; ST, 1966.7.30:7*

Jalan Penjara
Penjara means prison in Malay. This road was named after the prison nearby.

Jalan Peradun (Seletar Hills Estate)
Peradun means fine dressing in Malay. This road became a public street in 1967.

Source: *ST, 1967.9.16:19*

Jalan Perahu
Perahu is an undecked native ship. The boat used by Orang Laut in the past is called a *perahu*. See *Jalan Bahtera*.

Jalan Perang (e)
Perang means war in Malay.

Jalan Pergam
Pergam is a large wood-pigeon in Malay. See *Jalan Kuang*.

Jalan Peria (e) (Kampong Ubi)
Peria means bitter gourd in Malay. This road was named in 1957.

Source: *RBAR, 1957:9*

Jalan Perisai (e)
Perisai is a round shield in Malay.

Jalan Perkasa (e) (former Jalan Eunos Malay Settlement)
Perkasa means brave or gallant in Malay. This road was named in 1961. See *Jalan Panglima*.

Source: *SFP, 1961.6.1:3*

Jalan Permatang (e) (Pulau Tekong)
This road was named after Kampong Permatang. *Permatang* means bank or rising ground in Malay.

Jalan Pernama
This road is located beside Changi Prison. *Pernama* means one month in Malay.

Jalan Perwira (e) (former Jalan Eunos Malay Settlement)
Perwira is a hero or warrior in Malay. This road was named in 1961. See *Jalan Panglima*.

Source: *SFP, 1961.6.1:3*

Jalan Pesawat
Pesawat means tool or mechanical appliance in Malay.

Jalan Petai (e)
Petai is a plant that bears long, flat edible beans that smell offensively. It is a popular culinary ingredient in South East Asia. This road was named in 1957.

Source: *RBAR, 1957:9; ZB, 2008.10.31*

Jalan Petua (e)
Petua means rule for the guidance of others in Malay.

Jalan Phua Pak Tiong (e)
This road was named in 1948 and subsequently renamed Plantation Avenue in 1951. *See Plantation Avenue.*

Source: *RBAR, 1948:7; RBAR, 1951:8*

Jalan Piala (e)
Piala is a beaker, goblet or drinking cup in Malay. This road was renamed Caldecott Close around 2007.

Jalan Pinang (Kampong Glam)
This road is located near Arab Street. *Pinang* means betel or areca nut in Malay.

Jalan Pinggir (e)
Pinggir means edge or border in Malay.

Jalan Pintau
Pintau is a weaverbird in Malay.

Jalan Pipit (e)
Pipit is a small twittering bird, finch or sparrow in Malay. This road was named in 1956 together with Jalan Kluang and Jalan Puchong, which were all bird names. It was renamed Pipit Road in 1970.

Source: *RBAR, 1956:9*

Jalan Piring
Piring is a saucer or shallow-rimmed plate in Malay. *See Jalan Mangkok.*

Jalan Pisang (Kampong Glam)
This road was named in 1861. *Pisang* means banana in Malay. *See Jalan Klapa and Arab Street.*

Source: *SFP, 1861.1.17:3*

Jalan Pokok Serunai
Pokok Serunai is a mangrove, *Wollastonia biflora*.

Source: *Boo: 448*

Jalan Potong Pasir (e)
See Potong Pasir Avenue.

Jalan Puay Poon (e)

Jalan Puchong (e)
Puchong is a little green heron, *Butotides striatus* in Malay. This road was located in the Siglap area. It was named in 1956 together with Jalan Kluang and Jalan Pipit.

Source: RBAR, 1956:9

Jalan Punai (former Jalan Eunos Malay Settlement)
Punai is a small pigeon in Malay. See *Jalan Eunos*.

Jalan Puteh Jerneh
Puteh means white and *jerneh* means clear in Malay.

Jalan Puteri Jula Juli
Puteri means princess or mimosa in Malay. *Puteri Jula Juli* is a Malay film. See *Jalan Azam*.

Jalan Putu (e)
Putu is a kind of Malay rice cake.

Jalan Puyoh
Puyoh is the bustard-quail, *Turnix taigoor* in Malay.

Jalan Quee Chew
Quee Chew may be a Chinese personal name or a transcription of "Qui Zhou" in Hokkien. Qui Zhou is a province in the south west of China.

Jalan Rabu
Rabu means Wednesday in Malay. See *Jalan Isnin*.

Jalan Rachek (e)
Rachek means snare of suspended nooses for catching birds in Malay.

Jalan Ragi (e)
Ragi means yeast in Malay. See *Kampong Ubi*.

Jalan Rahmat (former Jalan Eunos Malay Settlement)
Rahmat means mercy or pity in Malay. See *Jalan Eunos*.

Jalan Raja Udang (e)
Raja udang means kingfisher in Malay.

Jalan Rajah (Raja)
This road is located off Balestier Road. It was listed as Jalan Raja in 1936. *Rajah* or *raja* means king or ruler in Malay. This road was named in 1901. See *Jalan Datoh*.

Source: MC, 1901.12.18; SG 1936

Jalan Rajawali
Rajawali is a falcon in Malay. *See Jalan Layang Layang.*

Jalan Rakit (e)
Rakit is a raft of long bamboo laid side by side or an arrangement, planning in Malay.

Jalan Rama Rama
Rama rama means moth or butterfly in Malay.

Jalan Rasok
Rasok or *rasuk* is a cross beam in Malay. *See Jalan Bumbong.*

Jalan Rawa (e)
Rawa is a marsh or a large tree, *Mangifera microphylla* in Malay.

Jalan Raya
Raya means large or great in Malay. However, since this road is among a group of flower roads, *raya* may refer to *bunga raya*, which is Hibiscus in English. *See Jalan Anggerek.*

Jalan Rebana
Rebana is a tambourine. *See Jalan Angklong.*

Jalan Rebong (e)
Rebong is young, edible bamboo shoot in Malay. This road was named in 1957.

Source: *RBAR, 1957:9*

Jalan Redop (Seletar Hills Estate)
Redop or *redup* means overcast in Malay. This road became a public street in 1967.

Source: *ST, 1967.9.16:19*

Jalan Rehat (e)
Rehat means rest in Malay. *See Quality Road.*

Jalan Remaja
Remaja means adolescent in Malay.

Jalan Remis
Remis is the generic name for many small bivalve shell fish in Malay.

Jalan Rendang
Rendang is a Malay word for cooking in a little oil or fat, roasting or frying.

Jalan Rengas (Seletar Hills Estate)
Rengas is the generic name for trees which yield timber and a sap that produces varnish. This road became a public street in 1967.

Source: *ST, 1967.9.16:19*

Jalan Rengkam
Rengkam is a growth, *Sargassum sp.* found on coral reefs in Malay.

Jalan Resak
Resak is the generic name for a number of timbers used in boat building, including *Shorea spp.* and *Hopea spp.*

Jalan Reteh (e)
This road was named after Kampong Reteh located nearby. *Reteh* or *retih* means springing up in little jerks in Malay. See *Kampong Ubi*.

Jalan Ria
Ria means joy or delight in Malay.

Jalan Riang
Riang means excitement or exaltation in Malay.

Jalan Rimau (former Jalan Eunos Malay Settlement)
Rimau means tiger in Malay. See *Jalan Eunos*.

Jalan Rindu
Rindu means loving longing in Malay.

Jalan Rukam
Rukam is a generic name for many thorny trees, such as *Flacourtia rukam*. This road was named in 1957. See *Jalan Chengam*.

Source: *RBAR, 1957:8; Boo: 603*

Jalan Rumah Tinggi
Rumah tinggi means tall house in Malay. This road was named when high rise apartments were built in this area.

Jalan Rumbia
Rumbia means sago palm in Malay.

Jalan Rumia
Rumia is a tree, *Bouea microphylla*; it is related to a mango tree with diminutive mango-like fruits.

Jalan Sabar (e) (former Jalan Eunos Malay Settlement)
Sabar means patience in Malay. This road was named in 1961. See *Jalan Panglima*.

Source: *SFP, 1961.6.1:3*

Jalan Sabit
Sabit means a native sickle or truth revealed in Malay.

Jalan Sagu (e)
Sagu is the sago pith of the sago palm tree in Malay. This road was named in 1957.
Source: *RBAR, 1957:8*

Jalan Sahabat
Sahabat means friend or comrade in Malay.

Jalan Sajak
Sajak means melodious harmony in Malay. *See Jalan Cherpen.*

Jalan Saksama (e)
Saksama means diligent enquiry in Malay.

Jalan Salabin (e) (Pulau Tekong)
This road was named after Kampong Salabin.

Jalan Salang
Salang is a hanging basket in Malay. This road was named in 1957.
Source: *RBAR, 1957:8; Kamus Perdana, 1997*

Jalan Saleh (e) (former Jalan Eunos Malay Settlement)
Saleh is a Malay personal name. *See Jalan Eunos.*

Jalan Sam Heng (Pulau Ubin)

Jalan Sam Kongsi
This road is located off 9 ms Tampines Road. This road was named in 1948.
Source: *RBAR, 1948:7*

Jalan Samarinda
Samarinda is the local name for Bengal currant, *Carissa carandas*. Samarinda is also the name of a town in East Borneo, Indonesia.

Jalan Sampurna
Sampurna or *sempurna* means perfect in Malay. This road is in Oei Tiong Ham Park.

Jalan Samulun
Samulun is the name of one of the aboriginal tribes in Singapore. This road leads to Pulau Samulun, off Jurong.
Source: *Haughton: 80*

Jalan Sankam
Sankam is a Hindi name for a type of sea shell. *See Kampong Wak Hassan.*

Jalan Sanyongkong (e) (Pulau Tekong)
See Kampong Sanyongkong.

Jalan Sappan
Sappan is a tree, *Dalium patens*. This road was named in 1957. See *Jalan Chengam*.
Source: *RBAR, 1957:8; Boo: 535*

Jalan Satu
See *Jalan Dua*.

Jalan Saudara Ku
Saudara means compatriot and *ku* means mine in Malay. *Saudara Ku* (My Compatriot) is the name of a Malay film. See *Jalan Azam*.

Jalan Sawi (e) (Kampong Ubi)
Sawi is an aromatic plant, *Brassica nigra*. This road was named in 1957.
Source: *RBAR, 1957:9*

Jalan Sayang
This road is located in the Kembangan area. *Sayang* means love, affection or pitying in Malay. See *Jalan Kembangan*.

Jalan Sayur (e) (Kampong Ubi)
Sayur is vegetable in Malay. This road was named in 1957.
Source: *RBAR, 1957:9*

Jalan Sea View

Jalan Sedap
Sedap means pleasant, nice or tasty in Malay.

Jalan Segam
Segam or *sagan* is nightingale in Malay. See *Jalan Kuang*.

Jalan Seh Chuan
This road was named after Seh Chuan Primary School which was established here in 1925. Subsequently, a secondary school was added. The schools have since been relocated and their English names have been changed to the pinyin version of "Shu Qun".
Source: *Shu Qun Schools 50th Anniversary Souvenir Magazine (1983)*

Jalan Sejarah
Sejarah means genealogy in Malay.

Jalan Selamat
Selamat means peace and safety in Malay. See *Jalan Kembangan*.

Jalan Selanting
Selanting is a long-billed partridge in Malay. See *Jalan Layang Layang*.

Jalan Selaseh
Selaseh or *selasih* is basil, *Ocimum basilicum* in Malay.

Jalan Selendang Delima
Selendang is shawl or hanging and *delima* is pomegranate. *Selendang Delima* is the name of a Malay film. See *Jalan Azam*.

Jalan Selimang
Ikan selimang is the Malay name for carp fish. See *Kampong Wak Hassan*.

Jalan Sembawang Kechil (e)
Kechil means small in Malay. See *Sembawang Road*.

Jalan Sembilang
Sembilang, as in *Ikan sembilang*, is the Malay name for Catfish.

Jalan Semechek (e)
This road was named after Pulau Semechek which used to face the end of this road.

Jalan Semerbak
Semerbak means diffused (of odour) in Malay.

Jalan Seminei (e)
This road was named after Sungei Seminei and Kampong Seminei.

Jalan Sempadan
This road was located off East Coast Road. *Sempadan* means boundary-mark in Malay. The road was just outside the old city limit.

Jalan Sena (e) (Sennett Estate)
Sena means an army in Malay. *Pokok sena* is the Angsana tree.

Jalan Senandong
Senandong means humming a tune to oneself in Malay.

Jalan Senang
Senang means easy or happy in Malay. See *Jalan Kembangan*.

Jalan Sendok (e)
Sendok means a spoon or a ladle in Malay.

Jalan Sendudok
Sendudok is a rhododendron-like shrub, *Melastoma malabathricum*.
Source: *Boo: 325*

Jalan Seng Giap (e)

Jalan Seni
Seni means art in Malay. See *Jalan Asuhan*.

Jalan Senja (e)
Senja means dusk or twilight in Malay.

Jalan Sentosa
Sentosa means calm and peaceful in Malay. See *Jalan Kembangan*.

Jalan Sentul (e) (Kampong Ubi)
Sentul is the Malay name for a lofty tree, *Sandoricum indicum*, producing an edible sour fruit and good timber. It has the common name of cottonfruit tree. This road was named in 1957.

Source: *RBAR, 1957:9*

Jalan Senyum
Senyum means smile in Malay. See *Jalan Kembangan*.

Jalan Serai
See *Geylang Serai Village*. This road was named in 1957.

Source: *RBAR, 1957:9*

Jalan Seranggong Kechil (e)
This road was located off 9 ms Punggol Road. *Seranggong* was one of the old names of Serangoon (see *Serangoon Road*). *Kechil* means small in Malay. Seranggong Kechil was located off Punggol Road, it was named in 1948.

Source: *RBAR, 1948:7*

Jalan Serene (Serene Centre)

Jalan Serengam
Serengam is a plant, *Desmodium latifolium* in Malay.

Jalan Serigading (e)
Serigading is a flowering plant, *Nyctanthes abortristis*. See *Kampong Ubi*.

Jalan Serindit (e)
Serindit is the Malay name for lovebird.

Jalan Seruling
Seruling is a flageolet or flute in Malay. See *Jalan Angklong*.

Jalan Setia (former Gillman Barracks)
Setia means fidelity, troth or allegiance in Malay.

Jalan Shaer
Shaer is a poem in Malay. See *Jalan Cherpen*.

Jalan Siantan
Siantan is the Malay name for a flowering tree, *Pavetta indica*, also known as angsoka, *Ixora spp*.

Jalan Siap
Siap means prepared in Malay. See *Jalan Asas*.

Jalan Sikudangan
Sikudangan is a kind of herbaceous plant in Malay. See *Jalan Anggerek*.

Jalan Silat Gayong (e)
Silat is a Malay sworddance. *Gayong* is a stick used as a weapon. *Silat gayong* is a Malay martial art for self-defence.

Jalan Sim Pah (e)
This road was located off 10.25 ms Tampines Road. It was named in 1948. From the road name, the land was probably a rural plantation that belonged to a Mr. Sim.
Source: *RBAR, 1948:7*

Jalan Simpang Bedok
Simpang is a crossroad in Malay. Simpang Bedok was probably the location of a crossing of Sungei Bedok. See *Bedok Road* for the etymology of Bedok.

Jalan Sinar Bintang/Bulan
Sinar means shining and *bintang* is star in Malay. *Sinar bintang* is star light.
  Bulan means moon in Malay. *Sinar bulan* is moonlight.

Jalan Sindor
Sindor or *sindoor* may refer to the plant, *Bixa orellana*. The pods of this plant are used to make *sindoor*, the red cosmetic powder worn by married Indian women along the parting of their hair.

Jalan Singa (former Jalan Eunos Malay Settlement)
The name was adopted by the Rural Board in 1941 because it was in the Malay Settlement. *Singa* means lion in Malay. See *Jalan Eunos*.
Source: *ST, 1941.08.15:7*

Jalan Siput (e)
Siput means snail in Malay.

Jalan Somapah Barat (e)/Timor (e)
See *Somapah Road*. *Barat* and *timor* are Malay words for west and east respectively.

Jalan Songket
Songket is a fabric that belongs to the brocade family of textile in Malaysia.

Jalan Songsong (e)
Songsong means going against the wind or tides in Malay.

Jalan Soo Bee
This road was first seen in the Street Directory of 1959. It was named after Tan Soo Bee. See *Simei Avenue*.

Jalan Sotong
Sotong means cuttlefish in Malay.

Jalan Suasa
Suasa is the Malay name for an alloy of gold and copper.

Jalan Suchi (e) (former Jalan Eunos Malay Settlement)
Suchi or *suci* means pure or clean in Malay. This road was named in 1961. See *Jalan Panglima*.

Source: *SFP, 1961.6.1:3*

Jalan Sudin (e) (former Jalan Eunos Malay Settlement)
Among notable persons with this name was Mohamed Sudin bin Abdul Rahman, a police officer. He was a treasurer of the Police Co-operative Society and a member of the Executive Committee of the Singapore Malay Union.

Source: *SFP, 1930.3.15:3*

Jalan Suka
Suka means pleasure, to like or to agree in Malay.

Jalan Sukachita
Sukachita or *sukacita* means enjoyment in Malay.

Jalan Sukun (e)
Sukun means breadfruit, *Artocarpus laevis* in Malay. This road was named in 1957.

Source: *RBAR, 1957:9*

Jalan Sulam (e)
Sulam means embroidery or replant in Malay.

Jalan Sultan (Kampong Glam)
This road was named after the Istana Kampong Glam. See *Sultan Gate*.

Jalan Sumbu (e)
Sumbu means a fuse, a slow match in Malay.

Jalan Sumpit (e)
Sumpit means shooting with a blowpipe in Malay.

Jalan Sungei Belang (e)
Sungei means river and *belang* means banded (in colouring) in Malay.

Jalan Sungei Buloh (e)
This road was named after Sungei Buloh, the name of a river that appeared in J T Thomson's survey map of 1852. *Buloh* means bamboo in Malay. See *Kampong Sungei Buloh*.

Source: *NAS, SP006362*

Jalan Sungei Pelandok (e)
Pelandok or *pelanduk* is a mouse deer in Malay. This road was located off West Coast Road and was named in 1954.

Source: *RBAR, 1954:8*

Jalan Sungei Poyan
This road was named after Sungei Poyan. *Poyan* means ancestor in Malay.

Jalan Sunggoh (e)
Sunggoh means truth or reality in Malay.

Jalan Surau (e)
Surau is a small place of worship for Muslims.

Jalan Ta'at (e) (former Jalan Eunos Malay Settlement)
Ta'at means obedient or faith in Malay. This road was named in 1961. See *Jalan Panglima*.

Source: *SFP, 1961.6.1:3*

Jalan Tabah (e) (former Jalan Eunos Malay Settlement)
Tabah means daring or boldness in Malay. This road was named in 1961. See *Jalan Panglima*.

Source: *SFP, 1961.6.1:3*

Jalan Taman
Taman means garden in Malay.

Jalan Tambah (e) (Kampong Kapor)
Tambah means increase by repetition or continuation in Malay. This road was seen in news reports as early as 1893. There was a Municipal decision to change its name to Inche Lane in 1906. However, the name change was not executed and it became a public street in 1914. It was finally changed to Veerasamy Road in 1927.

Source: *DA, 1893.12.19:3; ED, 1906.12.1:4; MC, 1914.11.27; MC, 1927.1.28*

Jalan Tamban
Tamban means sardine in Malay.

Jalan Tambur
Tambur is a drum. See *Jalan Angklong*.

Jalan Tampang
Tampang is a tree, *Artocarpus gomeziana* in Malay.

Jalan Tampoi (e)
Tampoi is a fruit tree, *Baccaurea malayana* in Malay. See *Kampong Ubi*.

Jalan Tan Tock Seng
Tan Tock Seng (1798-1850, Hokkien) was the first Chinese in Singapore to be conferred a Justice of the Peace title. The hospital he built for the poor in 1844 near Pearl's Hill was the modest beginnings of Tan Tock Seng Hospital.

Source: *Kua: 86*

Jalan Tanah Puteh
Tanah means soil or land and *puteh* means white in Malay. *Tanah puteh* is white soil.

Jalan Tanah Rata
Rata means flat in Malay. *Tanah rata* is flat land. This road is located in the Tanah Merah area.

Jalan Tangki (e) (former Jalan Eunos Malay Settlement)
Tangki is the water tanks on a ship in Malay. See *Jalan Eunos*.

Jalan Tani
Tani means farming in Malay.

Jalan Tanjong
Tanjong or *tanjung* means cape in Malay.

Jalan Tanjong Irau (e)
Irau is a variant of *hiru*, it means disturbance in Malay. See *Kampong Tanjong Irau*.

Jalan Tanjong Penjuru (e)
Penjuru means a corner in Malay. *Tanjong penjuru* is the corner of the cape. This road was named in 1950.

Source: *RBAR, 1950:9*

Jalan Tapisan/Ayer (e)
Tapisan means filter and *ayer* means water in Malay. *Tapisan ayer* is water filter.

Jalan Tari Dulang/Lilin/Payong/Piring/Serimpi/Zapin
Tari means dance in Malay.

> *Dulang* is a wooden tin wash board. *Tari dulang* is a dance with *dulang*.
>
> *Lilin* is candle in Malay. *Tari lilin* is candle dance.
>
> *Payong* is umbrella in Malay. *Tari payong* is umbrella dance.
>
> *Piring* is a saucer in Malay. *Tari piring* is a saucer dance.
>
> *Serimpi* is a court dancer in Malay. *Tari serimpi* is a court dance.
>
> *Zapin* is a Malay term for Arabian dance. *Tari zapin* is Arabian dance.

Jalan Tarum
Tarum is the Indigo plant. It is one of the original sources of Indigo dye. *See Jalan Chengam.*

Jalan Tauge (e) (Kampong Ubi)
Tauge is a Malay transcription of bean sprout in Hokkien. This road was named in 1957.

Source: *RBAR, 1957:9*

Jalan Teban (e)
This road was located off 7.75 ms Tampines Road. It was named in 1948 after Kampong Teban in the same location. *Teban* means money deposited or bet in Malay. *See Kampong Teban.*

Source: *RBAR, 1948:7*

Jalan Tebing Terjun (e)
Tebing means bank of river or canal. *Terjun* means rapid descent in Malay. *Terjun* originated from Ayer Terjun, a tributary to the Jurong River in H E McCallum's survey map of 1885.

Source: *NAS, TM000003*

Jalan Tebu (e) (Kampong Ubi)
Tebu means sugar cane in Malay. This road was named in 1957.

Source: *RBAR, 1957:9*

Jalan Teck Kee
This road was located off 6 ms Yio Chu Kang Road. It was named after Chop Teck Kee, the shop owned by Sim Lian Hong (1850–1921, Teochew). He was one of the founders of Sze Hai Tong Bank (subsequently merged with OCBC Bank). This road was named in 1948.

Source: *RBAR, 1948:7; Kua: 40*

Jalan Teck Whye
This road was named in 1957.

Source: *RBAR, 1957:8*

Jalan Tegas (e) (former Jalan Eunos Malay Settlement)
Tegas means firm, well-defined or precise in Malay. This road was named in 1961. *See Jalan Panglima.*

Source: *SFP, 1961.6.1:3*

Jalan Tegoh (e) (former Jalan Eunos Malay Settlement)
Tegoh means firm and strong in Malay. This road was named in 1961. *See Jalan Panglima.*

Source: *SFP, 1961.6.1:3*

Jalan Tekad
Tekad means determination in Malay. *See Jalan Asas.*

Jalan Tekukor
Tekukor is a turtle dove or cuckoo dove in Malay. *See Jalan Layang Layang.*

Jalan Tekun (e) (former Jalan Eunos Malay Settlement)
Tekun means perseverance in Malay. This road was named in 1961. *See Jalan Panglima.*

Source: *SFP, 1961.6.1:3*

Jalan Telaga (e)
Telaga is a well in Malay.

Jalan Telang
Telang is the Butterfly-Pea flower plant, also known as Blue-Pea. The flower is often used when making Nyonya cakes. *See Jalan Chengam.*

Jalan Telawi (e)
Telawi is the Malay word for the long and curving feather of chicken or bird.

Jalan Telipok
Telipok or *telepok* means water-lily in Malay.

Jalan Teliti
Teliti means care in Malay.

Jalan Tembikai (e)
Tembikai means watermelon in Malay. *See Geylang Serai Village.*

Jalan Tembusu
This road is located off Tanjong Katong. Tembusu, *Fagraea fragrans*, is a large evergreen tree that is native to Singapore. Its flowers are creamy white and strongly fragrant especially in late evenings.

Source: *ZB, 2008.10.31*

Jalan Tempua
Tempua is a weaver bird in Malay.

Jalan Tempunai (e)
Tempunai is a tree, *Artocarpus rigida*. This road was named in 1956.

Source: *RBAR, 1956:9*

Jalan Tenaga (former Jalan Eunos Malay Settlement)
Tenaga means strength in Malay. This road was named in 1961. *See Jalan Panglima.*

Source: *SFP, 1961.6.1:3*

Jalan Tenang
Tenang means still or calm in Malay.

Jalan Tengah (e)
Tengah means middle in Malay. This road was in the centre of Geylang Serai.
See *Geylang Serai Village*.

Jalan Tenggiri
Tenggiri is the Spanish mackerel in Malay.

Jalan Tenon
Tenon or *tenong* is a flat-topped circular basket or box of Javanese make.

Jalan Tenteram
Tenteram means peaceful in Malay.

Jalan Teo Ngoh Thong (e)

Jalan Tepi Sungei (e)
Tepi means edge or brink and *sungei* means river in Malay. *Tepi sungei* means edge of the river. This road was close to the upper reaches of Geylang River. See *Geylang Serai Village*.

Jalan Tepong
Tepong means rice flour in Malay.

Jalan Terang Bulan
See *Terang Bulan Avenue*.

Jalan Terap (e)
Terap is a tree, *Artocarpus elasticus*, in Malay.

Source: *Boo: 519*

Jalan Teratai (e)
Teratai means water lotus in Malay. See *Jalan Anggerek*.

Jalan Terentang (e)
Terentang is the Malay name for a large forest tree, *Camonosperma auriculata*.

Jalan Terong (e)
Terong or *terung* means brinjal in Malay. This road was named in 1957.

Source: *RBAR, 1957:9*

Jalan Tertib (e) (former Jalan Eunos Malay Settlement)
Tertib means order or correct conduct in Malay. This road was named in 1961. See *Jalan Panglima*.

Source: *SFP, 1961.6.1:3*

Jalan Terubok
Terubok is a fish, *Clupea kanagurta* in Malay.

Jalan Terusan
Terusan is a cutting or short canal in Malay. This road crosses a tributary of Jurong River.

Jalan Tiga
See *Jalan Dua*.

Jalan Tiga Ratus
Jalan Tiga Ratus Track (3, 6, 8, 11, 15, 16, 18) (e)
Tiga ratus is 300 in Malay. Jalan Tiga Ratus was named in 1950.
Source: *RBAR, 1950:9*

Jalan Timun (e) (Kampong Ubi)
Timun means cucumber in Malay. This road was named in 1957.
Source: *RBAR, 1957:9*

Jalan Tinggi (e)
The original spelling of *tinggi* was *tingi*, which means high in Malay. This road was named in 1956.
Source: *RBAR, 1956:9*

Jalan Tiong
Tiong is the transcription of cemetery in Hokkien. This road was named in 1954. The name implies that it was once a burial ground. See *Tiong Bahru Road*.

Jalan Tiong Bahru (e)
See *Tiong Bahru Road*.

Jalan Toa Payoh
See *Toa Payoh Central*. Jalan Toa Payoh began construction in 1964.
Source: *ST, 1964.6.19:5*

Jalan Todak
Todak is swordfish in Malay.

Jalan Toh Guan (e)
"Toh Guan" is the transcription of starfruit farm in Hokkien. There was a large starfruit farm in this area around the time of WW2 as the fruit was in demand and could fetch a high price.
Source: *NAS, 2780:17*

Jalan Tongkang Pechah (e)
This road was off 8.25 ms Yio Chu Kang Road. *Tongkang* is a barge-like seagoing cargo-boat and *pechah* means broken into fragments in Malay. This road was located at the upper reaches of Sungei Punggol and was the dumping ground for abandoned boats. This road was named in 1948.
Source: *RBAR, 1948:7; NAS, 172:3*

Jalan Traling (e)
Traling is a bird or the timber used in building houses from *Tarrietia simplicifolia* in Malay.

Jalan Tua Kong
In the Malay language, *tua* means senior or old and *kong* is a deity in the temple. *Tua kong* could also be a transcription of "Tua Peh Kong", the earth god in Hokkien. This road was named in 1950.

Source: *RBAR, 1950:9*

Jalan Tuah (e)
Tuah means luck in Malay.

Jalan Tuas (e)/Kechil (e)
See *Tuas Avenue*. *Kechil* means small in Malay.

Jalan Tukang
Tukang is a technician in Malay.

Jalan Tumpu
Tumpu means footing, base of operation in Malay. See *Jalan Asas*.

Jalan Tungku Kadir (e) (former Jalan Eunos Malay Settlement)
Tungku is a prince in Malay. The word may also be spelt as *tengku* or *tuanku*. *Kadir* means almighty in Malay. *Tungku kadir* was probably a descendant of the Sultan of Singapore. He was a Justice of the Peace and the vice-chairman of the Malay Silver Jubilee Committee in celebration of the silver jubilee of King George V's ascension to the throne on 6 May 1935. The road name "Tungku" was changed to "Engku" around 1955. *Engku* is a Malay title of high rank, prince. See *Jalan Engku Kadir* and *Jalan Eunos*.

Source: *ST, 1935.3.27:16*

Jalan Tupai
Tupai means squirrel in Malay. See *Jalan Arnap*.

Jalan Turi
Turi is a small tree, *Sesbania grandiflora*. This road was named in 1957.

Source: *RBAR, 1957:9*

Jalan Ubi (Kampong Ubi)
Ubi means tapioca in Malay. This road was named in 1957.

Source: *RBAR, 1957:9*

Jalan Ubin (Pulau Ubin)
Ubin means floor tile in Malay.

Jalan Udaya (e)
Udaya could be a variant of *daya upaya*, which means resources in Malay.

Jalan Uji
Uji means test in Malay. See *Jalan Asas*.

Jalan Ular (e)
This road was located off Sembawang Road. *Ular* is a snake or serpent in Malay.

Jalan Ulu Kuala Simpang (e)
Ulu is the Malay term for the upper reaches of a river. See *Jalan Kuala Simpang*. This road was named in 1948.

Source: *SFP, 1948.7.17:5; RBAR, 1948:5*

Jalan Ulu Seletar
See *Seletar Road*.

Jalan Ulu Sembawang
See *Sembawang Road*. This road was named in 1948.

Source: *SFP, 1948.7.17:5*

Jalan Ulu Siglap
See *Siglap Road*.

Jalan Unggas
Unggas is a bird in Malay.

Jalan Ungu (e)
Ungu means purple or deep reddish brown in Malay.

Jalan Unjam (e)
Unjam is a Malay term for a bunch of coconut leaves anchored at sea to attract fish. *Unjam* also means to thrust anything vigorously into the ground in Malay.

Jalan Unum (e)
Unum or *unun* means lotus in Malay.

Jalan Usaha
Usaha means assiduity, industry or persistent in Malay.

Jalan Utasan (e)
Utasan means craftsmanship in Malay. This road was renamed International Road around 1968.

Jalan Wah Ming (e)
This road was probably named after the Wah Ming School located in this area.

Source: *DSM: 399*

Jalan Wajek
Wajek is a sweetmeat in Malay.

Jalan Wak Selat (e)
Wak means uncle or aunty in Malay, or a title awarded by rulers of Malacca. *Selat* means straits in Malay. The road was named after Kampong Wak Selat, which in turn was named after an elder by the name of Wak Selat.

Source: *NAS, 1117:4*

Jalan Wakaff
This road was located off Changi Road. *Wakaff* or *wakaf* is a Malay word which means devoted to religious purposes. This name may be related to the Masjid Kassim in the same location. See *Jalan Masjid*.

Jalan Wangi
Wangi means fragrant in Malay.

Jalan Waringin
Waringin is a tree, *Ficus benjamina*.

Source: *Boo: 595*

Jalan Waspada (e)
Waspada means cautious in Malay.

Jalan Wat Siam (Pulau Ubin)
Wat is a temple in Thai. *Siam* is the old name of Thailand. There was a Siamese Temple along this road.

Jalan Wijaya (e)
Wijaya means victorious in Malay.

Jalan Woodbridge (e)
This road was renamed Gerald Drive in 1998.

Source: *BT, 1998.6.30:32*

Jalan Yahya (e) (former Jalan Eunos Malay Settlement)
One notable person with this name was Yahya A Rahman, who was the co-Secretary of the Singapore Malay Union from 1926–1931. See *Jalan Eunos*.

Source: *SFP, 1929.2.1:13*

Jalan Yahya Afifi (e)
This road was probably named after Shaik Yahya bin Ahmad Afifi. See *Jalan Afifi*.

Jalan Yasin (former Jalan Eunos Malay Settlement)
Yasin is a Muslim personal name. It is also the title of chapter 27 of the Koran. See *Jalan Eunos*.

Jalan Zamrud
Zamrud means emerald in Malay. *See Jalan Batu Nilam.*

Jamaica Road (former Singapore Naval Base)
Jamaica (land of water and trees in the indigenous Arawak Indian language) is an island country in the Caribbean Sea and was under British rule before WW2. *See Admiralty Road.*

Source: *ZB 2008.8.23*

Jambol Place/Walk
See Jalan Mat Jambol.

Jansen Close/Road
J M Jansen (Eurasian) was the Secretary of the Kuala Sawah Rubber Co. Ltd. He served on the Rural Board between 1935 and 1942. Jansen Road was repaired in 1952 at the frontagers' expense with the approval of the Rural Board. *See Dix Road.* Jansen Close was named in 1957.

Source: *RBAR, 1952:8; RBAR, 1957:8*

Japan Street (e)
Japan Street appeared in Municipal records as early as 1838 and was made a public street in 1895. It was one of the two streets renamed soon after WW2. The street name was changed to Boon Tat Street in 1946.

Source: *MC, 1895.2.27; MC, 1946.6.28*

Japanese Cemetery Road (e)
The cemetery was the burial place for Japanese who died during WW2. The road was named in 1948 and subsequently changed to Chuan Hoe Avenue in 1957.

Source: *RBAR, 1948:7; RBAR, 1957:8*

Japanese Garden Road
The Japanese Garden was opened in 1973.

Jasmine Road
This road was named in 1954. *See Carnation Drive.*

Source: *RBAR, 1954:8*

Java Road
This road was named after the Island of Java, Indonesia. It was listed as a street in town in 1853. *See Kampong Java.*

Jedburgh Gardens (Frankel Estate)
This road was named in 1954. Jedburgh is a town and former royal burgh in the Scottish Borders. *See Burnfoot Terrace.*

Source: *ST, 1954.6.15:5*

Jeddah Street (e) (Kampong Glam)
This street was named in 1870 after Jeddah, a Saudi Arabian city close to the Red Sea. *See Arab Street.*
Source: *ST, 1870.12.17:1*

Jelapang Road
Jelapang means paddy-barn in Malay.

Jelebu Road
Jelebu means far in Malay.

Jellicoe Road (WW1 roads)
This road was named after Admiral John Rushworth Jellicoe (1859-1935), one of the leading commanders in WW1. *See Allenby Road.*

Jellicoe commanded the Grand Fleet at the Battle of Jutland (off Denmark) during WW1. The road was converted to a public street in 1929.
Source: *ST, 1929.12.21:17*

Jelutong Road (e) (Thiam Siew Village, Tanjong Katong)
Jelutong is a town in Penang, Malaysia. *See Thiam Siew Avenue.*

Jervois Close/Hill/Lane/Road (off River Valley Road)
Jervois Crescent (e) (former Singapore Naval Base)
Based on a report in 1935, Jervois Road was named after Lieutenant General Sir William Francis Drummond Jervois (1821-1897). Jervois was a military engineer and the Secretary of a Commission set up to examine the state and efficiency of British land base fortifications against naval attacks. He became the tenth Governor of the Straits Settlements between 1875 and 1877.

Jervois Crescent at the Naval Base was probably named after the same person as mentioned above. *See Admiralty Road.*
Source: *SFP, 1935.9.19:3*

Jetty Road (e)
Jetty Road was on Pulau Blakang Mati (now Sentosa Island).

Jiak Chuan Road
This road was named in 1927 after Tan Jiak Chuan (1858-1909, Hokkien), the son of Tan Beng Gum. Tan Beng Gum was the second son of Tan Kim Seng. *See Kim Seng Road.*
Source: *ST, 1909.1.4:7; MC, 1927.9.30; Kua: 84*

Jiak Kim Street
This road was named after Tan Jiak Kim (1859-1917), cousin of Tan Jiak Chuan. He was the son of Tan Beng Swee. As Tan Beng Swee was the eldest son of Tan Kim Seng, Tan Jiak Kim was privileged to inherit his forebears'

position as the leader in the Chinese community (see *Beng Swee Place and Kim Seng Road*). He served as a member of the Municipal Commission from 1886 to 1893 and was a member of the Legislative Council from 1889 to 1893 and 1903 to 1915. He was conferred Justice of the Peace in 1891. During WW1, apart from making generous cash donations to the relief fund, he donated a fighter plane to the British government.

Jiak Kim Street was named by the Commissioners in 1920.

Source: *SFP, 1917.10.23:7; MC, 1920.2.27; Song: 194-196*

Jim Chuan Hill (e)
See *Cheang Jim Chuan Lane*.

Joan Road
Based on a news article in 1937, Joan Caldecott was the daughter of Andrew Caldecott, the Colonial Secretary. As this road is located in Caldecott Hill Estate, it was possible that Joan Road was named after her.

Source: *SFP, 1937.7.9:4; Dunlop*

Joe David Road (e)
This road was named after Joe V David by the Rural Board in recognition of the pioneering work done by him in the area. It was named in 1949 after he passed away.

Source: *RBAR, 1949:9; ST, 1949.3.18:6*

John Road
This road is located in Caldecott Hill Estate. It was reported that Andrew Caldecott, the Colonial Secretary, had a son and a daughter, although the name of the son is unknown. As the daughter was probably named in Joan Road, it was possible that John Road was named after another family member of Caldecott. See *Joan Road*.

Source: *Dunlop*

Johnston Pier (e)/Street (e)
A L Johnston (died 1850) was one of the earliest settlers in Singapore. The pier was named after him in 1853. It was spelt Johnston's Pier or Johnstons Pier. The pier was completed in 1855 and red navigation lights were used to guide boats into the pier. The red lights gave rise to its colloquial name of red light pier used by the Chinese. The pier was rebuilt in 1932 and renamed Clifford Pier (see *Clifford Pier*). Johnston Street was named in 1952.

Source: *ST, 1853.10.25:5; ST, 1952.10.18:4*

Johore Road (e) (Kampong Glam)
This road was a side road of Arab Street, part of the Muslim Quarter. It was named after the State of Johore in Malaysia. See *Arab Street*.

Joo Avenue

Joo Chiat Avenue/Lane/Place/Road/Terrace/Walk

Chew Joo Chiat (1857-1926) was the largest land owner in the Katong area after WW1.

A continuation of the original Joo Chiat Road to the sea (before land reclamation) was named in 1930.

Source: *SFP, 1926.2.9:8; MC, 1930.9.26; Kua: 140*

Joo Hiang Road (e)

This road was listed in the 1936 Gazetteer and was occasionally seen in news reports. It was actually a misprint of Joon Hiang Road.

Joo Hong Road

Joo Koon Circle/Crescent/Road/Way

Joo Koon Road was named after Joo Koon School, originally located at 18 ms Jurong Road. The English name of the school was changed to "Yu Qun" (in pinyin) and merged with Joo Hwa School in 2002. The merged school was named "Yu Hua", the pinyin name of Joo Hwa. Yu Hua School is now located in Jurong East.

Joo Seng Road

This road was named in 1930.

Source: *MC, 1930.7.29*

Joo Yee Road

This road was named around 1976. *See Chia Ping Road.*

Joon Hiang Road

Chew Joon Hiang (died 1916, Hokkien) was one of the founders of Tao Nan School. This road was named in 1929.

Source: *MC, 1929.10.25; Kua: 141*

Joon Tong Road (e)

Jubilee Road

This road was named to commemorate the Jubilee (25th year) celebration of the wedding of King George VI on 26 April 1948.

Source: *RBAR, 1948:7*

Jumbo Jet Drive (Singapore Turf Club, Woodlands)

Jupiter Road

Jupiter is one of the planets in the solar system. This road was named in 1961. *See Capricorn Drive.*

Source: *SFP, 1961.1.6:6*

Jurong Canal Drive/Jurong Crescent (e)
Jurong East Avenue 1
Jurong East Central/Central 1
Jurong East Street 11 to 13, 21, 24, 31, 32
Jurong Gateway Road/Jurong Hill/Jurong Island Highway
Jurong Lake Link
Jurong Pier Circus (e)/Road/Way
Jurong Port Road/Jurong Road
Jurong Road Track (3 to 6, 8, 9, 11, 13, 14, 17) (e), 18, 19 (e), 20, 21 (e), 22, 23 (e), (27, 28, 30, 32) e
Jurong Town Hall Road/Jurong Village (e)
Jurong West Avenue 1 to 5
Jurong West Central 1 to 3
Jurong West Street 21 (e), 22 to 25, 26 (e), 41, 42, 51, 52, 61 to 65, 71 to 76, 81, 82, 91 to 93

The word Jurong may be derived from *jerung* (greedy shark in Malay). The name of the district came from the Jurong River, which was shown in a survey map of Singapore c.1830. Jurong was a district name in the map of Singapore in 1852.

Jurong Port Road was renamed from Jalan Gudang in 1971.

Jurong Town Hall Road was opened in 1980.

Source: *SFP, 1837.8.10:2; SYrBk, 1971:12; ST, 1980.6.27:11; NAS, SP006362; NAS, SP006747; Buckley: 300; Koh: 270*

Jutland Road (e) (WW1 roads)

This road was named after the Jutland Peninsular in Denmark, one of the famous battlefields during WW1. *See Allenby Road.*

The Battle of Jutland was the largest and only full scale clash of battleships in WW1. It was fought between British and German Navy fleets over two days (31 May to 1 June 1916) with heavy losses of life and damage to ships on both sides. The road was named in 1928.

Source: *MC1, 1928.10.2*

Kadayanallur Street

Kadayanallur is a place in South India. This street was the place where Muslim immigrants from Kadayanallur used to congregate.

Source: *Dhoraisingam: 182*

Kaki Bukit Avenue 1 to 6
Kaki Bukit Crescent/Industrial Terrace/Place
Kaki Bukit Road 1 to 6

Kaki Bukit View
Kaki bukit means foot of the hill in Malay.

Kalidasa Avenue (Teachers' Housing Estate)
This road was named after Kalidasa, an Indian playwright and poet who lived around the 5th century. See *Iqbal Avenue*.

Kallang Airport Drive
Kallang Avenue/Bahru/Close (e)/Junction/Place
Kallang Paya Lebar Expressway
Kallang Pudding Road
Kallang Road/Sector/Square (e)/Tengah/Walk
Kallang Way/Kallang Way 1, 2, 2A, 3, 4, 5
Kallang was originally known as Kilang (as in Sungei Kilang) in a survey map of Singapore c.1830. In the 1838 survey map drawn by G D Coleman, the place name was changed to Kelang. Kallang as a place name was used from 1842.

The origin of Kilang, Kelang or Kallang may have come from an Orang Laut tribe known as Beduanda Kalang who originally settled at Kampong Glam, where *kajangs* (boat roof) and sails were made. Apparently the settlers were removed by the Temenggong upon the cessation of Singapore to Britain. The tribe had gone extinct after a small-pox epidemic at their new settlement in Johore. *Kalang* in Malay means roller skid for launching boats.

Translations of other Malay words used above are as follows:

Bahru means new, *pudding* or *puding* is a small tree and *tengah* means middle.

Kallang Road was one of the early roads which began construction in 1831.

Kallang Airport Drive was the location of the first airport in Singapore. The area has been redeveloped into a sports hub.

Kallang Pudding Road was named in 1921.

Source: *SFP, 1842.3.24:3; MC, 1921.12.20; DM, 1928:19-X; NAS, SP002997; NAS, SP006747; Buckley: 212, 340; Haughton: 77; Sophia: 377 map*

Kampong Amber (e)
Kampong was also spelt *campong* in the early days and is the Malay word for village. This village was named after Amber Road where it was located.

Kampong Amoy Quee (e)
This village was located at 10.5 ms Yio Chu Kang Road.

Kampong Ampat
This was one of the five villages in the MacPherson area that was named by Malay numerals.

See *Pachitan Dua* for numerals in Malay.

Kampong Satu to Kampong Ampat were named at the same time in 1921.
Source: *MC, 1921.12.20*

Kampong Arang Road
Arang means charcoal in Malay. This area was the centre for unloading charcoal imported from Thailand, Indonesia and Malaysia. *See Tanjong Rhu Road.*

Kampong Ayer Bajau (e)
Ayer means water and *bajau* means a sea gypsy in Malay. This village was located close to Sungei Ayer Bajau. There was also an island of the same name across the sea.

Kampong Ayer Gemuruh (e)
Gemuruh means thunder or roar in Malay. This village was located at the end of Wing Loong Road at the seaside in Changi.

Kampong Ayer Limau (e)
Limau means lemon, lime or orange in Malay. This village was situated at the former Pulau Merlimau.

Kampong Ayer Manis (e)
Manis means sweet in Malay. This village was located around Wing Loong Road.

Kampong Ayer Samak (e)/Kampong Ayer Samak Darat
Both villages were located in Pulau Tekong. *See Ayer Samak.*

Kampong Bahru (e)/Hill (e)/Kampong Bahru Road
Bahru means new in Malay. There were three villages named Kampong Bahru located at Neil Road, Nallur Road (Kampong Bahru Siglap) and Pulau Ubin. All have been expunged. Kampong Bahru Road was named in 1907.
Source: *MC, 1907.3.1*

Kampong Ban Siew San (e)
This place name only appeared once in the 1950 Street Directory. It was located at Wishart Road.

Kampong Banjai (e)
This was another place name that appeared only once in the 1950 Street Directory. It was located along Changi Road.

Kampong Batak (e)
Batak is a nomadic tribe in the northern part of Sumatra, Indonesia. This village was located along Changi Road.

Kampong Batu Koyak (e)
Batu means stone and *koyak* means broken in Malay. *Batu koyak* is broken stone. This village was in Pulau Tekong.

Kampong Belimbing (e)
Belimbing is star fruit in Malay. This village was located near 15 ms Choa Chu Kang Road.

Kampong Beremban (e)
Beremban is a cross beam in Malay. This village was located at the junction of Lorong Halus and Lorong Lumut.

Kampong Berih (e)/Road (e)
Berih is the name of a local tree, *Quercus spp*. Berih was written as Beireh in the 1950 Street Directory and Bereh in 1972 Street Directory.

Kampong Bintang (e)
Bintang means star in Malay. Kampong Bintang was probably named in 1907 after the Bintang Oil Mill (established in 1897). The village, if existed, was gone by the 1950s and Kampong Bintang was a dead end road.

Source: *SFP, 1907.12.17:1*

Kampong Blukang (e)
This village was named after Sungei Blukang.

Kampong Bugis/Bugis Crescent
See *Bugis Street*. The above two roads are located off Kallang Road.

Kampong Bunga Raya (e)
Bunga raya is the Malay name for Hibiscus. This village only appeared once in the Street Directory of 1950. It was located in Geylang Road.

Kampong Chai Chee (e)
See *Chai Chee Avenue*.

Kampong Chantek (e)/Kampong Chantek Bahru (e)
Chantek means pretty and *bahru* means new in Malay. In 1953, the land in Kampong Chantek was acquired and the villagers had to move to Kampong Chantek Bahru at 6.5 ms Dunearn Road. The village was named in 1953.

Source: *RBAR, 1953:8*

Kampong Che Jevah (e) (Pulau Ubin)
The village was located near Chek Jawa (at the cape).

Kampong Cheng Tong (e)
The village was located at Thomson Road, it was named in 1929.

Source: *MC, 1929.9.27*

Kampong Chia Heng (e)
This village was named after Leow Chia Heng (1874–1934, Teochew) who was in the rubber, pepper, gambier and textile business. He expanded into rubber plantations and became one of the founders of Sze Hai Tong Bank.

He was also one of the founders of the Chinese Chamber of Commerce. This village, located at 5 ms Thomson Road, was named in 1929.

Source: *MC, 1929.7.26; Kua: 203*

Kampong Chin Guan (e)
This village was located at 5 ms Thomson Road.

Kampong Coconut Plantation (e)
This village was located at 14.5 ms Woodlands Road.

Kampong Coronation (e)
There were two villages with this name, in Tengah and Jalan Haji Alias. However, the exact locations were not known.

Kampong Cutforth (e)
This village was located at 12 ms Choa Chu Kang Road.

Kampong Damar Darat (e)
Damar is the resin or gum exuded by certain trees and *darat* means land in Malay. This village was located around Boon Lay Road.

Kampong Darat Nanas (e)
Darat means land and *nanas* means pineapple. The village was located behind the Changi Prisons. *See Jalan Darat Nanas.*

Kampong Dua (e)
See Kampong Ampat.

Kampong Eng Ho Hng (e)
This village was located at Thomson Road and was seen in news reports as early as 1938.

Source: *ST 1938.1.17:1*

Kampong Eunos
See Jalan Eunos.

Kampong Gian Thye Road (e)
This village along Thomson Road was named in 1929 after Chua Gian Thye (1865–1911, Hokkien). He served as a Municipal Commissioner for eight years.

Source: *MC, 1929.9.27; Kua: 205; Savage & Yeoh, 2004*

Kampong Haji Karim (e)
This village was located at Tampines Road. It was vacated for the expansion of Paya Lebar Airport in 1971. *See Jalan Haji Karim.*

Kampong Harvey (e)
This village was located at Harvey Avenue. *See Harvey Avenue.*

Kampong Hock Soon (e)
This village was located at Lorong 3, Geylang.

Kampong Jagoh (e)
Jagoh is a creeper-vine in Malay. This was a village in Telok Blangah.

Kampong Java (e)/Kampong Java Road
Java is an island of Indonesia where its capital city is located. The island dominates Indonesia politically, economically and culturally. Based on a report in 1881, residents in Kampong Java were mostly Javanese immigrants. This was in line with the original town plan of segregating residential areas by races.

Source: *STOJ, 1881.5.12:2; NAS, 1255:3*

Kampong Java Teban (e)
Java is an Indonesian island (*see Kampong Java*). *Teban* means money deposited or bet in Malay, it is also a place name in Indonesia. The name Java was probably used for differentiation from Kampong Teban at Tampines (*see Kampong Teban*). In a news article in 1980, it was reported that before roads were built to the Jurong area, commuters from Pasir Panjang had to disembark at Kampong Java Teban to take a boat across the Jurong River, which was infested with crocodiles.

Source: *ST, 1980.2.14:6*

Kampong Jelutong (e)
See Jalan Jelutong.

Kampong Kachor (e)
Kachor or *kachar* means angling in Malay. This village was located at Alexandra Road.

Kampong Kallang (e)
This was one of the oldest villages in Singapore. Based on a news article in 1951, villagers here lived at the river shore on stilt houses until 1932 when it was vacated for the construction of Kallang Airport.

Source: *ST, 1951.8.11:6*

Kampong Kapor (e)/Kampong Kapor Road (Kampong Kapor)
Kapor, *Dryobalanops aromatic*, also spelt *Kapur* or *Kapore* in Malay, is the Camphor tree. Based on a news report in 1881, the villagers here mainly came from the Bawean Island of Indonesia. Kampong Kapor Road became a public street in 1914.

Source: *STOJ, 1881.5.12:2; MC, 1914.11.27; NAS, 1255:3; Boo: 574*

Kampong Kayu Road
Kayu means wood in Malay. *See Tanjong Rhu Road.*

Kampong Kebun Bahru (e)
Kebun means garden and *bahru* means new in Malay. This village was located in Ang Mo Kio, near the present Ang Mo Kio Industrial Park 2.

Kampong Kebun Ubi (e)
Kebun ubi is a tapioca garden in Malay. This village was located in the Dunearn Road area.

Kampong Kembangan (e)
This village was located at 5 ms Changi Road. *See Jalan Kembangan.*

Kampong Kitin (e)
This village was at the north coast facing Seletar Island.

Kampong Kling (e)
This village was located around 5 ms Pasir Panjang Road. *See Chulia Street.*

Kampong Kopit (e) (Pulau Brani)
Kopit means narrowly open in Malay.

Kampong Kranji (e)
This village was situated along Kranji Road.

Kampong Kuchai (Koo Chye) (e)
"Kuchai" is the transcription of chives in Hokkien. This village was located at the end of Lorong 3, Geylang across the upper reaches of Kallang River.

Kampong Ladang (e)
See Jalan Ladang. There were two villages with this name, one in Pulau Tekong and the other between Jalan Jumat and Jalan Checkor.

Kampong Lama Road (e)
Lama means old in Malay. This road was named in 1932 for a section of Kampong Bahru Road.
Source: *ST, 1932.8.15:16*

Kampong Lew Lian (e)
See Lorong Lew Lian.

Kampong Lima (e)
See Kampong Ampat.

Kampong Loyang (e)
This village was located at the end of Kuala Loyang Road. *See Loyang Avenue.*

Kampong Mamam (e) (Pulau Ubin)
See Jalan Mamam.

Kampong Mandai Kechil (e)
See Mandai Road. Kechil means small in Malay. This village was named in 1955.
Source: *RBAR, 1955:9*

Kampong Marican (e)
This village was located at 3 ms Serangoon Road.

Kampong Martin (e)
See *Martin Road*.

Kampong Melayu (e) (Pulau Tekong)
Melayu is the old name for Malays.

Kampong Noordin (e) (Pulau Tekong)

Kampong O'Carrol Scott (e)
This village was located at the present National University Hospital. It was named after Major General A G O'Carrol Scott, who was the GOC, Singapore from 1951 to 1954. British military facilities around this location included the Gillman Barracks, Alexandra Barracks and Alexandra Hospital.
Source: *ST, 1954.1.14:7*

Kampong Pachitan (e)
This village was located at 5.5 ms Changi Road. See *Pachitan Dua*.

Kampong Pahang (e)
This village was named after the State of Pahang in the east of Peninsula Malaya. There were two villages with this name, one in Radin Mas and the other in Pulau Tekong.

Kampong Pasir (e)/Kampong Pasir Merah (e) (Pulau Tekong)
Pasir means sand and *merah* means red in Malay.

Kampong Pasir Ris (e)
See *Pasir Ris Avenue*.

Kampong Pengkalan Kundor (e)
Pengkalan is a pier in Malay. *Kundor* or *kundur* means wax gourd in Malay. This village was located near MacRitchie Reservoir.

Kampong Pengkalan Pakau (e) (Pulau Tekong)
Pakau is a game of cards or trimming, framework in Malay.

Kampong Pengkalan Petai (e)
See *Jalan Petai*. This village was located at 10 ms Yio Chu Kang Road.

Kampong Permatang (e) (Pulau Tekong)
Permatang means rising lane in Malay.

Kampong Potong Pasir (e)
This village was located along the Kallang River near Woodleigh and was named in 1929. It was vacated in 1982. See *Potong Pasir Avenue*.
Source: *MC, 1929.12.27*

Kampong Pulau Damar Darat (e)
See *Kampong Damar Darat*. This village was located east of Jurong Pier Way, facing the Damar Laut Island.

Kampong Pulau Kerchil (e)
Kerchil means small in Malay. Kampong Pulau Kerchil means village in a small island. The small island was Pulau Seraya, now part of Jurong Island.

Kampong Punggol (e)
See *Punggol Road*.

Kampong Quarry (e)
This village was located near Hindhede Road, leading to the Hindhede Quarry.

Kampong Radin Mas (e)
See *Radin Mas*.

Kampong Reteh (e)
This village was situated near the Jalan Eunos Malay Settlement. See *Jalan Reteh*.

Kampong Rhu (e) (Tanjong Rhu Road)

Kampong Roko (e)
This village was located at Kallang Road in the town plan of 1886. *Roko* means cigarette in Malay.
Source: *SFP, 1886.7.17:33*

Kampong Salabin (e) (Pulau Tekong)
See *Kampong Selabin*.

Kampong Sambau (e)
This village was located at the end of Palmer Road at the seashore. See *Sambau Street*.

Kampong San Teng (e)
"San Teng" was derived from "Peck San Teng". See *Bishan Lane*.

This village was named in 1927. Residents in this village were relocated in the early 1980s to make way for the development of Bishan New Town.
Source: *MC, 1927.1.28; ST, 1985.5.28:14*

(Kampong Sanyongkong (Sam Yong Kong)/Kampong Sanyongkong Parit) (e) (Pulau Tekong)
Parit means groove or moat in Malay. The two villages above were probably named after the Pulau Sanyongkong across the sea.

Kampong Satu (e)
See *Kampong Ampat*.

Kampong Sek Lim (e)
See Koh Sek Lim Road.

Kampong Selabin (e) (Pulau Tekong)
Selabin, sometimes written as salabin, was once the property of the Sultan of Trengganu in Malaysia.

Kampong Semenei (e) (Pulau Tekong)

Kampong Seng Kong Parit (e) (Pulau Tekong)
Parit means groove or moat in Malay.

Kampong Serangoon Kechil (e)
See Jalan Seranggong Kechil.

Kampong Seraya (e)
This village was located at the former Pulau Seraya. See Seraya Avenue.

Kampong Silat (e)
See Silat Avenue.

Kampong Sireh
Sireh is the betal-leaf in Malay. This village was located at 6 ms Upper Serangoon Road.

Kampong Songa (e)
Songa or sunga is an edible leaf used to spice curry in Malay. This village was located at 16.5 ms Jurong Road.

Kampong Soo Poo (e)
Kampong Soo Poo was both a village and a road. They were located opposite Kampong Bugis and were named in 1906. This was an area occupied by the Boyans from Indonesia. According to a press article in 1951, the Boyans monopolised the employment of syce and stableboys in the horse era. It was left with a dead-end road by 1950.
Source: MC, 1906.11.30; ST, 1951.4.14:6; NAS, 1953:6

Kampong Sultan (e)
This village was located at 5.5 ms Pasir Panjang Road. This road was declared a public street in 1951.
Source: RBAR, 1951:8

Kampong Sungei Attap (e)
See Attap Road. Sungei means river in Malay. This village was near Jurong River.

Kampong Sungei Belang (e) (Pulau Tekong)
See Jalan Sungei Belang.

Kampong Sungei Blukar (e)
Blukar or *belukar* means secondary jungle in Malay. This village was named after Sungei Blukar, a small river that flowed into the Serangoon Harbour at Johore Straits in the past. Following land reclamation in this area, the river now flows into the Serangoon Reservoir.

Kampong Sungei Buloh (e)
Buloh was spelt Booloh in the early years. *Buloh* means bamboo, hollow cylinders in Malay. The village was located around Kranji Road.
Source: *SFP, 1848.5.18:3*

Kampong Sungei China (e)
Sungei China is a creek close to the Causeway to Johor. There could be a village along this creek. However, in the 1970s Kampong Sungei China was a road connected to Woodlands Road near the Causeway.
Source: *SD, 1972:115*

Kampong Sungei Jurong (e)
This village was located at 11 ms Jurong Road, north of the present Chinese Garden.

Kampong Sungei Nior (e)
Nior or *nyiur*, means coconut in Malay. This village was located at 9 ms Punggol Road.

Kampong Sungei Pandan (e)
See *Pandan Avenue*. This village was located at 9.5 ms Pasir Panjang Road.

Kampong Sungei Perempuan (e) (former Singapore Naval Base)
Perempuan means women in Malay.

Kampong Sungei Tengah (e)
Tengah means middle in Malay. This village was located at 9 ms Punggol Road, near the present location of Compassvale Lane.

Kampong Sungei Tuas (e)
This village was located at 18 ms Jurong Road. See *Tuas Avenue*.

Kampong Tanah Merah Kechil (e)
See *Tanah Merah Kechil Avenue*.

Kampong Tanjong (e)
Tanjong means cape in Malay. This village was located at Pasir Panjang Road.

Kampong Tanjong Balai (e)
This village was located at the south end of Jalan Tepong. See *Tanjong Balai*.

Kampong Tanjong Irau (e)
This village was located at the end of Sembawang Road, near Kampong Wak Hassan.

Kampong Tanjong Kling (e)
This village was located at the southeast end of Tanjong Kling Road. It was demolished to build the Jurong Industrial Estate in 1964. *See Chulia Street.*

Source: *ST, 1964.7.2:11*

Kampong Tanjong Pelandok (e)
Pelandok is a smaller chevrotin or mousedeer in Malay. This village was located around 11 ms West Coast Road.

Kampong Tanjong Penjuru (e)
See Tanjong Penjuru.

Kampong Teban (e)
Teban existed as a Malay village off Serangoon River in J T Thomson's survey map of 1852. Kampong Teban was located around 7 ms Tampines Road. *See Jalan Teban.*

Source: *STOJ, 1881.9.29:13; NAS, SP006362*

Kampong Tebing Terjun (e)
This village was located at 11 ms Jurong Road. *See Jalan Tebing Terjun.*

Kampong Tengah (e)
Tengah means middle in Malay. There were two villages with this name, one at 15 ms Sembawang Road and the other near RAF Tengah. There was also a Kampong Sungei Tengah at 9 ms Punggol Road.

Kampong Teo Chew (e)
This village was located along Grange Road with residents of mostly Teochew ancestry. It was named in 1926.

Source: *MC1, 1926.6.15*

Kampong Tiga (e)
See Kampong Ampat.

Kampong Todak (e) (Pulau Tekong)
Todak is swordfish in Malay.

Kampong Toh Guan (e)
This village was located at 10 ms West Coast Road. It was named in 1954. *See Jalan Toh Guan.*

Source: *RBAR, 1954:8*

Kampong Tongkang Pechah (e)
This village was located at 8.25 ms Yio Chu Kang Road, close to the end of Sungei Punggol. *See Jalan Tongkang Pechah.*

Kampong Tulloch (e)

This village was located near the campus of the National University of Singapore (NUS) at Ayer Rajah Road. It was named after Major General Derek D C Tulloch (born 1904). Tulloch was the GOC, Singapore Base District, from 1954 to 1957. *See Kampong O'Carrol Scott.*

Source: *ST, 1957.3.27:9*

Kampong Ubi (e)

Ubi means tapioca in Malay. This was the part of Geylang Serai which was designated for cultivation of tapioca during the Japanese Occupation. Due to shortage of rice, the Malays in this area were offered land to cultivate tapioca as an alternate staple food which gave its name. Roads in this village were named after vegetables such as *kobis* (cabbage), *bayam* (spinach), *tauge* (bean sprout), etc.

Kampong Ulu Jurong (e)

Ulu Jurong is the upper reaches of the Jurong River. This village was located around 12 ms Jurong Road. *See Jurong Road.*

Kampong Ulu Pandan (e)

Ulu Pandan is the upper reaches of Sungei Pandan. This village was located at 10 ms Jurong Road. *See Pandan Road.*

Kampong Unum (Onom) (e) (Pulau Tekong)

This village was named after Sungei Unum or Pulau Unum across the sea. *See Jalan Unum.*

Kampong Wak Hassan

Wak Hassan means Uncle Hassan in Malay. This road was named after the village of the same name which was relocated for the construction of the former Singapore Naval Base. The village was purportedly established by Wak Hassan bin Ali around 1914. Leading to Kampong Wak Hassan, is a group of road names of fishes, trees or plants.

Source: *NAS, 784:4; Tan: 27*

Kampong Wak Selat (e)

This village was located in the Kranji area. It was vacated in 1993. *See Jalan Wak Selat.*

Source: *ST, 1993.4.9:36*

Kampong Wak Tanjong (e)

Based on a news article in 1936, Wak Tanjong was a Muslim from Malacca. His grandson was Abdul Manan bin Mohamed Ali, a court translator for 34 years. This village was located in the Sims Avenue area.

Source: *ST, 1936.12.20:12*

Kampong Wayang Satu (e)
Wayang means opera and *satu* means first in Malay. The road name means first opera village and was located at the junction of Dunearn Road and Trevose Crescent. It was named in 1926.
Source: *MC1, 1926.7.1*

Kampong Wing Loong (e)
See Wing Loong Road.

Kampong Woodleigh (e)
See Woodleigh Close.

Kampong Yeo Tiong (e)
"Tiong" is a transcription of cemetery in Hokkien. Yeo is a Chinese family name. "Yeo Tiong" was a cemetery for the Yeo clan. This village was located in Telok Blangah, near the other Yeo clan cemetery at Heap Guan Village. *See Heap Guan Village.*

Kandahar Street (Kampong Glam)
This road lies within the Kampong Glam conservation area. It was named in 1909. Kandahar is the second largest city in Afghanistan. *See Arab Street.*
Source: *MC, 1909.10.1*

Kandis Lane/Walk
See Jalan Kandis and Kampong Wak Hassan.

Kang Ching Road
"Kang Ching" means hill view in Chinese. This road is in the vicinity of Jurong Hill. *See Ho Ching Road.*

Kang Choo Bin Road/Walk
This road was named in 1949.
Source: *RBAR, 1949:9*

Kanisha Marican Road (e)
Kanisha Marican could be the name of an Indian or a company. The company name was seen in the news in 1887. The road name was first seen in the press in 1905.
Source: *ST, 1887.7.13:2; ST, 1905.6.21:5*

Kaolin Lane (e)
Kaolin is a hill in Jin De Zhen, a town in the province of Jiangxi, China. Kaolin was so famous in the West for its fine clay (essential for the production of fine china) that it became the name of the clay.

Kapur Lane (e) (Kampong Kapor)
This lane was named in 1906. *See Kampong Kapor Road.*

Source: *ED, 1906.12.1:4*

Karamat Road (e)
This place name was a misprint of Keramat Road.

Karikal Lane (e)/Road (e)
Karikal Road was between East Coast Road and Karikal Mahal, the residence of Moona Kader Sultan, from Karikal in southeast India. He was the King of Cattle Trade. Both roads above were named in 1930. Karikal Road was declared a public street in 1968 and was renamed as Still Road South in 1978.

Source: *MC, 1930.6.27; MC, 1930.8.29; ST, 1968.5.31:19; NAS, 74:36*

Kasai Road
Kasai is a cosmetic face powder in Malay.

Katmandu Road
This road was named after Katmandu, the capital of Nepal. *See Nepal Park.*

Kay Hai Road (e)
The above road was named in 1948 after Chua Kay Hai (1891–1939, Hokkien) who was a Manager at Ho Hong Bank and United Overseas Bank. He was also a member of the Municipal Commission.

Source: *SFP, 1948.7.17:5; Kua: 205*

Kay Poh Road
This road was probably named in 1930 after Wee Kay Poh (died 1915), Manager of the trading company, Po Hin Chan. After buying some properties in Raffles Place at an auction for 2,000 dollars, he was embroiled in a law suit in 1890 as the ownership of the properties were under dispute. Nevertheless, Wee was awarded the rights to the properties by the Court.

Source: *ST, 1915.10.15:6; MC, 1930.10.31; Song: 316*

Kay Siang Road
This road was named in 1930 after Wee Kay Siang (1858–1925) as the Administrator of his Estate provided the land for this road without charge. Wee was a trader and landowner who started as a produce-storekeeper in Messrs. Brinkmann and Co. He was once the Managing Partner of spirit and opium farms in Singapore and Hong Kong and the Managing Director of Kwong Yik Bank.

Source: *ST, 1925.8.1:10; MC, 1930.6.27*

Keat Hong Close/Link/Village (e)
Keat Hong Village was named in 1938. It was located at Choa Chu Kang Road, close to RAF Tengah.

Source: *SFP, 1938.8.12:3*

Kedondong Road (e)
Kedondong is a tree bearing a fruit that resembles the hog-plum. This road was named in 1957.

Source: *RBAR, 1957:8*

Kee Ann Road (e)
Based on a news article in 1985, Kee Ann was one of the uncles of Lim Nee Soon.

Source: *ST, 1985.2.1:21*

Kee Choe Avenue (Sennett Estate)
This road was built during the first phase of development of Sennett Estate by the Sennett Realty Estate Limited on the original site of the old Alkaff Garden (see *Angsana Avenue*). Road names in this phase used personal names of directors of the company and other well known personalities. Beside Kee Choe Avenue, there were Kwong Avenue, Pheng Geck Avenue, Puay Hee Avenue, Siak Kew Avenue, Siang Kuang Avenue, Tai Thong Crescent and Wan Tho Avenue. These personal names were approved by the Public Works Committee of the City Council in 1951 on account of the fact that some of the names were already incorporated in legal documents. There is however no information about Mr. Kee Choe.

Source: *CC, 1951.9.28*

Kee Hua Road (e)
Kee Hua was the pen name of Lim Nee Soon. A report in 1985 said that Kee Hua was an elder in Shantou who was very well respected by Lim Nee Soon. If this was true, then it cannot be the pen name of Lim Nee Soon since it would be considered disrespectful in Chinese custom. Based on a news article in 1985, the road name was changed from West Hill Avenue 3 around 1962. See *Nee Soon Road* and *West Hill Avenue*.

Source: *ST, 1985.2.1:21*

Kee Seng Street
Tan Ti Seng was the head of a secret society; his name became Kee Seng when the road was named after him in 1901. Kee Seng Street is located in the Tanjong Pagar area.

Source: *MC, 1901.12.18; ST, 1989.4.5:5; T Pagar: 135*

Kee Sun Avenue/Drive (e)/Road (e)
Chan Kee Sun was a Cantonese who worked for the Asia Petroleum Company, the predecessor of Shell Petroleum. He was a public spirited man and was good at resolving differences between groups of people. With this skill he helped to end a number of industrial strikes. He was conferred the title of Justice of the Peace in 1927 and was on the honour roll of the Governor in 1939.

However, in the same year, part of Kee Sun Avenue was renamed Elliot Road. In 1947, the special names for all three roads above were replaced by the name of Tay Lian Teck. Finally in 1956, the road name of Kee Sun Avenue was reinstated. All these roads are located off Upper East Coast Road.

Source: *ST, 1939.3.23:12; ST, 1939.6.9:13; SFP, 1947.3.17:5; RBAR, 1956:9; Kong: 146*

Keene Road (former Tanglin Barracks)

Keene is an English name, meaning proud or brave. *See Barrack Road.*

Kelantan Lane/Road

Kelantan is a northern state of Malaysia. Pursuant to the Bangkok Treaty of 1909 between Britain and Thailand, the latter surrendered the governing rights to the British for Kedah, Kelantan, Perlis and Trengganu. This road was declared a public street in 1929.

Source: *SFP, 1929.7.27:11*

Kellock Road

J R Kellock was an Agent of the Peninsular & Oriental Steam Navigation Co. between 1875 and 1877. He resigned as a member of the Municipal Commission in 1877 and left for India. Kellock Road became a public street in 1960.

Source: *ST, 1877.5.26:15; CCAR, 1960:7; Dunlop*

Kelopak Road

Kelopak means sepal or calyx of a flower in Malay. *See Kampong Wak Hassan.*

Kelulut Hill

Kelulut is a small bee or a common shrub, *Uraena lobata* or *Cyathila prostrate* in Malay.

Kempas Road

This road was named in 1929 together with four other roads in the Lavender Street area: Idris Road, Petaling Road, Rawang Road and Tronoh Road. These were named after well known Malayan companies related to the tin mines and rubber industries which were mainly British-owned at that time. They were Kempas Ltd, Idris Hydraulic Tin Ltd, Petaling Tin Ltd, Rawang Tin Mining Company and Tronoh Mines Ltd.

Source: *MC, 1929.3.27; SIT 1158/28*

Kenanga Avenue (Sennett Estate)

Kenanga or *kenenga* is the Malay name for *Cananga odorata*, a tropical tree that is valued for the perfume extracted from its flowers called ylang-ylang. This road was named in 1951. *See Angsana Avenue.*

Source: *CC, 1951.9.28; Boo: 539*

Keng Cheow Street

Tan Keng Cheow (died c.1903) was a Hokkien in the business of ship chandlers. In 1879, he applied for a license to set up a steam laundry. The Singapore Steam Laundry was established at Stevens Road. However, the venture was met with strong resistance from the Indian laundry workers and closed after four years.

Source: *STOJ, 1879.4.19:3; Kua: 77; Song: 205*

Keng Chin Road

Chia Keng Chin (1865-1919) took over the ownership of Ann Lock & Co. from his elders. The company dealt with liquor and equestrian goods. Chia was one of the founders of the Straits Chinese Recreation Club. He was a Municipal Commissioner in 1910 and a member of the Legislative Council in 1913.

The descendents of Lim Keng Chin (1867-1934) claimed that this road was originally named after Lim Keng Chin as a private road and was conceded to Chia in 1927. Lim Keng Chin was the President of the Singapore Foo Chow Association.

This road was officially named in 1927.

Source: *ST, 1919.5.30:8; MC, 1927.1.28; Kua: 194; Savage & Yeoh, 2004; Song: 216*

Keng Kiat Street

Lee Keng Kiat (1851-1917) was an Assistant Manager of the Straits Steamship Co. Ltd. Keng Kiat Street is located in the (pre-war) Tiong Bahru housing estate and was named before 1936.

Source: *ST, 1917.2.19:10; SG-1936; Singam*

Keng Lee Road

Chng Keng Lee (1857-1934, Hokkien) was born in Malacca. His father was a rice merchant and shipowner. He ventured to Saigon (now Ho Chi Min City) at the age of 17 to work as a comprador in a rice milling factory. In 1911, Chng came to Singapore and established Chng Keng Lee Company with a friend. The company was in the property business as an auctioneer, valuer and broker. He was a member of the Municipal Commission for nine years (1905-1914). Keng Lee Road was named in 1928.

Source: *MC, 1928.10.26; SFP, 1934.9.3:3; Kua: 19*

Kenler Road (e) (former RAF Changi)

This road was named after RAF Kenler (1917-1959) outside London. RAF Kenler was one of the three main fighter stations during WW2. *See Abbotsingh Road.*

Kensington Park Drive/Road
Kensington Road (e) (Serangoon Gardens)
Kensington Park Road was named in 1953. Kensington is a district in West London. *See Alnwick Road.*

Source: *RBAR, 1953:8*

Kent Ridge Crescent/Drive/Road
Kent Ridge was originally named Gap Hill. It was renamed Kent Ridge in honour of the Duchess of Kent (Princess Marina of Greece, 1906-1968) and her son, the Duke of Kent (he was Prince Edward of Kent before he took over his father's title). The royals visited the British military installations on this hill in 1952. In 1954, the hill was renamed Kent Ridge and a plaque was erected to commemorate their visit. Two highest points on the hill were also named as Marina Hill and Prince Edward Point.

Source: *ST, 1954.2.24:4*

Kent Road (Race Course Road area)
This road was named in 1927. Kent is a county in South East England. *See Bristol Road.*

Source: *MC, 1927.9.30*

Kenya Crescent (former Singapore Naval Base)
Kenya was a British colony in Africa before WW2. *See Admiralty Road.*

Keong Saik Road
Tan Keong Saik (1850-1909, Hokkien) was a Director at a shipping company. He was one of the founders of the Chinese Chamber of Commerce. Keong Saik Road was named in 1926.

Source: *ST, 1909.9.30:7; MC, 1926.11.26; Kua: 90*

Keow Neo Road (e)

Keppel Bay Drive/View/Vista
Keppel Drive 2, 3, 5, 6
Keppel Hill/Keppel Road
Keppel Street C-G, I-L
Keppel Terminal Avenue
(Keppel Terminal Road K, M, N) (e)
(Keppel Terminal Street 6, 7) (e)
Keppel Way (e)
The above roads were named after Admiral of the Fleet Sir Henry Keppel (1809-1904). Admiral Keppel was credited for ensuring the safety of passage in the South China Sea by making successful operations against the Borneo pirates. He also took part in both Opium Wars against China.

Keppel Harbour was originally named New Harbour. It was renamed Keppel Harbour in 1900 when Admiral Keppel agreed to the change in name. The road leading to the harbour, New Harbour Road, which was commissioned on 2 January 1896, was accordingly renamed Keppel Road.

Source: *ST, 1886.1.30:7; SFP, 1900.2.10:2; Buckley: 493*

Keramat Road (former Singapore Naval Base)
Keramat means holy grave or shrine in Malay. *See Admiralty Road.*

Kerbau Lane (e)/Road
Kerbau means buffalo in Malay. There were cow sheds and abattoirs around this area. In 1896, frontagers paid for the repair to this road before the Municipality would declare it as a public street.

Source: *ST, 1896.8.15:3*

Keris Drive
See Jalan Keris and Jalan Azam.

Kerong Lane/Walk
Kerong kerong is a large-scaled Terapon (a type of fish) in Malay. *See Kampong Wak Hassan.*

Kerr Street (e) (Kampong Malacca)
This street was probably named in 1882 together with other roads in Kampong Malacca South. Its earliest press appearance was in 1892. It was likely to be named after William Graham Kerr, who started his business in 1852 under the name of W G Kerr & Co. in partnership with A Nugent. In 1857, he joined the partnership of Martin Dyce & Co. He was a member of the Grand Jury in 1856 to 1857 and was associated with W H Read in agitating against the introduction of the copper coin of India. *See Angus Street.*

The source of this road name was generally believed to be William P W Ker, the Director of Paterson, Simons & Co. This is doubtful as he arrived in Singapore in 1900, after the street was named.

Source: *SFP, 1853.4.8:2; SFP, 1856.7.18:1; MC, 1882.4.19; SFP, 1892.10.18:2; Makepeace, vol.2:450; Singam*

Kew Avenue/Crescent/Drive/Heights/Lane/Terrace/Walk
Kew Drive was named in 1955, probably after the renowned Kew Gardens in England.

Source: *RBAR, 1955:9; Watts*

Khalsa Crescent (former Singapore Naval Base)
Khalsa is a Sikh temple or religious rites for the Sikhs. This road was within the prison compound of the Naval Base.

Kheam Hock Road

Tan Kheam Hock (1862–1922) was the son of wealthy merchant Tan Teng Pong in Penang. He came to Singapore in 1889 and was connected with the opium and spirit farms. In 1901, he became a contractor to the Tanjong Pagar Dock Company for the supply of coolie labour to the dock. This continued later with the Singapore Harbour Board. He was appointed a Municipal Commissioner in 1910, a post he held till the time of his death. In addition, he was a member of the Hokkien Advisory Board and director of many public companies. This road was named in 1923.

Source: *ST, 1923.6.6:10; Song: 258*

Khiang Guan Avenue

Tan Khiang Guan was one of the founders of the Gambier and Pepper Association. This road was named in 1952.

Source: *ST, 1952.10.18:4; Savage & Yeoh, 2004*

Kian Hong Road (e)

This road was named in 1956 after Kian Hong Rubber Plantation at 12 ms Jurong Road. The plantation was owned by Toh Kim Chiu, a Hokkien businessman.

Source: *RBAR, 1956:9; ZB Special Supplement, 2014.11.20:19*

Kian Teck Avenue/Crescent/Drive/Lane/Road/Way

Kian Teck Road was first seen in the 1963 Street Directory.

Kilburn Estate (e)

This estate was located at 6.5 ms Bukit Timah Road. Kilburn is a multiple place name in England. *See Denham Close.*

Killiney Road

This road was named after Killiney House, which was probably named after Killiney, the seaside resort and suburb of Dublin. Based on a news article in 1886, Killiney House, built atop Oxley Hill in 1842, was the residence of Dr. Thomas Oxley, a government surgeon who was in Singapore from 1830 to 1857. *See Oxley Road.*

Source: *SFP, 1886.10.16:8*

Kim Cheng Street

Tan Kim Cheng (1829–1892, Hokkien), was the son of Tan Tock Seng. He was a Chinese community leader for more than 30 years and acted as consul in Singapore for Japan, Thailand and Russia. His English name was spelt as Kim Ching and Kim Cheng. This street in the (pre-war) Tiong Bahru housing estate was listed in the 1936 Gazetteer and was officially named in 1941. *See Seng Poh Road.*

Source: *MC, 1941.4.25; SG-1936; Kua: 82*

Kim Chuan Drive/Lane/Road/Terrace/Village (e)
Kim Chuan Road was named after Ng Kim Chuan (1885-1958, Hokkien) who owned a factory processing copra and rubber at Paya Lebar Road. The road was best known for the big fire in 1950 that destroyed the Aik Hoe Rubber Factory (owned by Tan Lark Sye) which resulted in losses of more than 10 million dollars.
Source: *Kua: 177*

Kim Keat Avenue/Close/Lane/Link/Road
Choa Kim Keat (1859-1907, Hokkien), was the son-in-law of Tan Kim Cheng (see *Kim Cheng Street*). He was in charge of Tan's rice business and at the same time was a horticultural enthusiast. The most recent news about him was the sale of his holiday bungalow in Marine Parade by his descendents in 2011.

Kim Keat Avenue was declared a public street in 1957.

Kim Keat Road was named in 1901.

Source: *MC, 1901.12.18; SFP, 1907.1.8:8; CCAR, 1957:5; Kua: 207*

Kim Pong Road
Low Kim Pong (died 1909, Hokkien) started his business in Chinese herbal medicine under the shop name of Chop Ban San (see *Ban San Street*) and expanded into the remittance business (see *Hock Lam Street*). He was one of the founder members of the Singapore Chamber of Commerce. Low was noted for building the Siang Lim (or Shuang Lin) Temple in the Kim Keat area jointly with Yeo Poon Seng. The temple was built from 1904 to 1910 at a cost of 500,000 dollars.

Kim Pong Road is located in the (pre-war) Tiong Bahru housing estate and was named before 1936. *See Seng Poh Road.*

Source: *ST, 1909.12.20:7; SG-1936; SD, 1954:15; Kua: 24*

Kim Seng Place (e)/Promenade/Road/Walk
Tan Kim Seng (1805-1864, Hokkien), was a prominent Peranakan merchant and philanthropist in the 19th century. Tan's contributions to the public included the building and maintenance of the Chui Eng Institute and Chong Fu Girls' School. He also paid for the building of Kim Seng Bridge across the Singapore River. He was noted for his generous donation to the first proposed public water works for fresh water supply to the town. However, due to delays and changes in the project, his donation was found to be too small for the huge water works which was eventually completed in 1878 at MacRitchie Reservoir. Nevertheless the Municipal Commission decided to commemorate his generosity by building the Tan Kim Seng Fountain, now located at the Esplanade Park.

Kim Seng Place was built by him. It was first named after him in 1859 and changed in 1928 to Beng Swee Place, the name of his elder son.

Source: *ST, 1859.10.8:3; MC1, 1928.5.1; Kua: 81*

Kim Tian Place/Road/Kim Tian's Pier (e)

Tan Kim Tian (died 1883) started working as a junior staff at Paterson, Simons & Co. He was later made an officer-in-charge of the warehouse. In 1849, he started his own Tan Kim Tian Shipping Company and owned Kim Tian's Pier at Havelock Road along the Singapore River. Kim Tian Road was named before 1936.

Source: *ST, 1883.1.8:3; SG-1936*

Kim Yam Road

Wee Kim Yam (1855-1914, Teochew), was the son of Wee Ah Hood (*see Ah Hood Road*). He was one of the founder members of the Chinese Chamber of Commerce and gave up his family mansion (House of Wee Ah Hood) for the Chamber's venue. This road was named in 1899.

Source: *MC, 1899.11.8; Kua: 176*

Kin Pong Street (e)

This street was reported to be located between Angullia Street and Ophir Road. It might have been named in 1904 after Low Kim Pong. However, it was only seen once in the press reports and was not listed in the Street Directories. *See Kim Pong Road.*

Source: *ST, 1904.1.30:5*

Kinara Lane

Kinara is a Hindi word that means river.

King Albert Park

King Albert Park (the housing estate) began construction in 1939, during the reign of King George VI (1936-1952). He was known as Prince Albert of York from birth. He ascended the throne after his brother Edward VIII abdicated to marry a divorced woman. Four kings in Britain had Albert as part of their name during the last century; they are George VI, Edward VIII, George V and Edward VII. *See King George's Avenue.*

King George's Avenue

This road was named in 1926, during the reign of King George V (1910-1936).

Source: *MC, 1926.8.26*

King's Avenue (former Singapore Naval Base)
King's/Close/Drive/Road/Walk (Bukit Timah)
King's Place (e) (Singapore River)
See Admiralty Road and Deptford Road for King's Avenue.

King's Road was originally named King Edward Road when it was officially opened to celebrate the coronation of King Edward VII on 11 August 1902. A Annamalai, a surveyor (see *Namly Avenue*) and the owner of this large parcel of land officiated the opening of this road. The name was changed to King's Road in 1905 by the subsequent owner, Choa Lam, with the approval of the Municipal Commission.

King's Place was named in 1907 but was changed to Empress Place at the same Municipal meeting.

Source: *ST, 1902.8.11:5; MC, 1905.7.14; SFP, 1905.7.15:5; MC, 1907.3.1; ED, 1907.3.2:3*

Kingsmead Road
This road was probably named after Kingsmead in Hampshire, South East England.

Kingswear Avenue (Serangoon Gardens)
This road was named in 1953. Kingswear is a village in Devon, South West England. Kingswear Castle, a 15th century artillery tower is situated nearby. *See Alnwick Road.*

Source: *RBAR, 1953:8*

Kingswood Road (e)
Kingswood is a multiple place name in England.

Kinta Road
Kinta is one of the ten administrative districts of Perak, Malaysia. This place was one of the major producers of tin in the 18th century.

Kintyre Park (e)
This small road led to the Kintyre Park Estate at the end of the road. Kintyre is the name of a Peninsular in southwest of Scotland.

Kirk Terrace
Kirk is a Scottish word meaning a church or the Church of Scotland. It is also a personal name. This road was named in 1901.

Source: *MC, 1901.12.18; Singam*

Kismis Avenue/Green/Place/Road
Kismis means raisins in Malay.

Kitchener Link/Road (WW1 roads)
Kitchener Road was named in 1928 after Field Marshal Horatio Herbert Kitchener (1850-1916), one of the leading commanders in WW1. *See Allenby Road.*

Kitchener visited Singapore on 2 September 1909. He was appointed the Secretary of State for War in 1914 during WW1. However, he drowned on 5

June 1916 when the HMS *Hampshire* struck a German mine in the west of Scotland.

Source: *MC1, 1928.10.2; Makepeace, vol.2:607*

Klang Lane/Road

Klang was a royal city and former capital of the state of Selangor, Malaysia.

Klang Road was declared a public street in 1896.

Klang Lane was named in 1923.

Source: *ST, 1896.8.15:3; MC, 1923.3.29*

Kling Street (e)

This street was renamed Chulia Street in 1921 due to objection to the name "Kling" by the Indian community. *See Chulia Street.*

Source: *MC, 1921.6.24; Buckley: 73*

Kloof Road (e) (former Singapore Naval Base)

This road was named after Kloof, a suburb in greater Durban, South Africa. *See Admiralty Road.*

Knightsbridge (e) (former RAF Seletar)

This road was named after Knightsbridge, an exclusive residential and retail district in Central London. *See Baker Street.*

Koek Lane (e)/Road

Edwin Koek (died 1891) was a Dutch lawyer. He married the daughter of William Cuppage, the Acting Postmaster General who owned a large nutmeg plantation in Emerald Hill. After the nutmeg bliss, Koek turned the plantation into an orchard but his venture failed and he went bankrupt. He died in New York in December 1891. As he lived in New York under a different identity, the news of his death did not reach his family until February 1892. Nevertheless he was respected in his profession and served as a Municipal Commissioner.

Source: *ST, 1892.2.24:112; Kua: 160*

Koh Sek Lim Road

Koh Sek Lim (1868-1948) was the Changi King of Coconuts as he owned a huge coconut plantation in Changi before WW2. This road was named in 1952. Xilin Avenue in the same vicinity was also named after him. *See Xilin Avenue.*

Source: *ST, 1948.8.22:6; RBAR, 1952:8; Kua: 33*

Kok Nam Lane (e)

This road was named in 1952.

Source: *RBAR, 1952:8*

Kolam Ayer Lane (e)
This lane was named in 1921. *See Jalan Kolam Ayer.*
Source: *MC, 1921.12.20*

Kolam Rumput Track (e)
Rumput kolam is a type of grass in Malay.

Koo Chan Road (e)
This road was located in the Kallang area. It was named after Chan Koo Chan who established an agency business in 1852 and became the owner of many properties. However, his business was mismanaged by his son-in-law when he made his trip to his ancestor home in China. He was made a bankrupt in 1861.
Source: *Song: 117*

Koon Seng Road
Cheong Koon Seng (1878–1934) was the founder of Cheong Koon Seng Auctioneers and Valuers, a surveyor firm with the longest history in Singapore. This road was known as Lorong E, East Coast Road before it was renamed Koon Seng Road in 1934.
Source: *SFP, 1934.7.18:8; Kua: 156*

Kovan Close/Road
Kovan Road appeared in the press in 1953 as a road requiring repair by the Rural Board. Kovan Close was named in 1956.
Source: *ST, 1953.5.29:4; RBAR, 1956:9*

Kowloon Road (e) (former Singapore Naval Base)
Kowloon Peninsula became a British colony in 1860 after the Opium War. Its sovereignty was transferred back to China on 1 July 1997. *See Admiralty Road.*

Koyli Road (e) (former Tanglin Barracks)
Koyli is the acronym for King's Own Yorkshire Light Infantry. After WW2, the regiment took part in peacekeeping and counter-insurgency operations in the Far East, headquartered in Tanglin Barracks. *See Barrack Road.*
Source: *SFP, 1910.3.4:4*

Kramat Lane/Road
Kramat, same as *keramat*, is a holy grave or shrine in Malay.

Kramat Road was near a cemetery. It became a public street in 1931.

Kramat Lane was named in 1925.

Source: *MC, 1931.2.27; MC, 1925.7.31*

Kranji Crescent/Expressway/Link/Loop/Road/Way
Kranji was also written as Kranjee and the roads were named after the Kranjee River as shown in the survey map of Singapore c.1800. *Kranji* is the Malay name of a local tree, *Dialium Indum*, also known as the Velvet Tamarind tree as the flavour of its fruit is similar to Tamarind. Kranji Road was constructed in 1855.

Source: *SFP, 1848.5.18:3; SFP, 1893.4.3:2; NAS, SP006448; Buckley: 350; Makepeace, vol.2:64*

Kreta Ayer Road
Kreta means wheeled vehicle and *ayer* means water in Malay. Before the fresh water supply system was installed, bullock carts were used to transport fresh water from Ann Siang Hill or Spring Street to this area for distribution to Chinatown and surrounding areas. It could also be used for supply of water to the ships via Boat Quay. Kreta Ayer Road was named in 1922.

Source: *MC, 1922.4.27*

Kreta Road (e) (Former RAF Changi)
This road was located in Selarang Camp of RAF Changi. See *Selarang Avenue*.

Kuala Loyang Road (e)
Kuala means the mouth of the river in Malay. See *Loyang Avenue* for the etymylogy of *Loyang*. *Kuala* Loyang is the mouth of the Loyang River.

Kuching Road (e)
This road was named in 1930 after the Sarawak capital of Kuching. See *Borneo Road*.

Source: *MC, 1930.7.29*

Kulim Place (e) (Thiam Siew Village, Tanjong Katong)
Kulim is the name of a town in Kedah, Malaysia. See *Thiam Siew Avenue*.

Kumquat Road (e)
Kumquat is the fruit of a flowering plant in the *Rutaceae* family. The edible fruit closely resembles the orange but is much smaller.

Kung Chong Road
This road first appeared in the 1958 Street Directory. The name "Kung Chong" is a transcription of factory in Cantonese. See *Hoy Fatt Road*.

Kuo Chuan Avenue
This road was named in 1941 after Lee Kuo Chuan (1887-1915), the father of Lee Kong Chian (1893-1967, Hokkien). The younger Lee was an entrepreneur, businessman and philanthropist. He was the founder of the Lee Foundation and made generous donations to education and other needs of the society.

Source: *MC, 1941.7.26; Kua: 43*

Kurau Grove/Place/Terrace/Walk (e)
See *Telok Kurau Road.*

Kwong Avenue (Sennett Estate)
This road was named after A C T Kwong, the Chinese diplomat from Canton. He was the Consul of the Chinese Consulate in Singapore before and after WW2. Subsequently, he became the Manager of Sennett Realty Estate Limited, the developer of Sennett Estate. This road was named in 1951. See *Kee Choe Avenue.*

Source: *SFP, 1951.8.25:5; ST, 1951.9.27:7; CC, 1951.9.28; Kua: 11*

Kwong Min Road
This road was first seen in the 1969 Street Directory. See *Chia Ping Road.*

La Salle Street
This name originated from the French Priest John Baptist de la Salle (1651–1719), the founder of the Institute of the Brothers of the Christian School. The organisation helped set up various Christian schools in Singapore, including St. Joseph's Institution in 1852.

Labrador Villa Road
Labrador is a type of retriever-gun dog, a favourite disability assistance breed in many countries. It is also a place name in the eastern part of Canada. Based on an advertisement in 1883, Labrador Villa was built around 1882 as the mansion of G J Mansfield, a Partner of W Mansfield and Co. At the end of this road was the shore where the Batu Berlayer was supposed to be situated. The rock was believed to be the Dragon Tooth Gate mentioned in ancient Chinese literature as the navigational landmark of Singapore. It was named Lot's Wife during colonial days and was blown up in August 1848. See *Bukit Berlayer Road.*

Source: *ST, 1883.1.11:3; SD, 1954:16; Edwards: 319;* 汪大渊, 岛夷志略校释: 213

Lady Hill Road
This road was named in 1929 after the Ladyhill Estate.

Source: *MC, 1929.6.28*

Lagos Circle (former Singapore Naval Base)
Lagos is the capital of Nigeria. See *Admiralty Road.*

Laguna Golf Green
This road was named after the Laguna Golf Club at the end of the road.

Lakepoint Drive/Lakeside Drive/Walk (e)

Lakeshore View (Sentosa)

Lakme Street/Terrace (Opera Estate)
Lakme is a French opera by Leo Delibes. *See Aida Street.* Lakme Street was named in 1953.

Source: *RBAR, 1953:7*

Lam Hoe Village (e)
This village was named after the Chop Lam Hoe Provision Store owned by Neo Tiew. It was the first provision store in the Lim Chu Kang area providing food and daily supplies to more than 400 workers clearing up the swamp in this area. *See Neo Tiew Crescent.*

Source: *ZB Special Supplement, 2014.11.20:19*

Lam San Village (e)
Lam San Village was named in 1948 after the name of the Chinese school which was instituted by the villagers. This place name was also spelt Nam San or Lam Sam. *See Jalan Lam Sam.*

Source: *ST, 1948.3.19:5*

Lambeth Walk (former RAF Seletar)
This road was named after Lambeth Walk, a street in Lambeth, London. *See Baker Street.*

Lancaster Gate (e) (former RAF Seletar)
Lancaster Road (e) (former RAF Tengah)
Lancaster Gate was named after a street in the Bayswater district of Central London. *See Baker Street.*

    Lancaster Road was named after Avro Lancaster, a WW2 heavy bomber built by Avro for the RAF. *See Hornet Road.*

Lange Road
This road was probably named after A Lange, a ship chandler who passed away in the early 20th century. His descendents used to live in Jansen Road which is connected to Lange Road. One account mentioned that this road was named after M Lange (1907–1956), a Danish textile and firearms merchant based in Singapore. This road was repaired by the Rural Board in 1953.

Source: *ST, 1953.5.29:4; Dunlop; Serangoon: 16*

Langsat Road
Langsat, *Lansium domesticum*, is a tropical fruit. This road was known as Lorong F before 1934. *See Tembeling Road.*

Source: *ST, 1935.12.21:10; SG 1936*

Lantana Avenue
Lantana is a genus of perennial flowering plants in the Verbena family. Lantana Avenue is one of the five roads in the same area with names

beginning with the alphabet L. The other roads were named Lasia Avenue, Lemon Avenue, Lily Avenue and Lotus Avenue.

Larkhill Road/Walk (e) (former Blakang Mati Artillery Barracks)
This road was named after Larkhill, a garrison town in Durrington, Wiltshire, South West England. The Royal School of Artillery, where many leading field commanders were trained, was established in Larkhill in 1915. *See Artillery Avenue.*

Larut Road
Larut is a district of the northern state of Perak, Malaysia. A discovery of rich tin ore in this area in 1850 led to conflicts among the local Chinese secret societies and the Malay royal families over the control of mining areas. The conflicts ended with the intervention from Britain in 1873 and the signing of the Pankor Treaty of 1874. Two towns in Larut were renamed: Klian Puah became Taiping and Klian Bahru became Kamunting. Taiping was the capital of Perak from 1876 to 1937.

Larut Road became a public street in 1910.

Source: *MC, 1910.1.21*

Lasia Avenue
Lasia is a genus of flowering plants in the *Araceae* family. *See Lantana Avenue.*

Laurel Wood Avenue
Laurel Wood is a large hardwood tree native to coastal California.

Lavender Street
The Lavender Street area was a vegetable farm in the early 19th century and was known for the pungent odour from the night soil which was used as fertilisers. The name of this road was probably given in 1858 with some sense of British humour.

Source: *SFP 1858.4.1:6; Singam*

Law Link (e)

Lee Yuan Road (e)

Leedon Heights/Park/Road
The name Leedon was probably taken from Leedon Village in Bedfordshire, South East England.

Leedon Park was named in 1949.

Leedon Road became a public street in 1952.

Source: *RBAR, 1949:9; RBAR, 1952:8*

Leese Road (e) (former RAF Changi)
This road was probably named after Lieutenant General Sir Oliver William Hargreaves Leese (1894–1978). He was a senior British Army Officer in both world wars. During WW2, he was the C-in-C of the Allied Land Forces, South East Asia in November 1944. He fought a successful campaign which led to the capture of Rangoon from the Japanese in May 1945. However, his position in the army was later replaced by his subordinate, William Slim. He returned to England and retired from the army in 1947. *See Slim Road.*

Leicester Road
Based on an article in 1933, this road was named after H N B Leicester (1856–1940), a clerk of the Singapore Harbour Board and a resident of this road.
Source: *ST, 1933.11.9:6; Singam*

Leith Park/Road
Leith is a district to the north of Edinburgh city at the mouth of the water of Leith. It was a major port in Scotland from the 12th to the 19th century. Leith Road was repaired by the Rural Board in 1953 and declared a public street in 1956. *See Dix Road.*
Source: *ST, 1953.5.29:4; RBAR, 1956:9*

Lembu Lane (e)/Road (Kampong Kapor)
Lembu means cow in Malay. These roads were occupied by the Indian cattle traders in early Singapore. Both roads were declared as public streets in 1914.
Source: *MC, 1914.11.27*

Lemon Avenue
See Lantana Avenue.

Lempeng Drive
See Jalan Lempeng.

Leng Kee Road
Leng Kee was the name of the shop owned by Gan Leng (or Gan Eng Leng), of Hokkien ancestry. In 1881, Gan successfully tendered for a large piece of land at a low price. He then donated part of the land for use as a cemetery for the public as well as the Gan clan.
Source: *Kua: 210*

Lengkok Angsa/Bahru/Mariam/Merak/Saga (e)
Lengkok is the generic name of Crescent in Malay. Translations of other Malay words are as follows: *Angsa* (goose), *bahru* (new) and *merak* (peacock).

Mariam is a female personal name equivalent to Mary in English.

Saga is the name of a tree. *See Jalan Merah Saga.*

Lengkong Dua/Empat/Enam/Lima/Satu/Tiga/Tujoh
These seven roads in the Kembangan area were named by numerals in Malay with a common generic name of "Lengkong" (cape in Malay). See *Pachitan Dua* for numerals in Malay.

Lengkong Dua, Lengkong Satu and Lengkong Tiga were named in 1953.

Source: *RBAR, 1953:7*

Lentor Avenue/Crescent/Drive/Green/Grove/Lane/Link/Loop/Place/Plain/ Road/Street/Terrace/Vale/Walk/Way
Lentor or *lentur* means a bend in Malay.

Leo Drive
Leo is one of the zodiac signs. This road was named in 1961. See *Capricorn Drive*.

Source: *SFP, 1961.1.6:6*

Leonie Hill/Leonie Hill Road
Leonie Hill is the residence of John H Robertson, a medical doctor. It was named after his hometown in Ayrshire, south west of Scotland. See *Robertson Quay*.

Leonie Hill was declared a public street after it was broadened in 1904.

Leonie Hill Road was officially named and made a public street in 1905.

Source: *ST, 1904.1.30:5; MC, 1905.11.5; Singam*

Lermit Road
This road was named in 1908 after A W Lermit (1850–1929), a Ceylonese surveyor who was an active participant in Municipal matters.

Source: *MC, 1908.2.28; SFP, 1929.12.19:10; Lee KL: 28; Singam*

Leuchars Road (former RAF Changi)
This road was named after RAF Leuchars in Fife County in Scotland. See *Abbotsingh Road*.

Lew Lian Vale
"Lew Lian" is the transcription of durian in Hokkien.

Lewin Terrace
This road is located in Fort Canning and was named after Major-General Ernest Ord Lewin (1879–1950). He was the GOC, Malaya Command between 1934 and 1935. See *Bond Terrace*.

Source: *SFP, 1935.11.9:10*

Lewis Road

This road was named in 1941 after D T Lewis (born 1885) who was the Manager of Borneo & Company. He was a member of the Municipal Commission (1921-1924) and Legislative Council (1925-1927). In 1928 he left for London to take up the appointment of General Manager in the London office of Borneo & Company.

Source: *SFP, 1921.4.7:215; ST, 1928.6.28:8; MC, 1941.4.25; ST, 1955.7.22:14*

Leyden Hill

Leyden Hill and Ross Avenue are both connected to University Road, which were all first listed in the Street Directory of 1954. Like Ross Avenue, it was probably named after another scholar, Dr. John Casper Leyden, a good friend of Raffles who completed the first translation of the Malay annals and was one of the earliest Anglo-Malay scholars. *See Ross Avenue.*

Source: *ST, 1957.6.21:6*

Li Hwan Close/Drive/Place/Terrace/View/Walk

Li Po Avenue (Teachers' Housing Estate)

This road was named after Li Bai or Li Po (701-762), one of the greatest Chinese poets who lived during the Tang Dynasty. *See Iqbal Avenue.*

Liane Road (Singapore Botanic Gardens)

Liane is a woody climbing plant, *Camellia sasanqua*. This road was named in 1913.

Source: *SFP, 1914.5.30:16*

Liang Seah Street

This street was named in 1926 after Seah Liang Seah (1850-1925, Teochew), the second son of Seah Eu Chin (*see Eu Chin Street*). He was a pineapple plantation owner and was a member of the Legislative Council from 1883 to 1890. In 1895, Seah acquired the Nam Sang Garden of Hoo Ah Kay and renamed it Bendemeer House (*see Bendemeer Road and Whampoa Road*). Bendemeer House was compulsorily acquired by the government in 1963 with a compensation of 28 million dollars. After years of negotiation by the Administrator of his Estate, the final compensation was raised to 72.2 million dollars in 1979.

Source: *MC, 1926.6.25; Kua: 105*

Libra Drive

Libra is the name of a zodiac. This road was named in 1961. *See Capricorn Drive.*

Source: *SFP, 1961.1.6:6*

Lichfield Road (Serangoon Gardens)
This road was named in 1953. Lichfield is a cathedral city in Staffordshire, West Midlands, England. It is notable for its three-spired medieval cathedral. *See Alnwick Road.*
Source: *RBAR, 1953:8*

Lichi Avenue (Sennett Estate)
Lichi, also known as Lychee, is a fruit tree native to Guangdong Province and Fujian Province in China. This road was named in 1951. *See Angsana Avenue.*
Source: *CC, 1951.9.29*

Lien Ying Chow Drive
Lien Ying Chow (1906-2004, Teochew), was a banker and philanthropist. He established the Overseas Union Bank and the Mandarin Hotel in Singapore and was one of the founders of the former Nanyang University and Ngee Ann College (now Ngee Ann Polytechnic). His Lien Foundation was set up in 1980 to help the needy and deprived in society as well as to help address environmental problems. This road was a rename of part of Nanyang Drive in 2008.
Source: *ST, 2008.12.30:26*

Lighthouse Beach Walk (e) (Sentosa Island)

Lilac Drive/Lilac Road/Lilac Walk

Lily Avenue
See Lantana Avenue.

Lim Ah Pin Road
This road was named after Lim Ah Pin, who made his fortune from manufacturing rice vermicelli ("bee hoon" in Hokkien), a popular staple food of the Hokkiens. Known as the Bee Hoon King during his time, Lim was a generous donour towards public amenities. He passed away during WW2. Lim Ah Pin Road was declared a public street in 1955.
Source: *RBAR, 1955:9*

Lim Ah Woo Road
Lim Ah Woo, a timber merchant under the trade name of Seng Moh & Co. in the 1920s, owned properties and a pineapple plantation in Mandai. He was the Secretary of Chui Huai Lim Club in 1929. This road was named Lim Road in 1922 and renamed Lim Ah Woo Road in 1935.
Source: *MC1, 1922.2.3; ST, 1935.6.24:12; NAS, 2780:4*

Lim Chiak Street (e)
This street was located between Beach Road and Clyde Terrace.

Lim Chu Kang Lane 1, 1A, (1B to 1D) (e)/Lane 2, (2A, 2B) (e)/Lane 3, 3A, (3B to 3E) (e)/Lane 4/Lane 5, 5A/Lane 6, 6A, 6B (e), 6C, 6D, 6E (e), 6F/Lane 7 (e)/Lane 8, 8A/Lane 9, 9A, 9B
Lim Chu Kang Road
Lim Chu Kang Track (3, 10) (e), 11 to 13
The people from the Lim clan were the first to develop the land in the northwestern part of Singapore, which was the source of the name of Lim Chu Kang (see *Choa Chu Kang for the explanation of "Kang Chu"*). By 1855, there were about 600,000 gambier plants and 100,000 pepper trees in the Lim Chu Kang area. When gambier was replaced by cheap chemicals, the plantations became unprofitable and Lim Chu Kang was reverted to a jungle. The land rights were then mainly acquired by M/s Cashin and Nemazie. The former hired Neo Tiew to clear up the land in 1914.

One account mentioned that the early "Kang Chu" of Lim Chu Kang was Lim Tui Qian (1868–1923, Hokkien), a Chinese community leader in that area. This is doubtful as Lim was not even born when the area was full of gambier and pepper trees. *See Neo Tiew Crescent.*

Lim Chu Kang Road was a new road under construction in 1931.

Source: *ST, 1855.5.15:5; SFP, 1931.4.10:12; SFP, 1931.4.10:12; Lim SH: 3*

Lim Eng Bee Lane (e) (Havelock and Park Roads)
This lane was first seen in the news in 1899. It was probably named after Lim Eng Bee who traded under the names of Lim Eng Bee and Co. and Chop Soon Seng with two other partners in the 1860s.

Source: *SFP, 1865.1.26:2; SFP, 1899.2.2:2*

Lim Liak Street
Lim Liak (1804–1875) was an entrepreneur in shipping, tin mining and tapioca plantation. This road was listed in the 1936 Gazetteer and was officially named in 1941. *See Seng Poh Road.*

Source: *MC, 1941.4.25; SG-1936; Kua: 132*

Lim Tai See Walk
See Jalan Lim Tai See.

Lim Teck Boo Road
Lim Teck Boo was the owner of a large coconut plantation in the Paya Lebar area before WW2.

Source: *NAS, 168:3*

Lim Teck Kim Road
This road was originally named Soon Teck Road in February 1929 and changed to Lim Teck Kim Road one month later. Lim Teck Kim (died 1936,

Hokkien) was the founder of Hoe Chiang Company. He was a grocery and coffee merchant and owned pineapple plantations.

Source: *MC, 1929.3.27; SFP, 1936.11.24:9; Kua: 137*

Lim Toh Road (e)
Based on a news article in 1985, Lim Toh was an assistant of Lim Nee Soon.

Source: *ST, 1985.2.1:21*

Lim Tua Tow Road
This road was named after Lim Tua Tow (1842–1912) a wealthy Teochew merchant and landowner. The road became a public street in 1931.

Source: *SFP, 1931.5.15:2; Singam*

Limau Garden/Grove/Rise/Terrace/Walk
Limau is lemon, lime or orange in Malay.

Limbok Terrace
Limbok is the generic name for pigeons in Malay.

Lincoln Road (Race Course Road area)
This road was named after Lincoln, the county town of Lincolnshire, East Midlands, England. Part of this road was declared a public street in 1951.

Source: *ST, 1951.5.1:8; CCAR, 1957:5*

Linden Drive
Linden is one of the English names for the tree *Genus Tilia*, also known as lime or basswood. This road was named in 1954.

Source: *RBAR, 1954:9*

Link Lane (e)/Road
Link Lane was named in 1953. It was connected to Boon Lay Road. The name was changed to Link Road in the 1971 Street Directory.

Source: *RBAR, 1953:7*

Little Cross Street (e)
This street was renamed Baghdad Street in 1909.

Source: *ST, 1909.10.2:8*

Little Road
This road could be linked to the three Little brothers who lived in Singapore between 1840 and 1900, Dr. Robert Little, John Martin Little and Mathew Little. They helped to co-found the departmental store John Little. Robert Little (died 1888) was a medical practitioner and a Coroner. He was a member of the Municipal Commission and the Legislative Council.

Source: *Buckley: 350*

Liu Fang Road (e)
This road in Jurong was first seen in the Street Directory of 1969. "Liu Fang" is a Chinese term that means leaving behind a good name. See *Chia Ping Road*.

Lloyd Gardens (e)/Road
Lloyd Leas (e) (former RAF Changi)
Lloyd Road is located in the Orchard/Oxley area. The road name was first seen in the press in 1865. It was probably named after Henry Lloyd, the Manager of Dr. Oxley's plantation in 1858. He became a plantation owner after purchasing a piece of land from the estate of Dr. Oxley.

Lloyd Leas was named after Air Chief Marshal Sir Hugh Pughe Lloyd (1894–1981). Sir Lloyd was the C-in-C, Air Command Far East from 1947 to 1950.

Source: *ST, 1858.8.7:4; ST, 1861.7.27:1; ST, 1947.9.20:3; Probert: 74*

Lock Road (former Gillman Barracks)
This road was probably named after Eric S Lock (1919–1941). He was a British RAF fighter pilot and the flying ace of WW2. It was reported that he shot down 21 German aircrafts during the Battle of Britain in 1940 and more after that. However, he was lost in action in August 1941. See *Gillman Close*.

Loewen Road (former Tanglin Barracks)
This road was probably named after Lieutenant General Sir Charles Falkland Loewen (1900–1986) from Canada. He was the C-in-C, Far East Land Forces from 1953 to 1956. This road was previously known as Inverness Road. See *Barrack Road*.

Source: *ST, 1953.10.20:2*

Lok Yang Lane (e)/Road (e)/Village (e)/Way
The special name of these roads was probably derived from the Lok Yang Estate (a rubber plantation) in Jurong, the Lok Yang Village or the Loke Yang Primary School.

Loke Yew Street
Loke Yew (1847–1916) from He Shan County in Canton started his career in Singapore as a shop assistant. He went into tin mining in Malaya and became very wealthy. This road was named in 1904.

Source: *ST, 1904.1.30:5; Kua: 66*

Lompang Road
Lompang means vacant space in Malay.

London Road (e) (former Nee Soon Cantonment), (former Pasir Panjang Barracks)

Loop Road (e) (former Nee Soon Cantonment)
The shape of the road is a loop. Loop Road was listed in the Street Directory as The Loop between 1950 and 1962. It was changed to Loop Road in 1963 and reinstated as The Loop in 1966.

Lornie Road/Walk
This road was named after James Lornie (1876–1959) in 1929. He started his career in Singapore in the Land Office in 1911. He was made the Commissioner of Lands before becoming the Vice President of the Municipal Commission in 1925. Two years later he was appointed the British Resident in Selangor. He retired in 1931.
Source: *SFP, 1929.8.13:2; ST, 1931.4.1:12; Makepeace, vol.1:301*

Lorong 1–5 Bukit Gombak (e)
See *Bukit Gombak*.

Lorong 1 (e), 101,102,104,105,106,107,108,110 Changi
Lorong 101 to 108 were the rename of Lorong 1, 2, 4, 5, 6, 7, 8, Changi in 1931. See *Changi Road*.
Source: *MC, 1931.4.29*

Lorong 1, 2 (e), 3–4, 5 (e), 6–42, 44, 14A (e), 21A, 24A, 25A, 27A Geylang
See *Geylang Bahru* for the etymology of *Geylang*.

Most of these lanes were named "Lorong" by the Commissioners in 1912. It was decided that they should be numbered consecutively from town outwards; even numbers to be on the right side (south) and odd numbers on the left (north) side of Geylang Road.

Subsequently, Lorong 34 was named in 1928, Lorong 41 in 1929, Lorong 21A in 1930, and Lorong 24A in 1931.
Source: *MC, 1912.9.29; MC, 1929.6.28; MC, 1929.11.29; MC, 1930.10.31; MC, 1931.2.27*

Lorong 1–7 Realty Park

Lorong 201, 205–209 Siglap (e)
See *Siglap Road* for the etymology of *Siglap*. All lanes were renamed in 1934 as follows:

Lorong 201 was renamed Marshall Road.

Lorong 205 was renamed Mangis Road.

Lorong 206 was renamed Rambutan Road.

Lorong 207 was renamed Chiku Road.

Lorong 208 was renamed Rambai Road.

Lorong 209 was renamed Pulasan Road.

Source: *ST, 1934.3.8:19*

Lorong 1-5, Soo Chow Garden (e)
See *Soochow Road.*

Lorong 1-8, 1A, 8A Toa Payoh
See *Toa Payoh Central.*

Lorong A-D, St. George's Road (e)
See *St. George's Road.*

Lorong A-C, Siglap (e)
These lanes were all renamed in 1934 as follows:

Lorong A, Siglap became Crane Road.

Lorong B, Siglap became Pennefather Road.

Lorong C, Siglap became Fowlie Road.

Source: *ST, 1934.3.8:19*

Lorong A-Leng
This lane was located at the lower reaches of a river. "A-Leng" is the transcription of lower reaches in Hokkien.

Source: *NAS, 168:4*

Lorong Abu Kassim (e)
Abu means ashes or father in Malay. Kassim is a Malay personal name.

Lorong Abu Talib
Talib means a seeker of truth in Malay. Abu Talib is a Malay personal name. A notable one was Abu Talib bin Ally (born 1911). He owned the Royal Press which was the publisher of *Hiboran*, a weekly magazine. This lane was named in 1949.

Source: *RBAR, 1949:9; NAS, 1216:1*

Lorong Abukaseh (e)
Kaseh or *kasih* means affection or love in Malay. Abukaseh appears to be a Malay personal name.

Lorong Achara (e)
Achara means a rule of conduct in Malay.

Lorong Ah Soo/Lorong Ah Soo Selatan (e)
These roads were named after Ng Ah Soo (died 1929), also known as Ng Thye Hiong, who owned a large coconut plantation at 7 ms Serangoon Road. His family was in the news over the distribution of his Estate after he passed away.

This area was also known as Hainan Garden as most of the residents were Hainanese. *Selatan* means south in Malay. Lorong Ah Soo was repaired in 1950 and became a public street in 1954.

Source: *ST, 1930.1.16:11; RBAR, 1950:8; RBAR, 1954:8; NAS, 158:42*

Lorong Ah Thia (e)
This lane was named in 1938 after Chia Ah Thia (1852–1930).
Source: *ST, 1930.8.1:6; SFP, 1938.8.12:3*

Lorong Ahadiat (e)
Ahadiat means unity in Malay.

Lorong Ahmad (e)
Ahmad is a Malay personal name. It also means much recommended.

Lorong Akar (e)
Akar means root, root fibre or a climbing plant in Malay.

Lorong Ampas
See Jalan Ampas and Balestier Road.

Lorong Anchak (e)
Anchak is the Malay term for offering of food placed in baskets for evil spirits.

Lorong Andong (e)
Andong is a palm of the nibong type, *Colodracon jacquinii*.

Lorong Anglo (e)
Anglo means English or a portable stove in Malay.

Lorong Antong (e)
This was a misprint of Lorong Atong in the 1970 Street Directory.

Lorong Asrama
Asrama means hostel in Malay.

Lorong Atong (e)
Atong means tripping the anchor in Malay.

(Lorong Ayam Belaga/Beroga/Betina/Bogel/Borek/Dara/Denak/Hutan/ Jalak/Jantan/Katek/Selaseh) (e)
These roads were all named after *ayam*, fowls in Malay.

Ayam belaga is a fighting cock.

Ayam beroga is a jungle fowl.

Ayam betina is a hen.

Ayam bogel is a tailless chicken.

Ayam borek is a spotted chicken.

Ayam dara is a hen that has not laid eggs.

Ayam denak is a jungle fowl.

Ayam hutan is a wild fowl.

Ayam jalak is a yellow-leg chicken.

Ayam jantan is a cock.

Ayam katek is a short chicken.

Ayam selaseh is a black-bone fowl.

Lorong Bachok
Bachok or *bacok* is a bamboo cup in Malay.

Lorong Bagas (e)
Bagas means steady and strong breeze in Malay.

Lorong Bajak (e)
Bajak means plough in Malay.

Lorong Bakar Batu
Bakar means being set on fire and *batu* means stone in Malay. *Bakar batu* is fire stone. This lane was named in 1921.

Source: *MC, 1921.12.20*

Lorong Balai (e)
Balai is a public building in Malay.

Lorong Baling (e)
Baling means circling round a central point in Malay.

Lorong Bandang
Bandang is the Malay name for a sea fish, salmon herring or milk fish.

Lorong Baning (e)
Baning is a tortoise in Malay.

Lorong Banir (e)
Banir means a buttress-like projection at the base of the tree trunk in Malay.

Lorong Basapah (e)
Bassappa was the son of wealthy Indian merchant Somapah. See *Somapah Road*. This road was named in 1948.

Source: *RBAR, 1948:7; NAS, 1179:4; NAS, 110:1*

Lorong Batawi
Batawi or *Batavia* (1619–1942) in English was an old name of Jarkata, the capital of Indonesia. This lane was named in 1948. See *Jalan Lye Kwee*.

Source: *RBAR, 1948:7*

Lorong Batu Giling (e)
Batu means stone and *giling* is a grind in Malay. *Batu giling* is a roller for grinding curry. It has been extended to mean the road roller.

Lorong Bayu (e)
Bayu means breeze or slave in Malay.

Lorong Bekalan Selatan (e)
Bekalan means provision and *selatan* means south in Malay.

Lorong Bekukong
Bekukong or *bekukung* is the Malay name of a sea-bream, *Sparus hasta*.

Lorong Bendul (e)
Bendul is the Malay term for crossbeam (from the house pillar) supporting the flooring of a house.

Lorong Bengkok
Bengkok means crooked or bent in Malay.

Lorong Beradab (e)
Beradab means courteous or polite in Malay.

Lorong Berhala (e)
Berhala means idol or graven image in Malay.

Source: *Haughton: 76*

Lorong Berkek (e)
Berkek or *berkik* is a snipe (type of bird), *Gallinago spp.*

Lorong Biawak
Biawak is a monitor-lizard in Malay.

Lorong Bingkai (e)
Bingkai means rim or border in Malay.

Lorong Binkiang (Pulau Ubin)

Lorong Bistari
Bistari means expert or skilled in Malay.

Lorong Buang Kok (Buangkok)/Lorong Buang Kok Kechil (e)
This area was the property of Singapore United Rubber Plantations Limited. "Buang Kok" was the transcription of its Chinese name Multi Nations in Teochew. Lorong Buang Kok was named in 1948. *Kechil* means small in Malay.

Source: *ST, 1948.10.22:6; RBAR, 1948:7; NAS, 799:6*

Lorong Bukit Pasoh (e)
This road was named in 1930. *See Bukit Pasoh Road.*

Source: *MC, 1930.2.28*

Lorong Bukit Tinggi (e)
See Bukit Tinggi.

Lorong Bunga
Bunga means flower in Malay.

Lorong Bunglon (e)
Bunglon means chameleon in Malay.

Lorong Chabai (e)
Chabai is a long pepper in Malay.

Lorong Chahaya (e)
Chahaya means lustre or glow in Malay.

Lorong Chamar (e)
Chamar is a sea mew or tern in Malay. Tern is a seabird related to gulls.

Lorong Chamcha (e)
Chamcha is a spoon in Malay.

Lorong Chanai (e)
Chanai means grinding by means of a roller in Malay.

Lorong Chemara (e)
Chemara is a pendant of horse hair (under the blade of a spear) in Malay.

Lorong Chembol (e)
Chembol or *cembul* is a small metal box in Malay.

Lorong Chenangau (e)
Chenangau is a foul smelling flying bug that preys on rice in Malay.

Lorong Chencharu
Chencharu means horse mackerel in Malay.

Lorong Cheng Lim (e)
This lane was named in 1948. See Cheng Lim Farmway.
Source: *RBAR, 1948:7*

Lorong Chengai (e)
Chengai is a tree, *Hopea curtisii*.

Lorong Cherdek (e)
Cherdek means bright or intelligent in Malay.

Lorong Chikar (e)
Chikar or *chekar* is a rough cart with solid wheels in Malay.

Lorong Chinchin (e)
Chinchin means finger ring in Malay. See *Lorong Jurai*.

Lorong Chuan
"Chuan" is the transcription of spring water in Hokkien. The name was probably given due to the presence of fresh water pipes in this area.

Source: *Serangoon: 15*

Lorong Chuntum (e)
Chuntum or *kuntun* means flower bud in Malay.

Lorong Dadah (e)
Dadah means drugs or cosmetics in Malay.

Lorong Danau
Danau means lake in Malay.

Lorong Dangai (e)
Dangai is a Malay cake made from sugar, coconut and glutinous rice.

Lorong Dedes (e)
Dedes is to browbeat or to question insistently in Malay.

Lorong Dendam (e)
Dendam is a Malay word that means yearning, longing, feeling of love or spite.

Lorong Dengkes (e)
Dengkes is a sea fish, black trevally, *Siganus spp.*

Lorong Desa (e)
Desa means region, county (village) or country in Malay.

Lorong Dirus (e)
Dirus means wetting, watering or irrigating in Malay.

Lorong Dodol (e)
Dodol is a tree, *Ficus rhododendrifolia* or sweetmeat of rice flour, palm sugar and coconut milk in Malay.

Lorong E, East Coast Road (e)
This lane was renamed Koon Seng Road in 1934.

Source: *SFP, 1934.7.18:8*

Lorong Elai (e)
Elai means sheet in Malay. This lane was between 47 and 49 Rochore Road.

Lorong Endah (e)
Endah or *indah* means fine or handsome in Malay.

Lorong Engku Aman (e)
This road was in Geylang Serai, location of the Alsagoff estate. It was named after Syed Abdulrahman bin Tana Alsagoff in 1930. The road was demolished

together with the redevelopment of the area in 1989. In August 1994, a new road was given the name of Engku Aman Road in a nearby location. See Engku Aman Road.

Source: MC, 1930.2.28

Lorong Ensel (e)
Ensel is a hinge in Malay.

Lorong Faham (e)
Faham means understand in Malay.

Lorong Fatimah (e)
This lane was probably named after a wealthy lady named Fatimah who developed this area. It was likely to be Princess Hadjee Fatima, a Bugis royalty in Malacca who maintained a trading post in Singapore. This lane was named in 1957.

Source: RBAR, 1957:8; NAS, 1097:5

Lorong G-H, J-N, P, Telok Kurau
See Telok Kurau Road.

Lorong M, Telok Kurau was listed as a road pending adoption by the City Council in 1957.

Lorong P, Telok Kurau was named in 1931 and was renamed St. Patrick's Road around 1935.

Source: MC, 1931.9.25; CCAR, 1957:5

Lorong Gambas (e)
Gambas means pumpkin in Malay.

Lorong Gambir
See Gambir Walk.

Lorong Gangsa (e)
Gangsa means goose or bronze in Malay.

Lorong Garpu (e)
Garpu means fork in Malay.

Lorong Garuda (e)
Garuda or geroda is a bird-headed man, a Hindu deity.

Lorong Gasal (e)
Gasal means odd number in Malay.

Lorong Gasing (e)
Gasing means spinning-top in Malay.

Lorong Gaung (e)
Gaung means ravine in Malay.

Lorong Gelora (e)
Gelora means storm or great wave in Malay.

Lorong Gemilap (e)
Gemilap or *gilap* means glitter or shimmer in Malay.

Lorong Gendi (e)
Gendi or *kendi* means goglet in Malay.

Lorong Getah (e)
Getah means rubber in Malay.

Lorong Geylang (e)
See *Geylang Bahru*.

Lorong Gimbul (e)
Gimbul means hump or bump in Malay.

Lorong Ginchu (e)
Ginchu or *gincu* means rouge or lipstick in Malay.

Lorong Golongan (e)
Golongan means classify or group in Malay.

Lorong Gulega Kechil (e)
Gulega means talismanic or curative bezoar in Malay. *Kechil* means small in Malay.

Lorong Hablor (e)
Hablor or *hablur* means crystal in Malay.

Lorong Hakikit (e)
Hakikit may be derived from *hakikat*, which means truth in Malay.

Lorong Halus
Halus means delicate or fine texture in Malay.

Lorong Halwa
Halwa means sugared preserve in Malay.

Lorong Handalan (e)
Handalan means renown in Malay.

Lorong Harapan (e)
Harapan means hope or expectation in Malay.

Lorong Hong Lee (e)
This lane was named in 1948.

Source: *RBAR, 1948:7*

Lorong How Sun
See How Sun Road.

Lorong Ingin (e)
Ingin means longing or strong desire in Malay.

Lorong Jelapang (e)
Jelapang is a paddy-barn in Malay.

Lorong Jelebu (e)
See Jelebu Road.

Lorong Jerneh (e)
Jerneh or *jernlh* means clear, limpid or transparent in Malay.

Lorong Jerun (e)
Jerun means turtle dove, *Turtur tigrinus* or a shrub, *Sida rhombifolia* in Malay.

Lorong Jirak (e)
Jirak is a small tree, *Eurya acuminate*, common in secondary jungles.

Lorong Jodoh (e)
Jodoh means match or a pair in Malay.

Lorong Jurai (e)
Jurai means long pendant thread in Malay. This road is linked to four other roads with names of adornment: *Rantai* (gold chain), *kerabu* (ear-rings), *sanggul* (hairpin) and *chinchin* (ring). *Jurai* in Malay is also a tree, *Chisocheton panei-floras.*

Lorong Kabong (e)
Kabong or *kabung* means sugar palm, *Arenga saccha refera*.

Lorong Kadut (e)
Kadut is a sack cloth in Malay.

Lorong Kail (e)
Kail means fishing (with rod or hand-line) in Malay.

Lorong Kalui (e)
Kalui is a freshwater perch in Malay.

Lorong Kanching (e)
Kanching or *kancing* means button in Malay.

Lorong Kapok (e)
Kapok is the Malay word for enfolding in the arms, not of embracing in fondness.

Lorong Kasemek (e)
Kasemek or *kesmak* means persimmon in Malay.

Lorong Kassim (e)
Kassim is a personal name for Muslims. This lane was located off North Bridge Road and was probably named after S Kassim (died 1915) or his Wayang Kassim Theatre Company which was located in North Bridge Road. It was named in 1908.
Source: *MC, 1908.1.17; ST, 1915.8.10:5*

Lorong Kebasi
Kebasi is a sea fish, *Dorosoma spp.*

Lorong Kechapi (e)
Kechapi, *Sandoricum koetjape,* is the Indonesian name for *Santol* or *Sentul* in Malay. See *Jalan Sentul.*
Source: *Boo: 697*

Lorong Keduang (e)
Keduang or *kedang* means stretched out in Malay.

Lorong Kelana (e)
Kelana is a climbing plant, *Dioscorea prainiana* or wanderer in Malay.

Lorong Kelopak (e)
Kelopak is a thin wrapper in Malay.

Lorong Kemabal (e)
Kemabal or *kebabal* means half grown jackfruit in Malay.

Lorong Kembang
Kembang means expansion or blossoming out in Malay.

Lorong Kembangan
See *Jalan Kembangan.*

Lorong Kemunchup
This lane was part of the Popular Estate which was located next to Princess Elizabeth Estate in Upper Bukit Timah Road. *Kemunchup* is burr or lovegrass in Malay. See *Jalan Malu Malu.*

Lorong Kenah (e)
Kenah or *kena* means contact, experience or to touch in Malay.

Lorong Kerabu (e)
Kerabu means ear stud in Malay. See *Lorong Jurai.*

Lorong Kerepek (e)
Kerepek means fried chips of banana, tapioca, sweet potato, etc.

Lorong Kerubut (e)
Kerubut means disorderly crowding or a plant bearing huge flower, *Rafflesia hasselti.*

Lorong Kesudian (e)
Kesudian or *sudi* means ready or willing in Malay.

Lorong Kesum (e)
Kesum or *kesom* is a herb, *Polygonum minus* with a fragrant edible leaf in Malay.

Lorong Ketam (e)
Ketam means crab in Malay.

Lorong Ketilang (e)
Ketilang means finches in Malay.

Lorong Khatijah (e)
Khatijah or *khatifah* is a rug in Malay.

Lorong Kijang (e)
Kijang means barking-deer in Malay.

Lorong Kikir (e)
Kikir is a file or grater in Malay.

Lorong Kilat
Kilat means flashing or lightning in Malay.

Lorong Kinchir (e)
Kinchir or *kincir* is a water-wheel in Malay.

Lorong Kingkit (e)
Kingkit is a small orange, *Triphasia trifoliate* in Malay.

Lorong Kismis
See Kismis Avenue.

Lorong Koo Chye (e)
See Jalan Kuchai. This location was a Chives plantation.
Source: *NAS, 168:4*

Lorong Krak (e)
Krak is a Malay word for refuse-rice sticking to the sides of the cooking pot or cracking sound.

Lorong Kranji (e)
See Kranji Road.

Lorong Krishna (e)
Krishna is one of the most revered and popular of all Hindu deities.

Lorong Kuasa (e)
Kuasa means power of attorney in Malay.

Lorong Kuini (e)
Kuini is a mango tree, *Mangifera odorata*.

Lorong Kukri (e)
Kukri is a Nepalese knife with an inwardly curved blade. It is a characteristic weapon of the Royal Ghurkha Rifles of the British army.

Lorong Kukus (e)
Kukus means cooking by steaming in Malay.

Lorong Kumara (e)
Kumara is a character from an Indian epic.

Lorong Kundang (e)
Kundang means control or bandage in Malay.

Lorong Lada Hitam/Merah (e)/Padi (e)/Puteh
These lanes were named after different types of *lada* (pepper in malay).

Lada hitam is black pepper.

Lada merah is red pepper.

Lada padi is small pepper.

Lada puteh is white pepper.

Lorong Ladang Kechil (e)
See *Jalan Ladang*. *Kechil* means small in Malay.

Lorong Ladang Pendek (e)
See *Jalan Ladang*. *Pendek* means low in Malay.

Lorong Lalat (e)
Lalat is the common fly in Malay. This lane was located off Jalan Besar and was named in 1920. It appears that the name was given because the lane adjoined the Municipal incinerator.

Source: *MC, 1920.10.29; SFP, 1920.11.4:8*

Lorong Landak (e)
Landak means porcupine in Malay.

Lorong Landasan (e)
Landasan means an anvil in Malay.

Lorong Langsir (e)
Langsir means curtains in Malay.

Lorong Lemang (e)
Lemang is the Malay word for rice and coconut milk cooked in bamboo container.

Lorong Lentor (e)
See Lentor Avenue.

Lorong Lew Lian
"Lew Lian" is the transcription of durian in Hokkien.

Lorong Liat (e)
Liat means tough or leathery in Malay.

Lorong Lichin (e)
Lichin or *licin*, means smooth or slippery in Malay.

Lorong Lidi (e)
Lidi means midrib of palm-frond, especially coconut-frond in Malay.

Lorong Lihat (e)
Lihat means to see or to inspect in Malay.

Lorong Limau
Limau is lemon, lime or orange in Malay.

Based on a news article in 1935, this lane was named in 1934.

Source: *ST, 1935.12.21:10*

Lorong Limbang (e)
Limbang means depression or low lying portion of ground in Malay.

Lorong Lingie (e)
Lingie or *linggi* means stem or stern of a ship in Malay.

Lorong Lintang (e)
Lintang means measurement of width or breadth in Malay.

Lorong Liput
Liput means flooding, covering or pervading in Malay.

Lorong Locheng (e)
Locheng means Chinese bell in Malay.

Lorong Lodeh (e)
Lodeh means boiled soft or pulpy in Malay.

Lorong Lompang (e)
See Lompang Road.

Lorong Longan (e)
Longan is the edible fruit produced by the *Sapinda ceae* family.

Lorong Lontong (e)
Lontong means Malay food made of rice and gravy.

Lorong Low Koon
"Low Koon" is the transcription of doctor from the Hokkien dialect. It is believed that there was a reputable Traditional Chinese Medicine practitioner who lived in this area. This lane was named in 1948.
Source: *RBAR, 1948:7*; Information kindly provided by Huang Bing Jie who lived near this lane

Lorong Loyak (e)
Loyak means soft (of wet ground or overboiled rice) or octopus in Malay.

Lorong Lumut (e)
Lumut means moss in Malay.

Lorong Lunak (e)
Lunak means soft in Malay.

Lorong Maha (e)
Maha means great in Malay.

Lorong Makam (e)
Makam means a grave in Malay. There was a Chinese cemetery near this lane.

Lorong Malai (e)
Malai is a pendant ornament worn in the hair in Malay.

Lorong Malayu (e)
Malayu was the old name for the Malay race. The name had been changed to Lorong Melayu.

Lorong Mambong
Mambong means empty or dried up internally (of fruit) in Malay.

Lorong Manchak (e)
Manchak means coconut milk obtained from the second pressing in Malay.

Lorong Mandai (e)
See *Mandai Road*.

Lorong Marican
This lane led to the Jalan Eunos Malay Settlement. Marican may be a Malay or Indian Muslim name. See *Jalan Eunos*.

Lorong Marsiling (e)
See *Marsiling Road*.

Lorong Marzuki
Marzuki is a Malay personal name.

Lorong Mat Ali (e)
Mat and Ali are both personal names for Malays. Mat is short for Muhamed or Ahmad. In 1937 a ship by the name of *Mat Ali* sailed from Singapore to England, which could be the source of this road name.
Source: *SFP, 1937.8.20:9*

Lorong Mayang (e)/Lorong Mayang Kechil (e)
Mayang means palm-blossom and *kechil* means small in Malay.

Lorong Mega
Mega means cloud in Malay.

Lorong Mekola (e)
Mekola or *mekula* is the Malay name for lotus.

Lorong Melayu
This lane led to the Jalan Eunos Malay Settlement. *See Lorong Malayu.*

Lorong Melukut
Melukut means broken rice grains in Malay.

Lorong Merawan (e)
Merawan is a tree, *Hopea mengarawan*.
Source: *Boo: 619*

Lorong Mesu
Mesu is Tembesu, *Fagraea spp.* in Malay.

Lorong Muallap (e)
Muallap or *muallaf* is a new Muslim convert. This lane was named in 1948.
Source: *RBAR, 1948:7*

Lorong Mudek (e)
Mudek means progress upstream in Malay.

Lorong Mutu (e)
Mutu means sorrowful or a measure of the purity of gold in Malay.

Lorong Mydin
This road was located between Kampong Parchitan (e) and Kampong Eunos (e). Mydin is a Malay personal name. Gulam Mydin was a wealthy cattle trader who also owned a pier. *See Robertson Quay.*
Source: *SFP, 1892.4.28:3*

Lorong Nangka
Nangka means jackfruit in Malay. This lane was named in 1937.
Source: *ST, 1937.12.10:18*

Lorong Napiri
Napiri is a royal trumpet in Malay.

Lorong Nibong (e)
Nibong is the Malay name for a palm tree with thorny trunk, *Oncosperma filamentosa*.

Lorong Nobat (e)
Nobat is the Malay name for the principal drum of the royal band.

Lorong Ong Lye
"Ong Lye" is the transcription of pineapple from Hokkien.

Lorong Pacheh (e)
Pacheh is an indoor board game in Malay.

Lorong Pahat (e)
Pahat means chisel in Malay.

Lorong Panchar
Panchar means gushing out or issue in Malay.

Lorong Panji (e)
Panji means streamer or pennant in Malay.

Lorong Pantai (e)
Pantai means beach or sea-shore in Malay.

Lorong Pasak (e)
Pasak is the Malay word for fastening or tightening with a bolt, peg or wedge. *Pasak Lingga* is the generic name for several trees, such as *Aphanamixis polystachya*.
Source: *Boo: 513*

Lorong Pasir Bedok (e)
Pasir means sand in Malay. *See Bedok Road.*

Lorong Pasu
Pasu means flower pot or bowl for gold fish in Malay.

Lorong Patong (e)
Patong means puppet in Malay. *Belalang patong* is a dragon-fly.

Lorong Pawai (e)
Pawai means insignia bore after a prince in Malay.

Lorong Paya Lebar
See Paya Lebar Road.

Lorong Payah
Payah means difficult in Malay.

Lorong Pekula (e)
Pekula means lotus in Malay.

Lorong Pelandok
See *Jalan Sungei Pelandok*.

Lorong Pelasari (e)
Pelasari is a yellow-flowered climber, *Alyxia stellata* in Malay.

Lorong Pelita (e)
Pelita is a lamp in Malay.

Lorong Peluang (e)
Peluang is a Malay word for lull, especially in the wind or a shrub, *Glycosmis sapindoides*.

Lorong Penchalak
Penchalak is a stick used to scrape out pounded areca-nut from the *gobek* (pounder in Malay).

Lorong Pendek
Pendek means short or low in Malay. This lane was named in 1921.
Source: *MC, 1921.12.20*

Lorong Pending (e)
Pending is a waist-buckle in Malay.

Lorong Perjanjian (e)
Perjanjian means contract or agreement in Malay.

Lorong Persatuan (e)
Persatuan means union or association in Malay.

Lorong Petir (e)
Petir means thunder in Malay.

Lorong Pikat (e)
Pikat is a horse-fly in Malay.

Lorong Pintu (e)
Pintu means door, gate or entrance in Malay.

Lorong Pisang Asam/Batu/Emas/Hijau/Raja/Udang
These lanes with names of different species of *pisang* (bananas in Malay) are located off Jalan Jurong Kechil.

Pisang asam (sour) is a sour banana.

Pisang batu (stone) is a green banana used for rojak, a Malay salad.

Pisang emas (gold) is a small yellow banana that is sweet.

Pisang hijau (green) is a green banana even when ripe.

Pisang raja a (big) is a big banana usually for deep frying which may be eaten raw as well.

Pisang udang (prawn) is a red banana.

Lorong Pulai (e)
Pulai is a lofty tree, *Alstonia scholaris* in Malay. Pulai is also the name of a river in Johor, Malaysia. It runs from Mount Pulai to Straits of Johore.

Lorong Puntong
Puntong means stump or butt in Malay.

Lorong Puspa (e)
Puspa means flower or flowery in Malay.

Lorong Puspita (e)
Puspita means flower in Malay.

Lorong Putek (e)
Putek means rudimentary fruit in Malay.

Lorong Puyu (e)
Puyu means whirlwind in Malay.

Lorong Ragam (e)
Ragam is a mode in Indian music.

Lorong Rajin (e)
Rajin means perseverance or diligence in Malay.

Lorong Rantai (e)
Rantai means gold chain in Malay. *See Lorong Jurai.*

Lorong Ranting (e)
Ranting means twig or small leafless branch in Malay.

Lorong Rapat (e)
Rapat means continuous in Malay.

Lorong Ratna (e)
Ratna means jewel or gem in Malay.

Lorong Renjong (e)
Renjong means blue/flower crab in Malay.

Lorong Resam (e)
Resam means custom or forest fern, *Gleichenia linearis* in Malay.

Lorong Rubah (e)
Rubah means jackal in Malay.

Lorong Rusa (e)
Rusa means deer, specifically the sambhur in Malay.

Lorong Rusuk
Rusuk means side, flank or edge in Malay.

Lorong Sabut (e)
Sabut means fibrous shell or husk in Malay.

Lorong Sakai (e)
Sakai is the term for aborigines who do not speak Malay.

Lorong Sakinat (e)
Sakinat means peace in Malay.

Lorong Salak (e)
Salak is a stemless thorny palm, *Zalacca edulis*, producing a fruit named *buah salak*.

Lorong Salleh
Salleh is a masculine personal name. Mat Saleh is the nickname for a European.

Lorong Salor Ayer (e)
Salor or *salur* means conduit or pipe in Malay. *Salor ayer* is water pipe.

Lorong Samak
See *Ayer Samak*.

Lorong Sang Kanchil (e)
Sang kanchil is the mousedeer in a Malay fable.

Lorong Sanggul (e)
Sanggul means coiffure or dressed hair in Malay. See *Lorong Jurai*.

Lorong Santun (e)
Santun means demure or sedate in Malay.

Lorong Sarhad
Sarhad is a place name in North Pakistan which means boundary.

Lorong Sari
Sari means flower or flower-like in Malay.

Lorong Sarina
Sarina is the wife of Prophet Ibrahim.
Source: *Dunlop*

Lorong Seburut (e)
Seburut is a plant, *Thottea grandiflora* in Malay.

Lorong Segala (e)
Segala means all or the whole of in Malay.

Lorong Segi (e)
Segi means side, corner or angle in Malay.

Lorong Selangat
Selangat is a fish known as basling shad, *Dorosoma spp.* in Malay.

Lorong Selangin (e)
Selangin or *senangin* is smaller threadfin, *Polynemus tetradactylus* in Malay.

Lorong Selden (e)
Selden is a place name and personal name. John Selden (1584–1654) was a jurist and reputed scholar in England.

Lorong Selderi (e)
Selderi means celery in Malay.

Lorong Seludu (e)
Seludu is a catfish, *Arius sp.* in Malay.

Lorong Semangka
Semangka means watermelon in Malay.

Lorong Senapang (e)
Senapang means gun or rifle in Malay.

Lorong Sengkang (e)
See *Sengkang Central*.

Lorong Senohong (e)
Senohong is a large threadfin, *Polenemus paradiseus* in Malay.

Lorong Sepakat (e)
Sepakat means reaching an agreement in Malay. See *Geylang Serai Village*.

Lorong Sepat (e)
Sepat is a fish of genus *Trichopodus* in Malay.

Lorong Serai (e)
Serai is the Malay name for lemongrass. There were two Lorong Serai (reported in the press as Lorong Seral) before 1940, of which one changed to Lorong Tai Seng in 1940.
Source: *ST, 1940.5.10:12*

Lorong Serambi
Serambi means a front verandah in Malay.

Lorong Serindit (e)
See *Jalan Serindit*.

Lorong Seroja (e)
Seroja means lotus, *Nelumbium speciosum* in Malay.

Lorong Sesuai
Sesuai means to match or to bring into harmony in Malay.

Lorong Setara (e)
Setara means to even or level in Malay.

Lorong Shahada (e)
Shahada means naughty in Malay.

Lorong Shukor (e)
Shukor is a Malay personal name.

Lorong Sidin (e)
Sidin or *siding*, means a line of rattan nooses or a fern in Malay. This lane was off North Bridge Road, parallel to Middle Road and named in 1908. Sidin is also a masculine personal name.

Source: *MC, 1908.1.17*

Lorong Sigar (e)
Sigar is a square headcloth in Malay.

Lorong Siglap
See *Siglap Road*.

Lorong Silat (e)
See *Jalan Silat Gayong*.

Lorong Simpang Pagak (e)
Simpang means crossroad in Malay. See *Jalan Pagak*.

Lorong Sinaran (e)
See *Sinaran Drive*.

Lorong Sinting (e)
Sinting is a thin pearly shell, *placuna sella* in Malay.

Lorong Sireh Pinang
Sireh is betel-leaf and *pinang* is betel nut in Malay.

Lorong Somapah Kechil (e)
See *Somapah Road*. *Kechil* means small in Malay.

Lorong Stangee
See *Stangee Close*.

Lorong Stephen Lee
See *Stephen Lee Road*.

Lorong Sudu (e)
Sudu is a coconut-shell spoon in Malay.

Lorong Sulur (e)
Sulur is the shoots of the roots of certain species of *Ficus* or lotus shoots in Malay.

Lorong Sungkai (e)
Sungkai is a plant, *Peronema canescens* in Malay.

Lorong Sunyi (e)
Sunyi means lonely or desolate in Malay.

Lorong Susila (e)
Susila means ethical in Malay.

Lorong Tahar
Tahar means to keep on a course in spite of bad weather in Malay.

Lorong Tai Seng (e)
This lane was known as Lorong Serai (reported in the press as Lorong Seral) until 1940. Tai Seng was named after the Ang Tai Seng Rubber Factory owned by Ang Chai Liat. The factory was closed following the economic depression of the 1930s and was converted into a wet market. *See Lorong Serai*.
Source: *ST, 1940.5.10:12; NAS, 168:2*

Lorong Taji (e)
Taji means artificial spur for fighting-cock in Malay.

Lorong Taluki (e)
Taluki or *teluki* means pink or carnation in Malay.

Lorong Tamok (e)
Tamok is a mullet, *Mugil waigiensis* in Malay.

Lorong Tanaman (e)
Tanaman means plants in Malay.

Lorong Tandan (e)
Tandan means stem of fruit that grows in a cluster in Malay.

Lorong Tanggam
Tanggam is a scarf-joint in Malay.

Lorong Tangkai (e)
Tangkai means stalk or stem in Malay.

Lorong Tapin (e)
Tapin is a shrub, *Croton griffithii* in Malay.

Lorong Tawas
Tawas means crude alum in Malay.

Lorong Tebera (e)
Tebera is a carp, *Labeobarbus tambra* in Malay.

Lorong Teck Hock (e)
This lane was named after Teck Hock Village. It was named in 1948.
Source: *RBAR, 1948:7; NAS, 1275:9*

Lorong Telok
Telok is a bay in Malay. Lorong Telok is located off Circular Road. This lane was in existence in 1829 as shown in G D Coleman's survey map printed in 1836.
Source: *NAS, SP002997*

Lorong Temechut
Temechut or *temuchut* is lovegrass in Malay.

Lorong Tempayan (e)
Tempayan is a water jar or large jar in Malay.

Lorong Tepak (e)
Tepak is a climber, *Melodorum cylindricum* in Malay.

Lorong Tepian (e)
This road was located in Tampines. *Tepian* means edge or border in Indonesian.

Lorong Terigu (e)
Terigu means wheaten flour in Malay.

Lorong Ternak (e)
Ternak means livestock in Malay.

Lorong Tingkap (e)
Tingkap is a long barred window in Malay.

Lorong Tombak (e)
Tombak means spear or lance in Malay.

Lorong Tombong (e)
Tombong is the seed bud in a coconut in Malay.

Lorong Tongkol (e)
Tongkol means tunny fish, *Thynnus tunnina* in Malay.

(Lorong Tukang Dua/Empat/Lima/Satu/Tiga) (e)
Tukang means technician in Malay. The third name for these lanes are numerals in Malay. See *Pachitan Dua*.

Lorong Tukol (e)
Tukol or *tukul* means hammer or mallet in Malay.

Lorong Tulin (e)
Tulin means pure blooded or genuine in Malay.

Lorong Tuwu (e)
Tuwu is a kind of cuckoo bird in Malay.

Lorong Ubi Tahun (e)
Ubi means tapioca and *tahun* means year in Malay. *Tahun ubi* is the cycle for planting tapioca.

Lorong Wali (e)
Wali means governor or guardian in Malay.

Lorong Watas (e)
Watas means boundary in Malay. This lane was just outside the city limit.

Lorong Woodlands Kechil (e)
Kechil means small in Malay. *See Woodlands Avenue.*

Lorong Zaitun (e)
Zaitun means olive tree in Malay.

Lothian Terrace (Frankel Estate)
This road was named in 1954. Lothian is a village in Midlothian, Scotland. *See Burnfoot Terrace.*

Source: *ST, 1954.6.15:5*

Lotus Avenue
See Lantana Avenue.

Low Hill Road (e) (former Singapore Harbour Board)
This road was the property of Singapore Harbour Board and was the connection between Old Keppel Road and New Keppel Road when it was named in 1922.

One account mentioned that this road was named after Major James Low (not a Chinese) as his residence was on this hill. This is doubtful as Low's residence in Singapore was at North Bridge Road according to Buckley's account and he left Singapore in 1844 for Penang. He subsequently returned to England in 1852.

Source: *MC, 1922.12.29; Buckley: 377; Makepeace, vol.1:86; Singam*

Lower Bourne Road (e)

Lower Delta Road
See Delta Road. This road was formed by two roads previously known as Gagak Selari Selatan and Gagak Selari Utara before 1970.

Lower Kent Ridge Road
See Kent Ridge Road.

Lower Ring Road (Singapore Botanic Gardens)

Lower Road (e) (former Nee Soon Cantonment, See Cliff Road)

Lower Seletar Close
See Seletar Road.

Lowland Road
Lowland Road is low relative to Highland Road in the same area; it was often flooded due to its terrain. This road was repaired in 1950 and was declared a public street in 1952.
Source: *RBAR, 1950:8; RBAR, 1952:8; Serangoon: 16*

Loyang Avenue/Besar Close/Crescent/Drive/Garden/Lane/Link/Place/Rise/Street/Terrace/View/Walk
Loyang Way/1/2/3/4/6
Based on the survey report on creeks and rivers of Singapore in 1848, Loiung was the name of a creek measuring about 30 feet (20 metres) wide. Loyang was probably a derivative of Loiung. By 1902, there were advertisements relating to the sale of properties in the Loyang area.

Loyang Industrial Estate was developed in the 1970s.

Loyang Avenue and Loyang Way were opened in 1979.
Source: *SFP, 1848.5.18:3; ST, 1979.11.22*

Lucky Crescent/Gardens/Heights/Rise/View

Ludlow Place (Serangoon Gardens)
This road was named in 1953. The road name was printed as Ludloxi in the Street Directory of 1954. Ludlow is a market town in Shropshire, West Midlands, England. The oldest part of this town is the 11th century medieval walled town and the Ludlow Castle. *See Alnwick Road.*
Source: *RBAR, 1953:8*

Lutheran Road
This road was named after the Lutheran Church of our Redeemer which was built in 1960.

Luxus Hill Avenue/Drive/Road

Lyndhurst Road (former Grove Estate)
This road was named in 1939 after Lyndhurst (meaning wooded hill growing with lime trees), a village in Hampshire, England. *See Grove Road.*
Source: *SFP, 1939.7.1:2; Watts*

Lyneham Road (e) (former RAF Changi)
This road was named after RAF Lyneham (1940-2012) in Wiltshire, South West England. *See Abbotsingh Road.*

Lynwood Grove (Braddell Heights Estate)
Lynwood is a place name in England. This street was named in 1950.
Source: *ST, 1950.8.26:7*

MacAlister Road
This road is located next to the College of Medicine Building near Singapore General Hospital. Based on a news article in 1951, this road was named in 1931 after Dr. George Hugh Kidd MacAlister (1879-1930). He was the Principal of the College of Medicine (now part of NUS) from 1918 to 1930.
Source: *SFP, 1930.11.6:10; MC, 1931.7.31; SFP, 1951.5.4:5*

Macao Street (e)
Macao, in Southern China, was a Portuguese colony until 1999. This street was renamed Pickering Street on 1 January 1925.
Source: *SFP, 1924.7.25*

MacKenzie Road
This road was probably named after Henry Somerset MacKenzie, the Resident Councillor and Police Commissioner from 1856 to 1859. Roads named after his contemporaries include Church, Marshall and MacPherson.

One account mentioned that this road was named after Reverend H L MacKenzie (died 1899). This is doubtful as Mackenzie Road was already seen in the map of Prinsep Estate in 1859. Reverend Mackenzie was in charge of gospel work in Shantou, China between 1860 and 1899.
Source: *ST, 1859.7.9:2; SFP, 1900.1.3:2; NAS, SP007298; Singam*

MacKerrow Road
This road was named after William McKerrow (died 1918). He commenced his business in 1880 under the name of William McKerrow and Co. The firm ceased business around 1910 when Mckerrow joined the partnership of Paterson, Simons & Co.

MacKerrow Road was listed in the 1936 Gazetteer.
Source: *SFP, 1918.5.30:340; SG-1936; Dunlop; Makepeace, vol.2:208*

MacPherson Lane/Road
These roads were named after Lieutenant Ronald A W MacPherson (1817-1869). After serving the British Army in the first Opium War, he was appointed Executive Engineer and Superintendent of Convicts as well as President of the Municipal Commission. When the Straits Settlements became a Crown Colony in 1867, he became the first Colonial Secretary.

On 11 February 1893, a Municipal notice for road closure indicated that MacPherson Road was previously known as Coconut Road.

Source: *ST, 1893. 2 15:2; SFP, 1935.9.19:3*

MacTaggart Road (MacPherson private roads)
This road was probably named after William MacTaggart (1827–1891). He became a Partner of Syme & Co. in 1857. He was a member of the Municipal Commission and one of the founding shareholders of the New Harbour in 1861.

This road was listed in the 1936 Gazetteer and it became a public street in 1960. *See Davidson Road.*

Source: *ST, 1891.7.15:3; SG-1936; CCAR, 1960:8; Makepeace, vol.2:230; Singam*

Madden Road (e) (WW1 roads)
This road was named in 1930 after Admiral Charles Edward Madden (1862–1935), one of the leading commanders in WW1. *See Allenby Road.*

Source: *MC, 1930.10.31*

Madras Road (e) (former Singapore Naval Base)
Madras Street
Madras Road was named after Madras (now Chennai), a city in South India. India was under British control before WW2. *See Admiralty Road.*

Magazine Road
Magazine in this context is a place within which ammunition or other explosive material is stored. This road was listed as a street in town in 1853.

Source: *SFP, 1853.7.8:4*

Maida Vale (former RAF Seletar)
This road was named after Maida Vale, an affluent residential district in north London. Maida refers to the Battle of Maida outside the town of Maida in Calabria, Italy during the Napoleonic Wars in 1806. The result was a one-sided British tactical victory. *See Baker Street.*

Maidstone Road (former Ayer Rajah Barracks)
Maidstone is a town in Kent, South East England. *See Dover Road.*

Main Entrance Road (e) (former Singapore Harbour Board)
This was the main entrance road to the port.

Main Exit Road (e) (former Singapore Harbour Board)
This was the main exit road from the port.

Main Gate Road (e) (former Tanglin Barracks)
This road was named in 1913. It was the main gate of the Tanglin Barracks, the headquarters of the British Far East Land Forces.

Source: *SFP, 1914.5.30:16*

Maju Avenue/Maju Drive
Maju means forward or progress in Malay.

Makepeace Road
Walter Makepeace (1859-1941) was the Editor of Singapore Free Press and one of the founders of the Singapore Swimming Club. He was one of the General Editors of *One Hundred Years of Singapore (1819-1919)*. The book was compiled in conjunction with the centenary celebration of Singapore. Makepeace Road was named in 1926.

Source: *MC1, 1926.7.1*

Makeway Avenue
Makeway is connected to Makepeace Road mentioned above. It was made a public street in 1968. It might have been named to complement Makepeace.

Source: *ST, 1968.5.31:19*

Malabar Street
Malabar is a region in Southern India. This street, close to Kampong Glam, was probably occupied by Muslims from Malabar. There is a Masjid Malabar in nearby Jalan Sultan, which was originally the burial ground for Malabar Muslims.

Malacca Street (In CBD)
Malacca is a plant from which *gula* (sugar) malacca is extracted. It is also the name of a state in Malaysia. Malacca Street was listed as a street in town in 1853.

Source: *SFP, 1853.7.8:4*

Malan Road (former Gillman Barracks)
This road was probably named after Colonel L N Malan, the Chief Engineer, Malaya of the British Army. In 1927, he was assigned, together with Lieutenant General Gillman, to report on the defense needed to protect the new Naval Base in Sembawang. Their proposal to build an artillery base in Changi was accepted and Malan was responsible for the initial work in Changi. See *Gillman Close*.

One account mentioned that this road was named after Major C H Malan, who was commissioned in Tanglin Barracks from 1869-1871. He was at the same time active in preaching the gospel. Further research on this is needed as this road name only appeared after WW2, about the same time as Gillman Barracks.

Source: *Probert: 7; Savage & Yeoh, 2004*

Malay Settlement, Ayer Gemuroh (e)
See *Kampong Ayer Gemuroh*. This settlement was located at Wing Loong Road, close to Kampong Ayer Gemuroh.

Malay Settlement, Jalan Eunos (e)
This settlement was located at the north end of Jalan Eunos with Kampong Eunos in the South, along Sims Avenue. See *Jalan Eunos*.

Malay Settlement, Sembawang (e)
This settlement was located at the end of 23 ms Sembawang Road, at the seashore between Jalan Selimang and Jalan Mempurong. Sembawang Village is located at 21 ms along the same road.

Malay Settlement, West Coast Road (e)
This settlement was located at West Coast Road near Sungei Pandan. West Coast Village was also in West Coast Road, close to Clementi Road.

Malay Street (Parallel to Bugis Street)

Malcolm Park/Road
General Neill Malcolm (1869–1953) was the GOC of the Troops in the Straits Settlements from 1921 to 1924. He was at the same time the Assistant General Manager of the Free Mason in 1923. After his retirement in 1924, he was appointed Chairman of the North Borneo Chartered Company. He remained in that position for 20 years.

Source: *SFP, 1924.4.24:7; Singam*

Malta Crescent/Road (e) (former Singapore Naval Base)
Malta is a South European island country in the Mediterranean Sea, which was part of the British Empire before WW2. See *Admiralty Road*.

Man Road (e)
This road led to the former Outram Road Prison.

Manasseh Lane (e)
This road was named after Manasseh Meyer in 1901. See *Meyer Road*.

Source: *MC, 1901.8.14*

Manchester Crescent (e) (former RAF Tengah)
This road was named after Avro Manchester, a British twin engine heavy bomber developed by Avro during WW2. See *Hornet Road*.

Mandai Avenue/Estate/Lake Road
(Mandai Lake Road Track 9/11/15) (e)
Mandai Link/Quarry Road/Road
Mandai Road Track 2 (e)/3/7/15, 16, 18/27 (e)/29 (e)/31A (e)
Mandai was derived from Sungei Mandai Besar, a river shown in J T Thomson's survey map of 1852 together with a hill named Bukit Ulu Mandai.

The name of the river and district became Mandi in H E McCallum's map of 1885. Bukit Mandai Road was mentioned in an 1883 Municipal minutes of meeting as a road needing repairs.
Source: ST, 1883.7.12:11; NAS, TM000003, NAS, SP006362

Mandalay Road
Mandalay is the second largest city and the last royal capital of Myanmar. It is located north of Yangon on the east bank of the Irrawaddy River. This road was declared a public street in 1957. *See Burmah Road.*
Source: CCAR, 1957:5

Mandarin Road (e)
Mandarin is the official form of the Chinese language. It is also the English name for a senior official in the former imperial Chinese Civil Service. This road was located in the Balestier Road area and was named in 1901.
Source: MC, 1901.12.18

Mangchoon Place (e)
Mangchoon is a small boat.
Source: *Savage & Yeoh, 2004*

Mangis Road
Mangis means mangosteen in Malay. This road was known as Lorong 205, Siglap until 1934. *See Tembeling Road.*
Source: ST, 1934.3.8:19

Manila Street
Manila is the capital of the Philippines. This street is close to Bugis Street.

Mansoor Street (e)
M C Mansoor, an Armenian, had a shop in Malacca Street in the jewellery and shipping business. This street was named in 1903.
Source: ST, 1903.7.4:5; Wright: 308

Manston Road (e) (former RAF Changi)
This road was named after RAF Manston in Kent, South East England. *See Abbotsingh Road.*

Mantlesham Road (e)
This is a misprint of Martlesham in the Street Directory of 1950.

Maple Avenue/Lane
See Cherry Avenue.

Mar Thoma Road
This road was named after the Eastern Orthodox Church in the vicinity.

Marang Road
This road was named after Abdul Hamid bin Marang, a Malay teacher. Marang was actually his father's name.
Source: *Hussain S Z, "Keeping the faith", ST, 2012: 111*

Maranta Avenue (Singapore Botanic Gardens)
Maranta is a flowering plant in the family *Marantaceae*. This road was named in 1913.
Source: *SFP, 1914.5.30:16*

Margaret Avenue (e) (Jurong Road)

Margaret Close (e)/Drive (Queenstown)
These roads were named after Princess Margaret, the sister of QE2.

Margate Road (former Grove Estate)
This road was named in 1928. Margate is a seaside town in Kent, England. *See Clacton Road and Grove Road.*
Source: *MC, 1928.9.28*

Margoliouth Road
L C Margoliouth (died c.1937) was a Manager in the South British Insurance Company and Director of several other companies. He was a member of the Municipal Commission for several years beginning in 1927.
Source: *ST, 1927.5.14:8; Dunlop*

Maria Avenue
Maria is an Italian name for a lady, equivalent to Mary in English. Maria Avenue, near Opera Estate, was opened in 1967.
Source: *ST, 1967.3.27:4*

Mariam Close/Walk/Way
Mariam is a Malay name for female, equivalent to Mary in English.

Marigold Drive
This road was named in 1954. *See Carnation Drive.*
Source: *RBAR, 1954:8*

Marina Boulevard/Marina Coastal Drive
Marina Coastal Expressway
Marina East Drive
Marina Gardens Drive
Marina Green/Grove
(Marina Lane 1/2/3/4) (e)
Marina Mall/Park (e)/Place (e)/Promenade (e)
Marina South Drive/Marina Station Road

Marina Street (e)/View/View Link/Way
Marine Crescent/Drive
Marine Parade Central/Road
Marine Terrace/Marine Vista
Marine Parade Road was named in 1931.

Source: *MC, 1931.9.25*

Maritime Avenue (e)/Maritime Square

Market Street
Market Street already existed in 1829 as it was included in G D Coleman's survey map printed in 1836. One other Market Street was changed to Crawford Street in 1858.

Source: *SFP, 1858.4.1:6; NAS, SP002997*

Marlene Avenue
Marlene is the name of a lady. This road was seen in the press in 1951. It was however a dead end road until the 1980s.

Source: *ST,1951.10.10:5*

Marne Road (WW1 roads)
This road was named in 1928 after The Marne, a river in an area east and southeast of Paris, the site of one of the famous battlefields during WW1. *See Allenby Road.*

Two battles were fought at The Marne during WW1, in 1914 and 1918, with casualties of more than 70,000.

Source: *MC1, 1928.10.2*

Marshall Lane/Road
Marshall Road was named after Captain H T Marshall, Superintendent of Peninsular & Oriental Steam Navigation Co. He was the first President of the Municipal Commission in 1856. The road was known as Lorong 201, Siglap before 1934.

Source: *ST, 1934.3.8:19; Buckley: 629; Singam*

Marsiling Avenue (e)/Crescent/Drive
Marsiling Industrial Estate Road 1-10
Marsiling Lane/Rise/Road/Village (e)
Marsiling may have been derived from the name of Lim Nee Soon's ancestral home in Maxi Village in the province of Canton (now Guangdong). The village is now in the suburb of Shantou City. His residence in Sembawang was named "Maxi Lu", translated as humble house in Maxi. Marsiling Village was named in 1949. *See Nee Soon Road.*

Source: *RBAR, 1949:9; Lim HS: 117; Song: 516-517*

Martaban Road

Martaban (now Mottama) is a small town in Mon State, south of Myanmar. This road was named in 1929. *See Burmah Road.*

Source: *MC, 1929.7.26*

Martia Road

This road was named after D M Martia (1851-1910) who worked in the Municipal Office for 35 years. He was an Assistant Engineer before his death. This road was declared a public street in 1957.

Source: *ST, 1910.12.22:6; CCAR, 1957:5; Braga: 95*

Martin Lane (e)/Place/Road

The Martin family were immigrants from Armenia and were dealing in liquor and local produce. Martin Lane was named in 1912.

Source: *MC, 1912.12.27; SFP, 1913.2.1:7; Singam*

Martlesham Road (former RAF Changi)

This road was named after RAF Martlesham Heath in Suffolk, South East England. Martlesham Road was originally named Artillery Road when the Changi area was a Royal Artillery Base before WW2. *See Abbotsingh Road.*

Source: *Probert: 19*

Maryland Drive

This road was named after Maryland Park Estate in 1954.

Source: *ST, 1954.3.26:4; RBAR, 1954:8*

Marymount Lane/Road/Terrace

The above were named after the Marymount Convent School in this vicinity. The school was established in 1939 by the Sisters of the Good Shepherd, a Catholic congregation founded by St. Mary Euphrasia. Marymount Road was commissioned in 1979.

Source: *ST, 1979.7.15:6*

Mas Kuning Terrace

See Jalan Mas Kuning.

Mata Ikan Road (e)/Village (e)

Mata means eye and *ikan* means fish in Malay. *Mata ikan* is fish eye.

Mata Ikan Road was located at 10 ms Changi Road. It was merged with Somapah Road in 1949. Mata Ikan Village was located at the end of the merged Somapah Road at the seashore and was demolished in the 1980s.

Mata Road (former Singapore Naval Base)

Mata means eye in Malay. *See Admiralty Road.*

Matlock Rise (Braddell Heights Estate)
Matlock is a place name in England. This street was named in 1951.
Source: *CC, 1951.11.28*

Mattar Road
This road was named after Shaikh Sallim Mattar, an Arabian who helped fund the building of Sallim Mattar Mosque.
Source: *Dunlop*

Maude Road (WW1 roads)
This road was named after Lieutenant General Frederick Stanley Maude (1864–1917), a British commander who was most famous for conquering Baghdad in 1917 during WW1. However, he became ill from cholera and abruptly died in Baghdad. This road was declared a public street in 1929. See *Allenby Road*.
Source: *SFP, 1929.7.27:11*

Maxwell Link/Road
Maxwell Road was named after the Maxwell family to commemorate their contributions to Singapore. Based on a news article in 1959, Sir Peter Benson Maxwell (1816–1893) was the Recorder of Singapore from 1866 to 1871. He became the first Chief Justice when the title of Recorder was changed to Chief Justice of the Straits Settlements in 1867. His four sons were all successful colonial civil servants in South East Asia and Australia.

Maxwell Road was named in 1925.
Source: *SFP, 1893.4.7:2; SFP, 1925.5.6:8; ST, 1959.8.26:6; Singam*

May Road

Mayfield Avenue
Mayfield is a multiple place name in England.

Mayflower Avenue/Crescent/Drive/Lane/Place/Rise/Road/Terrace/Way

Mayne Road
This road was probably named after J O Mayne, the Colonial Engineer who designed/constructed the bridges and water supply system as well as the reconstruction of the St. Andrew's Cathedral in Singapore. He served as a Municipal Commissioner for several years from 1862.
Source: *ST, 1862.8.23:1*

Mayo Road/Street (e) (Kampong Kapor)
Mayo Street was named after Lord Mayo, Richard Bourke (1822–1872), the fourth Governor-General and Viceroy of India from 1869 to 1872. He was

murdered in the course of his duty by a convict in Port Blair, Andaman Islands. *See Clive Street.*

McAlister Road (e)
This was a misprint of MacAlister Road in the Street Directories from 1961 to 1966.

McCallum Street
Sir Henry E McCallum (1852-1919) was a Colonial Engineer. He was in charge of building various military fortifications in Singapore, including Blakang Mati (now Sentosa Island) around 1878. After that he was a governor at several places, including Lagos, Newfoundland and finally Ceylon in 1907. McCallum Street was named and declared a public street in 1895.

Source: *MC, 1895.2.27; SFP, 1919.12.1:6; Makepeace, vol.2:461; Singam*

McNair Road
John Frederick Adolphus McNair (1828-1910) was the Executive Engineer and Superintendent of Convicts of the Straits Settlements. He employed Indian convicts in the construction of roads and buildings, including the St. Andrew's Cathedral and the Government House (now The Istana) between 1862 and 1869. This road was named in 1901.

Source: *MC, 1901.12.18; SFP, 1910.6.13:6*

McNally Street (e)
Joseph McNally (1923-2002), a brother from the La Salle Christian Brotherhood (*see La Salle Street*), was the founder of the Singapore La Salle-SIA College of the Arts.

Meadowgreen Avenue (e)

Medang Road (e) (Thiam Siew Village, Tanjong Katong)
Medang is the generic name for many trees in the order of *Laurinaceae* and for others with a timber of similar appearance, such as *Litsea firma*. See *Thiam Siew Avenue.*

Media Circle/Link/Walk (Mediapolis@One North)

Medical Drive (NUS)

Medway Drive (Serangoon Gardens)
This road was named in 1953. Medway is a unitary authority within Kent, South East England. Rochester Castle is a landmark in Medway. *See Alnwick Road.*

Source: *RBAR, 1953:8*

Mei Chin Road
Mei Hwan Crescent/Drive/Road/View (e)

Mei Ling Street
With the exception of Mei Hwan Road/View, the above roads were first seen in the 1969 Street Directory.

Mekong Walk (e) (Delta Estate)
Mekong River flows through the Indo-China Peninsular with its upper reaches in China, known as Lancang River. *See Ganges Avenue.*

Melbourne Road (e) (former Singapore Naval Base)
Melbourne is the capital of Victoria, Australia. *See Admiralty Road.*

Melrose Drive (Braddell Heights Estate)
Melrose is a place name in England. This street was named in 1951.
Source: *CC, 1951.11.28*

Meng Suan Road
This road was named in 1956. It is located close to Thong Bee Road (Nee Soon Village).
Source: *RBAR, 1956:9*

Mengkuang Road (e) (Thiam Siew Village, Tanjong Katong)
Mengkuang is the common screwpine in Malay. Mengkuang is also the name of a small village near Butterworth in Penang, Malaysia. *See Thiam Siew Avenue.*

Meragi Close/Road/Terrace
Meragi means painted snipe, *Rostratula capensis* in Malay.

Merah Road (e) (former Singapore Naval Base)
Merah means red in Malay. *See Admiralty Road.*

Meranti Avenue/Crescent/Drive (e)/Lane/Place (e)/Road/View
Meranti is a large emergent forest tree with a dense hemispherical crown, native to Singapore. The wood is a source of Light Red Meranti timber used for light carpentry. *See Banyan Avenue.*

There was another Meranti Road in Tanjong Katong which was expunged. *See Thiam Siew Avenue.*

Merbau Road
Merbau is a tree. *See Ayer Merbau Road.*

Merbok Crescent (e)
Merbok means barred ground-dove, *Geopelia striata* in Malay.

Merchant Lane (e)/Loop/Road
Merchant Road appeared in the Municipal minutes in 1876 with regard to property owners' request to build a road from New Market Road to Merchant Road.
Source: *STOJ, 1876.12.2:2*

Mergui Road
Mergui (now Myeik) is a city located in the extreme south of Myanmar on the coast of an island on the Andaman Sea. This road was named in 1922. *See Burmah Road.*

Source: *ST, 1922.2.23:8*

Merino Crescent
Merino is a breed of sheep prized for its wool. The breed origins are not known but are probably in North Africa. This road became a public street in 1957. *See Shepherds Drive.*

Source: *CCAR, 1957:5*

Merkeh Road (e)

Merlimau Lane/Place/Road
Merlimau is a scandent thorny wild orange, *Paramignya monophylia*. The above roads are found on Jurong Island. They were named after Pulau Merlimau, one of the offshore islands which were amalgamated to form the present Jurong Island. *See Ayer Chawan Place.*

Merlion Walk
Merlion is a word combining mermaid and lion. The Merlion creature was created as a Singapore symbol, a mascot. The first Merlion sculpture was completed in 1972.

Merpati Road
Merpati means dove or pigeon in Malay. This road was a rename of Jalan Merpati.

Merryn Avenue/Close/Drive/Road/Terrace
The above roads were probably named after St. Merryn, a village in north Cornwall. *See Berrima Road.*

Mersawa Road (e)
Mersawa is a tree, *Anisoptera spp.* in Malay.

Meteor Road (e) (former RAF Tengah)
This road was named after Gloster Meteor, the first British jet fighter during WW2. *See Hornet Road.*

Metropole Drive (Opera Estate)
Metropole is derived from the Greek metropolis for mother city. This road was named in 1957.

Source: *RBAR, 1957:8*

Meyappa Chettiar Road
Based on news articles in 1933 and 1977, this road was named after the owner of the land along this road, S N S M Meyappa Chettiar (died 1932). Meyappa Chettiar was well known in the Indian community as a generous person towards the poor. This road was declared a public street in 1960. See *Annamalai Chetty Avenue*.

Source: *ST, 1933.11.9:6; CCAR, 1960:7; ST, 1977.4.6:11; NAS, 1247:3*

Meyer Place/Road
Meyer Road was named after Manasseh Meyer (1843-1930) in 1921. Meyer started trading in opium which he sourced from India and became a big landowner. He was a Municipal Commissioner from 1893 to 1900.

Source: *MC, 1921.2.25*

Middle Road
Middle Road is the link between North Bridge Road and Victoria Street. The road existed in 1829 as it was included in G D Coleman's survey map printed in 1836.

One other Middle Road, located in the former Singapore Naval Base, was renamed Old Middle Road.

Source: *NAS, SP002997*

Middlesex Road (former Tanglin Barracks)
Middlesex was a county in South East England; it became part of Greater London in 1953. This road was named after the Middlesex Regiment which was active in Singapore between 1908 and 1930. See *Barrack Road*.

Mill Lane (e)
This lane was located in Kampong Bugis, near the gas works. It was named in 1906.

Source: *MC, 1906.11.30*

Miller Street
This street was named after 1936. It may be named after C D Miller who was a member of the Municipal Commission in 1934.

Source: *SFP, 1934.9.29*

Milne Road (e)
This road was named after Reverend W Milne, a Protestant missionary, who applied to Raffles for land in May 1819 to build a church.

Source: *Makepeace, vol.2:235; Singam*

Miltonia Close/Link
Miltonia is a kind of orchid.

Mimosa Crescent/Drive/Place/Road/Terrace/Vale/View/Walk/Way (e)
Mimosa is a plant that folds its leaves when touched or exposed to heat.

Min Hock Road (e)

Minaret Walk
The minaret is a distinctive architectural structure akin to a tower found adjacent to mosques. It provides a visual focal point and is used for the Muslim call to pray. This street is close to a mosque.

Minbu Road
Minbu, also known as Sagu, is a city in the centre region of Myanmar. *See Burmah Road.*

Minden Road (former Tanglin Barracks)
This road was named before WW2 as it appeared in the map of Tanglin Barracks in 1936. The road was named after the Battle of Minden in 1759; it was the most decisive engagement during the Seven Years War between the allied nations of Britain, Hanover, Prussia and France. In Britain, the victory was considered to constitute the Annus Mirabilis of 1759. *See Barrack Road.*

Source: *ST, 1913.7.10:8*

Ming Teck Park

Minto Road
Lord Minto (1751–1814) was the Governor-General of India between 1806 and 1813. He was the superior of Raffles when the latter was in Java and Bencoolen. Minto was succeeded by Marquess of Hastings.

    Minto Road was listed as a street in town in 1853.

Source: *SFP, 1853.7.8:4; Singam*

Miri Road (e)
Miri is a coastal city in northeastern Sarawak, Malaysia. It is noted for its oil and gas reserve as well as timber exports. This road was named in 1930. *See Borneo Road.*

Source: *MC, 1930.7.29*

Mistri Road
Navriji R Mistri (1885–1953) was the Parsi (*see Parsi Road*) entrepreneur who started the Phoenix Aerated Water Company in 1925. He donated a large part of his wealth towards medical services in Singapore.

Source: *SFP, 1953.10.29:1*

Moh Guan Terrace
Based on a news article in 1955, this road was named after See Moh Guan (died 1879). He was the son of See Hood Kee, the founder of the Hokkien clan in Singapore. *See Seng Poh Road.*

Source: *SFP, 1955.7.18:12; Kua: 213*

Mohamed Ali Lane
This lane was originally known as Mohamed Allie Lane and was named after Mohamed Allie in 1883.

The account that this lane was named after M M Ali Namazie (1864–1931), the owner of Capitol Theatre in 1929 is doubtful. Namazie was born in Madras and came to Singapore in 1909, after this lane was named.

Source: *MC, 1883.12.27; SFP, 1931.7.27:10; Dunlop*

Mohamed Sultan Road
Sultan is the title of a king in Malay. However, it is sometimes seen in personal names, such as Moona Kader Sultan, the cattle trader of Karikal Lane.

Colloquial Name: "Zui Long Tao", the main water factory. (*Phua, 1952:199*)

Monk's Hill Road/Terrace
Monk's Hill Terrace was named in 1926.

Source: *MC1, 1926.7.1*

Mons Road (e) (WW1 roads)
This road was named in 1928 after Mons-Conde Canal in Belgium, the site of one of the famous battlefields during WW1. *See Allenby Road.*

The Battle of Mons in August 1914 was the first major action of the British Expeditionary Force against the Germans in WW1.

Source: *MC1, 1928.10.2*

Montreal Drive/Link/Road (former Singapore Naval Base)
Montreal is the largest city in the Canadian province of Quebec. *See Admiralty Road.*

Moon Crescent (e)
Located in Changi Prison, this road was named in 1952.

Source: *RBAR, 1952:8*

Moonbeam Drive/Terrace/View/Walk

Moonstone Lane
Moonstone is a type of gemstone. This lane is located off Serangoon Road together with a few other roads which were named after gemstones, including Opal Crescent, Ruby Lane and Topaz Road. This road was named in 1952.

Source: *ST, 1952.5.1:7*

Moreton Close (Serangoon Gardens)
This road was named in 1953. Moreton village is a multiple place name in England. *See Alnwick Road.*

Source: *RBAR, 1953:8*

Morley Road
This name was probably taken from Morley, a market town in Leeds, England.

Mornington Crescent (former RAF Seletar)
This road was named after a street in Camden, London. *See Baker Street.*

Morrison Hill (e)
This road was probably named after Robert Morrison (died 1834), the first Protestant Missionary to China and who served there for 27 years. He was involved in the establishment of the Singapore Institution (renamed Raffles College) and was its first Vice Chairman of the Board.

Source: *Buckley: 54*

Morse Road
This road was named in 1908 after Morse, the name of the telegraphic code used extensively in the late 19th century for international communications. *See Pender Road.*

Source: *MC, 1908.2.28*

Mosque Square (e) (Masjid Malacca)

Mosque Street (Masjid Jamae Chulia)
Mosque Street was listed as a street in town in 1853.

Source: *SFP, 1853.7.8:4*

Mosquito Road (e) (former RAF Tengah)
This road was named after de Havilland Mosquito, a British multi-role combat aircraft which served during WW2. *See Hornet Road.*

Moss Avenue (e)
This road was probably named after S H Moss, a Partner in Derrick and Company, an accounting firm. He was a Municipal Commissioner. He retired in 1935 and returned to England.

Source: *SFP, 1935.10.10:1*

Moulmein Rise/Road
Moulmein (now Mawlamyine) is the fourth largest city of Myanmar. It is located south of Myanmar at the mouth of River Salween. Moulmein Road was named in 1900. *See Burmah Road.*

Source: *SFP, 1900.1.18:3*

Mount Echo Park

Mount Elizabeth/Link/Road

Mount Elizabeth was a nutmeg plantation and the residence of Thomas Hewetson, a clerk to the magistrate. It was described by Buckley as "the furthest house in Tanglin" in 1842.

Mount Elizabeth Road was named around 1901.

Source: *SFP, 1901.10.1:4; Buckley: 377*

Mount Emily Road (e)

Most accounts on Mount Sophia state that it was a rename of Bukit Selegie. However, information from newspapers seem to indicate that Bukit Selegie was more likely renamed as Mount Emily. This is due to the fact that Government Notifications between 1843 and 1847 used Mount Sophia and Bukit Selegie to describe the two hills along Selegie Road and both hills appeared in G D Coleman's survey map printed in 1836. Mount Emily only appeared alongside Mount Sophia in a later survey map drawn by J T Thomson in 1852 and in the news from 1864.

Based on a news article in 1950, Mount Emily and its surrounding land were part of the nutmeg estate owned by Charles Robert Prinsep ("CRP"), which he acquired around 1841 (see *Prinsep Street*). As the name of the hill was changed between 1847 and 1852, the hill may not be named after CRP's daughter Mary Emily Prinsep, as stated in most etymologies of this hill, since she was born in 1853.

As names of other smaller hills in the Prinsep Estate bore names of CRP's wife and sisters, it is possible that Mount Emily was named after his sister Amelia (nicknamed Emily).

Mount Emily Road was made a public street in 1929.

Source: *SFP, 1843.12.23:1; SFP, 1847.12.16:1; ST, 1929.1.18:10; ST, 1950.10.14:6; NAS, SP002981; NAS, SP002997; NAS, SP006362; Allbrook, Malcolm: Henry Prinsep's Empire [http://press.anu.edu.au?p=290761]*

Mount Faber Loop/Mount Faber Road

The above were named after C E Faber, the Chief Engineer who built the road to reach the top of Telok Blangah Hill in 1844. The hill was renamed Mount Faber the following year.

Source: *Buckley: 431*

Mount Pleasant Drive/Mount Pleasant Road

Mount Pleasant was also known as Bukit Brown. The hill was originally owned by G H Brown, one of the founders of the Tanjong Pagar Dock Company, who built his residence at Mount Pleasant. Mount Pleasant Road was named in 1929.

Source: *MC, 1929.7.26; Makepeace, vol.2:1; Singam*

Mount Road (e) (former Nee Soon Cantonment. *See Cliff Road*)

Mount Rosie Road/Terrace
T H Sohst (died 1912) was a nobleman from Germany. He married Rosalie de Souza, daughter of a wealthy merchant in 1868 and named his residence Mount Rosie Estate (*see De Souza Avenue*). In 1912, a proposal to officially name the road Mount Rosie Road was changed by the Municipal Commission to Sohst Road (*see Sohst Road*). However, it was eventually renamed Mount Rosie Road in 1920 after WW1.

Source: *MC, 1920.3.26; ST, 1939.2.1:12*

Mount Sinai Avenue/Crescent/Drive/Lane/Plain/Rise/Road/View/Walk
Mount Sinai is the sacred mountain in the bible.

Mount Sophia
There are two possible etymologies for Mount Sophia:
- Sophia Hull, the wife of Raffles, who was the original owner of this hill.
- Sophia Cooke, Head of Chinese Girls' School (now St. Margaret's School of the Anglican Church), a missionary teacher in Singapore for 42 years from 1853.

The first occupant of the hill was Captain William Flint, the brother-in-law of Raffles, after Raffles left Singapore in 1823. He named it Flint's Hill. Flint passed away in 1828 and the hill was renamed Mount Sophia around 1831.

C R Prinsep acquired the hill around 1841. His daughter Sophia was born in 1850. *See Mount Emily.*

From newspaper records, the hill was named Prinsep's Hill for a short period before 1874. From early 1874, the name of Mount Sophia reappeared in the news and by then, the Chinese Girls' School was already established in the hill from 1861 and it was therefore possible that the name of Sophia was reinstated for Sophia Cooke.

One account mentioned that the hill was named after Sophia Blackmore, the founder of Methodist Girls' School. This was not likely as Ms. Blackmore came to Singapore in 1887.

Source: *SCCR, 1831.5.25:3; ST, 1865.11.3:2; STOJ, 1874.1.29:9; ST, 1950.10.14:6, Makepeace, vol.2:450; Allbrook, Malcolm: Henry Prinsep's Empire [http://press.anu.edu.au?p=290761]*

Mount Vernon Road

Mount Vernon is a place name often used in Britain and USA, including the plantation estate and the final resting place of George Washington. Mount Vernon was first seen in J McNair's map of 1873.

Source: *NAS, SP006819*

Mount Washington (e)

Washington is the capital and the name of a state in USA. This place name was seen in the press in 1908. A 1932 news article mentioned that the Alkaff family mansion at the end of Pender Road was named Mount Washington. It is now known as Alkaff Mansion in Telok Blangah Hill.

Source: *ST, 1908.8.24:8; MSP, 1932.6.25:7*

Mountbatten Road

Admiral of the fleet Louis Mountbatten (1900-1979) was the Commander of South East Asia Command when he accepted the surrender of the Japanese in Singapore on 12 September 1945. After the war he was the last Viceroy of India and thereafter served as the Chief of Defence Staff. This road was renamed from Grove Road in 1946 upon the agreement of Lord Mountbatten.

Source: *MC, 1946.6.28*

Mowbray Road

Mowbray is a multiple place name in England.

Muar Road (e)

This road was named after Muar, a town in Johor, Malaysia. It was declared a public street in 1890.

Source: *ST, 1891.4.28:9*

Mugliston Gardens/Park/Road/Walk

Mugliston Garden/Park/Walk in the Yio Chu Kang area were built on land originally owned by the Bukit Sembawang Rubber Company Ltd and were named after its Chairman, Gerald Ronald Knight Mugliston (died 1953). See *Bukit Mugliston*.

Mugliston Road is located in the East Coast. It could be named after the above G R K Mugliston or his father, Dr. Thomas Crighton Mugliston (1854-1931). Both were members of the Municipal Commission. Dr. Mugliston arrived in Singapore in 1881 and was a Senior Surgeon in Penang and Singapore.

Source: *SFP, 1931.5.9:11; Makepeace, vol.1:518*

Muisian Lane (e)

Muisian is a county in Guangdong Province, China. Muisian Lane was renamed Faculty Road in 1971. See *Faculty Avenue and Nanyang Avenue*.

Mulberry Avenue (Sennett Estate)
Mulberry is the common name for *Morus*, a flowering plant. This road was named in 1951. *See Angsana Avenue.*

Source: *CC, 1951.9.28*

Munshi Abdullah Avenue/Walk (Teachers' Housing Estate)
Munshi Abdullah (1797-1854) was a Malay writer. He served as one of the Secretaries to Raffles. *See Iqbal Avenue.*

Murai Farmway
This road was named after Sungei Murai, which was dammed in the early 1980s. *Murai* is a kind of bird, such as Straits robin, in Malay. *See Jalan Murai.*

Murray Street/Terrace
The above were named after Colonel Alexander Murray (1850-1910), Colonial Engineer and Surveyor from 1897 to 1909. He was the Commander of the Singapore Volunteer Corps (1899-1905). Murray Street was named in 1930.

Source: *ST, 1910.4.25:7; MC, 1930.6.27; Makepeace, vol.1:391*

Muscat Street (Kampong Glam)
This street was named in 1909. Muscat is the capital of Oman in the Middle East. Muscat is also thought to be one of the possible origins of the Muscat family of grapes. *See Arab Street.*

Source: *MC, 1909.10.1*

Muslim Cemetery Path 1 to 12, 12A, 13, 15 to 22, 24, 26, 28

Muswell Hill (Braddell Heights Estate)
Muswell Hill is a multiple place name in England. This street was named in 1950.

Source: *ST, 1950.8.26:7*

Muthuraman Chetty Road
Based on press reports in 1923 and 1932, there were two Chettys with the name of Muthuraman. They were Moona Navena Moona Etaba Toona Muthuraman Chetty and S V S Muthuraman Chetty and both had monetary disputes with their debtors. *See Annamalai Chetty Avenue.*

Source: *SFP, 1923.12.31:2; SFP, 1932.6.14:2*

Nagapa Lane (e)
Nagapa is an Indian personal name, such as Nagapa Chetty. According to a news article in 1904, he was one of the trustees of the Hindu Temple in South Bridge Road.

Source: *ST, 1904.9.10:5*

Nallur Road
Nallur is a place in the northeast of Sri Lanka. This road became a public street in 1953.

Source: *RBAR, 1953:7*

Nam Lock Street (e)
Boey Nam Lock (died 1914, Cantonese) was the owner of a leather processing factory in Kallang Road. This road was off Kallang Road and was named in 1906.

Source: *MC, 1906.11.30; ST, 1914.3.24:8; Kua: 184; Song: 184*

Namly Avenue/Close/Crescent/Drive/Garden/Grove/Hill/Lane(e)/Place/Rise/Street (e)/View
Land around the Sixth Avenue was once owned by A Annamalai. The name Namly, an Anglicised word of Annamalai, was decided by the Rural Board in 1941. Nevertheless, the owner retained his name in Anamalai Avenue, located between Sixth Avenue and Bukit Timah Road. *See King's Road.*

Source: *ST, 1941.08.15:7; Information was provided by a senior government officer who knows the Annamalai family personally*

Nankin Street (e)
Nankin Street Mall
Based on a news article in 1837, Nankin was originally spelt Nankeen. It is now known as Nanjing, the capital of Jiangsu Province in China.

Source: *SFP, 1837.6.22:3*

Nanking Road (e)
This road was merged with Nanyang Avenue in 1971 and became Nanyang Drive. *See Nanyang Avenue.*

Nanson Road
William Nanson (1849–1911) was a prominent lawyer at the end of the 19th century. He was a Municipal Commissioner from 1892 to 1900.

Source: *SFP, 1911.5.24:6; Singam*

Nanyang Avenue/Circle/Crescent/Drive/Green/Hill/Link/Terrace/Valley/View/Walk
Nanyang Avenue was named in 1954, it was within the domain of the former Nanyang University established by the Chinese communities in South East Asia and was operational from 1955–1980. The university was then reconstituted as Nanyang Technological University with almost all road names in the campus renamed to suit the new use for the campus. *See Faculty Avenue.*

In 1971, Nanyang Avenue was merged with Nanking Road and the merged road was renamed Nanyang Drive. The present Nanyang Avenue is a new road at the campus. The following is a list of current road names against the original names:
- Nanyang Circle was Szechuan Road
- Nanyang Crescent was a merger of Peking Road, Sinkiang Road and Tientsin Road
- Nanyang Green was Hangchow Road
- Nanyang Hill was Hoi How Lane
- Nanyang Valley was Chungking Road

Source: *RBAR, 1954:8*

Nanyang Poly Drive

Napier Road
This road was named after William Napier (1804–1879), the first lawyer in Singapore and one of the founders of *Singapore Free Press and Mercantile Advertiser* in 1835. He was the editor of the weekly newspaper until 1846. From 1847 to 1851, he was appointed the Deputy Lieutenant Governor of Labuan. His residence in Tang Leng estate was named Tyersall. It was sold around 1857 to Sultan Abubakar of Johore who converted it into Istana Tyersall.

Napier Road was listed as a country road in 1853.

Source: *SFP, 1851.6.13:3; SFP, 1853.7.8:4; ST, 1935.9.19:13; NN, 1979.8.26:6; Buckley: 275*

Narayanan Chetty Road
This road appeared in the 1936 Gazetteer. Between 1905 and 1924 there were at least seven Narayanan Chettys with different first names in the newspaper reports. *See Annamalai Avenue.*

Narcis Street (Road) (e)
This street was occasionally misprinted as Narcis Road. It was named after Nerses Joaquim, the son of diamond merchant Parsick Joaquim (c.1818–1872). Narcis is a corruption of Nerses. This street was declared a public street in 1926.

Source: *SFP, 1926.9.17:6; T Pagar: 135*

Narooma Road
This road was possibly named after Narooma, a town on the far south coast of New South Wales, Australia. Narooma is an aboriginal word that means clear blue water. *See Berrima Road.*

Nassim Hill/Road
S Nassim was a Jewish merchant who owned a nutmeg plantation in the Tanglin area. In 1863 the Municipal Commissioner discussed the extension of Grange Road to Napier Road which required a part of his land. Nassim Road was officially named and made a public street in 1905.
Source: *ST, 1863.6.6:2; MC, 1905.1.27; Singam*

Nathan Road (former Sri Menanti Estate)
This road was named in 1910 after S J Nathan, a Jewish broker. It was confirmed as the official name again in 1912 when it became a public street.
Source: *MC, 1910.1.21; MC, 1912.12.27; Singam*

Naval Base Road (e) (former Singapore Naval Base)

Nee Soon Road/Village (e)
Nee Soon Road was officially named in 1950 by the Rural Board to facilitate postal services. It was named after Lim Nee Soon (1879–1936, Teochew) who owned a huge parcel of land in what is now the Yishun area. Not only was he the Pineapple King and Rubber King, he was a banker and a land-owner, and was active in public affairs. He was a member of the Rural Board from 1913–1921. Like many other wealthy Chinese community leaders of his time, Lim was a strong supporter of Sun Yat-Sen's revolutionary activities in China. It was reported that when he passed away in Shanghai, he was given a state funeral by the Chinese government and was buried close to Sun's mausoleum. Lim and his family once had the largest number of roads named after a single family in Singapore. Besides Nee Soon, he was also known as Bah Soon (peranakan name), Kee Hua, Wei Hua, Chong Sin and Chong Nee. Family members that have roads named after them include Teo Lee, Peng Nguan, Peck Hay, Chong Kuo and Chong Pang, etc.
Source: *RBAR, 1950:9; Kua: 118*

Neil Road
James George Smith Neil (1810–1857) was a Scottish military officer of the East India Company who served during the Indian Mutiny of 1857. He was infamous for the indiscriminate killing of native Indians during the uprising. He died in action in Lucknow. In 1858, the Municipal Commission decided to name a portion of Salat Road (now known as Silat Road) as Neil Road.
Source: *SFP 1858.4.1:6*

Nek Road (e) (former Gillman Barracks)
This road was located in Gillman Barracks next to Anzac Road. It was likely to be named after the Battle of the Nek in WW1. *Nek* is an African word for mountain pass. The Nek was a narrow stretch of ridge in the Anzac

battlefield on the Gallipoli Peninsular in Turkey. The campaign in Gallipoli started on 25 April 1915, a date now commemorated as the Anzac day.

Nelson Road (e)

This road was located close to the old Singapore Harbour Board. It was named in 1897 after Vice Admiral Horatio Nelson (1758-1805), the hero of the Battle of Trafalgar who died after the pivotal victory against the combined Napoleonic French and Royal Spanish fleets off the southwest coast of Spain in 1805. The Municipal Commissioners thought the name was suitable as this road would be much used by sailors arriving at the port.

Source: *ST, 1897.1.14:3*

Nemesu Avenue

Nemesu is the Malay name for a species of rainforest tree, genus *Shorea dipterocarpaceae*, also known as Dark Red Meranti. This road was first named Chempaka Avenue in 1956. However the name was changed to Nemesu in the same year.

Source: *RBAR, 1956:9*

Neo Pee Teck Lane

Neo Pee Teck was a part owner of a rubber factory. He passed away in 1947.

Source: *ST, 1947.11.20:2*

Neo Tiew Crescent
Neo Tiew Lane 1 to 3, (4 to 11) (e)
Neo Tiew Road

Neo Tiew (1884-1975, Hokkien) was a pioneer in the development of Lim Chu Kang in the early 20th century. In 1914, he organised workers to help estate owners to clear more than 1,500 acres of land in the Lim Chu Kang area. Subsequently, he rented and purchased 200 acres of land in Lim Chu Kang and converted it into a coconut plantation. Neo was a Chinese community leader who supported the anti-Japanese initiatives in Singapore during WW2. Two days before the Japanese landed in Singapore, he left for his hometown in China. However, 35 of his family members were killed. After WW2, he was awarded medals by the Chinese and British governments for his contributions.

Neo Tiew Lane was named in 1967.

Source: *ST, 1975.11.17:21;* 吕振瑞: *112-159*

Nepal Circus/Link/Park (former Pasir Panjang Barracks)

Based on an article in 1951, Nepal Park was used to house the officers of the Gurkha Regiment which was stationed in Singapore from 1948. The other army residential areas in the vicinity such as Hog's Back, Island View Estate, Rochester Park and Wessex Estate were used for British officers.

Source: *ST, 1951.4.22:3; SFP, 1951.6.9:4*

Neram Crescent/Road
Neram is a tree, *Dipterocarpus oblongifolius*.

Netheravon Road (former RAF Changi)
This road was previously named New Road when the Changi area was a Royal Artillery Base. It was renamed in 1946 after RAF Netheravon in Wiltshire, South West England. *See Abbotsingh Road.*

Source: *Probert: 8*

Networks Link (e)

New Bridge Road
This road name refers to Coleman Bridge, named after G D Coleman who designed the bridge. It was the second bridge across the Singapore River and was built in 1840. New Bridge Road was laid in the same year.

Source: *SD, 1954:3*

New Bugis Street
See Bugis Street.

New Cemetery Road (e)

New Changi Coast Road
See Changi Road.

New Industrial Road
This road was named after the New Industrial group of companies which owned five blocks of industrial buildings at this location.

Source: *ZB-Special Supplement, 2014.11.20:19*

New Loyang Link
See Loyang Avenue.

New Market Road
This road was named after the former Ellenborough Market which was completed in 1849.

Source: *SFP, 1849.5.31:2*

New Road (e)
This road was located at 14 ms Upper Changi Road and was designated a British military area (Royal Artillery Base) in 1933. It was renamed Netheravon Road in 1946.

New Upper Changi Road
This road was commissioned in 1975. *See Changi Road.*

Source: *ST, 1975.4.6:6*

Newton Circus/Road
Based on a news article in 1935, Newton Road was named after Howard Vincent Newton (1852–1897), the Assistant Engineer of the Municipality.

This road was originally named Syed Ali Road in 1854 after Syed Ali Aljunied. To avoid confusion with a similar road name (Syed Alwee Road in Little India), the Municipal Commission decided to change the road name to Newton Road in 1914. *See Syed Ali Road.*

In a related incident, a request in 1902 to change the name of a train station from Scott's Road to Newton (train line operative from 1 January 1903), for ease of communication between the Chinese, was accepted by the Commission.

Source: *SFP, 1897.8.7:2; ST, 1902.10.27:5; MC, 1914.10.30; SFP, 1935.9.19:3*

Neythal Road
Neythal is a Tamil word for weaving. There were large textile and knitting factories along this road in the 1970s.

Nicoll Drive/Highway
John Fearns Nicoll (1899–1981) was the Governor of Singapore from 1952 to 1955. Nicoll Drive is in the Changi area. It was named after the Governor in 1955.

Nicoll Highway was opened on 18 August 1956.

Source: *ST, 1955.7.15; RBAR, 1955:9; CCAR, 1956:14*

Nile Road (e) (Delta Estate)
This road was named after the Nile River, a major river (6,800 km long) in northeastern Africa, generally regarded as the longest river in the world. *See Ganges Avenue.*

Nim Crescent/Drive/Green/Road
Nim, also known as neem, is a tree, *Azadirachta indica.*

Source: *Boo: 521*

Niven Road
Lawrence Niven (died 1876) was the Manager of Prinsep's Estate and at the same time, the Manager of the Singapore Botanic Gardens. He managed the Gardens from 1859 to 1876 and was credited for the initial organisation of the Gardens.

Niven Road is located in Mount Emily (Prinsep's Estate) and became a public street in 1900.

Source: *MC, 1900.7.12; Singam*

Noordin Lane (e)
The land for this lane was owned by Lo Lam. There is no other information about him and the origin of the name Noordin.

Source: *Firmstone 1905, 114-115*

Norfolk Road (Race Course Road area)
Norfolk is a county in the East of England. This road was named in 1922. *See Bristol Road and Derbyshire Road.*

Source: *ST, 1922.2.23:8*

Norma Terrace (Opera Estate)
Norma is an opera by Vincenzo Bellini. *See Aida Street.*

Normanton Park (former Ayer Rajah Barracks)
This was named after Normanton, a town in West Yorkshire, England.

Norris Lane (e)/Road (Kampong Kapor)
Based on a news article in 1905, Norris Road was named after the family of Richard Owen Norris (and George Norris). Both roads were declared public streets in 1914.

Source: *ED, 1905.10.23:3; MC, 1914.11.27*

North Boat Quay
See Boat Quay.

North Bridge Road
The bridge refers to Elgin Bridge which strides the Singapore River and serves as the divider of North Bridge Road and South Bridge Road. It is the oldest bridge in Singapore. The first bridge was constructed in 1822 as a wooden footbridge called Presentment Bridge. It was replaced in 1844 by another wooden footbridge designed by J T Thomson (*see Thomson Road*) and named Thomson Bridge. It was replaced again in 1862 by an iron bridge imported from Calcutta and renamed Elgin Bridge in 1863.

Elgin Bridge was named after Earl of Elgin (James Bruce) for his success in the Second Opium War against China which ended in 1860. The war saw the complete destruction and looting of the Yuan Ming Palace in Beijing and resulted in the signing of the second unequal treaty by China. Elgin was made Viceroy of India in 1862 but died of a heart attack one year later.

North Bridge Road was seen in advertisements in the press as early as 1836.

Source: *SFP, 1836.4.7:1; ST, 1862.5.10:1*

North Buona Vista Drive/Road
Buona vista means good view in Italian. Buona Vista Road was divided into North and South sections in 1949.
Source: *RBAR, 1949:9*

North Canal Road
This was the north bank of the old canal that leads to the Singapore River.
Source: *NAS, SP002997*

North Church Road (e) (former RAF Changi)

North Coast Crescent (e)/North Coast Drive

North Perimeter Road (Singapore Changi Airport)

North Pier (e) (Telok Ayer Basin)

North Road (former Singapore Naval Base)
This road is located near the King George VI Dock.

Another North Road at Clarke Quay was renamed Read Street in 1896. This portion of Read Street is now a pedestrian mall.
Source: *NAS, SP000100*

North South Expressway

North Woodlands Drive/Link/Way

Northolt Road (former RAF Changi)
This road was named after RAF Northolt in South Ruislip, West London. *See Abbotsingh Road.*

Northshore Drive/Link/Walk

Northumberland Road (Race Course Road area)
Northumberland is the northernmost county of England. It borders Scotland to the north. *See Bristol Road.*

Northweald Road (e) (former RAF Changi)
This road was named after RAF North Weald in Epping Forest, Essex, England. *See Abbotsingh Road.*

Novena Rise/Terrace
These roads were named after the Novena Church which was built in 1935. *Novena* is a Latin word that means the number nine or the nine-day rites performed by the Catholic Church.

Nutmeg Road
Nutmeg is native to the Moluccas, known as the Spice Islands in Indonesia. That area commanded the world monopoly for the supply of nutmeg and mace until the early 17th century when the British introduced the tree to their colonies. Nutmeg plantations were an important part of agricultural production in Singapore in the 1830s until the trees were hit by a widespread disease in 1855. The plantations were located along the stretch that is present-day Orchard Road, where Nutmeg Road is located today. Branches of Nutmeg Road are roads of other spices: Jalan Lada Puteh (white pepper), Jalan Kayu Manis (cinnamon) and Jalan Jintan (generic name for cumin, anise and caraway seeds).

Oak Avenue
See *Cherry Avenue*.

Oakwood Grove
See *Ashwood Grove*.

Ocean Drive/Ocean Way (Sentosa Island)

Odin Square (e)
Odin is a widely revered god in Norse mythology. *See Bragi Road*.

Oei Tiong Ham Park
Oei Tiong Ham (1866–1924, Hokkien) was born in Semarang, Indonesia. He was nicknamed the Sugar King in South East Asia.
Source: *Kua: 173*

(Office Gate Road/Office Ring Road) (e) (Singapore Botanic Gardens)
These roads were named in 1913.
Source: *SFP, 1914.5.30:16*

Office Road (former Singapore Naval Base)

Old Airport Road
The old airport refers to the Kallang Airport which was completed on 12 June 1937. It was replaced in 1955 by Paya Lebar Airport. This road now connects the Tanjong Katong area to Mountbatten Road.

Old Anson Road (e)
See *Anson Road*.

Old Bah Soon Pah Road
See *Bah Soon Pah Road*.

Old Balmoral Road (e)
See *Balmoral Road*.

Old Birdcage Walk (former RAF Seletar)
The name of this road was changed from Birdcage Walk around 1977 to differentiate from another road named Birdcage Walk in the former Blakang Mati Artillery Barracks. *See Baker Street.*

Old Boy's Drive (e) (St. Andrew's School)

Old Canberra Road (e) (former RAF Tengah)
This was a rename of Canberra Road. *See Canberra Road.*

Old Choa Chu Kang Road
See Choa Chu Kang Road.

Old Clementi Road (e)
See Clementi Road.

Old Halifax Road (e)
See Halifax Road.

Old Holland Road
This road name was seen in the press in 1973. However, it was only listed in the Street Directory from 1981. It was originally part of Holland Road.

Old Jurong Road
This road name was seen in the press in 1971. However, it was only listed in the Street Directory from 1981. It was originally part of Jurong Road.

Old Keppel Road (e)
This road was located outside Gate 3 of the former Singapore Harbour Board. It was only listed in the Road and Street Directory in 1950 and 1953 and was not seen after that.

Old Lim Chu Kang Road
See Lim Chu Kang Road.

Old Middle Road (former Singapore Naval Base)
This road was originally named Middle Road. *See Admiralty Road.*

Old Nelson Road (former Singapore Naval Base)
This road was first seen in the 1978 Street Directory. This road leads to The Old Admiralty House in the Naval Base. It was probably named after Admiral Horatio Nelson (1758–1805). *See Nelson Road.*

Old Parliament Lane

Old Pier Road (former RAF Changi)

Old Sarum Road (former RAF Changi)
This road was named after RAF Old Sarum in Salisbury, Wiltshire County, South West England. *See Abbotsingh Road.*

Old Stirling Road (e)
See *Stirling Road in RAF Tengah*.

Old Tampines Road
See *Tampines Avenue*.

Old Terminal Lane (former Kallang Airport)

Old Toh Tuck Road
See *Toh Tuck Road*.

Old Upper Jurong Road
This road only appeared in the 1988 Street Directory. See *Jurong Road*.

Old Upper Thomson Road
See *Thomson Road*.

Old Valley Road (e) (former RAF Changi)
This was a rename of Valley Road.

Old Yio Chu Kang Road
See *Yio Chu Kang Road*.

Oldham Lane
This lane was named in 1920 after W F Oldham (1854–1937). He was the bishop of the Methodist Episcopal Church and founder of Anglo Chinese School, Singapore, in 1886.

Source: *MC, 1920.6.25; SFP, 1937.3.31:2; Singam*

Olive Road
Based on a report in 1939, this road was named after Olive Innes, the wife of Andrew Caldecott (1918–1943). Caldecott married his second wife Evelyn May in 1946. See *Caldecott Close*.

Source: *ST, 1939.5.1:10; Singam*

Omar Khayyam Avenue (Teachers' Housing Estate)
This road was named after Omar Khayyam (1048–c.1131), a Persian Mathematician and poet. See *Iqbal Avenue*.

Omar Road (e) (Kampong Malacca)
This road was first seen in the press in 1853. It was probably named after Syed Omar bin Al Junied (1792–1852) the trader from Palembang who founded the Masjid Omar Kampong Malacca in 1820. The Mosque, located at Keng Cheow Street, is the oldest in Singapore. It started as a wooden surau and was rebuilt a few times, the first by his son Syed Abdullah in 1955. See *Aljunied Road*.

Source: *SFP, 1853.7.7:4; MUIS-Mosque Directory*

Onan Road
Onan is a Muslim name. It was probably named after Onan bin Rajidin from Java, who built a mosque along this road.

Source: *NLB-Onan Road*

One North Avenue/Crescent/Gateway/Link

One Tree Hill
This road was named in 1926.

Source: *MC1, 1926.6.15*

Ong Ham Road (e)
This road was named in 1954.

Source: *RBAR, 1954:8*

Ong Lee Village (e)
This village was located at 10.5 ms Jurong Road. It was named in 1954 after Ong Ko Lee or Ong Lee, a Hokkien businessman.

Source: *RBAR, 1954:9; ZB Special Supplement, 2014.11.20:19*

Onraet Road
This road, located at the former Police Training School, was named after Rene H de Solminihac Onraet (1887-1952) who was the Inspector General of the Straits Settlements Police from 1935 to 1939. He published a book about his life in the police force after retirement.

Source: *SFP, 1939.2.13:7; ST, 1952.5.11:9*

Ontario Avenue
Ontario is a West Indian word that means village on the hill. This road was named in 1956 together with Florida Road and Toronto Road. Ontario is a province in the east of Canada.

Source: *RBAR, 1956:9; Wagner: 45*

Opal Crescent
Opal is a gem stone. This road was named in 1952. *See Moonstone Lane.*

Source: *ST, 1952.5.1:7*

Ophir Road
It was reported in the press in February 1887 that the government had agreed to the use of reserve land for the widening of Ophir Road. It was probably named after Mount Ophir (height: 1,276 metres) at the border of Malacca and Johore. Gold was discovered by European prospectors in Mount Ophir around 1850.

Orange Grove Road
This road was named after Orange Grove, the mansion of A L Donaldson, a lawyer. The road name first appeared in the press in 1893 and in Municipal minutes in 1897. It became a public street in 1926.
Source: *SFP, 1893.8.30:2; SFP, 1897.8.26:2; SFP, 1926.9.17:6; Singam*

Orchard Boulevard/Circus (e)/Drive (e)/Link/Road/Spring Lane/Turn
As mentioned under Nutmeg Road, European migrants began planting nutmeg on a large scale in Singapore in the 1830s. Notable ones are Prinsep's Estate, Oxley Estate, Cairn Hill, Sri Menanti Estate and Claymore Estate. These plantations covered an area from what is now Tanglin through Orchard Road to Prinsep Street. Nutmeg cultivation was profitable until the trees were fatally hit by a widespread disease in 1855. By 1862 the cultivation of nutmegs had entirely ceased and some were converted to orchards. The plantations were the source of the road name.

Orchard Road was listed as a street in town in 1853.
Source: *SFP, 1853.7.8:4*

Orchid Club Road/Orchid Drive
Orchid Club Road was named after Orchid Country Club.

Orchid Drive was named in 1954. *See Carnation Drive.*
Source: *RBAR, 1954:8*

Ord Road (e)
This road was named after Harry George Ord (1819–1885), an unpopular Governor of the Straits Settlements from 1867 to 1873. There were two Ord Roads in 1970 and both have been expunged.
Source: *Makepeace, vol.1:94; Singam*

Oriole Crescent
Oriole or Black-Nape Oriole is one of the most common garden birds in Singapore. This road was named in 1954.
Source: *RBAR, 1954:9*

Ottawa Road (former Singapore Naval Base)
Ottawa is the capital city of Canada. *See Admiralty Road.*

Outram Hill/Park/Road
Outram Road was named in 1858 after General J Outram (1803–1863), one of the military officers of the East India Company who crushed the Indian Mutiny in 1857.
Source: *SFP, 1858.4.1:6*

Owen Road
G P Owen was the Secretary General of the Singapore Cricket Club for more than 20 years from 1886. This road was named in 1902.

Source: *ST, 1902.1.16:5; Singam*

Oxford Crescent (e) (former RAF Tengah)
Oxford Road (Race Course Road area)
Oxford Street (former RAF Seletar)
Oxford Crescent (RAF Tengah) was named after Airspeed Oxford, a training aircraft used during WW2. *See Hornet Road.*

Oxford Street (RAF Seletar) was named after a major road of the same name in the West End of London, Europe's busiest shopping street. *See Baker Street.*

Oxford Road was named in 1927 after Oxford City in Oxfordshire, South East England. *See Bristol Road.* There was one other Oxford Road at 12 ms, Upper Changi Road which was expunged.

Source: *MC, 1927.9.30*

Oxley Garden/Rise/Road/Walk
Based on a news article in 1906, Oxley Road was named after Dr. Thomas Oxley (died 1886) who owned a nutmeg plantation in this area. He was a surgeon of the Straits Settlements in 1830 and became Senior Surgeon in 1844. He bought a massive land of uncleared jungle from the East India Company and converted it into a nutmeg plantation and named it Killiney Estate. However, when the nutmeg blight swept plantations in Singapore in 1855, he sold the estate and left for England in 1857.

Oxley Road was declared a public street in 1861.

In 1898, the nearby Love Lane was renamed Oxley Rise.

Source: *ST, 1861.12.28:1; MC, 1898.6.8; ED, 1906.4.24:3; Buckley: 405*

(Pachitan Dua/Duabelas/Empat/Enam/Lapan/Lima/Satu/Sebelas/Sembilan/ Sepuloh/Tiga/Tujoh) (e)
These lanes were named after the Kampong Pachitan which was located between Jalan Eunos Malay Settlement and the Chai Chee area. The name Pachitan (now spelt Pacitan) came from the eastern province of Java Island in Indonesia.

The second Specific Names are Malay numerals from 1 to 12: they are *satu, dua, tiga, empat, lima, enam, tujoh, lapan, sembilan, sepuloh, sebelas* and *duabelas.*

Packing Hill (e)
This hill was located in the Pasir Panjang area. *See Pepys Road.*

Padang Chancery
Padang means treeless plain in Malay. *See Chancery Road.*

Padang Jeringau
Jeringau or *jerangau* is a medicinal plant, *Acorus calamus* in Malay. This road was named in 1906.

Source: *MC, 1906.11.30*

Padang Terbakar (e)/Padang Terbakar Village (e)
Terbakar means on fire in Malay. Padang Terbakar in the East Coast Road area was a field with wild grass and was often on fire. It was renamed Greenfield Drive after the surrounding land was developed into a residential estate.

Padang Terbakar Village was located at Siak Kuan Road at the seashore in Changi. Both the road and village of the same name are now part of the south end of the Changi Airport runway.

Source: *NAS, 709:12*

Padi Dedap Walk (e)
Padi means small and *dedap* is a coral tree, *Erythrina variegate* in Malay.

Pagoda Street
The street was named after the pagoda-like gopuram of Sri Mariamman Temple. Pagoda Street was listed as a street in town in 1853. *See Pillai Road.*

Source: *SFP, 1853.7.8:4*

Pahang Street (Kampong Glam)
This street was named after the State of Pahang in Malaysia. *See Arab Street.*

Pakistan Road (former Singapore Naval Base)
Pakistan was a British colony before WW2. *See Admiralty Road.*

Palawan Beach Walk
This is the board walk on Sentosa Island along Palawan Beach, opposite Palawan Island. *See Jalan Pelawan.*

Palembang Road (e)
Palembang is the capital of the South Sumatra Province in Indonesia. This road was parallel to Java Road near Kampong Glam.

Source: *SFP, 1853.7.8:4*

Palm Avenue/Palm Drive/Palm Road (Siglap)
Palm Close (e) (former RAF Changi)
Palm Grove Avenue (Upper Serangoon)
Palm Valley Road (Botanic Gardens)
Palm Avenue and Palm Drive were named in 1954.

Palm Road became a public street in 1957.

Palm Grove Avenue was repaired by the Rural Board in 1953.

Source: *ST, 1953.5.29:4; RBAR, 1954:8; RBAR, 1957:8*

Palmer Road/Street (e)

The above were named after John Palmer (1766-1836), the influential Calcutta merchant who purchased Mount Palmer soon after Singapore became a settlement. When his Calcutta firm of Palmer & Co. became insolvent in 1831, part of the hill was sold to a Parsi who turned it into a Parsi burial ground (*see Parsi Road*). The hill became the site of Fort Palmer from 1859 until it was levelled for land reclamation around 1905.

Palmer Road was named in 1905.

Palmer Street was named and declared a public street in 1895.

Source: *MC, 1895.2.27; MC, 1905.4.7; SD, 1954:14*

Pan Island Expressway

Pandan Avenue/Crescent/Gardens/Loop/Road/Valley

Pandan is the smaller screwpine. These roads were named after Sungei Pandan. With the exception of Pandan Valley, the roads are situated at both sides of the river outlet to Selat Jurong. Pandan Valley is situated at the upper reaches of the river.

Pang Seng Road

Lee Pang Seng was the eldest son of Lee Choon Guan (*see Choon Guan Street*), a graduate of Cambridge University in 1915. He served as a Municipal Commissioner from 1920 to 1925.

Source: *SFP, 1925.8.13:16; Song: 214*

Paradise Island (Sentosa Island)

Parbury Avenue

This road was named in 1938 after Justice of the Peace George Parbury (1876-1954). He was a member of the Municipal Commission from 1928 to 1939.

Source: *SFP, 1938.8.12:3; ST, 1954.9.29:8*

Pari Dedap Road

Pari dedap is the Malay name for porcupine ray.

Park Crescent/Park Road (China Town)
Park Lane (former RAF Seletar)
Park Street (Marina South)
Park Vale (Bukit Timah)

Park Crescent and Park Road were named for their proximity to People's Park, a shopping area near Pearl's Hill. Both became public streets in 1891.

Park Lane in RAF Seletar was named after a major road in Central London. *See Baker Street.*

Source: *ST, 1891.7.9:2*

Park Villas Green/Rise/Terrace

Parkstone Road (former Grove Estate)

This road was named in 1928 after Parkstone, an area in Poole, Dorset, England. *See Grove Road.*

Source: *MC, 1928.9.28*

Parliament Lane (e)/Parliament Place

Parry Avenue/Road/Terrace/View/Walk

These roads are located in an area that once belonged to the Singapore United Rubber Plantations Limited. The roads were probably named after one of its Directors, E H Parry. *See Dix Road.*

Source: *Lim HS: 241*

Parsi Road

This road was named after the Parsi (or Parsee) Cemetery in this location up to 1969, after which it was relocated when the land was acquired by the government. Parsis are followers of the Iranian prophet Zoroaster in India. The first Parsi arrived in Singapore before 1830.

Source: *Koh: 405*

Pasar Lane

Pasar means market in Malay. This road in Little India was made a public street in 1910.

Source: *MC, 1910.1.21*

Pasir Ayer Samak (e) (Pulau Tekong)

Pasir means sand or sand bank in Malay. *See Ayer Samak.*

Pasir Laba Road

Laba means much gain or good returns in Malay. This road was situated in the Peng Kang district which was once full of gambier and pepper plantations. It is now a military area.

Pasir Panjang Avenue 7, 8
Pasir Panjang Drive 1-6, 8
Pasir Panjang MAY St 1,2
Pasir Panjang Terminal Avenue 1 to 3
Pasir Panjang Terminal Lane A, F, G
Pasir Panjang Terminal Link
Pasir Panjang Terminal Street A, E, F, LM, RS, Y1, Y2, Y7, Y30
(Pasir Panjang Terminal)

Pasir Panjang Close
Pasir Panjang Drive
Pasir Panjang Hill/Road
Pasir Panjang View/Village (e)
Pasir panjang means stretch of sandy beach in Malay. These roads are no longer close to the sandy beach after land reclamation in the early 1990s.

Pasir Panjang village was located at the former seashore near the junction of Clementi Road and West Coast Road.

Pasir Ris Avenue/Central
Pasir Ris Central Street 3/Pasir Ris Close
Pasir Ris Coast Industrial Park 1 to 3, 4 (e), 5 (e), 6
Pasir Ris Drive 1/2/3/4/6/8/10/12
Pasir Ris Farmway 1/2/3
Pasir Ris Green/Grove/Heights (e)
Pasir Ris Industrial Drive 1
Pasir Ris Lane/Link/Rise/Road
Pasir Ris Street 11/12/13/21/41/51/52/53/71/72
Pasir Ris Terrace/View/Village (e)/Walk/Way
Pasir Ris was written as Passier Reis or Passier Rice in the 1800s. *Ris* means bolt rope, rope-edging to sail or a rustling sound in Malay. Pasir Ris Road first appeared in the news in 1955.

Source: *SFP, 1955.3.9:5; Buckley: 565; Haughton: 78; URA: 14; Wise: 48*

Passenger Crescent (e)

Patani Street (e) (Malayan Streets in Tanjong Pagar)
This road was named in 1898 after Patani, a historical region in the northern part of the Malay Peninsula. It was under Thai rule until the Bangkok Treaty between UK and Thailand in 1909, when part of Patani region was annexed into the northern part of Kelantan. *See Bernam Street.*

Source: *MC, 1898.11.8*

Paterson Hill/Road
William R Paterson (1823-1898) joined Kerr Rawson and Company in 1840 as an assistant and became a Partner of the firm in 1853. When the firm was dissolved in 1859, he set up Paterson, Simons & Co. with two other partners. In 1861, Paterson, M Little and Rittershaus jointly signed an agreement to transfer the roads in their estate to the Municipal Commission as a public street. The combined road was named Paterson Road. Paterson returned to England in 1874 as Chairman of the Board of Chartered Bank (1874-1896).

Source: *ST, 1861.4.27:2; SFP, 1898.2.9:3*

Paul Little Drive
This road was named after the former Managing Director of Toll Holdings.

Pavilion Circle/Green/Grove/Place/Rise/Street/View

Paya Lebar Close (e)/Crescent/Place/Rise/Road/Street/Village(e)/Walk/Way
Paya was written as "Pyah", and then "Payah" in old documents. It became Paya Lebar (Pyah Laebar) in a survey map drawn in 1885 by Major McCallum, Colonial Engineer and Surveyor-General of the Straits Settlements.

Based on an 1881 news article, the meaning of Pyah Lebar was a wide valley. However, Paya Lebar is a wide swamp.

Paya Lebar Road was included in a plan of Amokiah District and Kallang in 1844.

Paya Lebar Crescent became a public street in 1955.

Paya Lebar Village was located along Upper Serangoon Road at the junction of Yio Chu Kang Road.

Source: *STOJ, 1881.5.12:2; RBAR, 1955:9; NAS, SP000218_2; NAS, TM000003*

Paya Road (e)
This road was renamed Sam Leong Road in 1928.
Source: *MC, 1928.11.30*

Peach Garden

Peakville Avenue/Grove/Terrace/Walk

Pearl Bank/Pearl Island
Pearl's Hill Road/Terrace
Based on a news article in 1935, Pearl's Hill was named after Captain James Pearl who purchased the hill from Chinese gambier and pepper planters in 1822. Captain Pearl was the owner and commander of Indiana, the vessel in which Raffles sailed from Penang to Singapore in 1819. The ship was also used in the trading and transportation of local produce, including opium. It was reported in 1835 that he was awarded a gold medal by the King of Netherlands for saving 198 people from drowning in the sea in 1822. He sold Pearl's Hill to the colonial government before his return to the UK in 1828.

Pearl Island is a road on Sentosa Island.
Source: *SFP, 1835.10.22:1; ST, 1883.2.5:1; SFP, 1935.9.19:13; Singam*

Pebble Lane

Peck Hay Road
This road was named after Wi Pek Hay, wife of Lim Nee Soon. She died during WW2 while leaving Singapore with her son (Lim Chong Pang) when the ship they were travelling in was sunk by the Japanese Air Force. Lim Chong Pang was however saved. *See Nee Soon Road.* Peck Hay Road was named in 1951.

Source: *MC, 1951.8.31; Information was kindly provided by great granddaughter of Lim Chong Pang; Kua: 34*

Peck Seah Street
Seah Peck Seah (died 1939, Teochew) was the fourth son of Seah Eu Chin (*see Eu Chin Street*). He was in the shipping business. This road became a public street in 1907.

Source: *MC, 1907.4.19; Kua: 106*

Peel Road
This road was named in 1930 after William Peel (1875–1945). He was the President of the Municipal Commission in Penang before being relocated to Singapore to assume the same position from July 1918 for a period of 11 months. He subsequently became the Governor of Hong Kong from 1930 to 1935.

Source: *SFP, 1918.7.27:12; MC, 1930.8.29; Singam*

Pegu Road
Pegu (now Bago), is an ancient capital city of Myanmar. *See Burmah Road.* Pegu Road was named in 1931.

Source: *MC, 1931.6.26*

Pei Wah Avenue
This road was named after Pei Hwa Primary School in the same locality. The school was established in 1889 and officially named in 1922. The school was renamed again in 1995 as Pei Hwa Presbyterian Primary School.

Peirce Drive/Hill/Place (e)/Road
The above roads were named after Robert Peirce (c.1854–1933) who was the Municipal Engineer from 1901 to 1916. He designed and carried out many large scale water supply and drainage systems in Singapore and Penang. Peirce Reservoir was also named after him. Peirce Road was named in 1921.

Source: *MC, 1921.3.2; SFP, 1933.3.31:7; Singam*

Pekin Street
Pekin is the old name of Beijing. Pekin Street existed before 1829.

Source: *NAS, SP002997*

Peking Road (e)
Peking was also the old name for Beijing, the capital of China. Peking Road was renamed Nanyang Crescent in 1971. *See Faculty Avenue and Nanyang Avenue.*

Pelton Link
Pelton Link runs along Pelton Canal which is linked to the Kallang River. The canal was probably named after Foster Pelton, Chief Engineer of the Public Works, who designed a comprehensive drainage system to beat the flood costing 32.7 million dollars in 1957.

Source: *ST, 1957.1.6:4*

Pemimpin Drive/Place/Terrace
See Jalan Berjaya.

Penaga Place
Penaga is a tree, *Calophyllum inophyllum* in Malay. *See Kampong Wak Hassan.*

There was another Penaga Place in Tanjong Katong which was expunged. In that case, Penaga was the old name of Penang. *See Thiam Siew Avenue.*

Source: *SFP, 1893.4.3; Boo: 537*

Penang Lane/Penang Road
Penang is a state in the northwest of Malaysia. Penang Road was listed as a street in town in 1853. Its extension to Tank Road was named in 1906.

Penang Lane was named in 1929.

Source: *SFP, 1853.7.8:4, MC, 1906.5.4; MC, 1929.2.27*

Pender Road
This road was named in 1908 after John Denison Pender (1855–1929), the President of the Eastern Telegraph Company. The company, a global business in submarine cables, was established by his father, John Pender. The Eastern Telegraph Company was responsible for the laying of undersea cables that linked the British Empire from London via Singapore to New Zealand in 1876. Pender Road is joined to Morse Road (after Morse code, also related to telegraph technology).

Source: *MC, 1908.2.28; SFP, 1929.3.16:9; Singam*

Pending Road
Pending means waist ornament in Malay.

Peng Ann Road (e)
"Peng Ann" is a transliteration of peace in Hokkien. The road was a branch of Peng Ghee Road in the Chai Chee area. Both roads were named in 1954.

Source: *RBAR, 1954:8*

Peng Ghee Road (e)
"Peng" or "Pheng Ghee" is a transcription of normal courtesy in Hokkien. This road was named in 1954 after the Peng Ghee Primary School and Peng Ghee Secondary School in this area. The name of the school had since been changed to the pinyin version of "Ping Yi".

Source: *RBAR, 1954:8; DSM: 394*

Peng Kang Avenue
"Peng Kang", or "Pengkang", meaning peace and health in Mandarin, was the name of a district around 1867. Peng Kang was also the name of a plantation estate, as seen in a press report in 1891. It is now a military area in Upper Jurong.

Source: *DA, 1891.4.1:3*

Peng Nguan Street
Lim Peng Nguan (died 1887) was the father of Lim Nee Soon. He arrived from Swatow (a Teochew area in Canton Province) in the 1860s.

Source: *Kua: 132*

Peng Siang Quay (e)
Lim Peng Siang (1872-1944) was the son of Lim Ho Puah, a shipowner (*see Ho Puah Quay*). He and his brother Peng Mao established Ho Hong and Company that owned oil and rice mills, and steamships. He was one of the founders of the Chinese Mercantile Bank and Ho Hong Bank.

Source: *Kua: 129*

Pengkalan Pekan (e)
Pengkalan is a pier and *pekan* is a town or market in Malay.

Penhas Road
R Penhas was a Jewish merchant who died during WW2 after being tortured by the Japanese. This road was named after him in 1929.

Source: *MC, 1929.2.27; Bieder: 87; Singam*

Penjuru Circle/Circus/Close/Lane/Place/Road/Slipway (e)/Street (e)/Walk
Penjuru is a corner in Malay. These roads are in the industrial estate between Sungei Jurong and Pandan Reservoir.

Pennefather Road
E G Pennefather (1851-1928) was the Commissioner of Police from 1895 to 1906. This road was a rename of Lorong B, Siglap in 1934.

Source: *SFP, 1928.5.3:16; ST, 1934.3.8:19; Singam*

Penshurst Place (Serangoon Gardens)
This road was named in 1953 after Penshurst, a village in Kent, South East England. Its notable landmark is the Penshurst Place, a mansion built in 1341 which has been used as a filming location for several films. *See Alnwick Road.*
Source: *RBAR, 1953:8*

Pepys Road
This road was named in 1948 after W E Pepys (1885-1966), the Commissioner of Customs and Excise from 1932 to 1938. This road led to the Customs Packing Plant where opium was packed.
Source: *SFP, 1932.5.14:5; SFP, 1948.7.17:5; RBAR, 1948:7; ST, 1966.11.19:13*

Perahu Road
See Jalan Perahu.

Perak Road (Kampong Kapor)
Perak is a state in the northwest of Malaysia. It was once famous for its wealth in tin ore which led to numerous conflicts between the Dutch, British, surrounding kingdoms and the Chinese immigrants. *See Larut Road.* Perak means silver in Malay, which was probably derived from the colour of tin, or it was mistaken for silver by the original settlers.

This road is located in Little India. It became a public street in 1914.
Source: *MC, 1914.11.27;* 黄尧, 星马华人志 *:85*

Perang Lane (e)
Perang means war or brown in Malay.

Percival Road
This road is located in Fort Canning and was named after Lieutenant General Arthur E. Percival (1887-1966). He was most noted for his defeat in the Battle of Singapore, which undermined the prestige of the British in the Far East. Percival surrendered to the Imperial Japanese Army on 15 February 1942 and was imprisoned in Taiwan and Manchuria. After the war, he returned to the UK in 1945 to write his despatch at the War Office which was revised by the British government and only published in 1946. He then published his own memoir, *The War in Malaya*, in 1949. *See Bond Terrace.*

Pereira Road (MacPherson private roads)
This road was probably named after Francisco Evaristo Pereira, a reputed lawyer and a member of the Municipal Commission. He was the son-in-law of Dr. Jose d'Almeida (*See D'Almeida Street*). It was reported in the press in 1883 that he passed away in London in 1881. *See Davidson Road.*
Source: *ST, 1883.1.22:2; Makepeace, vol.1:366*

Permatang Pasir Muah (e) (Pulau Tekong)
Permatang is bank or rising ground. *Pasir* is sand or sandy stretch and *muah* or *mua* is cheeky or pert (of spoilt children).

Perumal Road
Perumal is one of the names of Vishnu, the supreme deity for the Tamils. This road was named in 1934 after the Sri Srinivasa Perumal Temple at the same location. The temple was built in 1855.

Source: *ST, 1934.2.5:12*

Pesari Walk

Pesek Road
This road was named after Pulau Pesek, now part of Jurong Island. *Pesek* means flat nose in Malay or a coin in Buginese. *See Ayer Chawan Place.*

Source: *Haughton: 79*

Pesiaran Keliling (e)
Pesiaran or *persiaran* means to stroll about and *keliling* means around in Malay. This road joined Pipit Road to form a semi-circle around the MacPherson Road Housing Estate. It was renamed Circuit Road.

Petain Road (WW1 roads)
This road was named in 1928 after Marshal Henri Philippe Petain (1856–1951), one of the leading commanders in WW1. *See Allenby Road.*

Petain was viewed as a national hero of France for his outstanding military leadership in WW1, particularly during the Battle of Verdun. After the war he was made Marshal of France in 1918 and continued with his military and political careers. During WW2, Petain became Prime Minister of Vichy France that gave Germany control over more than half of French territory. He was charged for treason after the War and initially sentenced to death. The sentence was later commuted to life imprisonment by President De Gaulle due to his age and military contributions during WW1. He died in prison in 1951.

Source: *MC1, 1928.10.2*

Petaling Road (e)
This road was named after Petaling Tin Ltd in 1929. *See Kempas Road.*

Source: *MC, 1929.3.27; SIT 1158/28*

Petir Road
See Lorong Petir.

Petticoat Lane (e) (former RAF Seletar)
This road was named after Petticoat Lane, a fashion and clothing market in the East End of London. *See Baker Street.*

Pheng Geck Avenue (Sennett Estate)
Yap Pheng Geck (1901-1979, Cantonese) was a Chinese community leader. He was the Manager of OCBC Bank, Director and Vice Chairman of the Chinese Chamber of Commerce and a member of the Municipal Commission. This road in Sennett Estate was named in 1951. See *Kee Choe Avenue*.
Source: *CC, 1951.9.28; Kua: 14*

Philip Street
This street was occasionally spelt as Phillips Street. It was named after W E Phillips, Governor of the Straits Settlements in Penang (1820-1826).

One account mentioned that it was named after Charles Philip (1835-1904), the Superintendent of the Sailors' Home and a missionary. However, this street was seen in the press as early as 1830 before Charles Philip was born (see *Circular Road*).
Source: *SFP, 1837.6.22:3; SD, 1954:13; Buckley: 209; Dunlop; Savage & Yeoh, 2004; Singam*

Philip Walk (e) (Princess Elizabeth Estate)
This road was named in 1952. See *Clarence Walk*.
Source: *RBAR, 1952:8*

Philips Avenue
This road was marked as a private road in 1954 and situated in the former rubber plantation in Yio Chu Kang owned by the Bukit Sembawang Rubber Company Ltd. It was probably named after Sir Ivor Philips, the Chairman of the company in 1937. One other account mentioned that it was named after C M Philips, the Principal of Raffles Institution in the early 20th century.
Source: *Dunlop; Lim HS: 241*

Philips Street (e)
See *Philip Street*.

Phoenix Avenue/Garden/Park/Rise/Road/Walk

Piccadilly/Piccadilly Circus (former RAF Seletar)
These roads were named after roads of the same name in the City of Westminster, London. See *Baker Street*.

Pickering Street
Based on a news article in 1935, this street was named after William Pickering (1840-1907). Pickering was the first Chinese Protector appointed in colonial Singapore. He was able to speak Mandarin and a number of Chinese dialects from his ten years' experience in Hong Kong. Due to his control of the secret societies' activities he was physically attacked in 1888 and suffered serious injury but survived. This street was previously known as

Macao Street. In 1924, the Municipal Commission decided to rename it to Pickering Street from 1925.

Source: *SFP, 1924.7.25; SFP, 1935.9.19:3*

Pier Road (e)
There were two Pier Roads in British military installations: one in the Changi area and the other in Pulau Brani. Both have been expunged.

Pierce Road (e) (Misprint of Peirce Road)

Pigott Road (e)
This road was named after F J Pigott (1865-1939), the Chief Engineer and Chief Surveyor of the Colony for 16 years and who retired in 1921. It was declared a public street in 1960.

Source: *ST, 1939.9.11:10; CCAR, 1960:8; Singam*

Pillai Road
This road was named after N Pillai, the first Indian to arrive in Singapore together with Sir Stamford Raffles in 1819. He worked for a short while as a clerk in the Colonial Office before setting up his brick factory and becoming wealthy. In 1823, the East India Company granted him a site in South Bridge Road to build a Hindu Temple. The first version of the Sri Mariamman Temple was completed in 1827.

Pine Close/Lane (off Guillemard Road)

Pine Grove (Ulu Pandan)

Pine Walk (Bukit Timah)
Pine Walk is a short road off Linden Drive and was named in 1954.

Source: *RBAR, 1954:9*

Pinewood Grove
See Ashwood Grove.

Pioneer Circus/Crescent/Lane (e)/Place/Road
Pioneer Road North
Pioneer Sector 1 to 3
Pioneer Sector Lane/Walk/Pioneer Turn/Pioneer View/Pioneer Walk

Pipit Road
See Jalan Pipit.

Pitt Street
There were two British Prime Ministers with the name of William Pitt and they were father and son. William Pitt the Elder (1708-1778) was British Prime Minister from 1766 to 1768. William Pitt the Younger (1759-1806), was

British Prime Minister from 1783 to 1801 and 1804 to 1806. The latter was best known for leading Britain in the great wars against France and Napoleon.

Pitt Street became a public street in 1910.

Source: *MC, 1910.1.21; Singam*

Plantation Avenue

Based on a news article in 1951, this road was previously known as Jalan Phua Pak Tiong. Because "Tiong" was often used as a place name for cemetery and "Phua Pak" sounded like opening of stomach in Hokkien, the residents found the name offensive and requested for the change in name to Plantation Avenue.

Source: *ST, 1951.6.22:5; RBAR, 1951:8*

Platina Road

Platina means platinum in Malay.

Playfair Road (MacPherson private roads)

This road was probably named after Captain F L Playfair from the Madras Staff Corps, who was the Assistant Resident Councillor of Malacca in 1863. He became Acting Lieutenant-Governor of Malacca from 1867 to 1869.

This road was listed in the 1936 Gazetteer; it became a public street in 1960. See *Davidson Road*.

Source: *ST, 1863.5.30:3; ST, 1869.3.20:3; SG-1936; CCAR, 1960:8*

Plumer Road (WW1 roads)

Based on a report in 1936, this road was named after Field Marshal Herbert C O Plumer (1857–1932), one of the leading commanders in WW1. See *Allenby Road*.

Source: *ST, 1936.7.27:10*

Plymouth Avenue

This road was possibly named after Plymouth, (which means mouth of river), a city in the south coast of Devon, South West England.

Source: *Mills*

Plywood Road (e)

This road was named after the Singapore Plywood Factory at the end of the road.

Poh Huat Crescent/Drive/Road
Poh Huat Road West/Poh Huat Terrace

Poh Huat Road was approved for making up by the Rural Board in 1952. It became a public street in 1955. The roads were probably named after Ong Poh Huat, a land owner who passed away in 1949.

Author's note: "Making up" or "make up" were phrases used by the Municipal Commission for more than 100 years to mean "put a surface on a road and make it a public road".

Source: *ST, 1949.4.26:6; ST, 1952.12.19:4; RBAR, 1955:9*

Ponggol Road Track 19, 22, 24
Ponggol Seventeenth Avenue/Twenty-Fourth Avenue
See Punggol Road.

Poole Road (former Grove Estate)
This road was named in 1928 after Poole, a large coastal town and seaport. Poole is located next to Bournemouth in Dorset, England. *See Grove Road.*

Source: *MC, 1928.9.28*

Port Road (Tanjong Berlayar Pier)

Portchester Avenue (Serangoon Gardens)
This road was named in 1953 after Portchester in Hampshire, South East England. The medieval Portchester Castle was built within a well-preserved Roman fort and is now an English Heritage. *See Alnwick Road.*

Source: *RBAR, 1953:8*

Portsdown Avenue/Road (former Ayer Rajah Barracks)
These roads were named after Portsdown, a ridge located in Hampshire, England.

Potong Pasir Avenue 1 to 3
Potong means cutting, slicing or cutting off a portion. *Pasir* means sand in Malay. *Potong pasir* is a strip of sand bank.

Power Station Road (e) (former Tanglin Barracks)

Prene Road (e) (former Tanglin Barracks)
Prene in Middle English means to stab or pierce. *See Barrack Road.*

Preston Road (former Gillman Barracks)
This road was probably named after Preston, the administrative centre of Lancashire, England. During WW2, the Second Battalion of Loyal Regiment (North Lancashire) was stationed in the Far East. They first fought in Malaya as part of the delaying action against the Japanese but eventually surrendered along with the rest of the Singapore garrison. The survivors spent the rest of the war years as prisoners of the Imperial Japanese Army. *See Gillman Close.*

Primrose Avenue
Primrose is a flowering plant native to Western and Southern Europe.

Prince Charles Crescent/Square (e) (Queenstown)
Prince Charles Rise (e) (Princess Elizabeth Estate)
These roads were named after Prince Charles, the eldest son of QE2. He is also the current Prince of Wales, the heir apparent to the throne.

Prince Charles Crescent and Prince Charles Square, in the Alexandra area, were named by the City Council in 1952.

Prince Charles Rise was named in 1952 by the Rural Board. *See Clarence Walk.*

Source: *ST, 1952.5.1:7; RBAR, 1952:8*

Prince Edward Lane (e)/Link (e)/Road
Prince Edward (1894–1972) was the eldest son of King George V. He was created Prince of Wales in 1910. Edward became King Edward VIII on his father's death in early 1936. However he abdicated in December the same year to marry a divorced woman. He was then created Duke of Windsor and retired in France after WW2. Prince Edward Road was named after him in 1923.

Source: *MC, 1923.1.26*

Prince Edward Point (e)
Prince Edward Point (e) was named in 1954 after Prince Edward of Kent. It was a scenic point and the name of a village at the junction of Clementi Road and Kent Ridge Road. *See Kent Ridge Crescent.*

Source: *ST, 1954.2.24:4*

Prince George's Park (NUS)
This road was named after the Prince George's Park Residences, a student housing estate of the university.

Prince of Wales Road
This road is located next to Princess of Wales Road, off Bukit Timah. Prince of Wales is the title granted to the heir apparent to the British monarch. *See Coronation Road.*

Prince Philip Avenue
Prince Philip, born Prince Phillip of Greece and Denmark, is the Consort of the current Queen, QE2. He was created Duke of Edinburgh by King George VI just before the wedding with Princess Elizabeth in November 1947. This road was named in 1952.

Source: *ST, 1952.5.1:7*

Prince Road/Street (e)
Prince Road is located off Bukit Timah Road. *See Coronation Road.*

Singapore Gazetteer Since 1936 and Annotations

Prince Street (e) was located in Raffles Place and was named after Honourable John Prince of Bengal Civil Service, the first Resident Councillor of Singapore. He was the third Singapore Resident from August 1826 to November 1827. He had no royal title.

Source: *MC, 1898.7.20; Singam*

(Princess Anne Close/Princess Anne Hill) (e)
Princess Anne is the only daughter of QE2. Both roads were named in 1952.

Princess Anne Close is located in the Alexandra area.

Princess Anne Hill was located at Upper Bukit Timah Road. *See Clarence Walk.*

Source: *ST, 1952.5.1:7; RBAR, 1952:8*

Princess Circus (e) (off Princess Anne Close)

Princess Elizabeth Drive (e) (Princess Elizabeth Estate)
This road was named in 1952. *See Clarence Walk.*

Source: *RBAR, 1952:8*

Princess of Wales Road
Princess of Wales is the title held by the wife of the Prince of Wales. *See Prince of Wales Road and Coronation Road.*

Prinsep Court (e)/Link/Street
The above streets were named after C R Prinsep (1789–1864), standing counsel to the East India Company, who once owned the Prinsep Estate. The estate encompassed Mount Sophia and Mount Emily, which Prinsep acquired around 1841 and developed into a nutmeg plantation with 6,700 nutmeg trees. After 1860, when Princep's fortune dwindled, the estate was divided and sold. Prinsep Street was a rename of one of the two Flint Streets in 1858.

Source: *SFP 1858.4.1:6; ED, 1906.4.24:3; NAS BL 10RP/13/37, 1841; Buckley: 406*

Prome Road
Prome (now Pyay) is in the Bago region in Myanmar. It is located along the Irrawaddy River and is 260 kilometres northwest of Yangon. *See Burmah Road.*

Puay Hee Avenue (Sennett Estate)
Tan Puay Hee was a Director of Sennett Realty Estate Limited. This road was named in 1951. *See Kee Choe Avenue.*

Source: *CC, 1951.9.28*

Pukat Road (e)
Pukat means a big fishing boat or fish net in Malay. This road was located in the Martin Road area, and was known as Braddell Road before 1930.
Source: *MC, 1930.6.27*

Pulasan Road
Pulasan is a fruit tree, *Nephelium mutabile*, with fruits resembling the rambuttan. This road was known as Lorong 209, Siglap before 1934.
Source: *ST, 1934.3.8:19*

Pulo Saigon Circus (e)/Road (e)
Pulo is the old spelling of *pulau*. It means island in Malay. Saigon was the old name of Ho Chi Min City. Pulo Saigon was an islet located in the middle of the Singapore River around the Chin Swee Road/Magazine Road area. Its name might have been derived from the unloading of rice from Saigon at this location. The islet increased in size over time from the accumulation of debris from clearing the river. In addition, Singapore River beyond this point was drained off in stages such that by 1992, the islet was completely merged with the main land at the Magazine Road area. The bridge that went across the islet was dismantled and sold as scrap in 1986.
Source: *ST, 1986.9.29:10*

Punah Place (e) (Thiam Siew Village, Tanjong Katong)
Punah is the trade name of timber from *Tetramerista glabra*. See Thiam Siew Avenue.

Punggol Avenue/Central/Crescent (e)/Drive/East
(Punggol Farmway 1 /2) (e)
Punggol Field/Field Walk/Lane (e)/Link (e)/Place
Punggol Point Road/Port Lane (e)
Punggol Road/Walk
(Punggol Road Track 1 to 17, 19, 20, 22, 24, 26) (e)
Punggol Village (e)/Punggol Way
Punggol was also spelt Pongol, Pongul (in 1848) and Ponggol. Based on an 1848 survey report, Pongul was the name of a creek. The name Sungei Punggol was used in H E McCallum's survey map of 1885.

Punggol or *punggal* is a Malay word that means cutting off the sharp ends, collection point for fruits and timber or collecting fruits by throwing up a stick. An article in 1906 said that *pongul* is a rice cooking gathering in Tamil.
Source: *SFP, 1848.5.18:3; Sunday Times, 1883.4.16:5; ST, 1906.1.18:2; NAS, TM000003; Singam*

Purvis Street

This street was named after John Murray Purvis (1832-1893), who established John Purvis & Co. in 1822 and remained with the company until 1862. He was also the Sheriff of Kampong Glam. This road was named in 1902.

Source: *SFP, 1893.3.21:2; ST, 1902.10.11:5; Buckley: 232; Singam*

Quadrant Road (e) (former RAF Changi)

Quality Road

This road was previously known as Jalan Rehat. It was renamed Quality Road in 1968. This is one of the roads named after good wishes in the Jurong Industrial Estate. *See Chia Ping Road.*

Quarry Road (e) (former RAF Changi)

This road was acquired for British Military use in 1933. It was the access road to the quarry at Changi Hill when it was built as a Royal Artillery Base. The road was renamed Cranwell Road and Tangmere Road when the Artillery Base was taken over by the RAF. *See Abbotsingh Road.*

Source: *ST, 1933.10.29:9; Probert: 11*

Queen Astrid Gardens/Hill/Park

The above roads were named after Queen Astrid of Belgium (1905-1935). She was a Swedish Princess married to Crown Prince Leopold of Belgium in 1926 and who became a Queen in 1934. She was however killed in an accident in 1935. As a close relative of the British Royal family, she visited Singapore in 1929 and 1932. Queen Astrid Park was named around 1940. Astrid Hill was named in 1952.

Source: *RBAR, 1952:8*

Queen Elizabeth Walk

This road was named after QE2, the current Queen, and was commissioned in 1953.

Source: *ST, 1953.5.31:5*

Queen Street

Based on a news article in 1844, this road was named after Queen Victoria.

Source: *SFP, 1844.2.15:1*

Queen's Avenue (former Singapore Naval Base)
Queen's Circus (e)/Close/Crescent (Queenstown)
Queen's Road (Bukit Timah)

Queen's Avenue is located in the former Singapore Naval Base. At the time of construction in 1923, the queen was Queen Mary, consort of George V. *See Admiralty Road and Deptford Road.*

Queen's Circus, Queen's Close and Queen's Crescent are extensions of Queensway. *See Queensway.*

Queen's Road was named around 1905, during the reign of Queen Alexandra, consort of Edward VII. *See Coronation Road.*

Queensway
This road is located in Queenstown, a new residential town in the plan of the Singapore Improvement Trust in 1953. The queen at that time was QE2, the current Queen.

Source: *SFP, 1953.10.2:5*

Quemoy Road
Quemoy is now Jinmen, an island close to Xiamen, in the province of Fujian, China.

Race Course Lane/Road/Village (e)
Race Course Road was the location of the first race course in 1843. It was used until 1933 when the second race course at the Turf Club at Bukit Timah Road was opened.

Race Course Village was located at the junction of Bukit Timah Road and Maple Avenue, divided by two major trunk roads away from the former Turf Club.

Radin Mas (e)
Radin mas means golden princess. Radin Mas Ayu was a young Javanese Princess who migrated to Singapore with her father, a prince. She died and was buried in this location. This road was connected to Kampong Bahru Road.

Source: *ST, 1996.9.4:26*

Raeburn Park/Raeburn Park Road
Raeburn Park Road was named after Raeburn Spice Plantation. The first owner of this plantation was Charles Scott (died 1858), one of the earliest settlers and planters in Singapore. He was a Partner at Napier & Scott and was one of the first Magistrates in Singapore in 1823. The plantation with a bungalow and 31 acres of spice and fruit trees were sold to G F Davidson around 1826 and then to the d'Almeida family in 1835 when it was renamed Raeburn Estate.

Source: *SFP, 1835.11.12:1; SFP, 1836.3.10:1; Buckley: 667*

Raffles Avenue/Boulevard
Raffles Institution Lane (Bishan)

Raffles Link/Place/Quay
These places were named after Sir Thomas Stamford Bingley Raffles (1781–1825), the British colonial officer who founded modern Singapore. Raffles landed in Singapore on 29 January 1819. After signing a formal treaty with the Sultan of Johor that secured the transfer of control of the island to the East India Company, he appointed Major William Farquhar as the first Resident of Singapore and left on 7 February 1819. He returned in May the same year and stayed for a month. His last visit lasted eight months during which he drew up the city plan, a code of settlement for the populace and the first constitution for Singapore. He passed away in London in 1825.

Raffles Place was a rename of Commercial Square in 1858.

Raffles Quay was named in 1894 at the recommendation of the Colonial Governor.

Raffles Avenue/Raffles Boulevard/Raffles Link were opened in 1983.

Source: *SFP, 1858.4.1:6; ST, 1894.2.16:3; SM, 1983.10.26:6*

Raglan Grove (Serangoon Gardens)
This road was named in 1953. Raglan is a village in Monmouthshire, southeast Wales, it is the location of the magnificent 15th century Raglan Castle. *See Alnwick Road.*

Source: *RBAR, 1953:8*

Railway Hill (e) (Gillman Barracks)

Rain Tree Drive/Valley (e)
The raintree is native to South America. It was introduced to Singapore in the 19th century. Rain Tree Drive is in the Singapore Botanic Gardens.

Rakit Road (e)
See Jalan Rakit.

Ramah Street (e)
This road was named in 1883 after Ramah Chitty.

Source: *MC, 1883.12.27; MC, 1884.2.28*

Rambai Road
Rambai is a fruit tree, *Baccauree motleyana*. This road was a rename of Lorong 208, Siglap in 1934.

Source: *ST, 1934.3.8:19*

Rambau Street (e) (Malayan Streets in Tanjong Pagar)
This street was named in 1898 after Sungei Rambau in Pahang, Malaysia. *See Bernam Street.*

Source: *MC, 1898.11.8*

Rambutan Road
Rambutan is a tropical fruit. This road was a rename of Lorong 206, Siglap in 1934. *See Tembeling Road.*
Source: ST, 1934.3.8:19

Ramree Road (e) (former RAF Changi)
This road was named after Ramree Island, an island off the coast of Rakhine State, Burma. This was the site of the Battle of Ramree from January to February 1945 during which British land, sea and air forces fought for six weeks before capturing the island back from the Imperial Japanese Army. This could be the reason for two roads having Burmese names in RAF Changi. *See Rangoon Road and Abottsingh Road.*

Ramsgate Road (former Grove Estate)
This road was named in 1928 after Ramsgate, a seaside town in Kent, England.
See Clacton Road and Grove Road.
Source: MC, 1928.9.28

Rangoon Lane/Road
Rangoon, now Yangon, is the former capital of Myanmar (before 27 March 2005) and the capital of the Yangon Region. In 1896, frontagers paid for the repair of this road before it was declared a public street by the Municipality. *See Burmah Road.*

There was one other Rangoon Road located in the former RAF Changi domain which had been expunged. *See Ramree Road and Abbotsingh Road.*
Source: ST, 1896.8.15:3

Rappa Terrace (e)
George Rappa (1833-1906) was the first Secretary of the Police Force. He was once a Partner at Robinson and Company. This road was named in 1906.
Source: ST, 1906.7.28:4; MC, 1906.11.30; Singam

Rasok Drive
Rasok or *rasuk* means cross beam in Malay. *See Jalan Bumbong.*

Ratus Road (e) (former Singapore Naval Base)
Ratus is a Malay word and could mean hundred, or a plant, *Justica bracteata*. *See Admiralty Road.*

Raub Street (e) (Malayan Streets in Tanjong Pagar)
This road was named in 1898 after Raub, a town in Pahang. *Raub* means handful scoop in Malay and it was a historic gold mining settlement. The

gold mine in Raub was operated by Raub Australian Gold Mine until 1961. *See Bernam Street.*

Source: *MC, 1898.11.8*

Rawang Road (e)
Rawang is a town in the Gombak district in Selangor, Malaysia. It was famous for its tin and coal reserves. This road was named after the Rawang Tin Mining Company in 1929. *See Kempas Road.*

Source: *MC, 1929.3.27; SIT 1158/28*

Rayman Avenue (e)
Lazarus Rayman (1889-1948) was a civil servant of the colonial government. In 1939, he was made the President of the Municipal Commission after more than 20 years of service. After WW2, the head of the Municipal Commission was initially assumed by William Bartley until 1946, when Rayman was reappointed as the President. He died a few months after retirement. This road was named in 1949.

Source: *ST, 1948.12.31:5; SFP, 1949.12.3:5*

Read Crescent/Street
William Henry Macleod Read (1819-1909) was a Partner at A L Johnston & Co. and one of the first directors of Eastern Asia Telegraph Co. Ltd. He was credited for his exertions and influence in England for the eventual transfer of the Straits Settlements from the East India Company to the Colonial Office in London in 1867 ("Transfer"). He became one of the first European unofficial members of the Legislative Council during the Transfer. Read Bridge at Clarke Quay was also named after him. Read Street was a rename of North and South Road in 1896.

Source: *ST, 1896.8.3:3; SFP, 1909.6.5:7; NAS, SP000100; Makepeace, vol.2:201, 417; Singam*

Rebecca Road
This road leads to the residential estate of Rebecca Park. It was named sometime in 1951 or 1952. Rebecca could be a lady's name or the name of a stage play in vogue at that time.

Source: *SFP, 1948.3.12:5*

Recorder Road (e)
This road was located near Pender and Morse Roads. It was named in 1908 after SS *Recorder*, a cable ship of the Eastern Extension Telegraph Co. *See Pender Road.*

Source: *ST, 1893.12.5:9; MC, 1908.2.28*

Recreation Lane/Road
Recreation Road was named in 1921.

Source: *MC1, 1921.9.2*

Red Brick Path (Singapore Botanic Gardens)

Redhill Close/Lane/Road
See *Bukit Merah Central.*

Redwood Avenue/Grove (e)
See *Cherry Avenue.*

Refinery Lane/Road
The roads were named after the Exxon Mobil Refinery at this location.

Reformatory Road (e)
Reformatory Road was named after the Reformatory Centre situated along this road. It was renamed Clementi Road in 1947 following the government's decision to rename the centre to Bukit Timah House. See *Clementi Road.*
Source: *SFP, 1947.8.22:5; SFP, 1947.10.17:5*

Regent Street (former RAF Seletar)
This road was named after Regent Street, one of the major shopping streets in the West End of London. Regent Street in London was named after the Prince Regent (later King George V). See *Baker Street.*

Republic Avenue/Boulevard/Crescent/Link

Research Crescent (General Hospital)

Research Link (NUS)

Reservoir Link (Bedok Reservoir)

Reservoir Road (MacRitchie Reservoir)
Reservoir Road was named in 1929.
Source: *MC, 1929.9.27*

Residential Road (e)

Rhodesia Road (e) (former Singapore Naval Base)
Rhodesia was a British colony before WW2. See *Admiralty Road.*

Rhu Cross/Rhu Lane (e)
Based on a news article in 1881, *Rhu* or *Ru* is Casuarina tree, *Casuarina equisetifolia* in Malay. The above were named in 1927.
Source: *STOJ, 1881.5.12:2; MC, 1927.8.26; Boo: 545; Makepeace, vol.2:64*

Richards Avenue/Place
The above roads were named after Peter Richards (died 1936), the Chief Engineer of the Official Yacht of the Governor, who owned a large plot of land in this area. The land was sold by his daughter in 1980.

One other account said that the road was named after Reverend R Richards, the European missionary in charge of St. Andrew's School from 1902 to 1934.

Richards Avenue was repaired by the Rural Board in 1953.

Source: *ST, 1953.5.29:4; NAS, 202:1; Dunlop; Makepeace, vol.2:242*

Ridgewood Close

Ridley Park
Ridley Road (e) (former Tanglin Barracks)
Ridley Park was named after Henry Nicholas Ridley (1855-1956) who was known as the father of the rubber industry. He was the first Director of the Botanic Gardens (1888-1911). During this period he successfully cultivated the rubber tree, which was brought in from Brazil and found an effective way of tapping its sap. His findings led to the success of the rubber industry in South East Asia. Ridley Park was named in 1923.

Source: *MC, 1923.11.30*

Ridout Road
This road was named in 1921 after Major General Sir D H Ridout (1866-1941) who was the GOC Troops, Straits Settlements from 1915 to 1921.

Source: *MC, 1921.3.2; Makepeace, vol.1:384; Singam*

Rienzi Street (Opera Estate)
Rienzi is an early opera by Richard Wagner. See *Aida Street*.

Rifle Range Road
This road was built for the Bukit Timah Rifle Range.

(Rimau/Rimau Lane/Road) (e) (former Singapore Naval Base)
Rimau means tiger in Malay. Rimau is one of the few simplex road names and was seen in the Street Directory of 1969 and 1972. It was renamed Rimau Lane. See *Admiralty Road*.

Ring Road (e) (Singapore Botanic Gardens)
This road was named in 1913.

Source: *SFP, 1914.5.30:16*

Ringwood Road (former Grove Estate)
This road was named in 1928 after Ringwood, a market town in Hampshire, England. It is located on the River Avon and close to the northeast of Bournemouth. See *Bournemouth Road*.

Source: *MC, 1928.9.28*

Ripley Crescent (Serangoon Gardens)
This road was named in 1953. Ripley is a multiple place name in England. Ripley village in North Yorkshire is the location of the Ripley Castle. See *Alnwick Road*.

Source: *RBAR, 1953:8*

Ritchie Road (former Tanglin Barracks)
This road was probably named after General Sir Neil Ritchie (1897-1983) who was the GOC, Far East Land Forces from 1947 to 1949.

Source: *ST, 1949.9.9:1*

River Valley Close/Green/Grove/Road
River Valley Road refers to the valley of the Singapore River. It begins from North Boat Quay at the Singapore River and ends at Delta Road. The road was listed as a street in town in 1853.

Source: *SFP, 1853.7.8:4*

Riverina Crescent/View/Walk

Riverside Road
This road is along the riverside of Sungei Cina in Sembawang.

Rivervale Close/Crescent/Drive/Lane/Link/Street/Walk (Sengkang New Town)

Riviera Drive

Robert V Chandran Way
This road leads to the Oil Tanking Helios Terminal in Jurong Island. It was named after the Founder and Chief Executive Officer of Chemoil Energy Ltd, the owner of the terminal. The terminal was opened in 2008, shortly after the death of Mr. Chandran.

Source: *ST, 2008.2.28:48*

Roberts Court (e)/Roberts Lane
Roberts Lane was probably named after a Mr. Roberts, a teacher who lived at this lane for a long time.

Source: *Singam*

Robertson Quay
This quay was previously known as Gulam Mydin Quay. It was renamed Robertson Quay in 1888 after Dr. John H Robertson (1829-1896). He was appointed a Magistrate in 1874 and a Municipal Commissioner from 1883 to 1886. See *Leonie Hill*.

J H Robertson was a medical doctor who settled in Singapore in 1857. He was a member of the Municipal Commission for many years up to 1886 before leaving Singapore in July 1900.

Dr. T M Robertson (1860-1931), the son of J H Robertson, was often mentioned as the source of this place name. He was the city coroner and joined the Municipal Commission in 1903, after the quay was renamed after his father.

Source: *MC, 1888.1.6; SFP, 1896.2.25:14; ST, 1903.7.4:5; Makepeace, vol.1:502; Singam*

Robey Crescent

This road was named after Gordon Robey who developed this area. It became a public street in 1957.

Source: *ST, 1948.12.10:7; RBAR, 1957:8*

Robin Close/Drive/Lane/Road/Walk

Robin Road became a public street in 1957.

Source: *CCAR, 1957:5*

Robinson Road

This road was named after Sir William Cleaver Francis Robinson (1834–1897), Governor of the Straits Settlements from 1877 to 1879. He subsequently became the Governor of Western Australia. Robinson Road was built on part of the reclaimed land arising from the Telok Ayer Bay land reclamation project. The bund of the reclaimed land, named Robinson Quay, was also named after Sir Robinson in 1881. Robinson Road was built in 1891.

Source: *STOJ, 1881.4.18:2; ST, 1891.7.15:5; SFP, 1897.6.1:3*

Rochalie Drive

This road was probably named after Rochalie, a famous residence around the 1880s. Rochalie Drive was named in 1914.

Source: *ST, 1883.8.1:2; MC, 1914.8.28*

Rochdale Road

This road name was given by the Rural Board for the Paya Lebar Road Co-operative Estate in 1957. It was given on the basis that the co-operative movement was founded in Rochdale, Lancashire, England. The other road named at the same time was Thrift Drive.

Source: *ST, 1957.11.1:6; RBAR, 1957:8*

Rochester Drive/Park (former Pasir Panjang Barracks)

Rochester Park in the Pasir Panjang area was built in the 1950s to house officers of the British Army. *See Nepal Park.* Rochester is the name of a town in Kent, South East England.

Rochor Canal Road
Rochor Road/Street (e)

Rochor was more often written as "Rochore" in old documents. Rochor Road appeared as Rochor Street in G D Coleman's survey map of 1836 based on an actual survey in 1829. It was named after the Rochor River. Rochore (or Rochor) Road appeared in the press as early as 1850. This area from Rochore to the Esplanade was a residential area for the Europeans in the first half of the 19th century. It was largely taken over by the Chinese when the Europeans moved to the Tanglin Area after the 1850s.

In 1955, Ramachandra was of the opinion that Rochore originated from *Rochoh*, a Malay word that means prodding.

Source: *ST, 1955.3.8:6; SFP, 1850.12.6:2; NAS, SP002997; Chopard: 11*

Rodney Road (e) (former Singapore Naval Base)
This road was probably named after Admiral George Brydges Rodney (1718-1792), a British naval officer best known for his victory over the French in 1782. Several Royal Navy warships were named after him. See *Admiralty Road*.

Rodyk Street
This street was named after Bernard Rodyk (died 1898), who co-founded the legal firm of Rodyk and Davidson in 1877. See *Davidson Road*.

Source: *SFP, 1898.8.19:2*

Rose Lane
This road was named in 1922 pursuant to the results of a road-naming competition. See *Gray Lane*.

One account mentioned that this road was named after Alan Rose, the Chief Justice of Singapore. It is noted that he arrived in Singapore from Ceylon in 1959, after the road was named.

Source: *MC1, 1922.2.3; SFP, 1922.2.27:6; Dunlop*

Roseburn Avenue (Frankel Estate)
Roseburn is a suburb of Edinburgh. See *Burnfoot Terrace*.

Rosewood Avenue (e)/Close (e)/Drive/Grove (e)
See *Ashwood Grove*.

Ross Avenue
It is believed that this road was named after Ronald Ross (1857-1932). He was the Nobel Prize winner in 1902 for his research on the cure for Malaria.

Source: *Dunlop*

Rosyth Avenue/Road/Terrace
Based on a news article in 1951, Rosyth Road was named after Rosyth, a town on the Firth of Forth in Fife, Scotland. This road was repaired at frontagers' expense in 1952. See *Dix Road*.

Rosyth Avenue was named in 1953.

Source: *ST, 1951.4.7:6; RBAR, 1952:8; RBAR, 1953:8*

Rotan Lane

Rotan means rattan in Malay. This road was named in 1928.

Source: *MC, 1928.11.30*

Rowell Lane (e)/Road (Kampong Kapor)

Dr. Thomas Irvine Rowell (1840-1932) was appointed Acting Colonial Surgeon in 1868. It was mentioned in the press in 1896 that Rowell once collected donations of more than 20,000 dollars from wealthy Chinese citizens to build six large wards in Tan Tock Seng Hospital. He was the President of the Municipality from 1888 to 1889 before retiring in 1890. The roads became public streets in 1914.

Source: *ST, 1896.6.10:3; MC, 1914.11.27; ST, 1932.7.20:11; Singam*

Royal Road (former Alexandra Barracks)

See Berkshire Road.

Ruby Lane

Ruby is a red gemstone. *See Moonstone Lane.*

Rumah Bomba Circus (e)

Rumah bomba means fire station in Malay. This was a traffic circus near a fire station.

Russels Road (former Alexandra Barracks)

Russels was derived from Russell. This road was named after Sir Henry Russell, Second Baronet of Swallowfield in Berkshire. Henry Russell was the British Resident of Hyderabad from 1811-1820. *See Berkshire Road and Hyderabad Road.*

Rutland Road (Race Course Road area)

Rutland is a county in the East Midlands, England. *See Bristol Road.*

Saas Fee Avenue 1 (Singapore Turf Club, Woodlands)

Saga Village (e) (former Pulau Brani military area)

See Jalan Merah Saga.

Sago Lane/Street

The streets were named after the sago factories that were concentrated in this area. Before 1900, sago was processed in Singapore for export to England and India.

Sago Street became a public street in 1900.

Source: *MC, 1900.7.12; Buckley: 236; Makepeace, vol.2:83*

Saiboo Street
This street is in the Robertson Quay area. It was known as Saiboo Marican Street in 1902. Saiboo Marican was a money changer in the former Adelphi Hotel.

Source: *ST, 1902.12.31:2*

St. Andrew's Road
This road was named after the St. Andrew's Cathedral, the largest cathedral in Singapore. It is the cathedral church of the Anglican Diocese. The first church building was designed by G D Coleman and built from 1835 to 1836. The second version was designed by J T Thomson and built around 1842. It was demolished and rebuilt by Colonel R MacPherson in 1861. The cathedral became a national monument in 1973.

St. Andrew's Road was named in 1907.

Source: *MC, 1907.3.1*

St. Anne's Wood
This road was named after the St. Anne's Church at the same location. St. Anne is the mother of Virgin Mary.

St. Barnabas Lane
Four roads in this location were named in 1938 after saints of the Catholic church, including St. Barnabas Lane, St. Francis Road, St. Lawrence Road and St. Wilfred Road.

Source: *SFP, 1938.6.15:9*

St. Francis (Frances) Road
See *St. Barnabas Lane*. This road was named in 1938.

Source: *SFP, 1938.6.15:9*

St. George's Lane/Road
The name of St. George here may refer to the military saint of the Cavalry. See *St. Michael's Road*. St. George's Road was named in 1925.

Source: *MC, 1925.5.1*

St. Gregory's Place
This road was named after the Armenian Church of St. Gregory The Illuminator, located opposite the road.

St. Helena Road (former Singapore Naval Base)
This road was named after St. Helena, a British Overseas Territory in the South Atlantic Ocean. It is famous as the place of Napoleon's exile and death. The island was named after St. Helena (c.250-330) who was the Roman empress and mother of Emperor Constantine. See *Admiralty Road*.

St. Helier's Avenue (Serangoon Gardens)
St. Helier is the capital and resort town of Jersey, in the English Channel Islands. The town is named after St. Helier (died 555), a 6th century Frankish missionary who was reputedly martyred there. *See Alnwick Road.*

St. James Road (e) (former Nee Soon Cantonment)
This road was most likely named after St. James's district in the City of Westminster, London.

St. John's Crescent (former RAF Changi)
St. John's Road (former Singapore Naval Base)
St. John's Crescent was named after RAF Barford St. John in Oxfordshire, south of England. *See Abbotsingh Road.*

St. John's Road was named after St. John, capital of Newfoundland in Canada. *See Admiralty Road.*

St. Joseph's Lane (e)
St. Joseph is the worldly husband of Virgin Mary. This road was named in 1948. It was located at 6.75 ms Upper Serangoon Road.

Source: *RBAR, 1948:7*

St. Lawrence Road (e)
See St. Barnabas Lane. This road was named in 1938.

Source: *SFP, 1938.6.15:9*

St. Margaret's Road (former Pasir Panjang Barracks)
This road was probably named after St. Margaret's town in Kent, England. *See Dover Road.*

St. Martin Lane (former RAF Seletar)
St. Martin's Drive
St. Martin Lane was probably named after the street of the same name in Covent Garden in Central London that runs from the church of St. Martin-in-the-Fields. *See Baker Street.*

St. Martin's Drive cut through the original estate of the Armenian Martin family in Tanglin district. The road name was submitted as St. Martin's Road and approved as St. Martin's Drive by the Municipal Commission.

Source: *NAS, 291:2*

St. Michael's Road
This road name appeared in the press as early as 1900 but was only officially named in 1906. St. Michael was probably the military saint and patron saint of soldiers referred to in the Order of St. Michael and St. George, the most

distinguished British honour. It was awarded by the Queen to holders of high office in the British Empire. Mr. Whampoa, or Hoo Ah Kay, was the recipient of this honour in 1878. There were discussions in the Municipality on whether this road should be a public street in 1925, around the time when St. George's Road was named.

Source: *ST, 1900.3.17:4; MC, 1906.11.30; Buckley: 659*

St. Nicholas View
This road was named after St. Nicholas Girls' School.

St. Patrick's Road
This road was named after St. Patrick's School. It was a rename of Lorong P, Telok Kurau.

Source: *SG-1936*

St. Thomas Walk
This road was named after the St. Thomas estate, off River Valley Road.

Source: *ST, 1903.12.31:1*

St. Wilfred Road
See *St. Barnabas Lane*. This road was named in 1938.

Source: *SFP, 1938.6.15:9*

St. Xavier's Lane
St. Xavier (1506–1552) was a Roman Catholic missionary who led an extensive mission to Asia. He was the first to venture into Japan and Borneo. He died while travelling to start his mission to China. This lane was named in 1953.

Source: *RBAR, 1953:7*

Sakra Avenue/Place/Road/View
Sakra is sugar or a tree in Hindi. The above roads are found on Jurong Island. They were named after Pulau Sakra, one of the offshore islands which were amalgamated to form the present Jurong Island. See *Ayer Chawan Place*.

Source: *Dunlop*

Salam Walk
See *Jalan Haji Salam*.

Sallim Road
Sallim or *salim* means healthy in Malay. This road was probably named after Shaikh Sallim Mattar, an Arab who donated to the construction of the Sallim Mattar Mosque nearby.

Source: *Dunlop*

Sam Leong Road
This road was named after Ong Sam Leong (1857–1918, Hokkien), an entrepreneur. He was the father of Ong Boon Tat (see *Boon Tat Street*). Sam Leong Road was a rename of Paya Road in 1928.
Source: *MC, 1928.11.30; Kua: 2*

Sambau Street (e) (Malayan Streets in Tanjong Pagar)
Sambau Street first appeared in the press in 1903. It was named after Sungei Sambau, close to Raub, in Pahang. See *Bernam Street.*
Source: *ST, 1903.5.19:3*

Sampan Place
Sampan is a kind of small wooden boat. See *Tanjong Rhu Lane.*

Samudera Lane
Samudera means ocean or sea in Malay.

Sandilands Road
Sandilands is a multiple place name in England.

Sandown Place (Serangoon Gardens)
This road was named in 1953. Sandown could be the seaside resort on the Isle of Wrght, or the Sandown Castle in Kent, both in South East England.
Source: *RBAR, 1953:8*

Sandwich Road (former Pasir Panjang Barracks)
Named after the town of Sandwich (meaning sandy market in Old English), in Kent, South East England. See *Dover Road.*
Source: *Watts*

Sandy Island (Sentosa Island)

Sandy Lane
This lane was named in 1922. See *Gray Lane.*
Source: *MC1, 1922.2.3*

Sanja Link (e)/Road (e)
These roads were occasionally seen in the press. However, they were misprints of Senja Road.

Sapper Close (e)/Road (e) (former Tanglin Barracks)
Sapper is a private in the Corps of Royal Engineers, usually responsible for tasks such as building and repairing roads and bridges, laying and clearing mines. See *Barrack Road.*

Saraca Drive/Hill/Place/Road/Terrace/View/Walk
Saraca, *Saraca thaipingensis*, is a tree with attractive flowers.

Sarimbun Avenue/Lane
Sarimbun Avenue leads to Sungei Sarimbun in Lim Chu Kang, which was dammed in the 1980s to create a reservoir. This location is close to the spot where the first Japanese troops landed in Singapore in 1942 during WW2.

Sarkies Road
This road is located off Bukit Timah Road. It was named in 1923 after the Sarkies brothers who were Armenians. They were the operators (not owners) of Raffles Hotel in 1888.

Source: *MC, 1923.1.26; Makepeace, vol.2:214*

Sarum Road (e) (former RAF Changi)
See *Old Sarum Road*.

Saujana Road
Saujana means wide in Malay.

Saunders Road
C J Saunders was Acting Protector of Chinese, Acting District Judge, member of the Legislative Council, a Municipal Commissioner, a Commissioner of Currency and held several other senior positions in the course of his career in Singapore. He retired in 1923 and the road was named in 1927.

Source: *SFP, 1923.5.12:6; MC, 1927.5.27; Lee KL: 20; Singam*

Scharf Road (e)
Based on a report in 1985, Scharff was an engineer who built and cleared the drainage in Chong Pang Village to eradicate mosquitoes.

Source: *ST, 1985.2.1:21*

School Road (e) (former Blakang Mati Artillery Barracks)
Science Centre Road (Singapore Science Centre)
Science Drive 1 to 4 (NUS)
Science Park Drive/Road (Singapore Science Park)

Scotts Circus (e)/Scotts Green Road (e)/Scotts Road
Based on a report in 1906, Scotts Road was named after William Scotts (1786–1861), Harbour and Post Master from 1836 to 1847. He owned Claymore Estate, a nutmeg plantation in the Orchard Road area. His residence named The Hurricane was an attap roof house at the corner of Scotts Road and Orchard Road. He passed away at his residence in Singapore. See *Claymore Drive*.

Scotts Road was listed as a country road in 1853.

Source: *SFP, 1853.7.8:4; ED, 1906.4.24:3; Buckley: 310*

Sea Avenue (off East Coast Road)

Sea Town Lane (e)

Sea Breeze Avenue/Grove/Road/Walk (off Upper Changi Road)

Seac Road (e) (former Nee Soon Cantonment)
Seac is the acronym of South East Asia Command.

Seagull Walk

Seah Im Road
This road was named in 1907 after Ang Seah Im, a wolfram mine owner.
Source: *MC, 1907.8.16; Singam*

Seah Street
This street was named after the Seah family in 1902. The family members include Seah Eu Chin, his sons Seah Liang Seah, Seah Peck Seah and Seah Song Seah.
Source: *ST, 1883.12.8:5; ST, 1902.10.11:5*

Sealand Road (former RAF Changi)
This road was named after RAF Sealand in Flintshire in Wales. *See Abbotsingh Road.*

Second Avenue
See Fifth Avenue.

Second Chin Bee Road
See Chin Bee Road.

Second Hospital Avenue (General Hospital)

Second Link (to Malaysia)

Second Lok Yang Road
See Lok Yang Road.

Second Street, Siglap
This was a rename of Siglap, 2nd Street.

Segar Close/Road
Segar means refresh or active in Malay.

Selangor Street (e) (Malayan Streets in Tanjong Pagar)
Selangor is a state of Malaysia. Selangor Street was named in 1898. *See Bernam Street.*
Source: *MC, 1898.11.8*

Selarang Drive (e)/Park (e)/Park Road/Ring Road/Road/Square (e)/Way (former RAF Changi)
These roads are located in Selarang Camp within the former RAF Changi area. They were named after Sungei Selarang, a river that flows into the Serangoon Harbour. Based on a report in 1848, Sungei Selarang was known as Sungei Silarang. *See Abbotsingh Road.*
Source: *SFP, 1848.5.18:3*

Selegie Road
There are three explanations for the word *selegie*: Firstly, it is a Malay word that means a spear sharpened and hardened by fire. Secondly, it is the name of a Bugis headman. Thirdly, it is a corruption of Seligi, the name of a palm tree.

Based on a 1950 news article, the road was named after Seligi Hill (seen as Bukit Seligie in G D Coleman's survey map of 1836).

Selegie Road was one of the first roads that existed in 1821.
Source: *ST, 1950.10.14:6; NAS, SP002997; Buckley: 69, 534; Ramachandran: 50; Singam; Tyers: 158*

Seletar Aerospace Crescent/Drive/Heights/Link/Rise/Road 1/View/Walk (e)
Seletar Close/Club Road/Court/Crescent
(Seletar East Farmway 1 to 6) (e)
Seletar Expressway
Seletar Green Avenue/View/Walk
Seletar Hills Drive/Link/Seletar Lower Close (e)
Seletar North Lane 1/2/Seletar North Link/Seletar Road/Seletar Satellite Station Road/Seletar South Road/Terrace
Seletar West Farmway 1 to 9, 10 (e)
Seletar West Link
Based on an 1848 report, Seletar (also known as Saleta or Saletar) was the name of a river and the name of a tribe of Orang Laut.

Seletar (Saletar) Road was listed as a country road in 1853.

Seletar Airport was a RAF air station in Singapore from 1928 to 1971. The Airport now functions as an aerospace centre.
Source: *SFP, 1848.5.18:3 SFP, 1853.7.8:4; ST, 1928.2.17:9*

Sembawang Alley/Avenue/Close/Crescent/Drive
Sembawang Hill Circus (e)/Drive
Sembawang Lane (e)/Link/Place/Road/Street (e)

Sembawang Village (e)/Vista/Walk/Way

Sembawang tree is the Malay name for *Mesua ferruginea*. Sembawang was also the name of a river, seen as Sungei Sembawang in J T Thomson's survey map of 1852.

In 1939, the original Seletar Road was divided into Sembawang Road and Upper Thomson Road, with Sembawang Road taking the portion of Yio Chu Kang to the seaside at the north. Sembawang Village was named in 1929.

Source: *SFP, 1929.12.12:20; ST, 1939.2.14:14*

Sembawang Terminal Avenue 1-3
Sembawang Terminal Road A/B/C/D/E/F/G/H

These roads are located in PSA Sembawang Wharves.

Sembong Road

Sembong or *sembung* is a kind of herbaceous plant, *Blumea balsamifera* in Malay.

Senang Crescent

Senang means easy or happy in Malay. See *Jalan Kembangan*.

Seng Poh Lane/Road

Tan Seng Poh (1830-1879, Teochew) was the brother-in-law of Seah Eu Chin. He was one of the main opium and spirit farmers in Singapore. His residence in Loke Yew Street was one of the four famous Teochew mansions in Singapore and was the source of the colloquial name of "Seng Poh Au" (behind Seng Poh's residence) for Armenian Street. As a Chinese community leader he was the first Chinese to become a member of the Municipal Commission and was its President for a short period.

Seng Poh Road was located in the (pre-war) Tiong Bahru housing estate. As this district was considered an extension of Chinatown by the Municipal Commission, it was decided in 1930 that Chinese names for the roads in this district were preferred. With the exception of Moh Guan Terrace and Yong Siak Street (named in 1941), roads in the housing estate were all named before 1936.

Source: *STOJ, 1879.12.20:1; MC1, 1930.9.2; SG-1936; Kua: 75*

Sengkang Central
Sengkang East Avenue/Drive/Road/Way
Sengkang Ind Ave 1,2
Sengkang Square
Sengkang West Avenue/Road/Way

This area is located between Upper Serangoon and Punggol. "Sengkang" is a transcription of prosperous pier in Hokkien. The old name for this area was "Kang Kah", meaning the end of the pier in Hokkien.

Senja Link/Road/Way
Senja means dusk or evening in Malay.

Senjata Road (e) (former Singapore Naval Base)
Senjata means firearm in Malay. See *Admiralty Road*.

Sennett Avenue/Close/Drive/Lane/Place/Road/Terrace
C W A Sennett (born 1892) was the Commissioner of Lands and the Chairman of the Rural Board. He headed the Sennett Realty Estate Limited after his retirement in 1949.

Sennett Road was named after him in 1947 at the request of residents. It was a rename of Jalan Pasir.

Source: *ST, 1947.10.17:5; RBAR, 1949:1*

Senoko Avenue/Crescent/Drive/Link/Loop/Road/South Road/Way
Based on a report in 1848, Senoko was named after Sungei Senoko; Senoko was also known as Sinko.

Source: *SFP, 1848.5.18:3*

Sentosa Cove Avenue (e)/Sentosa East Gateway (e)/Sentosa East Mall (e)/Sentosa Gateway
Sentosa means calm and peaceful in Malay. Sentosa Island was originally known as Pulau Blakang Mati, meaning death upon entering the island. The name was changed in 1972 when the island was converted into a resort island. Sentosa Gateway joins the island to the main Singapore Island at Telok Blangah Road.

Sentul Avenue (e)/Crescent/Link
Sentul is a tree. See *Jalan Sentul*.

Seok Wee Road (e)
This road was named in 1901 after Kiong Seok Wee (1839–1888, Hokkien) who was in the business of ship chandlers and general merchants. The road was located near Chin Swee Road.

Source: *MC, 1901.12.18; Kua: 186; Song: 39*

Seow Kee Road (e)
Seow Kee Road was renamed Shanghai Road in 1914.

Source: *MC, 1914.7.31*

Sepoy Avenue (e)/Sepoy Lane (e)
Sepoy was the name given to a native infantry private in the British Indian Army and the British East India Company. For example, it was said that Raffles arrived in Singapore in 1819 with 120 sepoys from the Bengal Native Infantry. In 1820, an initial military cantonment for the sepoys was constructed at a site around Short Street. When greater protection of the island

was required, the 35th Regiment of the Madras Native Infantry was sent in 1827 and the barracks were sited near Pearl's Hill, seen as Sepoy Lines in G D Coleman's survey map of 1836, the approximate location of Sepoy Avenue/Lane. After the Indian Mutiny in 1915, the sepoys were gradually replaced by British and local Malay personnel and were completely gone after India's independence in 1947. Only eight Ghurkha battalions were left in Singapore and Malaysia after 1947.

Source: *NAS, SP002997*

Serangoon Avenue 1-4
Serangoon Central/Serangoon Central Drive
Serangoon Garden Circus/Way
Serangoon Lane/Link
Serangoon North Avenue 1 to 6
Serangoon Road/Terrace/Village (e)

Serangoon was known by many names in the past. It was shown as Rangung or Rangon in early maps. It was changed to Rangong in 1830, Sarangon in 1843, Sarangoon in 1844 and *Sirangoon* in 1845. In a press report in 1848, Sirangoon was the name of a river. From the Malay language perspective, *ranggong* is heron. *Sarangong* (or *serangoon*) means a heron. Other explanations for this road name are firstly, from the Malay phrase of *Serang degan gung* meaning beating the drum to scare (animals). Secondly, it was derived from Sri-Rengam, a place in India.

Serangoon Road started as a bridle path in 1821 and was a new road in 1839. It was one of the first country roads and was said to be named after the creek and district of Rangung, now known as Serangoon. In any case, Upper Serangoon Road still runs along Sungei Serangoon.

Serangoon Garden Way was a rename of Jalan Chye Lye in 1953.

Serangoon Garden Circus was named in 1956.

Serangoon Lane became a public street in 1914.

Source: *SFP, 1848.5.18:3; MC, 1914.11.27; RBAR, 1953:8; SD, 1954:3; RBAR, 1956:9;*

Buckley: 220, 363, 406; Haughton: 79; Perera: 55-57; Sophia: 377 map

Serapong Course Road/Hill (e)/Hill Road

These roads are on Sentosa Island (previously Pulau Blakang Mati). Based on a report in 1848, Serapong was the name of a river. Serapong Hill Road was part of the Blakang Mati Artillery Barracks area, where Fort Serapong is.

Serapong Course Road was built after 1970 and leads to Serapong Golf Course.

Source: *SFP, 1848.10.26:3*

Seraya Avenue/Jetty Road (e)/Place/Rise/Road 14, 18, 25
Seraya is a species of tree, *Shorea curfisii*, also called dark red Meranti. The above roads are found on Jurong Island. They were named after Pulau Seraya, one of the offshore islands which were amalgamated to form the present Jurong Island. See *Ayer Chawan Place*.

Seraya Crescent (Upper Thomson Road)

Seraya Road/Lane (Haig Road)
Seraya Crescent was originally named Cassia Crescent in 1956. The rename took place in the same year.
Source: *RBAR, 1956:9*

Serenade Walk

Seton Close/Walk (e)
This road was named after Sir Frederick Seton James (1870-1934), the Colonial Secretary in Singapore from 1916 for eight years. He was a Food Controller during WW1. Subsequently, he became Governor of the Windward Islands in the West Indies from 1924 to 1930.
Source: *ST, 1934.3.3:18; Singam*

Shaik Madersah Lane (e)
Shaik or *Sheikh* is an honorific title for descendents of the companion of Prophet Muhammad. Shaik Madersah was reputed in the business of arranging pilgrimage to Mecca.
Source: *NAS, 1255:3*

Shallot Lane (e)

Shamah Terrace
Shamah is a small passerine bird of the family *Muscicapidae*. See *Jalan Layang Layang*.

Shan Ching Road (e)
"Shan Ching" is mountain view in Mandarin. See *Ho Ching Road*.

Shan Road
Shan is a state in the east of Myanmar. See *Burmah Road*.

Shanghai Road/Way (e)
Shanghai Road was known as Seow Kee Road before 1914.
  Shanghai Way was renamed Students Walk. See *Nanyang Avenue*.
Source: *MC, 1914.7.31*

Shangri-La Close/Walk
Shangri-la is a fictional earthly paradise. These two roads are located in the Ang Mo Kio area.

Shaw Road (MacPherson private roads)
This road was probably named after Commander Edward Wingfield Shaw, Royal Navy (1827-1879), the Lieutenant-Governor of Malacca from March 1869 to April 1879. He was also Acting Colonial Secretary and President of the Municipal Commission between 1869 and 1870. This road was listed in the 1936 Gazetteer and was converted to a public street in 1960. See *Davidson Road*.

Other possible sources of this road name are: Walter Sidney Shaw, the Chief Justice of the Straits Settlements from 1921 to 1925 or the Partner of Shaw, Whitehead & Co.
Source: *STOJ, 1879.4.19:1; SG-1936; CCAR, 1960:7; Singam*

Sheares Avenue/Link
Dr. Benjamin Sheares (1907-1981) was the second President of Singapore. He was in office from 1971 to 1981. He died while serving his third term in office.

Shelford Road
Thomas Shelford (1839-1900) was a Partner at Paterson, Simons & Co. He was a member of the Legislative Council and Municipal Commission.
Source: *SFP, 1900.1.13:3; Makepeace, vol.2:447*

Shenton Circus (e)/Lane/Way
Sir Shenton W Thomas (1879-1962) was the last Governor and C-in-C of the Straits Settlements from 1934 to 1942. Following the fall of Singapore he was taken as a POW and was initially interned by the Japanese at Changi Prison and subsequently at Formosa and Manchuria. He retired from the Colonial Service and returned to London in 1946. Shenton Way was built on land from the Telok Ayer reclamation in 1932. The Municipal Commission decided to name this road after Sir Shenton in 1951 to commemorate him as a war time governor despite a suggestion to name it Raffles Way. The road was opened by Governor Sir Franklin Gimson on 20 July 1951.
Source: *ST, 1951.6.13:5; MC, 1951.6.29; ST, 1951.7.2:5*

Shepherds Drive
This road was previously known as Shepherd's Drive. It became a public street in 1957. In the same estate are a few roads named after species of goat and sheep, such as Angora, Barbary and Merino.
Source: *CCAR, 1957:5*

Sherwood Road (former Tanglin Barracks)
This road was in existence before 1936 and was probably named after Sherwood Foresters Regiment from the Normanton Barracks in Derby, England. The regiment was stationed in Singapore in 1905 to 1906. Sherwood Forest is a royal forest in Nottinghamshire, famous for its historical association with the legend of Robin Hood. *See Barrack Road.*

Shipyard Crescent/Road (Jurong Shipyard)

Short Street
This street is short but it has a long history. This was the area where the first sepoy cantonment was located in 1820. The road name was seen in the press as early as 1853.

Source: *ST, 1853.10.25:5*

Shrewsbury Road (Race Course Road area)
Shrewsbury is the county town of Shropshire in the West Midlands, England. This road was named in 1922. *See Bristol Road and Derbyshire Road.*

Source: *ST, 1922.2.23:8*

Shunfu Road
This road was known as Soon Hock Road. "Shunfu" is the pinyin version of "Soon Hock" in Hokkien.

Siak Kew Avenue (Sennett Estate)
This road was named after Tan Siak Kew (1906–1977, Teochew) who was a trader in pepper and other produce and was the Director and General Manager of Sze Hai Tong Bank. He donated generously to various universities and educational organisations. This road was named in 1951. *See Kee Choe Avenue.*

Source: *CC, 1951.9.28; Kua: 94*

Siak Kuan Road (e) (Sennett Estate)
This road was probably named after Tan Siak Kuan (1892–1952, Teochew) who was the son-in-law of Seah Liang Seah (*see Liang Seah Street*). He was the Company Secretary and Chief Accountant of OCBC Bank and later, Manager of the Bank. In 1932 he co-founded Tai Thong Rubber Factory. The factory was in the news when its workers went on strike in 1940. He became the Chairman of the Overseas Union Bank when the Bank was established. Siak Kew Avenue was named in 1951 after his younger brother. Tai Thong Crescent (also in Sennett Estate) was named after his factory.

Source: *SFP, 1951.10.12:5; Kua: 94*

Siak Street (e)
Based on a news article in 1951, this road was named after the Sultanate of Siak in Sumatra. Its main export was timber and agriculture produce. Siak Street was named in 1898. See Deli Street.

Source: *MC, 1898.11.8; ST, 1951.4.7:6*

Sian Tuan Avenue
Siang Kuang Avenue (Sennett Estate)
Tan Siang Kuang was a Director of Sennett Realty Estate Limited, the developer of Sennett Estate. This road was named in 1951. See Kee Choe Avenue.

Source: *ST, 1951.9.27:7; CC, 1951.9.28*

Siang Lim Park (e)
Thong Siong Lim, a Cantonese, inherited a tailor shop from his father. The shop was the oldest and most famous in town for tailoring Western suits. Thong expanded his business into sawmill and properties. He co-founded a school (Ying Xin School) in 1905 and was the Cantonese representative in the Chinese Advisory Board.

This road was named in 1928 at the request of Thong's Siang Lim Saw Mill Co.

Source: *MC, 1928.9.28; Kua: 33; Singam; Song: 435*

Sibu Road (e)
Sibu is the Malay name for the plant *Odenlandia corymbosa*. Sibu is also the second largest city in Sarawak. The city is nicknamed Little Fuzhou due to its large number of Chinese population with Fuzhou ancestry. See Borneo Road.

(Siglap, 1st Street/2nd Street/3rd Street/4th Street) (e)
Siglap Avenue/Avenue South
Siglap Bank/Close/Drive/Gardens/Hill/Link/Plain/Rise/Road/Terrace/Valley /View/Village (e)/Walk
Siglap is derived from the Malay word *si gelap* (this gloomy). This place was full of trees and was frequented by pirates.

Seglap Road (now known as Siglap Road) was listed as a country road in 1853.

Siglap Village was situated between Jalan Ulu Siglap and Jalan Tua Kong.

Source: *SFP, 1853.7.8:4; Buckley: 424*

Silat Avenue/Crescent (e)/Lane (e)/Road/Square (e)/Walk
Silat was known as *salat* or *selat*, which means straits in Malay. The Silat Road area was originally a dumping ground.

Salat Road (now known as Silat Road) was listed as a country road in 1853. In 1858, part of Salat Road (now known as Silat Road) was renamed Neil Road.

Source: *SFP, 1853.7.8:4; SFP, 1858.4.1:6*

Siloso Beach Walk/Siloso Road

Siloso may have been derived from *salusuh*, which is the name of a herb. Siloso Road leads to the fort of the same name on Sentosa Island. *See Artillery Road.*

Source: *Haughton: 80*

Sime Park Avenue (e)/Drive (e)/Hill/Road (e)/Sime Road

W M Sime (1873-1943) and Henry Darby established Sime Darby Rubber Plantation Management Company in 1910 in Malacca. It started a branch office in Singapore in 1915 and has expanded ever since to become a large conglomerate today.

During WW2, Sime Road was the strategic and command camp for the British army. The area became an intern camp for the Australian soldiers during the Japanese Occupation. In May 1942, there was an exchange of POWs in the Sime Camp and ordinary prisoners in Changi Prison.

Sime Park Avenue, Sime Park Drive, Sime Park Hill and Sime Park Road were named in 1953.

Source: *RBAR, 1953:8; Singam*

Simei Avenue/Lane/Rise/Road
Simei Street 1 to 6

These roads were named after Tan Soo Bee (1887-1964, Hokkien) who started business as a shipowner. He expanded his business into rubber, building materials and coconut produce. Jalan Soo Bee was also named after him.

"Simei" is the pinyin translation of "Soo Bee" in Hokkien. Somehow his name was interpreted as four beauties, referring to the four great classical beauties in China, instead of four virtues for a man. As a result, portraits of the four classical beauties can be seen on the walls of some apartment blocks in this area.

Source: *Kua: 72*

Simon Close (e)/Lane/Place/Road/Walk

These roads were probably named after Max Simon or Simon Aroozoo. Max Simon was a medical doctor in the 1890s. *See Aroozoo Lane.*

Simon Lane was approved for repair by the Rural Board in 1952. It became a public street in 1955.

Simon Walk was named in 1953.

Source: *ST, 1952.12.19:4; RBAR, 1953:7; RBAR, 1955:9; Dunlop*

Simpang Bedok Village (e)
See Jalan Simpang Bedok.

Sims Avenue/Avenue East
Sims Drive/Lane/Place/View/Way
William Arthur Sims (1875-1937) was the Manager of Commercial Union Assurance for many years from 1904. He was a member of the Municipal Commission from 1916 to 1922. Sims initially expressed an aesthetic dislike to the suggestion of naming Sims Road after him. The name was confirmed as Sims Avenue in December 1922.

The account that this road was named after Sim Kia Jan, a banker, is doubtful.

Source: *ST, 1922.11.25:9; MC, 1922.12.29; ST, 1937.9.5:1; Kua: 40; Singam*

Sin Koh Street (e)
Goh Sin Koh was the owner of sawmills and shipping companies in the 19th century. He was once wrongfully accused for a crime but was acquitted on appeal. This road was named in 1906.

Source: *MC, 1906.11.30; Singam; Song: 264*

Sin Koy Lane (e)
There was a misprint of this lane as Sin Kay in the 1936 Gazetteer.

Sin Ming Avenue/Drive
Sin Ming Industrial Estate Sector A/B/C
Sin Ming Lane/Road/Walk
These roads were named after Sin Ming School which was located here. It was reported in 2013 that its secondary school was established in 1945 with the help of Ye Fan Feng (in pinyin). Ye purportedly sold five pigs to rent three houses as the initial premises for the secondary school. However, he was deported to China in the 1950s for selling rubber to China.

Source: *DSM: 398; NAS, 650:1; ZB, 2013.10.16 Singapore News: 12*

Sin Poh Street (e)
This was a misprint of Sin Koh Street in the press in 1906.

Source: *SFP, 1906.12.1:8*

Sinaran Drive
Sinaran is a ray or a glitter in Malay.

Sing Avenue

Sing Joo Walk

Sing Nan Road (e)

(Singapore Harbour Board Gate No. 1 to 9) (e)
Singapore Harbour Board Main Entrance (See Main Entrance) (e)
Singapore Harbour Board was the predecessor of the Port of Singapore Authority.

Sinkiang Road (e)
Sinkiang or Xinjiang is an autonomous territory in northwest China. Sinkiang Road was renamed Nanyang Crescent in 1971. *See Faculty Avenue and Nanyang Avenue.*

Siok Wan Close (e)
Khoo Siok Wan (1874–1941, Hokkien) was a poet from a wealthy family. He was revered as the Father of Poetry in South East Asia. Khoo established a poetry society, a newspaper and was generous towards funding for schools. Politically he supported the Manchurian government in China unlike many fellow wealthy Chinese who supported Sun Yet-Sen's revolution. Due to his generosity in all the above endeavours, he was made a bankrupt and died a poor man.
Source: *Kua: 102*

Sirat Place/Road
Sirat was a Malay businessman in the business of supplying satay and Indonesian delicacies. He became rich as a result of his business.
Source: *Serangoon: 19*

Sireh Place
See Kampong Sireh.

Sit (Seet) Wah Road
Seet Wah (died 1923) was a building contractor who cultivated yam and vegetables on a large scale in the Tiong Bahru area. This road in Tiong Bahru was named in 1905.
Source: *MC, 1905.3.10; ST, 1923.3.1:8*

Sixth Avenue/Sixth Crescent
See Fifth Avenue.

Sixth Lok Yang Road
See Lok Yang Road.

Slim Barracks Rise/Road (e) (former RAF Changi)
These roads were named after Field Marshall William Slim (1891–1970). Slim was famous as a leader of the Burma campaign to victory during WW2 and took over his superior's position as the C-in-C of the Allied Land Forces, South East Asia in September 1945. After the war he returned to England and was subsequently made the Chief of the Imperial General Staff in 1949.

He retired from the army in 1952 and was appointed Governor-General of Australia from 1952 to 1960. *See Leese Road.*

Source: *ST, 1945.9.18: 1*

Smart Road (former Tanglin Barracks)
See Barrack Road.

Smith Street
This street name appeared in the minutes of the Municipal Commission in 1853 discussing a request to repair Smith Street by J C Smith, the agent for the Estate of J T Dickenson. Dickenson was the owner of a large part of Bukit Pasoh (*see Bukit Pasoh Road*) where Smith Street is located.

John Colson Smith (died 1863) was the headmaster of Penang Free School. He came to Singapore in 1844 to be the headmaster of Raffles Institution ("RI") when Dickenson returned to America on account of his health. He became the librarian of the Singapore Library situated in RI from 1844 until he passed away in 1863. He was also the Treasurer of the Masonic Lodge in Singapore.

The account that this street was named after Cecil Clementi Smith (1840–1916), Governor of Singapore from 1887 to 1893, is doubtful because Governor Smith arrived in Singapore as a Colonial Secretary in 1878, long after the existence of Smith Street.

Source: *SFP, 1853.2.25:3; ST, 1863.3.16:1; Buckley: 134, 497; Singam*

Sohst Road (e)
This road was named in 1912 after wealthy German aristocrat T H Sohst (died 1912). Due to hostility against Germany arising from WW1, the road was renamed Mount Rosie Road (named after his wife) in 1920. *See Mount Rosie Road.*

Source: *MC, 1912.12.27; MC, 1920.3.26*

Solomon Street
Abraham Solomon (1789-1884) was a successful merchant and one of the earliest Jewish settlers in Singapore. He took part in the construction of the first Synagogue, the Maghan Aboth Synagogue, at Synagogue Street. He lost most of his fortune from speculation in opium and died a poor man.

Source: *ST, 1884.5.20:2; Singam*

Somapah Estate (e)/Somapah Changi Village (e)/Somapah Road/ Somapah Serangoon Village (e)
H Somapah (died 1919) was a wealthy Indian broker and property owner. His father Harumalpah was one of the Indian convicts who served his sentence as a labourer in Singapore. After his term he decided to settle down in Singapore.

Somapah Road was constructed in 1950 and became a public street in 1955.

Somapah Changi Village was located at the junction of Somapah Road and Upper Changi Road.

Somapah Serangoon Village was located at the junction of Upper Serangoon Road and Tampines Road.

Source: *SFP, 1919.1.29:6; RBAR, 1950:8; RBAR, 1955:9; NAS, 110:1*

Somerset Road

This road runs parallel to Devonshire Road in the Orchard Road area. It was probably named after the county of Somerset in South West England, which borders Devonshire to the southwest. The word "Somerset" is derived from Old English suthmorset, meaning the people living at Sumortun. This road was declared a public street in 1930.

Source: *SFP, 1931.8.17:12; Wagner: 135*

Somme Road (WW1 roads)

This road was named in 1928 after Somme, the site of one of the famous battlefields during WW1. *See Allenby Road.*

The Battle of the Somme was fought by the British and French armies against the German empire between July and November 1916 on both sides of the River Somme. It was one of the largest battles of WW1 with casualties of more than one million.

Source: *MC1, 1928.10.2*

Sommerville Estate Drive (e)/Road (Holland Road)
Sommerville Road/Walk (Upper Serangoon Road)

Sommerville Estate Road first appeared in the press in 1951.

Sommerville Road was listed in the 1936 Gazetteer as a private road. It appeared in the press in 1952. Likely sources for this name could be A C Sommerville who was a Partner at Paterson, Simons & Co. in 1900 or D K Sommerville, a Director at Straits Steamship Co. Ltd.

Source: *Singam*

Soo Bin Road (e)

This road was named after Tan Soo Bin (1882–1939), the great grandson of Tan Kim Seng and the second son of Tan Jiak Kim (*see Jiak Kim Street*). He was a sharp shooter and a member of the Singapore Volunteer Infantry. In 1940, his widow donated a motorboat valued at 3,500 sterling pounds to the RAF in his memory. Soo Bin Road, located in Queenstown, was named in 1956 but was changed to Stirling Road in the same year at the request of the Tan family. *See Stirling Road.*

Source: *SFP, 1939.8.14:7; SFP, 1940.9.10:9; RBAR, 1956:9*

Soo Chow Drive/Garden Road/Rise/View/Walk/Way
See Soochow Road.

Soochow Road (e)
Soochow (now Suzhou) is a city near Shanghai. It is famous for its beautiful gardens. Soochow Road was located in the former Nanyang University. *See Nanyang Avenue.*

Soon Hock Lane/Road (e)
Soon Hock Lane is located off Jurong Port Road.

Soon Hock Road was named in 1950. It is now known as Shunfu Road. *See Shunfu Road.*

Source: *RBAR, 1950:9*

Soon Keat Road (e)
Based on a report in 1985, this road was named after one of Lim Nee Soon's elders. During the Japanese Occupation, this road was known for its comfort women outside the Singapore Naval Base.

Source: *ST, 1985.2.1:21; NAS, 977:1*

Soon Lee Drive/Road/Street
This road was first seen in the 1969 Street Directory. *See Chia Ping Road.*

Soon Teck Road (e)
This road was located between Cantonment Road and Tanjong Pagar Road. It was named in 1929.

Source: *SFP, 1929.2.7:8*

Soon Wing Road

Sophia Road
See Mount Sophia. Sophia Road became a public street in 1877.

Source: *ST, 1877.3.31:2; Singam*

Sops Avenue/Boulevard/Crescent/Drive/Lane/Street/Terrace/Way (e)
This area was renamed Loyang Industrial Park.

Sorby Adams Drive
Reverend R K Sorby Adams (1901–1976) was an Australian missionary who came to Singapore in 1927 to take up a teaching position at St. Andrew's School. He was its Principal from 1934 to 1956.

Source: *ST, 1976.11.28:9*

South Boat Quay (e)
See Boat Quay.

South Bridge Road

The bridge here refers to Elgin Bridge, which was discussed under North Bridge Road. The road was probably built following the completion of the first bridge in 1822. South Bridge Road was seen in the press as early as 1831.

Source: *SCCR, 1831.6.30:1*

South Buona Vista Road

This road was created from the splitting of the original Buona Vista Road into north and south sections. This road is hilly and commands a good view. It had a colloquial name of "9 bends and 13 turns" (九曲十三弯) in Mandarin. *See North Buona Vista Road.*

Source: *RBAR, 1948:7*

South Canal Road

This was the south bank of the old canal leading to the Singapore River.

Source: *NAS, SP002997*

South Perimeter Road (Singapore Changi Airport)

South Pier (e) (Telok Ayer Basin)

South Quay (e) (Telok Ayer Basin)

South Road (e)

This road was renamed Read Street in 1896.

Source: *NAS, SP000100*

South Woodlands Drive/Way

Spitfire Road (e) (former RAF Tengah)

This road was named after Supermarine Spitfire, a British fighter aircraft which was used from 1938 to 1961. *See Hornet Road.*

Spooner Road

This road was named after Charles Edward Spooner (1853-1909). He was the Manager of the Federated Malay States Railways from 1901 to 1909.

Source: *ST, 1909.5.17:7*

Sports Drive 1/2 (NUS)

Spottiswoode Park Road

This road was named after William Spottiswoode (died 1859). W S Spottiswoode arrived in Singapore in 1824 with John Conolly and established the firm of Spottiswoode and Conolly. After Conolly's death, the company was renamed Wm Spottiswoode & Co. in 1849. According to Buckley's account, Spottiswoode was the Executor of Choa Chong Long's Estate after the latter was murdered in Macao in 1838 (see *Chong Long Road*). Wm Spottiswoode & Co. prospered for some time and even owned a building in Commercial Square (renamed Raffles Place) until around the 1860s. Spottiswoode left Singapore in 1856. In 1859, Spottiswoode Park was up for auction sale by the Estate of William Spottiswoode (deceased).

One other account mentioned that the road could be named after Charles Spottiswoode who took over Wm Spottiswoode & Co. in 1856.

Source: *SFP, 1849.8.24:1; SFP, 1859.12.1:4; Buckley: 216, 233; Singam*

Spring Street
Spring Street was named for the source of fresh water found at this location.

Springleaf Avenue/Crescent/Drive/Garden/Height/Lane/Link/Rise/Road/View/Walk

Springside Avenue/Crescent/Drive/Green/Link/Place/Road/View/Walk

Springwood Avenue/Close/Crescent/Height/Terrace/Walk

Sri Menanti Estate (e)/Road (e)
The name of Sri Menanti could be taken from the royal capital of the State of Sembilan, Malaysia. *Sri* is Goddess of rice in ancient Javanese and *menanti* means awaiting in Malay. Sri Menanti Estate, located at Grange Road, was the nutmeg plantation of G G Nichol in 1843. Nichol was a Partner at the firm of Hamilton, Gray and Co. (1832–1886). *See Chatsworth Avenue*.

Sri Menanti Road was named in 1921.

Source: *MC, 1921.12.20; Buckley: 406, 677*

Stable Loop (Singapore Turf Club, Woodlands)

Stadium Boulevard/Crescent/Drive/Lane/Link/Place/Road/Walk/Way (Singapore Sports Hub)

Stagmont Ring/Road
These roads are located in the Choa Chu Kang/Woodlands area. Stagmont Ring was named in 1955.

Source: *RBAR, 1955:9*

Stamford Road
This road was named after Sir Stamford Raffles. It was previously named Hospital Street as it was the location of a hospital. Stamford Road was listed as a street in town in 1853.

Source: *SFP, 1853.7.8:4; Makepeace, vol.2:491*

Stangee Close/Place
Stangee is incense made from fragrant wood.
   Stangee Place was named in 1951.
Source: *CC, 1951.10.31; Dunlop*

Stanley Street
This road was named after Captain E Stanley who led a successful operation in 1836 to clear pirates in the Straits of Malacca.
Source: *SFP, 1836.3.24:3; Dunlop*

Starlight Road/Terrace (off Rangoon Road)

Stars Avenue (Mediapolis)

Stephen Lee Road
This road in the Mandai area was named in 1957 after Reverend Father Stephen Lee, Parish Priest of the Church of St. Anthony at Mandai Road.
Source: *RBAR, 1957:8*

Stevens Close/Drive/Road
Stevens Road was originally named Stephen's Road as Municipal records from 1850 to 1861 showed that this road was connected to Bukit Timah Road and Dalvey Road. The road was probably named after James Stephen, a Partner at Shaw, Whitehead & Co., and a member of the Grand Jury in 1838. He was generous towards public causes and on one occasion put up funds together with Tan Tock Seng to build two water tanks for the public. He died in England in 1851.

   A news article in 1935 mentioned that this road was named after A Stevens, the Assistant Superintendent of the Police Force. This is unlikely as A Stevens came from India in 1881 with a Sikh contingent from Punjab to strengthen the police force in Singapore. As can be seen from the above, the road name existed prior to his arrival.
Source: *SFP, 1838.11.29:3; ST, 1845.1.23:1; ST, 1851.11.11:4; SFP, 1850.12.6:2; ST, 1861.10.12:21; SFP, 1935.9.19:3*

Still Lane/Road/Road South
Alexander William Still (1860–1931) was the editor of *The Straits Times* from 1908 to 1925. Still Road was named in 1931. Still Road South was a rename of Karikal Lane in 1980.
Source: *MC, 1931.4.29; ST, 1980.1.11:14; Singam*

Stirling Drive (e) (Serangoon Gardens)
This road was named in 1953 and renamed Berwick Drive in 1955.
Source: *RBAR, 1953:8*

Stirling Road (e) (Nee Soon Cantonment, RAF Tengah)
Stirling Road in the Nee Soon Cantonment was listed only once in the 1953 Street Directory.

Stirling Road in RAF Tengah was named after Short Stirling, manufactured by the Short Brothers. The plane was the first four-engine heavy bomber of WW2. It was renamed Old Stirling Road. *See Hornet Road.*

Source: *SD 1953*

Stirling Road/Walk (Queenstown)
Stirling Road in Queenstown was a rename of Soo Bin Road in 1956.

Source: *RBAR, 1956:9*

Stockport Road (former Pasir Panjang Barracks)
This name was taken from Stockport, a market town in Cheshire, England.

Stokesay Drive (Serangoon Gardens)
This road was named in 1953. Stokesay is a historic hamlet in Shropshire, West Midlands, England. It is famous for its 13th century Stokesay Castle, one of the best preserved castles and the oldest of its kind. *See Alnwick Road.*

Source: *RBAR, 1953:8*

Stone Avenue

Stonehills Road (e)

Stores Road (e) (former Singapore Naval Base)
Stores Road is close to the Store Basin at the Wharf of the Naval Base. *See Admiralty Road.*

Straits Boulevard/View

Strathmore Avenue/Road
Strathmore Valley is situated in Forfar in Angus County, North East England. *See Forfar Square.*

Strathmore Avenue was declared a public street in 1957.

Source: *CCAR, 1957:5*

Stratton Drive/Green/Place/Road/Walk
Stratton means a dwelling place along a Roman road; it is a multiple place name in England.

Source: *Watts*

Street TNP (Pasir Panjang Terminal)

Students Crescent (e)/Walk
These roads are located in the Nanyang Technological University campus. Students Crescent and Students Walk were previously Wuchang Road and Shanghai Way respectively.

Sturdee Road/Road North (WW1 roads)
Sturdee Road was named after Admiral Sir Frederick C D Sturdee (1859-1925), one of the leading commanders in WW1. Sturdee Road was first named in 1928 and was reconfirmed as a new road by the MC in 1930. See *Allenby Road*.

In the Battle of the Falkland Islands on 8 December 1914, Sturdee's forces almost sank the entire German squadron. For his part in this important naval action Sturdee was created a baronet in 1916.

Source: *MC1, 1928.10.2; MC, 1930.6.27*

Sturrock Road (e)
This road was named after G Sturrock (born 1880), a professional engineer and architect who worked in Singapore and Malaya for 28 years. He was the colony's first Director of Public Works from 1932-1935 and a member of the Legislative Council. This road was declared a public street in 1960.

Source: *SFP, 1935.4.6:6; CCAR, 1960:8; Singam*

Suara Avenue (e)/Suara Road (e) (former Singapore Naval Base)
Suara has several meanings in Malay. In the context of Naval Base, it probably means radio. See *Admiralty Road*.

Sudan Road (former Singapore Naval Base)
Sudan is a country in northeast Africa. See *Admiralty Road*.

Suez Canal Road (e)

Suffolk Road/Walk (Race Course Road area)
Suffolk is a county in South East England. See *Bristol Road*. Suffolk Road was named in 1929.

Source: *MC, 1929.7.26*

Sultan Gate/Road (e) (Kampong Glam)
Sultan Gate is the location of the Istana Kampong Glam. Kampong Glam was the land set aside for Sultan Hussein Mohamed Shah and his 600 family members upon his ceding of Singapore to the British East India Company in 1823. The Istana was built by Sultan Mohamed's eldest son, Tengku Mohammed Ali, in 1840. The Istana is now part of the Malay Heritage Centre. See *Arab Street*.

Sultan Road was listed as a street in town in 1853 and was renamed Bussorah Street in 1909.

Source: *SFP, 1853.7.8:4; ST, 1909.12.16:12*

Sum Wah Chee Drive (e)

Sumang Lane/Link/Walk

Sumang means donation in Malay.

Sumbawa Road (e)

Sumbawa is an Island in Indonesia. Sumbawa Road was the area allocated to immigrants from Sumbawa Island. Sumbawa Road was listed as a street in town in 1853 and was subsequently renamed Crawford Lane.

Source: *SFP, 1853.7.8:4; Salam is "peace; the blessing at the end of a mosque service" in Malay. ST, 1919.11.1:9*

Summer Place

Summit Lane (e)

Sunbird Avenue/Circle/Road

Sunderland Road (e) (former RAF Tengah)

This road was named after Short Sunderland, a British flying boat patrol bomber developed for the RAF by the Short Brothers. See *Hornet Road*.

Sundridge Park Road (Braddell Heights Estate)

Sundridge Park is a place name in England. This road was named in 1951.

Source: *CC, 1951.11.28*

Sungei Belang (e) (Pulau Tekong)

See *Jalan Sungei Belang*.

Sungei Berih Road (e)

The road was named after Sungei Berih in 1949 and was located off 16 ms Choa Chu Kang Road. *Berih* in Malay means a fish or a tree *Quercus spp.*

Source: *ST, 1949.12.16:7; RBAR, 1949:9; Haughton: 80*

Sungei Bomban (e)

This road was listed in the 1950 Street Directory as "off 7.5 ms Tampines Road". According to a news article in 1938, Bomban is a shrub that gave the town of Seremban its name.

Source: *ST, 1938.2.13:21*

Sungei Gedong Road

Named in 1949, this road was between Sungei Gedong and Sungei Karang in Lim Chu Kang. *Gedong* means godown in Malay.

Source: *RBAR, 1949:9*

Sungei Kadut Avenue/Central/Crescent/Drive/Lane/Loop/Road (e)
Sungei Kadut Street 1 to 6
Sungei Kadut Way
Kadut is a cloth sack in Malay. Sungei Kadut Road was named in 1949.

Source: *RBAR, 1949:9*

Sungei Mandai Village (e)
This village was named in 1953. See *Mandai Road*.

Source: *RBAR, 1953:7*

Sungei Nipah (e)
See *Jalan Nipah*.

Sungei Road
This road was declared a public street in 1925.

Source: *SFP, 1925.3.28:9*

Sungei Simpang Village (e)
Simpang means a crossroads in Malay. This village was located around Chong Pang Road.

Sungei Tengah Road (e)
Tengah means middle in Malay. Sungei Tengah is a tributary of the Punggol River at its upper reaches. It was the location of Kampong Sungei Tengah. The road was named in 1949.

Source: *RBAR, 1949:9*

Sungei Tuas (e)
See *Tuas Avenue*.

Sunrise Avenue/Close/Drive/Lane/Place/Terrace/Walk/Way

Sunset Avenue/Close/Crescent/Drive/Grove/Heights/Lane/Place/Square/Terrace/Vale/View/Walk/Way
Sunset Avenue was named in 1954.

Source: *RBAR, 1954:9*

Sunshine Terrace
This road was named in 1956.

Source: *ST, 1956.2.1:8*

Sunview Road/Way

Supreme Court Lane

Surin Avenue/Lane/Road
The above were named after the Eurasian Surin family who owned silent movie theatres. Surin Avenue was printed as Surina Avenue in the 1936 Gazetteer.

Surrey Road (Race Course Road area)
This road was named after Surrey, a county in South East England. *See Bristol Road*. The road name first appeared in the press in 1936.

Source: ST, 1936.1.12:22

Sussex Garden (former RAF Seletar)
This road was named after Sussex Garden, a major road in the Bayswater area, City of Westminster, London. *See Baker Street*.

Sut Avenue
Sut is the acronym for Sembawang Utilities Terminal.

Swallow Street (e) (former RAF Seletar)
This road was named after Swallow Street in Mayfair, City of Westminster, London. *See Baker Street*.

Swan Lake Avenue (Opera Estate)
Swan Lake is a ballet composed by Pyotr Tchaikovsky. *See Aida Street*.

Swanage Road (former Grove Estate)
This road was named in 1928 after Swanage, a coastal town in Dorset, six miles south of Poole. *See Grove Road*.

Source: MC, 1928.9.28

Swatow Lane (e)/Street (e)
Swatow (now Shantou) is a city in Guangdong Province. Swatow Lane was renamed Faculty Avenue in 1971. *See Faculty Avenue and Nanyang Avenue*.

Swatow Street was known as Fish Court before May 1928.

Source: MC1, 1928.5.1

Swee Hee Lane (e)
Yeo Swee Hee (1861–1909) was the General Manager of Huttenbach & Co. and the first lessee of the Singapore Cold Storage retail depot at Orchard Road.

Source: ST, 1909.10.12:7; Song: 308

Swettenham Close/Green/Road
These roads were named after F A Swettenham (1850–1956), Governor of the Straits Settlements from 1901 to 1903. He wrote two books on Malaya. Swettenham Road was named in 1921.

Source: MC, 1921.3.2; Singam

Swiss Club Avenue/Lane/Link/Road
The Swiss Club was established in 1871 in Balestier Road as a social meeting place for its members. It housed a rifle range (see *Target Road*). The club moved to its current premises at Swiss Club Road in 1902. See *Clarke Road*.

Swiss Club Lane was named in 1953.

Source: *SFP, 1947.10.17:5; RBAR, 1953:8*

Swiss Cottage Estate/Swiss View

Sydney Road (e) (former Singapore Naval Base)
Sydney is the largest city in Australia. See *Admiralty Road*.

Syed Ali (Allie) Road (e)
This road was named after Syed Ali bin Mahomed Al Junied (1814-1858), a community leader who financed the building of four wells to ensure a supply of drinking water to the public. The road name was changed to Newton Road in 1914 to avoid confusion with Syed Alwi Road, which was named after Syed Ali's son. When a request to reinstate the name was raised by a member of the Commission in 1924, it was decided to put the name on hold for a Muslim area. This may be linked to the naming of Aljunied Road in 1926.

Source: *MC, 1914.10.30; SFP, 1924.8.30:9; Buckley: 564*

Syed Alwi (Alwee) Road
Based on a news article in 1881, this road was originally named Syed Alwee Road, also known as Jalan Bahru. After 1900, the simpler "Alwi" began to be used together with "Alwee" and by 1937 only "Alwi" was used. Syed Alwee (Allowie) was the son of Syed Ali bin Mahomed Al Junied (*See Syed Ali (Allie) Road*); he sold his inheritance to help build three bridges on behalf of the Municipality.

Source: *STOJ, 1881.9.9:7; Buckley: 564*

Synagogue Street
This street was named after the Maghain Aboth Synagogue which had since been relocated to Waterloo Street in 1973. Synagogue Street was listed as a street in town in 1853.

Source: *SFP, 1853.7.8:4*
Colloquial Name: "Po Lei Au", behind the Police Station. (*Phua, 1952:219*)

Szechuan Road (e)
Szechuan (now Sichuan) is a province in southwest China. Szechuan Road was renamed Nanyang Circle in 1971. See *Faculty Avenue and Nanyang Avenue*.

T1 Airport Boulevard/Arrival Crescent/Basement Drive/Boulevard/Departure Crescent
T1 Link East/West

T1 Passenger Crescent/VIP Drive (Terminal 1 of Changi Airport)
T2 Arrival Drive/Basement Drive/Boulevard/Departure Drive
T2 Link North/South/T2 VIP Drive (Terminal 2 of Changi Airport)
T3 Arrival Crescent/Basement Drive/Departure Crescent
T3 Link North/South (Terminal 3 of Changi Airport)

Tagore Avenue/Drive/Industrial Avenue/Lane/Road
These roads were named after Tagore (1861–1941), an Indian writer and painter. He visited Singapore in 1924 and 1927.

This area is located next to the Teachers' Housing Estate. *See Iqbal Avenue.*

Tah Ching Road
"Tah Ching" is pagoda view in Mandarin, it refers to the pagoda in the Chinese Garden nearby. *See Ho Ching Road.*

Tai Gin Lane (e)/Road
Tai Gin Road was named in 1901 as Tai Jin Road. "Tai Jin" is the dialect version of the Mandarin term of "Da Ren", a polite address for a Senior Official. It was used by local Chinese in early days as a polite address for senior colonial officials such as the Chinese Protector. Similar names in the vicinity are Jalan Datoh, Jalan Rajah and Mandarin Road.

Source: *MC, 1901.12.18*

Tai Hwan Avenue/Close/Crescent/Drive/Grove/Heights/Lane/Place/Terrace/Walk
"Tai Hwan" means big garden in Mandarin. This estate was built around 1973.

Tai Keng Avenue/Gardens/Lane/Place/Terrace
"Tai Keng" means big celebration in Mandarin. This estate was built around 1970.

Tai Seng Avenue/Crescent (e)/Drive/Link/Street/Village (e)
See Lorong Tai Seng.

Tai Thong Crescent (Sennett Estate)
This road was named in 1951. *See Siak Kuan Road and Kee Choe Avenue.*

Source: *CC, 1951.9.28*

Tai Yuan Heights
"Tai Yuan" means peaceful garden in Mandarin.

Taipeng Road (e)
The original name for this road was Cheang Wan Seng Road. The name was first changed to Taipeng Road in 1914 and renamed again in 1924 to Beng Hoon Road. The road was located between Chin Swee Road and Havelock Road.

Source: *MC, 1914.7.31; MC, 1924.10.31*

Taipu Lane (e)
Taipu (now Dabu) is a county in the province of Guangdong, China. Taipu Lane was renamed Faculty Road in 1971. *See Faculty Avenue and Nanyang Avenue.*

Talbot Road (e) (former Singapore Naval Base)
This road was probably named after Admiral Sir John Talbot (c.1769-1851). He was a senior Royal Navy officer who served in the French Revolution and Napoleonic Wars. Several ships in the Royal Navy were named after him. *See Admiralty Road.*

Talma Road
This road was named after Edwy Lyonet Talma (1874-1930, Eurasian) who was a Partner at the law firm of Battenberg and Talma and a member of the Municipal Commission.

Source: *SFP, 1930.7.7:10; Singam*

Taman Bedok
Taman means garden in Malay. *See Bedok Road.*

Taman Ho Swee
See Jalan Bukit Ho Swee.

(Taman Jurong/Taman Jurong 1 to 10, 12) (e)
See Jurong Road for the etymology of Jurong.

The above roads were renamed in 1971 as follows:

Taman Jurong became Corporation Drive.

Taman Jurong 1 became Yung Loh Road.

Taman Jurong 2 became Yuan Ching Road.

Taman Jurong 3 became Yung Ping Road.

Taman Jurong 4 became Hu Ching Road.

Taman Jurong 5 became Yung Kuang Road.

Taman Jurong 6 became Tao Ching Road.

Taman Jurong 7 became Yung Sheng Road.

Taman Jurong 8 became Ho Ching Road.

Taman Jurong 9 became Yung An Road.

Taman Jurong 10 became Shan Ching Road.

Taman Jurong 12 became Tah Ching Road.

Taman Kembangan
See Jalan Kembangan.

Taman Mas Merah
Mas merah is rose gold in Malay. *See Jalan Mas Kuning.*

Taman Nakhoda
Nakhoda is the Malay word for shipmaster, specifically of the master of a Persian or Indian trading-dhow.

Taman Permata
Permata means precious stone in Malay.

Taman Selamat
See *Jalan Selamat*.

Taman Serangoon (e)
This road was renamed Chuan Garden.

Taman Serasi
Serasi means suitable or harmonious in Malay.

Taman Siglap
See *Siglap Road*.

Taman Sireh
See *Kampong Sireh*.

(Taman Tampines/Dua/Satu/Tiga) (e)
See Tampines Avenue for the etymology of Tampines.
    See Pachitan Dua for numerals in Malay.

Taman Warna
Warna means colourful or attractive in Malay.

Tamarind Road
Tamarind fruit pulp is a popular ingredient in South East Asian cooking. It is also known as Assam Java.
Source: *Boo: 732*

Tambah Lane (e) (Kampong Kapor)
See Jalan Tambah for the meaning of *tambah*. This road became a public street in 1914.
Source: *MC, 1914.11.27*

Tampines Avenue/Avenue 1 to 12
Tampines Central 1 to 8
Tampines Close (e)/Tampines Concourse/Tampines Drive (e)/Tampines Expressway/Tampines Grande
Tampines Industrial Avenue 1 to 5
Tampines Industrial Crescent/Drive
Tampines Industrial Street 61/62
Tampines Lane (e)/Tampines Link
Tampines North Drive 1, 2

Tampines Place/Tampines Road
Tampines Street 11, 12, 21 to 24, 31 to 34, 41 to 45, 52, 61, 62, 64, 71 to 73, 81 to 86, 91, 92, 93, 94 (e)
Tampines Way (e)
Tampines was written as Tampenis or Tempenis before 1939. Based on a survey report in 1848, Tampenis was the name of a creek. Tampines is the name of hardwood timber from *Sloetia sideroxylon* or *Streblus elongates*.

Tampenis Road was constructed in 1864. Its maintenance became the responsibility of the Rural Board when the Board was formed in 1908. The current name of Tampines was adopted by the Board in 1939.

Tampines Street 94 was merged with Tampines Street 92.

Source: *SFP, 1848.5.18:3; SFP, 1886.10.30:8; ST, 1887.9.2:3; ST, 1939.2.19:12; Buckley: 714; Koh: 535; Makepeace, vol.2:64*

Tan Boon Chong Avenue
Tan Boon Chong (died 1957, Hokkien) was in the building construction and import-export business and was the owner of a large plantation. This road was named around 1958.

Source: *ST, 1958.12.2:5*

Tan Kim Cheng Road
See Kim Cheng Street.

Tan Quee Lan Street
Tan Quee Lan was a Hainanese merchant who was active in the 1880s to the early 1900s. From limited information available, it appears that he was the owner of at least two plantations, one in Tanjong Katong and the other at 6 ms Bukit Timah Road. His residence at Gemmil Hill was the former club house of Chwee Lan Ting Club. In late 1891 his household furniture at Gemmil Hill (more than 1,000 items) was offered for sale by auction. He probably passed away sometime in 1904. *See Club Street.*

Source: *ST, 1889.9.3:2; ST, 1891.4.14:4; SFP, 1891.11.23:2; ST, 1904.6.9:1*

Tan Sim Boh Road
Tan Sim Boh (1902-1941, Hokkien) was a lawyer. He often represented Lee Kong Chian (founder of Lee Foundation, one of the richest men in the 1950s and 1960s) in supervising the operations of subsidiaries of Lee's Nam Aik Group. He was a member of the Municipal Commission.

Source: *Kua: 93*

Tan Tock Seng Link
See Jalan Tan Tock Seng.

Tan Tye Alley/Place
Tan Tye or Tan Cheng Tye (1839-1898, Hokkien) was a Chinese community leader. Tan Tye Alley was declared a public street in 1925.

Source: *MC, 1925.6.26; Kua: 88*

Tanah Merah Besar Lane/Road/Walk
Tanah Merah Coast Road/Tanah Merah Ferry Road
Tanah Merah Kechil Avenue/Link/Ridge/Rise/Road
Tanah Merah Kechil Road South
Tanah merah means red land in Malay. The name was derived from the red laterite cliffs along the coast in this area that were visible from the sea. Two red cliffs were marked along the northeastern coast of Singapore island in *Sophia's Sketch of the Island of Singapore* (c. 1830). Other Malay words used above are *besar* (big) and *kechil* (small).

Tanah Merah Road was listed as a country road in 1853.

Source: *SFP, 1853.7.8:4; NAS, 709:12; Sophia: 377 map*

Tanglin Circus (e)
Tanglin Gate Road (Singapore Botanic Gardens)
Tanglin Halt Close/Road
Tanglin Hill/Road (e)
Tanglin Rise/Road/Walk
The name Tanglin probably originated from the Teochews who were the earliest to develop this area, which was said to have tigers. The Teochews referred to this area as "Toa Tang Leng" as it was considered the greatest hill peak in the east. The name was further confirmed by William Napier when he named his residence Tang Leng.

Tanglin Hill was named in 1903 at the request of the Estate of the late Mr. Baxter.

Tanglin Halt was named after the train stop of the Malayan Railway.

Source: *ST, 1903.5.23:5; Koh: 548*

Tangmere Road (former RAF Changi)
This road was named after RAF Tangmere in Tangmere, West Sussex, England. See Abbotsingh Road.

Source: *Probert: 11*

Tanjong Balai (e)
Tanjong means cape and *balai* means public building in Malay. Tanjong Balai was named after the main city of Karimun island, Indonesia, located in the southwest of Singapore.

Tanjong Beach Walk (Sentosa Island)

Tanjong Irau (e)
See *Irau Avenue*. This road was located at 15 ms Sembawang Road.

Tanjong Katong Road/Road South
Tanjong means cape in Malay. *Katong*, also a Malay word, may mean a tortoise, *Dermochelys coriacea* or a tree, *Cynometra ramiflora*. This area was a large coconut plantation before 1920. Tanjong Katong Road was approved for construction in 1905.
Source: *STOJ, 1881.5.12:2; MC, 1905.4.7*

Tanjong Kling (e)/Road
The above was named after Kampong Tanjong Kling which was located at the end of the road and demolished in 1964. See Chulia Street for the explanation of "Kling".

Tanjong Pagar Plaza/Road
Tanjong Pagar Terminal Avenue
Tanjong Pagar Drive 1, 2
Tanjong Pagar Street B, CG, DE, DF, E, H, HW
Pagar was spelt Paggar in the early days; it means native stake fence in Malay, a name which reflects its origin as a Malay fishing village. The road existed before 1823 as it was one of the roads requiring repairs by the Municipality that year.

Tanjong Pagar was the site of the first harbour facility in Singapore. It was built by the Tanjong Pagar Dock Company in 1823. The harbour operations were taken over by the Singapore Harbour Board (the predecessor of Port of Singapore Authority) in 1905.
Source: *STOJ, 1881.5.12:2*

Tanjong Penjuru/Crescent
Penjuru means angle or side in Malay.

Tanjong Plandok (e)
Plandok is the English translation of the Malay word *pelandok*. See *Jalan Sungei Pelandok*.

Tanjong Rhu Lane (e)/Place/Road/View
Based on a news article in 1848, Rhu was spelt as Ru in the early days. It is the Malay name for *Casuarina equisetifolia* or Casuarina tree. Tanjong Rhu was once a logistics centre for charcoal and timber, and boatyards. This explains the road names of Kampong Arang Road (charcoal village) and Kampong Kayu Road (timber village). There are also different kinds of boats:

Sampan Place, Tongkang Place and Twakow Place. By 1973, the traditional trade of handling charcoal and timber dwindled; the boatyards however remained until the 1980s when it was relocated to Jurong. The vacated land was zoned for residential development.

Source: *STOJ, 1881.5.12:2; ST, 1848.11.22:2; ST, 1973.3.15:16*

Tank Road

Tank refers to the tanks used to store water flowing from Fort Canning Hill before tap water was available in Singapore.

Tank Road was listed as a street in town in 1853. It was the location of Singapore Station, the terminal station of the railway which started operations on 1 January 1903.

Source: *SFP, 1853.7.8:4; ST, 1903.1.2:5*

Tannery Lane/Road

Tannery Lane was named in 1921.

Source: *MC, 1921.12.20*

Tao Ching Road

The island view of Tao Ching Road refers to offshore islands that may be seen from the tall buildings along this road. *See Ho Ching Road.*

Tapah Street (e) (Malayan Streets in Tanjong Pagar)

This street was named in 1899 after the town of Tapah, the main entry point to the old Cameron Highlands route, in Perak Malaysia. *See Bernam Street.*

Source: *MC, 1899.12.20*

Target Road (e)

This road was located in the Balestier Road area, the original site of the Swiss Club which also housed the Swiss Rifle Club. This could be the source of the road name in 1901.

Source: *MC, 1901.12.18*

Tasmania Road (former Singapore Naval Base)

Tasmania is the biggest island of Australia. *See Admiralty Road.*

Tavistock Avenue (Serangoon Gardens)

This road was named in 1953. Tavistock is an ancient market town in Devon, South West England. It traces its recorded history to AD 961 when Tavistock Abbey was founded. *See Alnwick Road.*

Source: *RBAR, 1953:8*

Tay Lian Teck Avenue (e)/Drive/Road

These roads were named after Tay Lian Teck (died 1942, Hokkien) who worked for Ho Hong Steamship Company and was a member of the

Legislative Council and Municipal Commission. He died during WW2 while leaving Singapore on a ship that was sunk by the Imperial Japanese Army. In 1947, three roads with the special name of Kee Sun were renamed. See *Kee Sun Avenue*. However, Tay Lian Teck Avenue was reinstated as Kee Sun Avenue in 1956.

Source: *SFP, 1947.3.17:5; RBAR, 1956:9; Kua: 116*

Teban Gardens Crescent/Road
This road was named after Kampong Java Teban in the same location. See *Kampong Java Teban*.

Tebing Lane/Walk (e)
Tebing means bank of river or canal, sandbank rising sharply from the sea in Malay.

Tech Park Crescent
Technology Crescent/Drive

Teck Chye Terrace
This road was named in 1929 after Lim Teck Chye who provided the land for this road. Lim, a Hokkien, was also known as Lin Zhu Zhai (in pinyin). He was the Secretary of the Chinese Chamber of Commerce around 1919.

Source: *MC, 1929.5.11; Singam; Song: 562*

Teck Guan Street (e)
This road was renamed from Tampenis Street (in Kampong Malacca) in 1907 after Tan Teck Guan (1846–1892), son of Tan Tock Seng. His keen interest in agriculture was carried on by his son, Tan Chay Yan, who was a pioneer in rubber planting.

Source: *MC, 1907.08.23; Song: 178*

Teck Hock Village (e)
This village was located at 8 ms Tampines Road. The name Teck Hock was changed to "Defu" in pinyin. See *Defu Avenue 1*.

Teck Lim Road
This road was named after Ong Teck Lim (1896–1912, Hokkien) who was the Manager of the family business of Ong Kew Ho Company, Chop Guan Tong. He was a member of the Municipal Commission from 1910 to 1912 and a member of the Rural Board in 1910. This road was named in 1927.

Source: *ST, 1906.12.15:10; ST, 1910.4.2:6; MC, 1927.9.30; Kua: 10*

Teck Whye Avenue/Crescent/Lane/Walk
See *Jalan Teck Whye*.

Tekka Lane
"Tekka" was a transcription of a Hokkien term that means the end of the bamboo forest. There was a large bamboo plantation in this area.

Tekong Highway
Tekong was known as Takung in the early days and was changed to Tukang in 1830. The name became Tikong (as in Tikong Besar) in J T Thomson's survey map of 1852. The present name of Tekong (as in Pulau Tekong) was used in H E McCallum's survey map of 1885. In Malay, *tukang* is a skilled craftsman. *Tekong* is navigating officer of a junk or a measurement of weight.

Source: *NAS, TM000003; NAS, SP006362; Buckley: 406; Haughton: 80; Sophia: 377 map*

Telegraph Street
The Telegraph Office was situated along this street. This street was named and declared a public street in 1895.

Source: *MC, 1895.2.27*

Telok Ayer Street
Telok was spelt as Teluk (1833), Telloh (1845), Telloo (1855) or Tulloh (1855). It means bay and *ayer* means water in Malay, i.e., water bay. This street was shown as Teluk Ayer Street in G D Coleman's survey map of 1836. It was changed to Telok Ayer in J Mcnair's survey map of 1873.

Telok Ayer Street was a coastal road until land reclamation took place in 1879. It was declared a public street in 1886.

Source: *STOJ, 1881.5.12:2; ST, 1886.12.20:8; NAS, SP002997; NAS, SP006819*

Telok Blangah Crescent/Drive/Green/Heights/Rise/Road/Street 31/Street 32/Way
Blangah was spelt Blanga or Belanga in the early days. *Blangah* means an earthen cooking pot in Malay. The name was given to the bay as its shape was like a cooking pot. Telok Blangah Road existed since the end of the 19th century. It was officially named as Teluk Blangah Road in 1907.

Source: *STOJ, 1881.5.12:2; MC, 1907.3.1*

Telok Kurau Road
Kurau is a medium-size threadfin in Malay.

Telok Mata Ikan (e)
Mata ikan means fish eye in Malay. This road was located at 11 ms Changi Road and was in the vicinity of Mata Ikan Village. See *Mata Ikan Village*.

Telok Paku Circus/Road
Paku means fern in Malay.

Temasek Avenue/Boulevard

Temasek originated from the Javanese word of *Tumasik* (which means watertown in English), the old Malay state name for Singapore. Tumasik as a name in Mandarin existed in Chinese historical books as early as the Yuan Dynasty (1271–1368).

Both roads were opened in 1983.

Source: *ST, 1983.10.26*

Tembeling Lane/Road

Tembeling is a place name in the State of Pahang, Malaysia. Kuala Tembeling is a transfer point to the Taman Negara National Park. This may be the reason that some streets around Tembeling Road were named after trees and fruits.

Tembusoh Road (e)

This road was located at 7.5 ms Thomson Road. It was named together with Cassia Crescent, Casuarina Road, Chempaka Avenue and Jacaranda Road at the same location in 1956. The name of Tembusoh was subsequently changed to Tembusu (*see Tembusu Avenue*).

Source: *RBAR, 1956:9*

Tembusu Avenue/Crescent/Drive/Road

The above are roads on Jurong Island. Tembusu is a large evergreen tree that is native to Singapore. *See Banyan Avenue and Jalan Tembusu.*

Temenggong Road

Temenggong is a high Minister of State usually ranked after the Premier. The treaty that transferred the control of Singapore to the East India Company on 6 February 1819 was signed by Raffles, Sultan Hussein and Temenggong Abdul Rahma of Johore. The latter's grandson Abu Bakar was installed as the Sultan of Johore in 1862.

This road was located next to Tanah Kubor Temenggong and was named in 1928.

Source: *MC, 1928.10.26*

Temple Hill (e)/Temple Hill Road (former RAF Changi)

There was a Chinese temple on this hill when the land was taken over by the British Army in 1927 to build a Royal Artillery Base. The temple was removed when barracks were built on this hill. Temple Hill is also a district in Dartford, Kent, England. *See Abbotsingh Road.*

Source: *Probert: 13*

Temple Street
Temple Street was named after the Sri Mariamman Temple, located at the corner of South Bridge Road and Temple Street. It was known as Almeida Street before 1908 and was named after Joaquim d'Almeida, the eldest son of Jose d'Almeida. See *D'Almeida Street and Pillai Road*.

Source: *MC, 1908.2.28*

Teng Tong Road
This road name was first seen in the press in 1947. In 1929, an auction sale of a rubber estate in Johore of 976 acres was said to be owned by Kwek Teng Tong and others.

Source: *ST, 1929.9.27:4*

Tengah Avenue
Tengah means middle in Malay. This is one of the roads around the Singapore Armed Forces Training Institute (SAFTI) Military Institute in Jurong.

Teo Hong Road
Teo Hong or Teo Wang (1847–1942, Hokkien) was a prominent building contractor. His building projects included the Fullerton Building, the National Museum and the former Ministry of Labour Building. His residence was at 9 Teo Hong Road.

Source: *Kua: 148*

Teo Kim Eng Road
See *Jalan Guan Choon*.

Source: *Kua: 111*

Teo Lee Road (e)
Teo Lee (1833–1899, Teochew) was the maternal grandfather of Lim Nee Soon. He derived his wealth from the textile business and property investments.

Source: *Lim HS: 118; Kua: 108*

Teow Hock Avenue

Terang Bulan Avenue
Terang means bright and *bulan* means moon in Malay. "Terang Bulan" was adapted from a French song and made popular as an Indonesian/Malay song in the 1930s. Terang Bulan Avenue, near Opera Estate, was opened in 1967.

Source: *ST, 1967.3.27:4*

(Terminal Crescent/Link East/Link West) (e)

Terrasse Lane
Terrasse is terrace in French.

Tessensohn Road
This road was named in 1927 after John Edwin Tessensohn (1857–1926, Eurasian) who was a Municipal Commissioner.
Source: *SFP, 1926.9.27:8; MC, 1927.5.27; Singam*

Tew Chew Street
This street was the area for the Teochews in Chinatown. The street name was seen in the press as early as 1883.
Source: *ST, 1883.4.3:2*

Tham Soong Avenue
Tham Soong was the daughter-in-law of Cheong Chun Tin. *See Chun Tin Road.*

The Arcade (e)
Arcade was a lane that was named after a building of the same name. It was renamed The Arcade in the 1963 Street Directory. The lane has been expunged but the building remains. *See Arcade.*

The Cut (e) (former Nee Soon Cantonment, See Cliff Road)

The Duckway (e) (former Blakang Mati Artillery Barracks)
This road was named after DUKW, colloquially known as Duck, an amphibious transport vehicle used during WW2. *See Artillery Avenue.*

The Inglewood
Inglewood is a multiple place name in Britain.

The Knolls (Sentosa Island)
The Knolls is a multiple place name in Britain.

The Loop (e) (former Nee Soon Cantonment)
See Loop Road.

The Oval (former RAF Seletar)
This road follows the shape of an oval. *See Baker Street.*

Theam Ting Road (e) (Joo Chiat Road)

Theng Hai Place (e)
Theng Hai Place was first named as Alexandra Place in 1907 and renamed as Theng Hai Place in 1928.

"Theng Hai" is the Teochew transcription of Cheng Hai, a county in Guangdong Province. It was the ancestral home town of Seah Eu Chin and Lim Nee Soon.
Source: *MC1, 1928.5.1; MC, 1907.9.20*

Thiam Siew Avenue (Thiam Siew Village, Tanjong Katong)
Ooi Thiam Siew (1894–1972, Hokkien) was in the tobacco business with strong connections in Penang. He owned the Lion City Hotel and the Hollywood Cinema in Singapore and was the developer of Thiam Siew Village in 1937. Thiam Siew Village was a large residential development in Tanjong Katong with roads named after places around Penang such as Ipoh, Butterworth, Kulim and Penaga. Penage in this case was the old name of Penang.

Source: *ST, 1972.2.10:6; Kua: 182*

Third Avenue
See Fifth Avenue.

Third Chin Bee Road
See Chin Bee Road.

Third Hospital Avenue (General Hospital)

Third Lok Yang Road
See Lok Yang Road.

Third Street, Siglap
This is a rename of Siglap, 3rd Street.

Thomson Close/Green/Heights/Hill/Hills Drive/Lane/Ridge/Road/Terrace/ View/Village (e)/Walk
Based on a 1926 news article, John Turnbull Thomson (1821–1884) was the Government Surveyor in Singapore from 1841 to 1853. He made a number of elaborate surveys of Singapore in the 19th century and played an instrumental role in the development of its infrastructure. He migrated to New Zealand subsequently and became the Chief Surveyor of that country. *See Ang Mo Kio Avenue 1.*

Thomson Village was located at 5.25 ms Upper Thomson Road.

Source: *ST, 1926.12.15:10; Buckley: 570-571*

Thong Aik Road (e)
Thong Aik was the name of the rubber factory owned by Lim Nee Soon. This road was named in 1955. *See Nee Soon Road.*

Source: *RBAR, 1955:9; Lim HS: 118; Phua, 1952:221*

Thong Bee Road
Thong Bee was the name of Lim Nee Soon's main shop at Beach Road. This road was named in 1955. *See Nee Soon Road.*

Source: *RBAR, 1955:9; Lim HS: 118; Phua, 1952:221*

Thong Hoe Village (e)
This village was named in 1949 after Thong Hoe, the shop name of Neo Tiew (1884–1975). *See Neo Tiew Crescent.*

Source: *RBAR, 1949:9;* 吕振瑞: *112-159*

Thong Soon Avenue/Green/Road
Thong Soon was one of the business units of Lim Nee Soon. *See Nee Soon Road.*

Source: *Lim HS: 118*

Thor Terrace (e)
Thor is a Norse (Viking) god, the hammer-wielding god associated with thunder. *See Bragi Road.*

Three Rings Drive (Singapore Turf Club, Woodlands)

Thrift Drive
This was one of the roads named by the Rural Board in 1957 for the Paya Lebar Road Co-operative Estate. *See Rochdale Road.*

Source: *ST, 1957.11.1:6; RBAR, 1957:8*

Tian Lye Road (e)/Street (e)
Tian Lye Street was located near the entrance of the Tanjong Pagar Dock and was named in 1898 after Lee Tian Lye (1841–1921), the Chief Coal Clerk of the Tanjong Pagar Dock Company Limited. He retired from the company between 1901 and 1906.

Source: *MC, 1898.11.8; ST, 1901.3.22:2; ED, 1906.10.27:5; SFP, 1921.7.27:6; Singam*

Tibet Road (e)
Tibet is an autonomous region of China. Tibet Road was renamed Faculty Road in 1971. *See Faculty Avenue and Nanyang Avenue.*

Tientsin Road (e)
Tientsin (now Tianjin) is a metropolis in coastal northeastern China. Tientsin Road was renamed Nanyang Crescent in 1971. *See Faculty Avenue and Nanyang Avenue.*

Tigris Walk (e) (Delta Estate)
Tigris is a river that flows from southeastern Turkey through Iraq and empties into the Persian Gulf. It is about 1,750 kilometres in length. *See Ganges Avenue.*

Tiong Bahru Road
The word Tiong was written as Tiang (in 1863 press reports) and Teong in 1875. "Tiong" was a transcription of cemetery or middle in Hokkien. *Bahru* means new in Malay. Based on an 1875 cemetery report, Tiong Bahru was a

new cemetery for the Chinese in 1859. The old cemetery (Tiong Lama) was located in Harbour Road, now Keppel Road.

Source: *SO, 1875.9.21:3*

Tiong Poh Avenue/Road

The above roads were named after Khoo Tiong Poh (1830–1892, Teochew), a brother-in-law of Seah Eu Chin. He was the sole proprietor of Bun Hin & Co., a shipping company that operated between China and South East Asia. *See Eu Chin Street and Seng Poh Road.*

Tiong Poh Road is located in the (pre-war) Tiong Bahru housing estate and was named before 1936.

Source: *SFP, 1892.3.3:2; SG-1936; Kua: 101*

Tiverton Lane

This lane is off Devonshire Road. Tiverton village in England is in Devonshire.

Tiwary Street (e)

Tiwary was a wealthy Indian merchant. The street became a public street in 1909.

Source: *MC, 1909.6.25; NAS, 1184:5*

Toa Payoh Central (Toah Pyoh)/Crescent (e)/Drive (e)/East/Industrial Park/Lane/North/Rise/Road (e)/West

Toa Payoh existed as a district under the name of Toah Pyoh in the early days. An 1849 article in the press provided the interpretation of "Toah" as long or large and "Pyoh" was an irregular path formed by wooden planks thrown into marshy or muddy place by the Chinese. The wooden plank formation looks like duckweeds floating in a pond, hence, "Pyoh" in Hokkien.

The present name of Toa Payoh appeared in H E McCallum's survey map of 1885. Up to the early 1900s, the Toa Payoh area was mainly used as burial grounds, brick kilns and perhaps, plantation. In 1859 a licence was granted by the Municipality to Gilbert Angus (*see Angus Street*) to build a brick kiln in Toa Payoh. Mr. Angus' property in Toa Payoh and a huge Government Brick Field between Kallang and Toa Payoh were indicated in the Singapore Maps of 1873 and 1885. It could be the brick kilns that changed the name of "Toah Pyoh" to "Toa Payoh", which means kiln in big undeveloped land in Mandarin.

In a recent interpretation, the word "payoh" was said to originate from the Malay word *paya*, meaning swamp. This is unlikely because in the same map by H E McCallum, the word Paya was already used for Paya Lebar.

Toa Payoh Road was named in 1929.

Source: *SFP, 1849.11.2:2; SFP, 1859.10.6:3; MC, 1929.9.27; NAS, TM000003; NAS, SP006819*

Toh Avenue/Close/Crescent/Drive/Heights/Street
These roads were named after Toh Chin Joo and Toh Chi Ghee (1908-1979), the father and son who came from Nan An County in the Fujian Province of China. They were in the transportation and building construction business; and were noted for developing the Toh Heights Estate.

Source: *ZB-Special Supplement, 2014.11.20:19*

Toh Guan Loop (e)/Road/Road East
See *Jalan Toh Guan*.

Toh Tuck Avenue/Close/Crescent/Drive/Lane (e)/Link/Place/Rise/Road/Terrace/Walk
Toh Tuck Road was named around 1959.

Toh Yi Drive/Road
Toh Yi Road was named around 1973.

Tomlinson Road
This road was named in 1921 after S Tomlinson (1895-1900), the Municipal Engineer who was responsible for the construction of the reservoir at Pearl's Hill.

Source: *MC1, 1921.6.7; Makepeace, vol.2:233; Singam*

Tong Lee Road
This road was named in 1955 after Tong Lee Realty Private Limited, a real estate company owned by Ang Oon Hui. Ang built schools in Jalan Kayu and donated land for building a nursing home for the poor. See *Hong San Terrace*.

Source: *RBAR, 1955:9; ZB-Special Supplement, 2014.11.20:19*

Tong Watt Road
Tan Tong Watt (1861-1907, Hokkien) was a big land owner who started as a store clerk in Behn Meyer. In 1901, he was one of the donours for the purchase of land to rebuild a "Tua Pek Kong" temple on Mohamed Sultan Road. Tong Watt Road was named in 1897 at the owner's request.

Source: *MC, 1897.6.9; SFP, 1907.1.14:4; Kua: 71; Singam*

Tongkang Place (e)
Tongkang is a type of wooden boat for carrying goods. It was commonly seen along the Singapore River running between the ships anchored at sea and the godowns at the shore of the River. See *Tanjong Rhu Road*.

Topaz Road
Topaz is a gem stone. This road was named in 1952. See *Moonstone Lane*.

Source: *ST, 1952.5.1:7*

Tops Avenue 1 to 3, 6, 8, 12, 21 to 23
TOPS is the acronym for Toll Offshore Petroleum Services. See *Paul Little Drive*.

Toranto Road
Toranto is an old name of Toronto, see below.

Toronto Road
Toronto is the provincial capital of Ontario, Canada. This road was named in 1956 together with Florida Road and Ontario Avenue.

Source: *RBAR, 1956:9*

Tosca Street/Terrace (Opera Estate)
Tosca is an opera by Giacomo Puccini. See *Aida Street*. Tosca Street was named in 1953.

Source: *RBAR, 1953:7*

Tower Hill Road (e) (former RAF Changi)
This road was probably named after Tower Hill of London. See *Abbotsingh Road*.

Towner Road
This road was named in 1934 after Henry Venus Towner (born 1875), the Colonial Engineer who came to Singapore as an Assistant Superintendent of Works and Surveys, Public Works Department of the Straits Settlements in 1901. He retired in 1929 and returned to England.

Source: *MSP, 1929.10.12:35; SFP, 1934.7.18:8; Dunlop*

Town Hall Link (Jurong)

Townsend Road (WW1 roads)
This road was named after Major General Sir Charles Vere Ferrers Townsend (1861–1924), one of the leading commanders in WW1. See *Allenby Road*.

During WW1 Townsend led an overreaching military campaign against the Ottomans in Mesopotamia and was defeated on 29 April 1916. While Townsend was well treated as a POW in Turkey, 70% of his men died from starvation or brutal treatment in the POW camps. Townsend returned to England in 1919 and entered politics.

Source: *Singam*

Track 24 (Lentor Avenue)

Tractor Road
This road was named after Tractors Singapore Limited moved to this road. The company is the agent for Caterpillar Tractors of USA.

Trafalgar Street (e)
This street was named after Trafalgar, a famous landmark in London commemorating Britain's victory in the Battle of Trafalgar in 1805 against France and Spain. This street, named in 1898, was situated on reclaimed land near the Singapore Harbour Board.
Source: *MC, 1898.6.8*

Transford Road (e) (former Tanglin Barracks)
This road appeared only in the Street Directory of 1950 and 1953. *See Barrack Road.*

Transit Road (former Nee Soon Cantonment)
This road was part of Loop Road in the Nee Soon Cantonment before 1964. The latter road had been expunged.

Tras Link/Street (Malayan Streets in Tanjong Pagar)
This street was named in 1899 after the sub-district of Tras, part of the Raub district in Pahang. The Raub district was a historic gold mining settlement. *See Bernam Street.*
Source: *MC, 1899.12.20*

Treasure Island (Sentosa Island)

Trengganu Street
Trengganu (previously Tringanu), is a State of Malaysia in the northeast of the Malayan Peninsular. It came under British control after the Bangkok Treaty of 1909 between UK and Thailand. *See Kelantan Lane.*

Trent Way

Trevose Crescent/Place
Trevose means a farm on a river bank. This road was possibly named after the Trevose district in Cornwall, South West England.
Source: *Watts*

Tronoh Road (e)
This road was named after Tronoh Mines Ltd in 1929. *See Kempas Road.*
Source: *MC, 1929.3.27; SIT 1158/28*

Truro Road (Race Course Road area)
Part of this road became a public street in 1931. The town of Truro is in Cornwall, South West England. *See Bristol Road.*
Source: *SFP, 1931.8.17:12*

Tu Fu Avenue (Teachers' Housing Estate)
This road was named after Tu Fu (712-770), one of the greatest Chinese poets who lived during the Tang Dynasty. *See Iqbal Avenue.*

Singapore Gazetteer Since 1936 and Annotations

Tua Kong Green/Place/Terrace
Tua Kong Lye Village (e)/Tua Kong Walk
See *Jalan Tua Kong*. Tua Kong Lye Village was first seen in the 1957 Street Directory, it was located around Jalan Kebaya in Ulu Pandan. Other roads are located along Upper East Coast Road.

Tuah Road (former Singapore Naval Base)
Tuah means magical power in Malay. See *Admiralty Road*.

Tuas Avenue 1 to 14, 16, 18, 18A, 20
Tuas Basin Close/Lane/Link
Tuas Bay Circle/Close/Drive/Lane/Link/Street/Walk
Tuas Crescent/Drive 1, 2/Lane/Link 1 to 4/Loop/Road
Tuas Second Link
Tuas South Avenue 1 to 10, 12, 14, 16
Tuas South Boulevard/Drive/Lane
Tuas South Street 1 to 3, 5 to 13, 15/View/Way
Tuas Street/Tuas Terminal Road
Tuas View Circuit/Close/Crescent/Drive/Hook (e)/Lane/Link/Loop/Place/Plain (e)/Square/Walk 1/Walk 2
Tuas Village (e)
Tuas West Avenue/Drive/Road/Street
The name Tuas was probably derived from Toas, which was the name of a river in the 1848 Government Surveyor's report on creeks and rivers at the west side of the island. The report mentioned a Sungei Toas in the extreme west.

Tuas View Hook was named after the shape of the road, it was subsequently renamed Tuas South Avenue 3.

Source: *SFP, 1848.10.26:3; Haughton: 81; Koh: 571*

Tudor Close
This road was located off Kheam Hock Road. The location was the residence of D R Waters, Partner at the Chartered Surveyors firm of Waters & Watson. The house he built here in 1940 was completely Tudor in design.

Source: *SFP, 1940.9.28:7*

Tukang Innovation Drive/Grove/Lane
Tukang means skilled worker in Malay.

Tung Po Avenue (Teachers' Housing Estate)
This road was named after Su Tong Po or Su Shi (1037–1101), a famous Chinese poet from the Song Dynasty. See *Iqbal Avenue*.

Tunggal Road (e)
Tunggal means unique or alone in Malay. This road was named in 1907.
Source: *MC, 1907.7.5*

Turf City Road/Turf Club Road (Bukit Timah)
The Singapore Turf Club was established in 1924. Turf Club Road led to the second race course which was used from 1933 to 2001. The club has since been relocated to Woodlands. *See Turf Club Avenue and Farrer Park Road.*

Turf City Road was opened in 2001.

Turf Club Avenue (Woodlands)
Turf Club Avenue is the main road leading to the third race course in Singapore. It was opened in 2001.

Turnhouse Road (former RAF Changi)
This road was named after RAF Turnhouse in Ingliston in the city of Edinburgh, Scotland. After WW2 the air station began to provide commercial services in 1947 and it is now known as the Edinburgh Airport. RAF Turnhouse was finally closed in 1997. *See Abbotsingh Road.*

Turriff Road (e) (former Changi Barracks)
This road was probably named after the market town of Turriff in Aberdeen County, Scotland. *See Gordon Road.*

Turut Track
Turut means following suit or going by advice in Malay.

Twakow Place (e)
Twakow is a flat bottom wooden boat for carrying goods. *See Tanjong Rhu Road.*

Tyersall Avenue/Park (e)/Road
Tyersall was the mansion in Tang Leng Estate built by William Napier in 1854. The property was sold to Sultan Abu Bakar of Johor (1833–1895) who rebuilt it as an Istana (palace), and named it Istana Tyersall. However the Istana was destroyed by a fire in September 1905. *See Napier Road.*

Tyersall Road became a public street in 1890.

Tyersall Avenue was a rename of Garden Road in 1924.

Source: *ST, 1891.4.28:9; MC, 1924.11.28*

Tyrwhitt Road (WW1 roads)
This road was named after Admiral Reginald Yorke Tyrwhitt (1870–1945), one of the leading commanders in WW1. *See Allenby Road.*

In August 1914 Tyrwhitt participated in the Battle of Heligoland Bight led by Sir David Beatty which caused heavy losses to the German Navy. After the war, Tyrwhitt took up several naval appointments and visited Singapore in 1928 as a C-in-C, China. This road was originally named Fisher Road and renamed Tyrwhitt Road in 1932.

Source: *SFP, 1928.1.16:9; ST, 1932.8.15:16; Singam*

Ubi Avenue 1 to 4
Ubi Close/Crescent/Link
Ubi Road 1 to 4
Ubi View
See Kampong Ubi.

Ulu Bedok Village (e)
Ulu is the Malay word for upper reaches of a river. This village was located along Upper Changi Road at the present Chai Chee area. *See Bedok Road.*

Ulu Pandan Road
See Pandan Avenue.

Union Lane (e)/Road (e)/Street
Union Lane (e) was a back lane to the Union Building along Fullerton Road.

Union Street is located in Marina Bay.

Unity Street
This street was probably named after United Engineers Ltd or its building (Uniteers Building) at the same location.

University Road/Walk
The university here refers to the University of Singapore which was relocated and renamed NUS.

Upavon Road (former RAF Changi)
This road was named after RAF Upavon in Wiltshire, South West England. RAF Upavon is known as the birthplace of the Royal Air Force. *See Abbotsingh Road.*

Upper Aljunied Lane/Link/Road
See Aljunied Road. Upper Aljunied Road was named in 1929.

Source: *MC, 1929.12.27*

Upper Ayer Rajah Road (e)
See Ayer Rajah Road.

Upper Bedok Road
See Bedok Road.

Upper Boon Keng Road
See Boon Keng Road.

Upper Bukit Timah Road/View
See Bukit Timah Road. Upper Bukit Timah Road was named in 1959.

Source: *ST, 1959.4.23:5*

Upper Chan (Cheang) Wan Seng Lane (e)
This road name was renamed Chin Swee Road in 1898 to avoid confusion with Cheang Wan Seng Road in the same area. *See Chin Swee Road and Cheang Wan Seng Lane.*

Source: *MC, 1898.6.8*

Upper Changi Link/Road/Road East/Road North
Upper Changi Road Track (2 to 8, 29, 35, 37) (e), 39
Upper Changi Road was the rename of the rural part of Changi Road in 1953.

Upper Changi Road North was the rename of a stretch of Upper Changi Road in 1987. *See Changi Road.*

Source: *ST, 1953.8.2:6; ST, 1987.10.30:23*

Upper Chin Chew Street (e)
See Chin Chew Street.

Colloquial Name: "Tao Hoo Kwe", Toufu Street. (*Phua, 1952:223*)

Upper Circular Road
See Circular Road.

Upper Cross Street
See Cross Street.

Colloquial Name: "Hai San Kwe", Street of the Hai San Secret Society. (*Phua, 1952:223*)

Upper Dickson Road
This road was originally known as Dunman Street, which was named after Thomas Dunman, the first Police Commissioner in Singapore. It was renamed Upper Dickson Road in 1930. *See Dickson Road and Dunman Street.*

Source: *MC, 1930.10.31*

Upper East Coast Road
This road was renamed by the Rural Board for the rural part of East Coast Road.

Source: *ST, 1953.8.2:6*

Upper Hokien Street
See Hokien Street.

Upper Jalan Eunos (e)
See Jalan Eunos.

Upper Jurong Road
(Upper Jurong Road Track 29, 31, 33, 38, 39, 40, 41, 42, 42A, 43, 44, 45, 46, 48, 51) (e)
See Jurong Road.

Upper Macao Street (e)
This road was renamed Upper Pickering Street on 1 January 1925. See *Macao Street*.

Source: *MC, 1924.7.25*

Upper Nankin Street (e)
See Nanking Street.

Upper Neram Road
See Neram Road.

Upper Palm Valley Road (Singapore Botanic Gardens)

Upper Paya Lebar Road
See Paya Lebar Road.

Upper Perak Road (e)
This road was named in 1928. See *Perak Road*.

Source: *MC, 1928.10.26*

Upper Pickering Street
The road was known as Upper Macao Street until 1 January 1925. See *Pickering Street*. This street had the colloquial name of "Dan Bin Kwe" or single sided street as buildings were constructed only on one side of the road.

Source: *MC, 1924.7.25*

Upper Ring Road (Singapore Botanic Gardens)

Upper Serangoon Crescent/Road/View
Upper Serangoon Road was named in 1906. See *Serangoon Road*.

Source: *MC, 1906.11.30*
Colloquial Name: "Au Gang", behind the Pier. (*Phua, 1952:223*)

Upper Thomson Road
This road was named in 1939. See *Thomson Road*.

Source: *ST, 1939.2.14:14*

Upper Tientsin Road (e)
See *Tientsin Road*. This road was renamed Faculty Avenue in 1971. See *Faculty Avenue and Nanyang Avenue*.

Upper Toh Tuck Terrace
See Toh Tuck Road.

Upper Weld Road (Kampong Kapor)
This road was declared a public street in 1914. *See Weld Road.*
Source: *MC, 1914.11.27*

Upper Wilkie Road
See Wilkie Road.

UT Avenue 1 (Jurong Island)

Valley Road
There were three Valley Roads listed in the 1954 Singapore Street Directory: one in Nee Soon Cantonment (*see Cliff Road*), one in RAF Changi and the third in the Upper Serangoon area. Only the Valley Road in Upper Serangoon remains today.

Vampire Road (e) (former RAF Tengah)
This road was named after de Havilland Vampire, a British jet fighter developed during WW2. *See Hornet Road.*

Vancouver Road (e) (former Singapore Naval Base)
Vancouver is a coastal seaport in British Columbia, Canada. *See Admiralty Road.*

Vanda Avenue/Crescent/Drive/Link/Road
Vanda is a genus in the orchid family. Vanda Miss Joaquim is the national flower of Singapore.

Vaughan Road
Jonas Daniel Vaughan (died 1891) was a midshipman in the East India Company who served in the Opium Wars against China. After that he served in various posts in the Straits Settlements and eventually became a lawyer. He died at sea in 1891 on his way home from Perak.
Source: *ST, 1891.10.21:13; Makepeace, vol.1:223*

Veeragoo Close
Veeragoo Naidoo (Veeragu Naidu) was a member of staff in the Public Works Department. His son was the owner of the land for this road and had the road named after his father in 1956.
Source: *RBAR, 1956:9; NAS, 1179:4*

Veerappa Chitty Lane (e)
See Chitty Lane.

Veerasamy Road
N Veerasamy (1864–1926) was an Indian doctor who served in the Municipal Commission for 11 years. This road was originally named Jalan Tambah. The name change was proposed by K K Pathy, a Municipal Commissioner, and approved in 1927.
Source: *MC, 1927.1.28*

Venture Avenue/Drive

Venus Drive/Road
Venus Road was named in 1961. *See Capricorn Drive.*
Source: *SFP, 1961.1.6:6*

Verapillay Road (e)
This road was originally named West Hill Avenue 7. Based on a report in 1985, the name was changed around 1955 to be named after Verapillay, an Indian elder in Chong Pang Village.
Source: *ST, 1985.2.1:21*

Verde Avenue/Crescent/Grove/Place/View/Walk
Verde means green in Italian.

Verdun Road (WW1 roads)
This road was named in 1928 after Verdun, in northeastern France, the site of one of the famous battlefields during WW1. *See Allenby Road.*

The Battle of Verdun between the German and French armies was fought from February to December 1916. It was one of the largest battles and the single longest battle of WW1 with more than one million casualties.
Source: *MC1, 1928.10.2*

Vernon Park
This road became a public street in 1957. *See Mount Vernon Road.*
Source: *CCAR, 1957:5*

Victoria Lane/Victoria Street (city)

Victoria Park Close/Road (off Farrer Road)
These roads were named after Queen Victoria (1819–1901) who was the Queen of the UK from 1837 to 1901. Her reign is known as the Victorian era during which Britain went through the Industrial Revolution and marked the expansion of the British Empire.

Victoria Street is an old street that was known as Marbro Street based on G D Coleman's survey map of 1836. The change took place after the Queen's accession to the throne in 1837 as the street name began to appear in the press in December 1842.
Source: *SFP, 1837.9.21:2; SFP, 1842.12.15:1; NAS, SP002997*

View Road (former Singapore Naval Base)

Vigilante Drive (Kent Ridge Park)

Viking Road (e)
The Vikings were Germanic seafarers who raided and traded from their Scandinavian homelands across Northern and Central Europe. *See Bragi Road.*

VIP Drive (e)

Vista Exchange Green (North Buona Vista)

Vista Terrace (South Buona Vista)

Vocational Drive (e)

Vulcan Terrace (e)
Vulcan is the god of fire in Greek mythology. *See Bragi Road.*

Waddington Road (e) (former RAF Changi)
This road was named after RAF Waddington in Lincolnshire, East of England. *See Abbotsingh Road.*

Wajek Walk
Wajek is a Malay sweetmeat made from glutinous rice, then served up with a sauce of coconut milk and sugar.

Wak Hassan Drive/Place
See Kampong Wak Hassan.

Wallace Way
This road was probably named after Alfred Russel Wallace (1823–1913), a naturalist. He was in Singapore from 1854 to 1862 as part of his extensive research on the fauna in Asia and Australia.
Source: *ST, 1913.11.10:9; Buckley: 611; Dunlop*

Wallich Street
Dr. Nathaniel Wallich (1785–1854, Danish) was a surgeon and botanist who worked for the East India Company in Calcutta. He came to Singapore in 1822 on the invitation of Sir Stamford Raffles to help establish the first Botanic Garden at Government Hill (Fort Canning Hill). This road was named in 1899.
Source: *MC, 1899.12.20; SFP, 1935.9.19:3*

Walmer Drive (Serangoon Gardens)
This road was named in 1953. Walmer is a town in Dover, Kent, South East England. It is the location of Walmer Castle, an English Heritage site. *See Alnwick Road.*
Source: *RBAR, 1953:8*

Walshe Road
This road was first seen in the Street Directory of 1953. There are two possible sources for this name: First was Captain H Walshe, Inspector General of Police in 1877 and a member of the Municipal Commission. The second was N P Walshe, Manager of Straits Steamship Co. Ltd and Mansfield & Co. Ltd. He left for Australia in 1932.

Walton Road (former Grove Estate)
This road was named in 1928 after Walton-on-Thames in Surrey, a seaside town in Kent, England. *See Clacton Road and Grove Road.*

One account mentioned that this road was named after P Walton, a lawyer from Donaldson and Burkinshaw. He was a Gunner from the Singapore Volunteer Artillery who was accidentally killed during the 1915 Indian Mutiny. *See Harper Road.*

Source: *SFP, 1921.5.9:12; MC, 1928.9.28; Singam*

Wan Lee Road
This road was first seen in the 1969 Street Directory. *See Chia Ping Road.*

Wan Shih Road (e)
See Chia Ping Road.

Wan Tho Avenue (Sennett Estate)
This road was named after Loke Wan Tho (1915–1964). He was a co-founder of Cathay Organisation, a company in the cinema and movie business. Unfortunately he died in an air crash in 1964. This road is in Sennett Estate and was named in 1951. *See Kee Choe Avenue.*

Source: *CC, 1951.9.28; Kua: 66*

War Cemetery Road (Woodlands)

Wareham Road (former Grove Estate)
This road was named in 1928 after Wareham, a market town southwest of Poole in Dorset, England. *See Grove Road.*

Source: *MC, 1928.9.28*

Waringin Park/Walk
Waringin is a tree, *Ficus benjamina* in Malay.

Warna Road
Warna means colour or hue in Malay.

Warwick Road (former Pasir Panjang Barracks)

Warwick Road (e) (former RAF Tengah)
Warwick Road in Pasir Panjang was named after Warwick, a county town of Warwickshire in West Midlands, England. *See Nepal Park.*

Warwick Road in Tengah was named after Vickers Warwick, a multi-purpose British aircraft used during WW2. *See Hornet Road.*

Waterloo Street
This was a rename of Church Street in 1858 to avoid confusion with another street of the same name in the city. Waterloo refers to the battle fought in 1815 near Waterloo in Belgium, in which Napoleon met his final defeat.
Source: *SFP 1858.4.1:6*

Watling Street (e) (Pasir Panjang Barracks)
Based on a report in 1924, Watling Street in London was built by the Romans during their occupation of Britain as an important track way between Dover to Wroxeter. *See Nepal Park.*
Source: *ST, 1924.12.4:13*

Watten Close/Drive/Estate (e)/Estate Road/Heights/Park/Rise/Terrace/ View
Watten Estate was an English garden style residential estate designed by Swan & Maclaren in 1919 for use as staff quarters of European companies. Under the first scheme, five houses were built for Barker & Co. This was followed by houses built for Firestone, Eastern Extension Telegraph Co., Borneo Company and Hongkong & Shanghai Bank, etc.

Watten Estate (the road) was renamed Watten Park in 1926 and reinstated later. In 1970 the name was changed again to Watten Estate Road. The name Watten was probably taken from Watten Village in Highland County, north of Scotland.
Source: *ST, 1919.11.11:8; MC1, 1926.7.1*

Wayang Street (e)
Wayang means opera in Malay. There was an open air performance area along this street.

Wee Cheng Soon Estate (e)
There were two prominent Singaporeans with the name of Wee Cheng Soon before WW2. The first was the fourth son of Wee Ah Hood and the other was a building contractor, granite quarry and rubber estate owner.
Source: *SFP, 1930.11.24:9*

Wee Nam Road
Lee Wee Nam (1880–1964, Teochew) was a banker. He was the Chairman and Managing Director of Sze Hai Tong Bank and the co-founder of Ngee Ann Girls' School. Due to his pro-China activities, he was jailed and tortured twice during the Japanese Occupation.
Source: *ST, 1964.1.24:6; Kua: 44*

Wei Hua Road (e)
Wei Hua was one of many names of Lim Nee Soon. Based on a news article in 1985, Wei Hua was the name of an elder in China deeply respected by Lim Nee Soon and the road name was changed from West Hill Avenue 2 around 1962. *See Nee Soon Road and West Hill Avenue.*
Source: *ST, 1985.2.1:21*

Weld Lane (e)/Road (Kampong Kapor)
Frederick Aloysius Weld (1823-1891) was the Governor of the Straits Settlements from 1880 to 1887. He initiated the building of the Raffles Library and Museum in Singapore. The facilities were opened by him before his departure in 1887. As a Governor, he was credited for the annexation of Pahang and was considered a Native States Governor. Weld Lane was made a public street in 1914.
Source: *ST, 1891.7.29:8; MC, 1914.11.27; Makepeace, vol.1:555*

Wellington Circle/Link/Road (former Singapore Naval Base)
Wellington Road was named after Wellington, capital of New Zealand. *See Admiralty Road.*
Source: *Watts*

Wellwyn Road (e) (former RAF Changi)
This road was probably named after Wellwyn, a town in Hertfordshire, South East England.

Wessex Estate (e) (former Ayer Rajah Barracks)
Wessex, meaning West Saxons, was an Anglo-Saxons kingdom in the south of England which was established in 519. Winchester was once its capital. Wessex Estate, along Ayer Rajah Road, was built in the 1950s to house officers of the British Army. All road names in this estate begin with letter W. They include Westbourne Road, Weyhill Close, Whitchurch Road, Wilton Close and Woking Road. *See Nepal Park.*

West Camp Road

West Coast Avenue/Drive/Road/Green/Grove/Lane/Park/Place/Rise/Road/Terrace/View/Village (e)/Walk/Way
West Coast Crescent/Ferry Road/Highway/Link
(Pasir Panjang Terminal and West Coast Pier)

West Gate Road (e) (former Nee Soon Cantonment)
This road was at the west end of the Cantonment.

(West Hill Avenue/Avenue 1 to 9) (e)

(West Hill Road/Village) (e)
West Hill Avenue was renamed Chong Pang Road in 1957.
> West Hill Avenue 1 was renamed Hock Chwee Road around 1962.
> West Hill Avenue 2 was renamed Wei Hua Road around 1962.
> West Hill Avenue 3 was renamed Kee Hua Road around 1962.
> West Hill Avenue 4 was renamed Eng Hock Road around 1962.
> West Hill Avenue 5 was renamed Huang Long Road around 1962.
> West Hill Avenue 6 was renamed Chong Sin Road around 1962.
> West Hill Avenue 7 was renamed Verapillay Road around 1955.
> West Hill Avenue 8 was renamed Chong How Road around 1962
> West Hill Avenue 9 was renamed Chong Nee Road around 1962.
> West Hill Road was renamed Chong Pang Road in 1957.
> West Hill Village was renamed Chong Pang Village in 1957.

Source: *RBAR, 1957:8; ST, 1985.2.1:21*

West Perimeter Road (Singapore Changi Airport)

West Wharf Road (e)

Westbourne Road (former Ayer Rajah Barracks)
Westbourne is a district in Bournemouth, Dorset. *See Wessex Estate.*

Westerhout Road
Jonannes Bartholomew Westerhout (1871–1937) was a famous architect who designed many residences in Emerald Hill. He served in the Municipal Commission from 1929 to 1934.

Source: *ST, 1937.11.19:12; Lee KL; Makepeace, vol.1:366*

Western Avenue (e) (former RAF Seletar)
This road was named after Western Avenue, a major road (about ten miles in length) leading out of London in a northwesterly direction. *See Baker Street.*

Westlake Avenue

Westmoreland Road (e)
Westmoreland is a historic county in North West England. It is now part of Cumbria.

Westridge Walk

Westwood Avenue/Crescent/Drive/Road/Terrace/Walk

Weyhill Close (former Ayer Rajah Barracks)
Weyhill is a village west of Andover, Hampshire. *See Wessex Estate.*

Whampoa Drive/East/North (e)/Road/South/Square (e)/West

Hoo Ah Kay (1816-1880) came from Whampoa in the province of Canton, China at the young age of 14. He established Whampoa & Co. in 1849 and supplied foodstuff to the British Royal Navy. From this he became wealthy and started to invest in land, property and plantations. He built a large mansion with a grand Chinese garden in the Serangoon area and named it Nam Sang Garden (Nam Sang was his other name). As he was known as Mr. Whampoa by the Europeans, Nam Sang Garden was known as Whampoa Garden to the public. Hoo was the first Chinese to become an unofficial member of the Legislative Council at the Transfer in 1867. He was made a C.M.G. in 1878 (see *St. Michael's Road*).

Source: *ST, 1880.4.3:1; Kua: 150*

Wharf Ave

This road is located near the jetty at Sungei Loyang.

Whitchurch Road (former Ayer Rajah Barracks)

Whitchurch is a town in Hampshire, England. *See Wessex Estate.*

White House Park/Road

White House Park is situated in Dalvey Road and was referred to as White House, Dalvey Road in 1891. It was once a nutmeg and betel plantation owned by Gilbert Angus (see *Angus Street*). The land was developed in the 19th century and divided into four houses: White House, Glencaird, Cree Hall and Sentosa. Only Glencaird remains today and was given conservation status in 1991. Both roads were listed in the Street Directory in the 1950s.

Source: *SFP, 1891.9.1:4*

Whitley Heights/Road

M H Whitley was the Attorney-General in Singapore from 1925 to 1929. Whitley Road was named in 1929.

Source: *MC, 1929.7.26; Singam*

Wholesale Centre (West Coast Highway)

Wilby Road

Wilby is a multiple place name in England.

Wilkie Road/Terrace

This road first appeared in the meeting minutes of the Municipal Commission in 1879 discussing a request by the residents of Wilkie Road to convert the road to a public street. One account mentioned that this road was named after a Captain Wilkie who lived in this location.

Source: *STOJ, 1879.5.27:3; Singam*

Wilkinson Road (former Grove Estate)
This road was named in 1921 after Richard James Wilkinson (1867–1941). He was the British Resident in Negri-Sembilan, the Colonial Secretary of the Straits Settlements from 1911 to 1916, and the Governor of Sierra Leone in Africa from 1916 to 1921. He returned to live in Malaya after his retirement. During his long stay in Singapore and Malaya, he romanised the Malay language and published an English-Malay dictionary.
Source: *MC, 1921.2.25; SFP, 1941.12.13:3; Singam*

Willow Avenue (Sennett Estate)
This road was named in 1951. *See Angsana Avenue.*
Source: *CC, 1951.9.28*

Wilmonar Avenue
This road was part of Kilburn Estate and was named in 1956. *See Denham Close.*
Source: *RBAR, 1956:9*

Wilton Close (former Ayer Rajah Barracks)

Wilton Gardens (Siglap)
Wilton Close was named after Wilton, a town in Wiltshire. *See Wessex Estate.*

Wiltshire Road (former Tanglin Barracks)
This road was named after Wiltshire South Regiment in 1934. The Regiment arrived at the Tanglin Barracks in November 1932. Wiltshire is a county in the south of England.
Source: *ST, 1934.11.23:17*

Wimborne Road (former Grove Estate)
This road was named in 1939 after Wimborne, a market town in East Dorset, five miles north of Poole. *See Grove Road.*
Source: *SFP, 1939.7.1: 2*

Winchester Road (former Alexandra Barracks)
This road was named after Winchester, a castle city and county town of Hampshire, South East England. A notable landmark in the city is the Winchester Cathedral. *See Berkshire Road.*

Windsor Drive (e)/Park Hill/Park Road
Windsor is an English name, the most famous of which is the town in Berkshire, the site of Windsor Castle.

Windsor Drive was located at 10 ms Upper Changi Road. *See Ang Chuan Lam Park.*

Wing Loong Road (e)
This road was named after a tailor shop Wing Loong that belonged to Wu Shen Cai (in pinyin), the Vice Chairman of Chung Khiaw Bank. Wu (1887-1960, Cantonese), was a member of the Municipal Commission.

Source: *ST, 1960.5.21:18; Kua: 35*

Winstedt Drive/Road
This road was named after Richard Olaf Winstedt (1878-1966) who was the Director of Education from 1920 to 1931 and the British General Adviser to Johore State from 1931 to 1935. He compiled a Malay-English Dictionary.

Source: *SFP, 1931.6.25:11; SFP, 1935.5.10:7; ST, 1966.6.5:5; Singam*

Wishart Road
Charles Wishart (1834-1905) was from Scotland. He was the Manager of New Harbour Dock till his retirement in 1895. This road was named in 1908.

Source: *SFP, 1905.11.27:2; MC, 1908.2.28; Buckley: 720; Singam*

Wittering Road (former RAF Changi)
This road was named after RAF Wittering in Northamptonshire, England. *See Abbotsingh Road.*

Woking Road (former Ayer Rajah Barracks)
Woking is a large town located in the west of Surrey, England. *See Wessex Estate.*

Wolskel Road
This road was named after H Wolskel (died 1951), Chairman of H Wolskel and Co. He served as a Municipal Commissioner from 1924 to 1932.

Source: *ST, 1951.2.13:1*

Wong Chin Yoke Road

Woo Mon Chew Road
Woo Mon Chew (1887-1958, Cantonese) was a major building contractor of his time. The former Hill Street Police Station and Barracks (1931), the Kallang Airport Terminal Building (1937, demolished) and the St. Andrew's School at Woodville (1939) were some of his projects. He was President, Trustee and Board Member of the Kwong Wai Siu Free Hospital at various times (1931-1957).

Source: *ST, 1931.8.8:17; ST, 1937.6.12:9; ST, 1939.4.23:7; Information kindly provided by Ms. Woo Pui Leng, granddaughter of Mr. Woo.*

(Woodfield Avenue/Lines/Road) (e) (former Singapore Naval Base)
See Admiralty Road.

Woodgrove Avenue/Drive/View/Walk

These roads are in the Woodlands area and are connected with a group of roads with names of different species of wood. Woodgrove is a new word. *See Ashwood Grove.*

Woodhaven Drive

Woodlands Avenue 1 to 10, 12
Woodlands Causeway
Woodlands Centre Road/Circle/Close/Crescent
Woodlands Drive 14 to 17, 19, 40, 42 to 44, 50, 52, 53, 60 to 65, 70 to 73, 75, 91, 93
Woodlands Height
Woodlands Industrial Park D Street 1/2
Woodlands Industrial Park E/E1 to E9, E10 (e)
Woodlands Lane/Link/Loop
Woodlands Ring Road/Rise
Woodlands Road/Sector 1, 2/Woodlands Square
Woodlands Street 11 to 13, 31, 32, 41, 81 to 83
Woodlands Terrace/View/Village (e)/Walk

Woodlands Road was part of Bukit Timah Road before 1929.

Source: *SFP, 1929.12.12:20*

Woodleigh Close/Lane/Park/Track

Woodleigh Close was named in 1926 after Woodleigh, the name of a mansion in Woodleigh Estate.

Source: *MC, 1926.5.28; Singam*

Woodstock Drive (e)

This road was probably named in 1922 after Woodstock in Oxfordshire, England.

Source: *MC, 1922.1.27*

Woodsville Circus (e)/Close/Road (e)

These roads were named after Woodsville, the mansion of Robert Carr Woods (1816–1875). Woods was the editor of *The Straits Times* (established in 1845). In 1861, he partnered with James Guthrie Davidson to establish the firm of Woods & Davidson, the first legal practice in Singapore. He was appointed Attorney General and Puisne Judge.

Woodsville Road was named in 1933.

Woodsville Close became a public street in 1960.

Source: *ST, 1933.11.4:10; CCAR, 1960:7; Makepeace, vol.2:72*

Woollerton Drive/Park
These roads were named after Edwin N C Woollerton (died 1942) who was the General Manager of Asia Petroleum Company (predecessor of Shell Petroleum) before WW2. He was a member of the Legislative Council (1937-1941).

Woollerton Park was a rename of Gallop Hill in 1949.

Source: *ST, 1937.8.21:13; MC, 1949.5.27*

Woolwich Loop (e)/Woolwich Road (former Blakang Mati Artillery Barracks)
These two roads were named after Woolwich, a historic town in southeast London and an important military and industrial town from the 18th to 20th century. It was home to the first Royal Military Academy (1741-1939) where cadets for the Royal Artillery were trained.

Woolwich Loop is now part of Allanbrooke Road. *See Artillery Avenue.*

Worcester Road (Race Course Road area)
This road was named after Worcester, a county town of Worcestershire in the West Midlands, England. *See Bristol Road.*

Workshop Road (King George VI Dock in Sembawang)

Worthing Road (Serangoon Gardens)
This road was named in 1953. Worthing is a seaside town in West Sussex, South East England. *See Alnwick Road.*

Source: *RBAR, 1953:8*

Worthy Down Road (e) (former RAF Changi)
This road was named after the RAF Worthy Down Air Station (1918-1950) at Winchester, Hampshire in England. *See Abbotsingh Road.*

Wuchang Road (e)
Wuchang is now part of Wuhan, a city in the province of Hubei, China. This road was renamed Students Crescent. *See Nanyang Avenue.*

Xilin Avenue
This road was named after Koh Sek Lim. "Xilin" is the pinyin version of his name. However, the Chinese name for this road was then translated to mean west woods, far from Koh's original name; the new Chinese name is also a duplicate of Westwood Avenue in Jurong. *See Koh Sek Lim Road.*

Source: *Kua: 33*

Yan Kit Road/Terrace (e)/Village (e)
Loke Yan Kit (1849-1931, Cantonese) was a qualified dentist from Hong Kong. He arrived in Singapore in 1877 and established his own dental practice at South Bridge Road. He became a big landowner with 70 houses and two rubber plantations. Yan Kit Road is in town and it was a public street since 1957.

Yan Kit Village was located at the junction of Upper Changi Road and Tampines Road.

Source: *CCAR, 1957:5; Kua: 66*

Yang Peng Street (e)

This road was connected to Peck Seah Street and declared a public street in 1907. However, it has not been seen in the press since 1910.

Source: *MC, 1907.4.19*

Yarrow Gardens (Frankel Estate)

This road was named in 1954. Yarrow is a tributary of Ettrick Water at the Scottish Borders in southeast Scotland. *See Burnfoot Terrace.*

Source: *ST, 1954.6.15:5*

Yarwood Avenue

This road in Kilburn Estate was named in 1947 after E S Yarwood, a director of George Wimpey. *See Denham Close.*

Source: *ST, 1947.11.30:7*

Yew Siah Village (e)

Based on a news article in 1948, this village was situated in Woodlands. However, this village was not listed in the Street Directory.

Source: *SFP, 1948.4.19:5*

Yew Siang Road

This road was named after Cheah Yew Siang who lived in this area. The road was named in 1948.

Source: *RBAR, 1948:7*

Yew Tee Close/Yew Tee Village (e)

Yew Tee Village was located near the Mandai Quarry. The village used to have some oil storage facilities for use at the Quarry and was named Yew Tee in 1938. "Yew Tee" is the transcription of oil pond in Hokkien. The storage facilities were destroyed during WW2.

Source: *SFP, 1938.8.12:3; Lim SH: 12*

Yio Chu Kang Drive/Gardens/Link/Road
(Yio Chu Kang Road Track 12, 14, 17 to 19, 21 (e) to 24, 26 to 29, 32, 33, 35) (e)
Yio Chu Kang Terrace/Yio Chu Kang Village (e)

The Yio family was the first to develop the Yio Chu Kang area. *See Choa Chu Kang.*

Yio Chu Kang Road appeared in a Singapore survey map in 1892.

Yio Chu Kang Link was opened in 1980.

Source: *NN, 1980.11.15:5; NAS, SP000006*

Yishun Avenue 1 to 9, 11
Yishun Central/Central 1, 2
Yishun Close
Yishun Central Service Road
Yishun Industrial Park A/Industrial Street 1
Yishun Northview Drive (e)/Ring Road
Yishun Street 11, 20 to 23, 31, 41 to 44, 51, 52, 61, 71, 72, 81, 101 (e)
These roads were named after Lim Nee Soon. "Yishun" is the pinyin of Nee Soon in Mandarin. *See Nee Soon Road.*

Yong Kim Road (e)

Yong Siak Street
This street was named in 1941 after Tan Yong Siak (1831–1914, Teochew) a textile trader and shipowner. *See Seng Poh Road.*

Source: *MC, 1941.4.25; Kua: 73*

York Hill (Chin Swee Rd)
York Road (former Alexandra Barracks)
These two roads were named after the Duke of Cornwall and York who visited Singapore in April 1901. He became King George V of the UK in 1910. *See Berkshire Road and Cornwall Road.*

Source: *MC, 1901.12.18*

York Lane (e)/York Road (e) (former RAF Tengah)
These two roads were named after Avro York, a British transport aircraft used during WW2. Both roads have been expunged. *See Hornet Road.*

York Place (Serangoon Gardens)
This road was named in 1953. York is a historic walled city in North Yorkshire, England. Besides the city wall, York Castle is an English Heritage site. *See Alnwick Road.*

Source: *RBAR, 1953:8*

Youngberg Terrace
This road was named after the Youngberg Hospital in the same location. The hospital was in turn named in 1948 after Reverend G B Youngberg who died as a POW during WW2.

Source: *SFP, 1948.2.13:5*

Yow Ngan Pan Street (e)
This street was named in 1910 after Yow Ngan Pan (1863–1930, Cantonese) who was a Director at the Straits Steamship Co. Ltd, and Lee Wah Bank.

Yow Ngan Pan Street was approved as a new street name again in 1919.

Source: *MC, 1910.5.18; MC, 1919.7.25; SFP, 1930.6.7:10; Kua: 103*

Yuan Ching Road
The garden view of Yuan Ching Road refers to the nearby Chinese Garden and Japanese Garden. *See Ho Ching Road.*

Yuk Tong Avenue
This road was named after Cheng Yuk Tong, wife of Cheong Chin Nam. *See Chun Tin Road.*

Source: *Kua: 112*

Yung An/Yung Ho/Yung Kuang/Yung Loh/Yung Ping/Yung Sheng Road
See Ho Ching Road.

Yunnan Crescent
Yunnan Drive 1 to 3
Yunnan Road
Yunnan Walk/Yunnan Walk 1 to 3
Yunnan is a province in the southwest of China. These roads were named after the Yunnan Estate, a rubber plantation owned by Yunnan Rubber Co. The roads are within the Nanyang Technological University.

Zehnder Road
This road was named in 1948 after H R S Zehnder, a Eurasian who came to Singapore in 1909 and became a land owner in the Pasir Panjang area. He was President of the Rent Conciliation Board and a member of the Legislative Council.

Source: *RBAR, 1948:7; Braga: 95*

Zion Close/Road
This road was named after Mount Zion in the same location. Mount Zion is the name of a biblical mountain in Jerusalem. The hill was probably named by the Keasberry's Mission, an American missionary, who established a Malay school at this location in the 1850s.

Source: *Buckley: 322, 573*

Zubir Said Drive
This road was part of Kirk Terrace before 2009. It leads to the School of the Arts and was renamed in 2009 in honour of Zubir Said (1907–1987). Zubir Said was a composer from the Minangkabau highlands of Indonesia. He was the composer of the national anthem of Singapore, "Majulah Singapura".

Source: *Today, 2009.5.9:4*

ABBREVIATIONS AND REFERENCES

ABBREVIATIONS USED IN TEXT:

(e) =	expunged
c =	circa
C-in-C =	Commander-in-Chief
C.M.G. =	Companion of St. Michael and St. George
GOC =	General Officer Commanding
LC =	Legislative Council
MC =	Municipal Commission
ms =	milestone
MRT =	Mass Rapid Transit (subway)
NUS =	National University of Singapore
POW =	Prisoner of War
QE2 =	Queen Elizabeth II
RAF =	Royal Air Force
Raffles =	Sir Thomas Stamford Raffles
SBNB =	Street and Building Names Board
Transfer =	Transfer of the Straits Settlements from the East India Company to the Colonial Office in London in 1867
UK =	United Kingdom
USA =	United States of America
WW1 =	World War One
WW2 =	World War Two

ABBREVIATIONS USED IN REFERENCES:

Newspapers:

XX, yyyy.mm.dd: pp = Name of Newspaper, year.month.date: page number

BT =	Business Times
DA =	Daily Advertiser
ED =	Eastern Daily Mail and Straits Morning Advertiser

MSP =	Malayan Saturday Post
NN =	New Nation
NP =	New Paper
SCCR =	Singapore Chronicle and Commercial Register,
SFP =	The Singapore Free Press in various names
SM =	Singapore Monitor
SO =	Straits Observer
ST =	The Straits Times
STOJ =	The Straits Times Overland Journal
Today =	Today
ZB =	新加坡《联合早报》("Lianhe Zaobao")

Government Records:

CC =	Minutes of Proceedings of the City Council at an Ordinary Meeting
CCAR =	City Council Annual Report
MC =	Minutes of Proceedings of the Municipal Commissioners at an Ordinary Meeting
MC1 =	Minutes of Meeting of Sub-Committee No. 1 of the Municipal Commission
NAS =	National Archives of Singapore NAS, XXXX:TTT = Special Project, New Project No. XXXX, Tape No. TTT; NAS, AAnnnnnn = Access Number for map
NLB =	National Library Board Infopedia
PWC =	Minutes of Meeting of the Public Works Committee
RBAR =	Rural Board Annual Report
SIT =	Singapore Improvement Trust, Minutes of Meeting
URA =	Urban Redevelopment Authority of Singapore

Chinese Books:

Lim SH =	林顺福 ("Lim Soon Hock")
Kua =	柯木林 ("Kua Bak Lim")
Lim HS =	林孝胜 ("Lim How Seng")
Phua =	潘醒农 ("Phua Chay Long")

English Books:

Bieder =	Joan Bieder
Braga =	Braga-Blake and Oehlers
Boo =	Boo Chih Min
Buckley =	Charles Burton Buckley
Chopard =	Kelly Chopard

Dhoraisingam =	S S Dhoraisingam
DM =	Directory of Malaya
DSM =	Directory of Singapore and Malaya 1928
Dunlop =	Peter Dunlop
Edwards =	Edwards, N & Keys
Evers =	H Evers and J Pevadarayan
Firmstone =	H W Firmstone
Haughton =	H T Haughton
Koh =	Tommy Koh
Kong =	Lily Kong
Lee KL =	Lee Kip Lin
Lee LT =	Lee Lai To
Malcolm =	Malcolm Allbrook
Millet =	Edition Didier Millet
Mills =	A D Mills
Makepeace =	Walter Makepeace, volume 1 (vol. 1) or volume 2 (vol. 2)
Perera =	V Gopalakrishnan and Ananda Perera
Probert =	Henry Probert
SD =	Street Directory
Ramachandran =	Ramachandran S
Song =	Song Ong Siang
Savage & Yeoh =	Victor R Savage & Brenda S A Yeoh
Serangoon =	Serangoon Gardens: 35th anniversary 1959-1994
SG-1936 =	Singapore Gazetteer, 1936
Siddique =	Sharon Siddique
Singam =	Raja-Singam
Sophia =	Sophia Raffles
SYrBk =	Singapore Year Book
T Pagar =	Tanjong Pagar, Singapore's Cradle of Development.
Tan =	Tan Sumiko
Tyers =	Tyers R
Wagner =	Leopold Wagner
Watts =	Victor Ernest Watts
Wise =	A M Wise
Wright =	N H Wright

REFERENCE MATERIALS

测量局编:《新加坡指南•附英华对照街道索引》, 新加坡文化部, 初版, 1970年.

崔贵强著:《新加坡华人-从开埠到建国》,新加坡宗乡会馆联合总会,
　　1994年.
杜祥明、王淑萍编译:《地名学术语词汇》, 中国中央研究计算中心,
　　2000年.
方百成等编:《头路》,新加坡福建会馆,2008年.
韩山元:《新马史话一千年》,八方文化创作室,2006年.
韩山元编写:《新马历史讲义》,未出版.
韩山元著:《从大坡到小坡》,新加坡八方文化创作室,2004年.
华林甫著:《中国地名学史考论》,中国社会科学文献出版社,2002年.
黄尧:《星马华人志元生基金会》,马来西亚黄氏联合总会,2003年.
柯木林主编:《新华历史人物列传》, 新加坡教育出版私营有限公司,
　　1995年.
李健才:《星加坡指南与街道名录》,新加坡知识出版社,1967年.
历年的新加坡《南洋商报》、《星洲日报》、《联合早报》及杂志.
梁立基主编: 印度尼西亚语-汉语大词典, Pt Elex Media Komputindo
　　Kelompok Gramedia, 1997年.
林宝卿编: 《普通话闽南方言常用词典》,厦门大学出版社,2007年.
林顺福、陈昭连、陈顺和编辑:《蔡厝港-从乡村到新镇》,新加坡蔡厝
　　港区公民资讯委员会,1986年.
林孝胜等编:《义顺社区发展史》,国家档案馆,1987年.
鲁白野著:《狮城散记》,星洲世界书局,1972年.
罗佩恒与罗佩菁合编:《新加坡简史》,新华文化事业(新加坡)有限公
　　司,2004年.
吕振瑞等编:《新加坡南安先贤传》,新加坡南安会馆,1998年.
南洋民史纂修馆:《南洋名人集传》,槟城南洋民史纂修馆,1939年.
南洋商报编:《新加坡一百五十年》,新加坡南洋商报,1969年.
潘醒农编:《新加坡游览指南》,新加坡南岛出版社,1936年.
潘醒农编:《东南亚地名街名录》,新加坡南岛出版社,初版,1952年.
潘醒农编:《东南亚地名街名录》,新加坡南岛出版社,二版,1957年.
邱新民著:《新加坡先驱人物》,新加坡胜友书局,1991年.
世界书局编:《星马通鉴》,世界书局,1959年.
汪大渊著、苏继顾校释:《岛夷志略校释》,中华书局,1981年.
王标桐主编:《地名学概论》,中国社会出版社,1993年.
王振春著:《石叻老街》,新加坡胜友书局,1997年.
王振春著:《话说海南人》,新加坡青年书局,2008年.
吴彦鸿著:《新加坡风土志》,潮州八邑会馆文教委员会出版组,1997年.
吴彦鸿著:《新加坡街名由来》,宏观工作厅,2006年.
许教正主编:《东南亚人物志》,未列出版社,1965年.
许永顺撰:《记得牛车水》,未列出版社,2002年.
许云樵著:《文心雕虫续集》,东南亚研究所,1980年.

许云樵著:《新加坡一百五十年大事记》, 青年书局, 1969年.
中国民政部地名研究所编:《数学地名》, 新华出版社, 2000年.
钟松发与黎煌才: 最新马华大词典 (Kamus Perdana), United Publishing House (M) Sdn Bhd, 1997年.
庄钦永:《新甲华人史史料考释》, 青年书局, 2007年.
周长楫主编: 《南方言大词典》, 福建人民学出版社, 2007年.

Allbrook, M (2014): *Henry Prinsep's Empire: Framing a Distant Colony*, Australian University Press.
Balestier: *A Heritage Trail*. Presentation by the National Heritage Board and the Central Singapore Community Development Council, 2006.
Bieder, Joan (2007): *The Jews of Singapore*, Subtree Media Pte Ltd.
Braga-Blake, Myrna & Ann Ebert-Oehlers (1992): *Singapore Eurasians: Memories and Hopes*, Times Editions.
Boo, Chih Min, Omar-Hor, Kartini & Ou Yang Chow Lin (2006): *1001 Garden Plants in Singapore*, NParks' Publication.
Buckley, C B (1902): *An Anecdotal History of Old Times in Singapore*, University of Malaya Press.
Chopard, Kelly (1989): *Rochore Eyewitness*, Rochore Citizen's Consultative Committee, Landmark Books.
Clement, Michael (2003): *Passage of Indians*, Singapore Indian Association.
Corfield, Justin (2010): *Historical Dictionary of Singapore*, The Scarcrow Press Inc.
Cribb, Robert & Kahin, Audrey (2004): *Historical Dictionary of Indonesia*, The Scarcrow Press Inc.
Dhoralsingam, K D Dhoralsingam & Samuel D S (2003): *Tan Tock Seng*, Natural History Publication.
Dhoraisingam, S S (2006): *Peranakan: Indians of Singapore and Melaka*, Institute of South East Asian Studies.
Dunlop, Peter K G (2000): *Street Names of Singapore*, Who's Who Publishing.
Edwards, Norman & Keys, Peter (1988): *Singapore : A Guide to Buildings, Streets and Places*, Times Books International.
Evers, H & Pevadarayan J (1985): *Asceticism and Ecstasy: The Chettiars of Singapore*, University of Bielefeld (Germany).
Firmstone, H W (1905): "Chinese names of streets and places in Singapore and the Malay Peninsula", *Journal of The Straits Branch of the Asiatic Society*.
Gopalakrishnan, V & Perera, Ananda (1983): *Singapore Changing Landscapes (Geylang • Chinatown •Serangoon)*, FEP International Pte Ltd.

Haughton, H T: "Notes on Names of Places in the Island of Singapore and its Vicinity", *Journal of The Straits Branch of the Royal Asiatic Society (AS 1889 vol. 20:80)*.

Jurong Journeys (1996): Published by Oracle Works for PAP Jurong Branch.

Koh, Tommy (2006): *Singapore : The Encyclopedia*, Editions Didier Millet.

Kong, Lily & Chang, T C (2001): *Joo Chiat: A Living Legacy*, Joo Chiat Citizens' Consultative Committee in association with National Archives of Singapore.

Lee, Kip Lin (1984): *Emerald Hill*, National Museum Singapore.

Lee, Lai To, et al. (1996): *Bukit Merah : From a Hilly Kampong to a Modern Town*, Federal Publications.

Lim, L C and Chan, S O (2004): *Pioneers of Singapore*, Asiapac Books Pte Ltd.

Liu, Gretchen (2000): *Singapore Pictorial History 1819-2000*, Editions Didier Millet.

Makepeace, W, Brooke, G E & Braddell, R J (1921): *One Hundred Years of Singapore*, John Murray.

Maya, Jayapal (1992): *Old Singapore*, Oxford University Press.

Mills, A D (2003): *Dictionary of British Place Names*, Oxford University Press.

Ministry of Communications and Information: *Singapore Yearbook 2004*, Singapore National Printers.

Majlis Ugama Islam Singapura (MUIS)-Mosque Directory: https://www.muis.gov.sg/mosque/mosque-directory.html.

National Achives of Singapore: *Compilation of Singapore Street Names, 1993*, Updated in 1999, unpublished.

New Directory of Malaya (1949). United Commercial.

Probert, Henry (2006): *The History of Changi*, Changi University Press.

Raffles, Sophia (1830): *Memoir of the Life and Public Services of Sir Thomas Stamford Raffles*, reprinted by Oxford University Press, 1991.

Singam, Raja (1939): *Malayan Street Names*, The Mercantile Press, Ipoh, Malaya.

Rajesh, Rai (2014): *Indians in Singapore*, Oxford University Press.

Savage, V R & Yeoh, B S A (2004): *Toponymics — A Study of Singapore Street Names*, Second Edition, Eastern University Press.

Serangoon Gardens: 35th Anniversary 1959-1994 (1994), Serangoon Gardens Commemorative Magazine Editorial Committee, Singapore.

Singapore Gazetteer Index to Roads 1936. Published by The Survey Department F.M.S & S.S. (Federated Malay States & Straits Settlements)

Siddique, Sharon (2000): *Nutmeg, and a Touch of Spice: The Story of Cairnhill Road*, Sembawang Properties.

Singapore Year Book (various years).

Song, Ong Siang (1923): *One Hundred Years' History of the Chinese in Singapore*, Oxford University Press (1984 reprint).
Survey Department: *Road and Street Directory and Guide to Postal Districts, 1950 &1953*, Government Printing Office.
Survey Department: *Singapore Street Directory, 1954-2007*, Government Printing Office.
Street Directory, 2010-2016, Mighty Minds.
Tanjong Pagar, Singapore's Cradle of Development, Tanjong Pagar Citizens' Consultative Committee (1989).
Tan, Sumiko (1993): *Chai Chee Revisited*, Kampong Chai Chee Citizens' Consultative Committee.
Tang, K F (1993): *Kampong Days : Village Life and Times in Singapore Revisited*, National Archives of Singapore.
Toh, Jason (2009): *Singapore through 19th Century Photographs*, Editions Didier Millet.
Turnbull, C M (1989): *A History of Singapore 1819-1988*, Oxford University Press.
Tyers, Ray K (1976): *Singapore, then & now*, University Education Press.
Wagner, Leopold (1891): *Names: And their Meanings, a Book for the Curious*.
Watts, Victor Ernest (2004): *Cambridge Dictionary of English Place-Name*, Cambridge University Press.
Wee, Yeow Chin (1989): *A Guide To The Wayside Trees of Singapore*, Singapore Science Centre.
Wilkinson, Sir Richard James (1901): *A Malay-English Dictionary (romanised)*, Kelly & Walsh.
Wilkinson, Sir Richard James (1926): *An Abridged Malay-English Dictionary (romanised)*, Kelly & Walsh.
Wilkinson, Sir Richard James (1932): *A Malay-English Dictionary (romanised)*.
Wise, M (1953): *Travellers' Tales of Old Singapore*, Times Books International.
Wong, Meng Voon (1970): *Report of the Committee on the Standardisation of Street Names in Chinese*, Ministry of Culture, 10 February 1970.
Wright, N H (2003): *Respected Citizens. The History of Armenians in Singapore and Malaysia*, Victoria, Australia.
Wright, Arnold and Cartwright, H. A (1908): *Twentieth Century Impression of British Malaya, Lloyd's Greater*, London. 1989 reprint.

Survey Maps from National Archives of Singapore:
SP000137: Plan of the District of Tannah (Tanah) Merah Ketchill (Kechil).
SP002981: Map of the Town of Singapore by Lieutenant Jackson.

SP002997:   Map of the Town and Environs of Singapore from an Actual Survey by G D Coleman in 1829, drawn and printed in 1836.
SP000218_2:   Plan of Amokiah District and Kallang, 1844.
SP006362:   Map of Singapore Island and its Dependencies, 1852 by J T Thomson.
SP000196:   Plan of Property of C H Prinsep, 1859.
SP006819:   Map of the Island of Singapore and its Dependencies, 1873, by F A McNair.
SP006818:   Map of the Island of Singapore and its Dependencies, c.1850s.
SP000041:   Plan showing the lands belonging to the Botanical Gardens and the adjourning property.
TM000003:   Map of the Island of Singapore and its Dependencies, 1885, by H E McCallum.
SP000006:   Map of Singapore, 1892.
SP002987:   Plan of Singapore Town showing Topographical Detail and Municipal Numbers, 1893.
SP006064:   Map of Singapore showing the Principal Residences and Places of Interest, 1913.
SP006448:   Plan of the Island of Singapore.
TM001148:   Singapore & Johore (part), 1932, Australia.

Government Records:
1. City Council Annual Report.
2. Rural Board Annual Report.
3. Minutes of Proceedings of the Municipal Commissioners at Ordinary Meeting.
4. Minutes of Meeting of Sub-Committee No. 1 of the Municipal Commission.
5. Minutes of Meeting of Sub-Committee No. 2 of the Municipal Commission.
6. Singapore Improvement Trust, Minutes of Meeting.
7. Singapore National Archives tape recordings and transcriptions.

ACKNOWLEDGEMENTS

I would like to thank the following friends and organisations who provided tremendous help in the completion of this project:

Mr. Roy Lee Kian who spent precious time reading through the book and offering advice to make the book more reader-friendly;

Ms. Tay Yu Shan for her excellent editing capability and Mr. Jimmy Low for his eye-catching cover design;

Mrs. Chua Ek Kay for the use of her late husband's paintings for the cover of this book;

Staff of the Reading Room at the National Archives of Singapore, who offered their untiring assistance in providing archived records and maps for this research;

National Heritage Board for the financial assistance to produce this book;

National Library Board for digitising all the historical newspapers; and

Last but not least members of my family for giving me the encouragement and support to write this book. My son, Chiang Wei, for solving all my computer hardware and software problems.

www.ingramcontent.com/pod-product-compliance
Lightning Source LLC
Chambersburg PA
CBHW050524300426
44113CB00012B/1951